MARITIME HISTORY

VOLUME 1:

The Age Of Discovery

Was hilfft der wechter in der statt/
Dem geweltigen schiff im meer sein fart/
So sie Gott beyde nicht bewart.

"What use is the watchman to the city and the navigator to the safety of the mighty ship in its voyage at sea, if God does not protect them both."

Portuguese seamen using a cross-staff to measure lunar distance to determine longitude and an astrolabe to determine latitude by the altitude of the sun. Illustration from Hans Staden, *Warhaftige Historia und Bescreibung einer Landschaft der wilden nacketen Grimmigen Menschenfresser Leuthen in der Newunwelt America gelegan* (Hamburg, 1557). Born at Hamburg in 1520, Staden took passage in a Portuguese ship to America. He was shipwrecked and later captured by Indians. He spent nine and half months in captivity before he was ransomed, after which he returned to Hamburg to write this enormously popular work. *Courtesy of the John Carter Brown Library at Brown University.*

MARITIME HISTORY

VOLUME 1:

The Age Of Discovery

Edited by
John B. Hattendorf
Ernest J. King Professor of Maritime History
Naval War College, Newport, RI

KRIEGER PUBLISHING COMPANY
MALABAR, FLORIDA
1996

Original Edition 1996

Printed and Published by
KRIEGER PUBLISHING COMPANY
KRIEGER DRIVE
MALABAR, FLORIDA 32950

FROM A DECLARATION OF PRINCIPLES JOINTLY ADOPTED BY A
COMMITTEE OF THE AMERICAN BAR ASSOCIATION AND COM-
MITTEE OF PUBLISHERS:

This Publication is designed to provide accurate and authoritative information in regard to the subject matter covered. It is sold with the
understanding that the publisher is not engaged in rendering legal,
accounting, or other professional service. If legal advice or other expert assistance is required, the services of a competent professional person should be sought.

Library of Congress Cataloging-In-Publication Data

Maritime history volume 1: the Age of Discovery/edited by John B.
Hattendorf.
    p.   cm.—(Open forum series)
    "A selection from the lectures delivered . . . at the John Carter Brown
Library's month-long Summer Institute in Early Modern Maritime
History held during August 1992"—Foreword.
    Includes bibliographical references and index.
    ISBN 0-89464-834-9 (alk. paper)
    1. Navigation—Europe—History—15th century. 2. Navigation-
Europe—History—16th century. 3. Europe—History, Naval.
I. Hattendorf, John B. II. Series.
VK55.M373 1996
387'.0094'09024—dc20   94-24805
                                          CIP

10 9 8 7 6 5 4 3 2

TABLE OF CONTENTS

LIST OF ILLUSTRATIONS

ABOUT THE CONTRIBUTORS

Felipe Fernández-Armesto is a member of the faculty of History at the University of Oxford. He is the author of a number of works, including, *Before Columbus* (1987), *Columbus* (1992) and editor of the *Times Atlas of Exploration* (1992).

John B. Hattendorf is Ernest J. King Professor of Maritime History at the Naval War College, Newport, Rhode Island, and was the academic director and organizer of the Summer Institute in Early Modern Maritime History at the John Carter Brown Library, 1992–1993.

Carla Rahn Phillips is Professor of History at the University of Minnesota. She is the author of the prize-winning, *Six Galleons for the King of Spain* and co-author of *The Worlds of Christopher Columbus* (1992).

William D. Phillips, Jr., is a specialist in Mediterranean and early modern Spanish history. He is Professor of History at the University of Minnesota and co-author of *The Worlds of Christopher Columbus* (1992).

A. N. Ryan was reader in modern history at the University of Liverpool until his retirement in 1992. He is well known for his many contributions to British naval history and was co-author of *England's Sea Empire* (1983).

Richard W. Unger is Professor of History at the University of British Columbia. A specialist in medieval history, he is the author of *Dutch Shipbuilding Before 1800: Ships and Guilds* (1978), *The Ship in the Medieval Economy* (1980) and *The Art of Medieval Technology: Images of Noah the Shipbuilder* (1991).

Charles Verlinden is Professor Emeritus, University of Ghent, Belgium. He was President of the International Commission for Maritime History (1980–1985), and awarded the Galileo Prize in

Italy as well as honorary doctorates from the universities of Coimbra and Sevilla. The leading scholar of the history of Portuguese exploration, *The Beginnings of Modern Colonization* (1970) is only one of his 26 books and 700 articles in many languages.

George Winius has been professor of history at the University of Florida, University of Leiden and visiting Professor at Brown University and the University of Charleston. He is the co-author of *Foundations of the Portuguese Empire, 1415–1600* (1977) and *The Merchant-Warrior Pacified: The VOC (The Dutch East India Company.) and its Changing Political Economy in India* (1991) as well as editor of *Portugal, the Pathfinder; Journeys from the Medieval towards the Modern World* (1995).

PREFACE

This volume is a selection from the lectures delivered in Providence, Rhode Island, at the John Carter Brown Library's month-long, Summer Institute in Early Modern Maritime History held during August 1992. This was the first of two such summer institutes, supported by the National Endowment for the Humanities, recognizing a national need for academic support of the maritime humanities. The first institute focused on European oceanic voyages in the fifteenth and sixteenth centuries, while the second focused on the seventeenth and eighteenth centuries.

As the Institute's program director, I designed the month's course of study as a broad outline of maritime history, from the first European impulses in maritime expansion during the late medieval period, continuing through the major exploring expeditions, and extending as late as the voyages to find a northwest passage in the early seventeenth century. The Institute was held at the John Carter Brown Library in order to utilize its rich collections of maps and charts, and published materials emphasizing the discovery, exploration, settlement and development of the New World, with its associated collection of navigation treatises, voyage and battle narratives, trade reports, seamen's training manuals, works on naval architecture, works on naval architecture and rigging, accounts of shipwrecks and sailing guides. In addition, the library's location on the campus of Brown University placed it close to the major maritime museums and related activities in the New England area, including Mystic Seaport, The Peabody Museum, and the Kendall Whaling Museum. During the course of the Institute, the participants visited these museum collections and were able to examine closely the replicas of the Spanish caravels on the 500th anniversary of Columbus's departure from Palos from the New World. Complementing seminar discussions and examination of original materials, they heard more than 25 lectures that were intended to illuminate the full scope of issues relating to nautical and oceanic affairs, embracing technology, economics, sociology, art and literature, politics, ideas, ship design, navigation and cartography.

The Summer Institute educated nearly 20 university and college-level teachers in maritime history, and nearly everyone of them has put the results of the summer institute to work by integrating it on their home campuses into their own courses in such disciplines as history, literature, and anthropology. This volume is an attempt to capture the work of that summer institute and to create from it an introductory survey of this period in maritime history that could serve as a basic text at the high school or undergraduate level, leading new students into a deeper appreciation of a topic that has become widely neglected.

As the product of the Summer Institute in Early Modern Maritime History at the John Carter Brown Library, this volume owes much to the many people who supported and encouraged the Institute, in a wide variety of ways. Among these, I would like to acknowledge foremost my colleagues on the staff of the Institute: the director of the John Carter Brown Library, Norman Fiering, who was the administrator in charge of the Institute; Mary Malloy, a graduate student in the American Civilization Department at Brown University and a member of the teaching staff at the Sea Education Association of Woods Hole, Massachusetts, who was the energetic assistant director of the Institute; and Melissa Marshall, a graduate student in the History Department at Brown, who was our student assistant for the project. Together, the four of us worked effectively and cooperatively as a team to make the Institute a success.

A number of others contributed to the origins and the successful functioning of different factors of the Institute: Elizabeth Welles from the National Endowment for the Humanities; staff members of the John Carter Brown Library, in particular, Susan Danforth, Susan Newbury, Daniel Slive, Gunther Buchheim, Vivian Tetreault, Karen DeMaria, Richard Hurley, and Lynne Harrell; and members of the Ad Hoc Maritime Studies Committee at Brown University, chaired by Professor Richard Gould.

Newport, Rhode Island   John B. Hattendorf

INTRODUCTION
THE STUDY OF
MARITIME HISTORY
John B. Hattendorf

Maritime history is a broad theme, within general historical studies, that by its nature, cuts across standard disciplinary boundaries. A student who pursues the theme may approach it from a variety of vantage points, and at the same time, touch upon a wide variety of other, related approaches, including science, technology, industry, economics, trade, politics, art, literature, ideas, sociology, military and naval affairs, international relations, cartography, comparative studies in imperial and colonial affairs, institutional and organizational development, communications, migration, intercultural relations, natural resources and so on. In short, maritime history is a humanistic study of the many dimensions in man's relationship with the sea.

Maritime history focuses on ships and the sailors who operated them, relating an identifiable segment of society to a specific range of technological development and to a hostile geographical area covering seven-tenths of the globe. The relative importance of maritime affairs varies from one period to another in general history; it stands out in some periods and in some cultures and not in others. For example, maritime affairs were an essential aspect of general European and European colonial history of the period from the fifteenth century to the twentieth century. Only recently, in the twentieth century, have alternative means of communication and transport developed and displaced much of the technological, social, economic and industrial fabric that surrounded maritime affairs, although a number of aspects continue.

While the subject may seem to brighten and fade for the general historian, a specialist in the subject of maritime history must keep in mind the continuity of maritime development through all periods. Maritime affairs are rarely, if ever, absent in history. At the same time, ships and sailors are not isolated phenomena. They are very much a part of larger developments. In order to understand what happened at sea and to analyze the effect of those events, one needs to relate them and interpret them in the context of broad issues that were occurring on land. Maritime history is, in many respects, only an extension of events on land, but it does involve a variety of very technical and specialist issues, such as shipbuilding, navigation, naval gunnery and tactics, marine engineering, hydrography, and so on. In order to understand these elements, which are key factors in maritime history, maritime historians must explain them in terms of the broadest context, while at the same time, they must come to grips with the details and make sense of the specific developments within that special area.

One of the main problems for maritime historians is the need to see events at sea in terms of a variety of perspectives. For example, a ship that was built in a particular country was a product of certain national political, economic, social, technological and industrial factors. When the same ship sailed at sea, it entered a different realm with an international dimension that may involve such additional factors as wars, cross-cultural relations, imperial competition, scientific research, the exchange of goods or the accumulation of capital through international trade.

Additionally, when ships left land and the network of activities that created and prepared them, they spent long isolated periods at sea. This unusual experience created a social dimension within the ships that, itself, became a new factor, creating microcosms of land-based societies while bringing them into various new environments and new experiences. These experiences, in turn, were reflected into land-based societies as sailors returned from the sea. In this area, as in others, maritime affairs typically acted as both a conduit as well as a separate channel of development.

Although focusing on ships and sailors, maritime historians deal in the interrelationship of events on land and at sea, dealing simultaneously with integrated, parallel, and unique aspects. As maritime historians move forward in their researches, they must also strive to compare and to contrast maritime events at different times, in different circumstances, and in different contexts. As a theme in general history, maritime history is not separate from other aspects of historical study. Nevertheless, it involves a wide range of specialized learning and knowledge that justifies the identification of maritime history as one of the many legitimate fields for historical research and writing. Identifying the field in this way, however,

neither removes it from the accepted standards of the best historical scholarship nor creates any unique standards or exclusive pre-
rogatives for those who follow it. It merely recognizes that the topic
is broad enough to identify fully a range of specialization and that it
is complicated enough to sustain the wide-ranging work of a number of scholars devoting their scholarly careers to working on differing aspects of the theme.

The Age of Discovery has some characteristics that define it as one
of the periods within the theme of maritime history. In the first
place, it lies chronologically within the general period of the late
Middle Ages and the end of the sixteenth century. In addition, it is
concerned with the outward expansion of Europe. In this respect, it
is part of the first phase in the historical theme that embraces the
way in which western European ways in technology, culture, languages and institutions, came to dominate the globe. This phase in
maritime history is largely a Eurocentric one, and scholars have traditionally emphasized this aspect. Nevertheless, this viewpoint can
not now be entirely accepted, as the importance of Arab scientific
knowledge to the development of European navigational science and
the relationships of European seamen with the peoples and cultures
of other parts of the globe amply demonstrate. As the first phase in
European expansion, maritime history necessarily touches on the
internal forces in Europe which allowed the voyages to take place,
but the voyages themselves resulted in contacts, cultural interac-
tion, and trade which quickly brings maritime historians back again
to the characteristic feature which forces them to cut across standard disciplinary boundaries.

In the Age of Discovery, maritime affairs were an essential element to Europe and to the expansion of Europe as they were key to
the reaction to that expansion. To understand sea affairs in this period, maritime historians must analyze it within the context of the
broadest issues, while at the same time understanding and explaining the specific maritime aspects. As with any good piece of historical analysis on a specific theme, historians working in maritime history strive to make a positive contribution to knowledge on a small,
but not isolated sector of that front. While they may limit themselves in scope to maritime matters, the questions that they answer
have a discernible relationship with problems of more general interest. The essays that follow in this volume outline many such
broad themes, providing an introduction to some specific and general aspects involved in the subject of maritime history and of maritime history of the Age of Discovery.

Part I
The Late Medieval Background

Figure I. The artist tried to depict in one image all the major activities of the busy harbor of Hamburg in the late fifteenth century. Here are three-masted cogs, having their cargoes, in barrels, unloaded into lighters by a large crane on the quayside, while the merchants, in the right fore-ground, are discussing business. A miniature from the *Hamburger Stadtrecht* (1497). *Courtesy of Staatsarchiv Hamburg.*

1

POLITICS, RELIGION AND THE ECONOMY OF RENAISSANCE EUROPE

Richard W. Unger

The voyages across the seas of the world to distant lands, one of the distinctive features of sixteenth-century Europe, grew out of the maritime history, the politics and the economy at the end of the Middle Ages. The first voyage of Christopher Columbus will always hold a fascination because it can be and, indeed has been, imbued with symbolic value, the nature of the symbol depending on the observer. That voyage, on examination, turns out to be one part of a pattern created by seamen, merchants and politicians dating back two hundred years or more. Among many other things, that first voyage of Columbus serves as a symbol of the importance of maritime history to the development of the world in the last millennium. It was not the report of a New World to Europeans so much as the opportunities created by the ability to travel efficiently and economically over long distance between continents which was the critical result of trips like those of Columbus and other highly skilled European navigators of his time. The Scottish philosopher and economist, Adam Smith, in 1776 already counted the opening of maritime traffic to the New World as the most important event in the history of man. Karl Marx in the *Communist Manifesto* followed Smith in pointing to the effects on social and economic structures from the integration of other economies with that of Europe. More recently scholars have described the effects on economies and societies outside of Europe which had to adjust and usually dramatically to the changed circumstances.

Relations between Europe and the rest of the world were, however, not new in 1492. The voyages of the great explorers were not isolated events. In the fourteenth and fifteenth centuries that pattern of adjustment forced by the opening of contact between Europe and other parts of the world was already established. The pattern simply became more striking in the following centuries. Contacts were principally by sea so the maritime history of Europe and its role in international contact dates, at the very least, from the late Middle Ages.

It is certainly no longer possible to see the navigators of the fifteenth and sixteenth centuries as heroes larger-than-life. That was a view popular among historians harboring the Romantic vision common in the nineteenth century. The insistence on the facts and careful examination of the facts have detracted from if not destroyed such ideas. There may be no possibility of resurrecting those great men but there is a possibility of making something now out of the role of men in shaping events, not just seeing them as tools of impersonal forces. The story of what they did, the narrative of the sailors and of the governments and merchants who supported them, shows the voyages as part of the long-term development of the relations of people with the sea. That is true of all parts of the world as much as it is of Europe. That is true of all voyages at sea and not just those made by explorers commissioned by governments. A myriad of choices and forces, complex, varied and hard to assess shaped maritime history. Among the more easily identifiable forces which shaped that maritime history were the structure of the European economy, the character of religious devotion and institutional religion, and the development of politics in the fourteenth and especially the fifteenth century.

Europe was above all a center of settled agriculture. Farming dominated the economy. Agricultural societies have always been bordered by two types of open spaces which required technologies very different from their own. Agricultural societies have always had contact with both types of open spaces. The first type was the sea. The second was the vast open stretches of arid land such as, for Europe, the steppes of central Asia and the deserts of Arabia and northern Africa and the frozen wastes of the Arctic north. In the fourteenth and fifteenth centuries Europe faced the closing of land routes across those open stretches and the shrinking of settled agriculture both in and outside the continent. The expansion of open spaces at the expense of farmed land came as a result of climatic changes. The fall in average temperatures through the fourteenth and fifteenth centuries combined with changes in rainfall to make lands in Scandinavia and in the Alps unusable for farmers. Drylands expanded too forcing back arable farmers. The outbreak of the

Bubonic Plague in 1346, virtually unknown in Europe since the early Middle Ages, led to a fall in the population of some 40% in a period of less than five years. Even more devastating were the recurrences of Plague through the rest of the fourteenth century which repeatedly wiped out any gains in numbers and so kept populations well below their levels of the 1330s. With fewer people both to produce and to consume food farmland was abandoned, often on the borders with the open spaces. The changes in physical and demographic circumstances combined with political changes outside Europe and inside to make travel more difficult in the expanses of land surrounding Europe. Movement across the Sahara Desert became increasingly difficult. Much more serious, though, was the breakdown of Mongolian hegemony which had offered some unity to Central Asia from the Black Sea to China. Travel was not easy because of distances and because of weather but it had been safe. It was not just Marco Polo and his family who found the way from Italy to China overland in the thirteenth and fourteenth centuries. The increasing danger of attack drove merchants to abandon, reluctantly, the lucrative trade with China. In that case as in others when merchants found land routes closing they looked outward toward the other frontier on the borders of Europe. They looked to the sea.

European political change was a product of, among many other things, the economic and technical changes of the fourteenth and fifteenth centuries. The political circumstances as much as those economic and technical changes, however, laid the basis for the long-term development of European maritime history. The "New Monarchies" is a standard topic and indeed a standard way of describing the political history of Europe in the years around that first voyage of Columbus. The idea that royal governments transformed themselves in the period grew up in the nineteenth century, especially after 1870 and the unification of Germany when historians felt obliged to find the origins of national states. It is certainly true that the nation state is one of the most powerful inventions of western Europe. Nations states which could command extremes of loyalty from millions of people certainly existed in 1914 but did not in 714 so something must have happened in the time in between. In the search for signposts along the way, the fifteenth century was taken to be one point of novelty. In the late fifteenth and sixteenth centuries states could and did take on a broader range of tasks. Among those tasks was sponsoring, subsidizing and directing geographical exploration.

Kings tried to assert the principle that they enjoyed the greatest authority since they had no superior. In the course of the twelfth and especially the thirteenth century kings found themselves able to establish what amounted to imperial authority, power to act as the ultimate judicial ruler in their own lands. Popes did try to insist on the right of appeal from royal justice to their own, thus claiming an authority higher than that of kings, but changes in religious thinking and in religious institutions in the fourteenth and fifteenth centuries undermined the position of the Church and its ability to act as a counterweight to royal power.

The political role of the papacy was hopelessly sabotaged in 1303 when a group of French knights held the pope captive for a short time. It was not just any pope, though. It was Boniface VIII who brought about the attack on himself and his office by extreme claims of papal supremacy. His capture and death a few days later, from the shock of being treated so much like just another actor on the political stage, exposed the vulnerability of the papacy. The moving of the popes away from Rome to Avignon in 1305, a move designed to find a safer home for the spiritual leader of western Christianity, meant a further reduction in the status of papal authority. The Great Schism which began in 1378 with two popes, one in Avignon and the other in Rome, not only shattered what esteem the popes still enjoyed but also embroiled the popes deeply in the mundane power politics of Europe. It took a church council in 1414–17 to put the papacy back together again, but that left popes for the next one hundred years and more fighting a battle within the church over the authority of a universal council compared to the authority of the pope. With popes preoccupied with competition among rival claimants to the throne of Saint Peter, with internal church questions, and with establishing stability and authority over lands near the city of Rome, the papacy could not thwart effectively the expanding power of kings.

In addition to the political troubles of the papacy there were attacks of a more fundamental nature on the established church. The philosophy of William of Occam (c. 1280–1349), known as the *via moderna,* became the norm for university instruction. His extreme views, even if only partially accepted, tended to undermine the authority of traditional practice. Some churchmen, most notably John Wyclif (d. 1384) in England and, in his train, John Hus (c. 1370–1415) in Bohemia, launched direct assaults on the powers of the clergy. The heretical ideas of these pre-Reformation reformers might be repressed or driven underground by actions of the Church and royal governments but those authorities could not subvert all novelty in religion. The *devotio moderna* was a more pious and more mystical program of worship which originated in the Low Countries and became popular there. It was symptomatic of a much broader trend toward more individualized, personal religion divorced from the grand public ritual which had developed in the high Middle Ages. There were signs of an increase in piety, of a more deeply felt Christianity among Europeans at the end of the Middle Ages. The changes in thought and religious practice tended to subvert the authority of the papacy in particular and the Church in general. Churchmen were very conscious of their weakened position and, often relying on secular powers for assistance, acted to shore up the damage. So rather than forming an institution to resist the growth of state power the Church often found itself a supporter of secular governments. The same shift from opposition to support of the crown was common among the aristocracy as well.

In the thirteenth century kings relied on feudal contracts as a basis for authority, for power over the more powerful in society and for a conception of the proper functioning of government. The king was seen as the first among equals, the leading aristocrat with all the finest attributes of a nobleman. Feudal monarchies in England, France, and elsewhere had a powerful nobility with local and regional power. Such feudal monarchies changed in the later Middle Ages, transformed into something very different.

The new monarchs relied not just on feudal contracts but on a broad range of tools to extend their authority. Much of what they did was at a practical level. Royal courts became more efficient, delivering speedy justice and so drawing cases to them. Kings established new courts which reached into areas of life formerly covered by other judicial arrangements. Courts responsible for overseeing taxation became more common and more effective so that royal governments were better able to collect and administer income. Kings came to be able to levy what were by medieval standards universal taxes such as taxes on salt (*gabelle*), head or poll taxes, and direct levies (*aides*). In Italy but elsewhere too diplomats appeared and even diplomatic services with individuals regularly involved in dealing with foreign powers for the king. Kings established noble orders such as the Knights of the Golden Fleece in the Low Countries and the Knights of the Garter in England. Aristocrats relied on the king for admission to these new exclusive clubs and, once members, the aristocrats found it difficult not to be loyal supporters of the crown. With the new funds from taxes, with more effective judicial systems, with a weakened opposition both among churchmen and aristocrats late medieval monarchs were able to generate paid armies and even collections of employees that began to look like paid bureaucracies.

In theory as well, the political position of monarchs was enhanced, creating a basis for the further extension of their authority. An emphasis on the primacy of the human will in forming the universe of human action was combined with novel ideas, derived from Aristotle, about sovereignty resting ultimately with the governed. Three writers from the fourteenth through the early sixteenth century demonstrated dramatically the changing views of the place of the prince in government; Marsiglio of Padua, Coluccio Salutati and Nicolo Machiavelli. It is no coincidence that they were all from northern Italy. It was in the evolution of Italian government in the Middle Ages that monarchs and theorists found the basis for arguments for what was to be called the Renaissance state.

Italy had a political history very different from that of the rest of Europe. It was not like the emerging new monarchies in England, France, Castile, Aragon, Portugal, Flanders, Bohemia, and Bavaria. Roman influence lasted longest in Italy. The Lombards, the German tribe which eventually conquered part of the peninsula, failed to establish a kingdom like those to the north or west. The Carolingian conquest in the eighth century proved only an interlude and the lack of a powerful royal state or for that matter any state left power to devolve to local authorities. Among those were the bishops in the towns who fostered virtually independent urban governments. In struggles in the eleventh and twelfth centuries churchmen lost their authority to sworn associations of town residents. Those groups established republican institutions which in turn fell apart in the course of the fourteenth century, that in all towns except for Florence and Venice. Those two became defenders in practice and in theory of a tradition of government run by and responsible to a citizenry.

Marsiglio of Padua (c. 1278–1342) was a propagandist for the Holy Roman Emperor in the papal-imperial struggle of the first half of the fourteenth century. He rejected claims of papal supremacy, like those of Boniface VIII, but he went much further in his principal work, the *Defensor Pacis* of 1324. Not only did he say the pope was responsible to a church council but the priesthood, in all parts including the pope, had to be subject to the single authority of the state. For Marsiglio, religious obligation was voluntary but political obligation was subject to coercion. The secular ruler for him had a function in maintaining the benefits of order and so ruled by divine right. The only restriction Marsiglio perceived was that the secular monarch was not to violate divine law, but then Marsiglio thought it highly unlikely that the monarch would choose to do so. The ideas of two powers side-by-side, one sacred and the other secular, which existed in the Early and High Middle Ages, disappeared in the writings of Marsiglio. Instead of a dualism of power for him, there was a singular secular power and one with divine sources.

Coluccio Salutati (1331–1406) was chancellor of the Florentine Republic and enjoyed annual reappointment from about 1375 until his death. In the fourteenth- and fifteenth-century wars, all parties found persuasion an effective tool in winning over opposition, often more effective than military force. Even if the pen did not prove mightier than the sword, it certainly proved less expensive. The use of propaganda gave skilled writers like Salutati an invaluable function and gave political ideas greater importance. As a republican and defender of Florence, Salutati promoted ideas about responsibility to the public good as well as ideas about the state as a public unit which has a function and value which thus deserves the loyalty of citizens. For him rulers were elected and thus authority, as for Marsiglio, was created by the people. That made the rulers responsible to the people. Loyalty was not the personal loyalty of, for example, feudal contracts but rather institutional loyalty to some abstract body politic.

Nicolo Machiavelli (1469–1527), also a Florentine politician but a less successful one than Salutati, was fully absorbed in the literary style of his day. He, like other Renaissance humanists, relied heavily on classical authors for guidance and for examples to help in describing the best practice for politicians. He derived a political morality which dictated the best actions for rulers measured in a purely political sense. That is not to say that he was not a Christian or that he had no use for traditional Christianity. Rather he thought that political figures, in order to accomplish their legitimate goals, could not and should not act consistently with those Christian principles. The result was a world which horrified many of his contemporaries, one in which seeming unprincipled opportunism was lauded. By no means were Machiavelli's ideas accepted immediately or universally. But the principles derived from the history of Italian city-states in the fourteenth and fifteenth centuries, articulated by the likes of Marsiglio of Padua, Coluccio Salutati and Nicolo Machiavelli, became the guide for Europe's monarchs and increasingly so through the Renaissance.

Monarchs found themselves with little effective opposition. The ideas coming from Italy offered them theoretical support or at least offered excuses for governments to be nasty to their own people and to others. Kings had a sense that their actions should be unrestrained, unrestrained by church, aristocracy, traditional practice or any earthly institution. England was perhaps the first kingdom outside Italy to imitate the novel kind of monarchy though the claim could be made for the Iberian kingdoms, where Italian influence was strong in virtually every category, or for France where King Louis XI (1461–83), the "universal spider," succeeded both domestically and externally in enhancing the authority of the crown.

The Renaissance state was a polity with a single powerful authority bent on expanding and extending that authority. By definition the Renaissance state aimed at undermining if not destroying completely traditional institutions, the most obvious example being representative estates. The state or, more precisely, the monarch became the center of all political action. Thanks to the drive toward centralization, the eradication of traditional institutions and the constant and often successful search for new sources of tax income, governments found themselves with more money and more ways to get money and with more interest in getting more money. There was over the long term an increase in the importance of monarchies, a decline in the power of aristocrats, in the influence of the Church, in the power and independence of smaller political units and, most notably in the sixteenth century, a relative decline of Italian city-states. The Renaissance state was something new in Europe. Though there might be among theorists reliance on classical examples and superficial imitation of Rome among politicians, in fact the Renaissance state was very different from anything that existed before. The medieval origins of the Renaissance state created the distinction. Renaissance states had the resources to support ventures of various types; technical, artistic, military, and diplomatic. Renaissance states both in and outside of Italy had an interest in supporting ventures to expand their authority, power, income and prestige. The Renaissance states found themselves able to subsidize shipping and exploration and so found themselves able to direct the maritime history of fifteenth- and sixteenth-century Europe.

Some monarchs may have come to believe that they could do anything that they wanted. It was of course not true. Directing maritime activity and for that matter directing any part of social and economic activity was not simply a matter of will. Renaissance monarchs typically did embark, unencumbered by any limitations that they could perceive or understand, on extensive programs of scientific and technological research. As part of those programs the mon-

11

Figure II. Under the Pont Neuf and Petit Pont on the Seine in Paris, a shipper sells wine brought in barrels by small river boats to the city, while another potential buyer sits sampling the vintage. On the bridges, five travelers cross in a coach while, on the right, a woman is paying a doctor while he examines a urinal. From a late fourteenth century illustrated life of St. Denis. © *cliché Bibliothèque Nationale de France, Paris.*

archs could and did pay for voyages of exploration. For various reasons, over which the monarchs had no control, the programs paid off
and for various reasons the successes had deep effects on many
facets of life both in and beyond Europe. The monarchs expected effects on the economy from their research programs. It was in the
economy of Europe, in both the short and the long term, that probably the explorations and related developments in shipping had the
greatest effect.

Looking at the late medieval economy in a very general way in-
troduces degrees of error because of the large scale of the description
and because of the sporadic and inconsistent nature of surviving
data. The range of answers produced is broad, the accuracy almost
invariably a subject of debate. Even accepting a relatively high level
of inaccuracy what is surprising is how often disparate data from different locations adds up to the same result. There is by no means
universal agreement on exactly what happened to the economy
throughout Europe in the fourteenth and fifteenth centuries. The
complaints, however, are more with details and with precise dating
of change than with the general outline of what happened. As a result the same broad story about the economy has dominated discussion among historians for some time.

The collapse of the Roman Empire in the West in the fourth and
fifth centuries was accompanied by and perhaps caused by a general
decline in population and in production. The failure of government
and the disorder which followed contributed to the deterioration of
the economy, deterioration by any measure. The shrinking of the
European economy continued to some point in the eighth or ninth
century. Though there were fluctuations in the economy during the
Dark Ages from the fifth through the tenth centuries it was really
around the time of the emperor Charlemagne (768–814) that signs
of economic revival and sustained expansion become clear. Christian Europe owed much to the Muslims to the south. Saracens did
repeatedly attack Christian states, trying to conquer France and
Italy. Though those attacks failed Muslims did, in the new Islamic
empire which stretched from the Indian subcontinent to the shores
of the Atlantic Ocean, create a large single trading area. Ideas, goods
and techniques flowed more easily across that great expanse and
European traders, just on the edge of the prosperous empire, found
ways to exploit opportunities created by Muslim success. Italian
traders exploited opportunities to export various goods, including
armaments, to the growing Muslim empire. Italian traders served
as intermediaries in the exchange of luxury goods between the

Levant and Europe. If peaceful trade did not prove profitable there was recourse to piratical attacks on Muslim ships and ports, action which yielded positive religious and political as well as economic results. At the same time that shippers from Italian towns were testing the possibilities of trading with the enemy, Scandinavian seafarers were extending the scope of shipping and trading in northern and eastern Europe. The volume of trade carried on by those Vikings was small compared to that in the Mediterranean. They did, however, open a new and alternate trade route between northwest Europe and the eastern Mediterranean, along the great rivers of Russia. The route also proved an avenue for the transfer of silver to the North from the Middle East.

The commercial revival in Italy and later Catalonia spread northward through overland trade to towns in France and the Low Countries. The emerging trading pattern proved extremely durable through the high Middle Ages. Luxury goods came from the Mediterranean, including spices, cloth of high value, works of art, gold and silver. Starting in the eastern Mediterranean the goods passed through Italy and from there went northward, overland, to Germany and France and the Low Countries. Along the shores of the Mediterranean there were very few rivers which were navigable for any length. Coastal shipping was more important. On the other hand in northern Europe river transport offered an effective alternative to land shipment because of the many navigable rivers. Of course, not all goods shipped were luxury goods. The movement of bulk goods was common throughout Europe. The standard trade goods of the Roman Empire were wheat, wine and olive oil and that did not change in the medieval Mediterranean. Rather, trade in those goods expanded with the growth in population and in production in the high Middle Ages. Traders carried increasing quantities of wool and also cotton for the growing textile industries of the towns. Those industries also needed dyes, some of them exotic, and mordants for fixing colors, such as alum. The industrial raw materials and some finished products joined a growing variety of foodstuffs in the holds and on the decks of ships in the Mediterranean and also in the North and Baltic Seas. Once in place the trading network which evolved could handle a broad range of goods and easily add new goods to the cargoes carried from port to port. By 1100 the barebones of the trading network were in place and the pattern was set. The trades would grow in range, volume and value over the next two hundred years.

The economy of Europe in the twelfth and thirteenth centuries was much more diversified than its predecessor and that in turn promoted the development of waterborne trade. Agriculture remained the primary activity for most workers and society was still overwhelmingly rural and agrarian. Perhaps 90% of the population was involved in primary agriculture. Urbanization even in Italy was still weak. Agricultural productivity was low compared to later levels but was rising thanks to technical changes in the ploughing and managing of fields. Villages, whether parts of large estates or home to independent farmers, had, in addition to arable land, forests and pastures which were critical to the productive process. The forests provided wood for heating and construction, the pastures forage for beasts of burden and manure, the principle fertilizer of medieval agriculture. There were also small plots, gardens and orchards to give some variety to the diet. Despite claims of historians to the contrary villages, farms, estates were not self-sufficient. The largest of estates did produce a broad range of goods including even some industrial goods and more commonly with the spread of the use of the water mill. But virtually all estates needed or wanted other things that could not be produced locally. Most had in some years a surplus to sell. The growing demand in the countryside along with rising production and so growing supply of goods led to a growth in trade and also to a spreading of trade to an ever greater area of Europe.

Urbanization came first in Italy but followed soon after in the Low Countries and then slowly in the rest of western Europe. Towns were always small by modern standards, though London may have reached 100,000 by 1300 and Ghent and Bruges almost certainly had 40,000 residents each at the same date. Italian towns were larger than their Flemish counterparts but less than the 800,000 of Constantinople. The size of the towns depended on the volume of trade through the port, on the production of industry in the town and on the scale of government services, both secular and religious, performed in the town. Since waterbone commerce was cheaper than overland it was preferred and so waterways dictated much about the location of towns and of economic activity. Europeans did increase the number and quality of roads in the twelfth and thirteenth centuries. They built bridges and by 1200 even some of the streets of Paris were being paved. Despite those improvements overland transport was typically by pack animal because of the poor quality of the roads. Shippers uniformly preferred carriage by ship up and down rivers, along the coasts, or across the open seas.

The industry in the growing towns was not exclusively devoted to the production of textiles. Woolen textiles were the biggest export of northern Europe to the South though those exports came under threat as Italian towns such as Florence developed their own woolen textile production. That did aggravate balance of payment problems for the North since northerners counted on textile exports to cover much of the cost of their luxury imports from the Mediterranean. Textiles enjoyed some diversification over time as towns made more linen and cotton cloth as well. At end of Middle Ages silk cloth was added to the list. Other industries thrived alongside textiles and in many towns outstripped cloth making. Tanning and related leather trades were necessary given the extensive use of leather. Most towns, especially in northern Europe had breweries and brewing was a growth industry in the thirteenth century. There were always many woodworking trades including coffinmakers, various sorts of metallurgical trades including gold and silver smithery, a range of defense industries and in port towns shipbuilding and related trades such as sailmaking and ropemaking. As seaborne commerce grew so too did the industries which supplied the vehicles for that trade.

By the late thirteenth and the first half of the fourteenth century the European economy was showing signs of strain. The long-term growth in population was, given the state of technology, putting some pressure on available resources. The climatic change, with warm and long summers in the thirteenth century, had favored the expansion of the area under cultivation. As the climate turned, on average colder in the fourteenth century, farmers on the periphery found it more difficult to continue. That compounded an already existing pressure on the available supply of cultivatable land. Already by about 1200 the cost of pasture had risen markedly compared to the price of arable land, suggesting that farmers were trying to grow ever more grain to feed a growing population. Farmers added to the supply of land first by internal clearing, which started even in the eleventh century, turning forests into farmland, and then by finding new lands to the east. Migration eastward continued and even perhaps increased in the thirteenth century. There was internal migration, that to the towns, which gained pace in the thirteenth century. It appears that by the early fourteenth century Europe had a relatively large population, that is compared to past history and in light of existing resources. There is clear evidence that Europeans developed a broad range of positive strategies to deal with the pressure on resources. Migration, greater investment such as the use of more horses, expansion of industry through investment in water mills all are signs that methods were being found to sustain the economic growth which had become the norm. When the Great Famine of 1315–17 subsided, there was a total population loss of perhaps as much as 20%, but losses were replaced rather quickly which suggests a healthy economy. The economic welfare of Europeans might not have been improving as fast as the economy or even improving at all. Still Europe had a larger population than ever before in 1340 and though income per person may have been declining it was still higher than Roman levels. Europe was able to feed an ever larger urban population suggesting that agricultural productivity was on the rise. Trade served to keep population growing since one of its functions was to alleviate short-term food shortages in one region by moving foodstuffs from areas of surplus. There are signs by 1300 of common price movements in the Rhine Valley, northeastern France and southeastern England. That pattern suggests that the trade in grain was having some effect and that people were relying on maritime trade to alleviate shortages and so to keep them alive.

The European economy enjoyed long-term economic growth from around 950 until the mid-fourteenth century. Though there were certainly variations from year to year and even month to month still the trend is and was clear. Europeans were able to use to advantage a wide range of technical improvements which led to increased output. The economic growth was broadly based in both agriculture and commerce. The expansion extended over time to all parts of Europe and increasingly extended eastward. It was in the circumstances of a long history of growth and developing strategies to deal with pressure on resources that Europe was devastated from 1346 to 1350 by a recurrence of the Bubonic Plague. That demographic disaster, with massive losses of labor and of consumers, must have had sizeable effects on the economy which in turn had implications for many facets of trade, industry, and agriculture. Those changes in the economy in turn ultimately had serious implications for political institutions and for society at large. Though it is always hard to define periods of history the loss of life from 1346 to 1350 must be seen as a breaking point.

The reduction in population raised the value of labor since fewer people were left to work. Consumption fell, but farmers, by concentrating their efforts on only the more productive lands, increased the average output of food for each hectare cultivated and for each day of labor used to produce that food. Farm laborers were typically able to increase their incomes in one form or another, that at the expense of landlords. Grain prices went down because production for each worker was up and there were fewer mouths to feed. It was landlords who bore the brunt of any decline in agricultural incomes. They had to pay workers more while getting lower prices for grain.

The more land a man or institution owned the greater the erosion of income. To combat the decline landlords tried different tactics to protect their position. They turned to producing crops of higher value such as meat, butter and cheese, or crops with lower labor costs, such as wool. The danger, and one that was quickly realized, was that other landowners would do the same thing, lowering the prices of the new crops. If incomes of agricultural workers went up those of industrial workers went up even more. Craftsmen had to be trained and it took time to replace the urban workers who had a higher death rate than their rural counterparts. Quality of workmanship deteriorated, training was opened to a broader range of individuals, and people left the countryside for towns in search of higher paying work. Landlords could try to counteract the trend by further promoting the development of industry in the countryside. Some did with success. The rising incomes of workers and especially urban workers created a pressure on their betters, on greater merchants and aristocrats, to maintain by symbols such as clothes the social distance which they perceived as normal and just. As the less well-off found themselves able to buy better textiles so industrial workers bought even finer cloths and merchants in their turn sported clothes of greater luxury in quality and in color. Aristocrats could not be outdone but at the same time, as landowners, they faced serious threats to their incomes. Caught in the squeeze between eroding incomes and rising costs of ostentation landlords often found themselves turning to entirely different sources of income.

The greatest landowners were the Church and the crown. While the Church enjoyed the benefits of many bequests in the wake of sharply increased mortality it also faced all the problems of a landlord. The confusion in the Church, the problems of fragmentation and conflict over who was the rightful pope multiplied difficulties. Monarchs, on the other hand, could counteract the threat to landed incomes by using taxing powers. In the past they had faced resistance from the aristocracy to such acts but those men, now in search of ways to defend their social and economic position, often supported the crown in hope that they might, as supporters or sustainers of the monarch, be able to lay their hands on a part of the king's greater income.

The rise in demand for luxury goods meant a rise in trade from the Mediterranean to northern Europe. The spices, luxury cloths, and works of art had to be paid for and northern Europeans did not export goods of sufficient value to cover the imports. Growth in direct voyages from northwest Europe to the Mediterranean and vice versa through the Straits of Gibraltar made moving those good easier. To make up for the shortfall western Europe continued the pattern of exporting gold and silver to Italy. From there the specie made its way to the Middle East and on to India and China. Though there were short-term and often local and technical reasons as well, Europe through the second half of the fourteenth and much of the fifteenth century suffered from a shortage of cash, of gold and silver. Ready money was critical for governments bent on carrying on wars but cash was also critical for merchants and for consumers so that they could pay bills and keep buying the luxuries that they believed they needed. There can be little doubt that the specie shortage was a policy consideration of European governments even after late fifteenth-century German miners found ways to extract more silver from pits in central Europe and even after the flow of gold and then silver started from the New World in the early sixteenth century.

The immediate effect of the Black Death in the mid-fourteenth century was to reduce the total volume of trade. The volume per person probably fell as well. But as the economy developed over the following two centuries, as population recovered and as landlords, peasants and merchants explored varying strategies under the changing economic circumstances trade increased absolutely and probably per person. The shifting relative balance of the number of workers and available resources over the last two centuries of the Middle Ages created a more integrated economy in Europe and one which relied more on trade carried out over long distance. For late medieval Europe, greater commercial exchange meant trade by sea.

There was a significant transformation of the European economy in the fourteenth and fifteenth centuries which in turn deeply effected politics. There was a change in both the social and political balance in the wake of the Black Death. There were also the first signs of a change in the international economic balance of power with a shift toward western and northern Europe which would become obvious through the sixteenth century. In the face of a declining and then slowly recovering population, there were continuing signs of a vibrant and highly flexible economy and of flexible economic institutions. In the wake of the disruption of the economy, the changing costs of supplies and prices of final products there were also signs of continued and possibly even accelerated technological change as producers struggled to deal with new conditions. It may be hard to measure and assess the extent of technological change but it is easy to identify an expansion in the role of the state in the late fourteenth and fifteenth centuries. Ideas, political and economic circumstances all played into the hands of governments and especially royal governments. Monarchs used their enhanced power in a number of ways, but most saw in navigation and seaborne commerce not only a source of increased income for the crown through taxation but also a source of new knowledge which could lead to greater power and even distinction for themselves and their royal houses. It was in the changing and charged atmosphere of the close of the Middle Ages that Europe began a process of maritime expansion and technical advance which would lead to dominance of the oceans of the world.

20

Figure III. A great galley in the harbor of Rhodes (left) and a two-masted carrack with a square mainsail and lateen mizzensail (right) in the harbor of Nothoni, Greece. From woodcuts of 1486 by Erhard Reuwich that appears in Bernhard von Breydenbach, *Bevareden tot dat heilighe grafft* (Mainz, 1488). *Photo courtesy of Richard W. Unger.*

2

THEORETICAL AND PRACTICAL ORIGINS OF METHODS OF NAVIGATION

Richard W. Unger

The history of navigation is normally taken to be a branch of history of science. That choice demonstrates a lack of understanding of the practical considerations which dominated the lives of sailors and also a greater concern for the results in the twentieth century than for the history of men in the Middle Ages finding their way from one port to another. The solution to the problem of finding the desired way on the open sea was ultimately found through science. Navigation is taken to be, especially in the twentieth century, an exact science. For sailors at the end of the Middle Ages, navigation was far from that. Even those sailors who made their way across the Atlantic and Indian Oceans still relied on old, simple methods to establish their position, methods based on traditional practice divorced from the theories of geographers and astronomers. Navigation needs to be understood in a broad sense. It may well be and has increasingly become, first an idea or understanding of what the natural world might be like. But second, and more important in earlier centuries, it was a bundle of knowledge which helped solve the problem of getting from one spot to another by water.

It was not just the captains and crews, not just the men on board who set the goals for sailors. The demands put on navigation came from a variety of sources, those demands directing if not dictating choices made about where to go and how to get there. Even going to sea at all was a decision not to be taken lightly. Travel was dangerous, the work on board hard, heavy and often tedious. Conditions on ships were always bad and often terrible, that in comparison both to later years and to contemporary life on land. Evidence from pilgrim ships of the late Middle Ages, where passengers were often of noble status and able to afford the best of accommodation and food, show that life at sea was hard. Disease was common, conditions were unsanitary, shortages of essentials were to be expected, conditions were cramped, leading to conflict, and there was always a great deal of time when nothing happened. If life at sea was so boring and so hard and so dangerous, then there must have been a compelling reason for sailors to take up the challenge. The answer must lie in the profit to be made from moving goods from areas of surplus to regions of shortage. The gain for those who did it can not and should not be ignored. Sailing, navigation was not a romantic adventure, at least not until the end of the nineteenth century. Before that it was a business proposition with all the potential for employment, profit and conflict which goes with any business.

In order to make the sailors' effort worthwhile the cost of the trip had to be less than the returns from it, that is barring some government action which might skew the relationship between cost and returns. By carrying something from a place of lower price to a place of higher price, merchants generated revenue, the difference between purchase price and sale price. Revenue then depended on demand and supply in both ports. It also depended on the quality of the good when delivered because travel would alter any good if in no other way than it was older. The profit to the shipper was the difference between revenue and costs, the outlay to move the good from one port to another. In turn, shipping costs were made up of capital costs, that is cost of the ship including repairs and the chance of losing the ship at sea, and of operating costs, that is wages and victuals for the crew.

The interest of shipowners was clear. They had to anticipate the return to them on their investment after all of their expenses to cover their capital outlay and repairs had been deducted. To get the most from their investment, they wanted to move as large a volume of goods from areas of low price to areas of high price and as quickly as possible. The interest of the captain and crew was less clear. Of course they too liked the idea of high returns from any voyage. That was especially true if they were traders as well, and often they were, having the right to space for a small amount of cargo on voyages. For those on board though safety was their primary concern. There was for them a constant tension between the need for safety and the need for prompt delivery of goods in the largest possible quantity.

Improvements in navigation throughout the Middle Ages and in general were always directed at the two goals of safety for ship and crew and the maximum income for all parties engaged in the shipping enterprise. Those goals were not necessarily in conflict but often were. The number of shipwrecks suggests that the participants did not always get the balance right. The equation was complicated by the fact that the return to owners was also determined by factors which had nothing to do with navigation. For example, the time it took in port after unloading and waiting for the lading of a new cargo, the turnaround time, was a period when the owners' investment was earning no return. The shorter the time in port the better for owners and crew alike. But the ability to reload a ship had little or nothing to do with how well she sailed or the skill of the captain in finding his way to sea. Similarly, the structure of supply in one region and demand at the destination might play a significant role in what sailors and shipowners got paid, but neither depended on navigational skill. From the late Middle Ages, however, improvements in navigation did combine over time and in varying degrees with better information and more efficient ports to open new routes for commerce and to allow for an ever greater volume of commerce to be handled by Europe's ships. The changes in technique and in organization and in the economy in general expanded the scale and scope of maritime activity and gave seafaring an increasingly important place in European society and history. It made it easier for sailors to answer the question of why they went to sea.

The choice of where those sailors were to go was determined by economic goals, by the desires of those who invested in sailing ventures. The choice of where to go and how was also constrained by the tools in use, that is by the ships and their ability to deal with the weather. Sailing ships were, in the end, always at the mercy of the weather and to forget that overwhelming fact is to obscure the most important consideration for any captain when dealing with getting to his goal. Adverse weather conditions could and often did make theoretical knowledge totally useless. At times, conditions even made practical knowledge and years of experience totally useless. When that happened the answer was to resort to prayer, something sailors often did.

Everyone in the Middle Ages knew the world was round. If they did not always show it as round that was largely because virtually everyone knew that fact, so it was meaningless. If visual representations of geography show a lack of interest in demonstrating that the world was round, it was because such representations had other purposes. Making a picture of the physical world is more difficult than would appear at first glance. No representation can possibly be all inclusive and all representations have specific functions which dictate how they show what. Geographic representations of the high Middle Ages fall into two large categories: world maps which had a propaganda function and showed Jerusalem in the center of the world, and strip maps showing roads, only the roads and what travelers would encounter as they went along them. Sailors got the equivalent of those strip maps but not until the thirteenth century. Portolan charts were the equivalent of strip maps. They showed coastlines giving the distance between ports and the direction from one to the next. Portolans were to give sailors some sense of how far they had to go but also what they might sight and what landmarks they could use to judge their position. They were for sailors who planned to be out of sight of land only for extremely short periods.

Sailors in the Middle Ages did not have charts of the type produced in the twentieth century or used in the eighteenth and for two reasons. Intellectuals, theoreticians, did not understand the earth in a way that would allow them to develop charts or, for that matter, make them seek out ways to make charts. Practical navigators themselves had no need of or use for charts. Their trips and methods of navigation had no place, at least not before the thirteenth and in many cases not before the nineteenth century, for charts. Inventions, new methods do not appear when a theory is enunciated nor does technical change occur when needed or at the moment some need is realized. The history of technology is not so simple. Still it is the case that in the early and high Middle Ages intellectuals could not think of charts and even if sailors had had charts they could not have used them. The ships they sailed could not keep to a course. The limitations of the design of their ships but much more important the power of the weather made staying on course, typically, impossible. They could get from one place to another, but the choice of a course was determined as much by prevailing winds and weather as by the navigator's desire to cover the distance in the shortest possible time. Sailors did have a compass, that as early as the eleventh century though then it was a very primitive instrument. Improvements over time made it more serviceable and by the fourteenth century the compass was an expected sight near the helmsman. He could use the indication of the needle to correct his steering, to compensate for changes in winds and, in the open sea, give some confirmation to sightings of the sun and stars as to general direction. The compass, however, was not followed slavishly as a guide to which direction to take, which course to follow. In the Baltic and North Seas as well as in the Mediterranean, the trips mariners took did not entail any need to plot a course and, in any case, the ships they sailed, at least up until the fifteenth century, did not have the ability to keep to a prescribed course.

European vessels up to the thirteenth century almost always made coastal voyages. If captains did not stay close to shore or at least within sight of land it was not by choice. In the Mediterranean ships went from island to island using landfalls as a navigational guide and stopping frequently at ports along the way to replenish supplies and to trade. The needs of navigating gave certain islands great strategic importance so that possession of Crete or Rhodes, for example, dictated the naval balance of power in the Mediterranean. Navigators relied on their experience, on their knowledge of landfalls. Pilots could be of great help but their use, especially for other than getting in and out of specific ports, appears to have been a later phenomenon, not well-known until the fifteenth century. Even in the thirteenth century, sailors did not travel in winter. Only after about 1250 did captains begin to venture out in the winter months. It was not the use of the compass which allowed that change in practice. It was still a simple floating device and which offered little more than a supplement to celestial and visual navigation. It is true that navigators did worry about poor weather obscuring the skies in winter but what kept most captains in port was increased chances of storms in the dead of winter, storms which their vessels could not handle.

In the Atlantic Ocean as well as the North and Baltic Seas, navigation was completely coastal. That was to be largely true until the closing years of the Middle Ages. Lead and line were the principal tools of navigation. Mariners worried about going aground since they were often close to shore. Scandinavian sailors in the Viking period went so far as to portage their ships or to travel along narrow inland waterways in order to keep navigation coastal. Even the Viking voyages into the North Atlantic, impressive voyages from Norway to Canada, were made as coastal as possible. The trips meant island hopping with the distances short or rather kept short by stops along the way at the Faroes, Iceland and Greenland. Even when the Vikings got to Canada their progress seems to have been made from one coast to the next. That made finding the way easier, decreased the danger, but also made it simpler to pass on knowledge to others who wanted to repeat the trips.

Sailors typically throughout the Middle Ages and down into the twentieth century relied to a greater or lesser degree on celestial navigation. Sailors knew about the stars as did many people on land through lengthy observation. Prehistoric Europeans had structured their astronomical knowledge in ways to pass it on and sailors continued that tradition. The information about positions of the stars and sun, collected over a very long term, could be and was consistently put to use by sailors. Though sailors may not have had a concept of the globe as banded by a series of parallel lines or latitudes, they did know that at its zenith the sun casts a shadow of the same length on the same day at each latitude. They realized that if they wanted to get to a certain port they needed to know the length of the shadow at that port and then simply reach a position at sea which produced a shadow of the same length and then head in a straight line toward the port. This was tantamount to running down a latitude and it appears that the Vikings may have done something along those lines though the evidence for it is extremely sparse. By the high Middle Ages, navigators would have been able to follow a procedure like that. Though their process of dead reckoning was more sophisticated, more accurate and more firmly based on acquired knowledge by the time of Columbus, the method was much the same.

The tools mariners had at the end of the fifteenth century were better than those of their predecessors even of the high Middle Ages. The compass did come into use more extensively in the Mediterranean in the thirteenth and fourteenth centuries. Improvements carried out around 1300 and attributed to Flavio Gioja at Amalfi in southern Italy gave the compass something like its modern form. The compass got a card indicating wind directions to go with the magnetized needle. It was not until 1485 that there is the first mention of gimbals, of some form of suspension which would allow the compass to remain somewhat stable even though the seas were rough. The limitations of the compass restricted its use, but in the sixteenth century, thanks to improvements in the instrument and to travel on open oceans far from land, the compass came to play a greater role in the predominant method of navigation by dead reckoning.

The portolan charts which cartographers began to produce in the thirteenth century offered a guide and opened new possibilities as makers added rhumb lines. From various arbitrary points on the charts, a series of lines radiated covering a broad range of angles. These lines crossed each other all over the chart and so, at first glance, they appear confusing. The lines gave different courses, different angles from north which could be measured with a compass. With those rhumb lines, sailors could not only run down a latitude as the Vikings may have done, keeping at the same distance from

Figure IV. A Viking vessel from the period of decline in the use of such ships. From a Fourteenth Century painting on the roof of Skamstrup Church, Denmark. *Photo Courtesy of Richard W. Unger.*

the North Pole, but they could run down a line following almost any direction. Knowing where they were and where they wanted to end up, all that was needed was for the mariner to find a rhumb line parallel to a line joining those two points and then read the needed course off the chart. Taking the distance along the imaginary line and knowing the speed of his vessel the navigator could more effectively estimate his position at any time. If for some reason his ship was blown off course, then the navigator, once he established where he was by, for example, making a landfall, could then carry out the same operation, find a new rhumb and then try to come as close as he could to that new course. The chart decreased the need for relying on sighting land to establish the position of the ship. With good data on speed and course, combined with sightings of stars or the sun, it was much easier for the navigator to estimate where he was.

To use rhumb lines effectively a captain needed a good portolan chart, an accurate compass, a way of measuring speed so he could know how far down a rhumb line he had run, clear weather and consistent, favorable winds. Such ideal conditions never prevailed in the fourteenth and fifteenth centuries. The equipment was not up to the task and weather was always the ultimate determinant of where the ship went and how fast it got there. How often portolan charts were taken to sea and how often they were used is subject to conjecture. Surviving portolans seems to be much too good and in too good a condition for having been used on pitching decks in variable weather. The portolans captains took with them were not likely to survive, so exactly what they were like is difficult to say. In fact, most captains may not have used rhumb lines on charts even as a rough guide. They often, it seems, fell back on the known methods of celestial navigation or simply relied on their knowledge of the coasts and islands along which they sailed. Position after all mattered only when trying to get into the chosen port. Until the ship was close to the destination all that mattered was that the ship was making as much headway in the general direction of the next port of call as possible under prevailing weather conditions.

In the open ocean there was more scope for the use of charts and compass and even for the use of the astrolabe, a device for measuring the altitude of the sun and other stars well-known to astronomers long before such devices made their way aboard ships. Originally brought along to carry out research on astronomy and navigation, they may have by the end of the fifteenth century become practical tools for open ocean sailors. On the high seas, in the Atlantic or the Indian Ocean, winds could be consistent both in direction and in strength. It was possible there to measure speed of the ship with some accuracy and to hold a course using the compass and hold to it even for days. In inland waters such conditions did not prevail. Most of the time in the Mediterranean sailors worked their ships in confined areas with sparse room to maneuver and with varying winds, weather and currents. Sailors there and in the North and Baltic Seas rarely found themselves out of sight of land. It was not that they necessarily wanted the reassurance of seeing land. In heavy storms in fact they wanted to get away from land for fear they might be blown on shore. It was rather the geography of those seas which makes it difficult to find places where ships would not be within sight of land. The ability of mariners to overcome adverse weather conditions depended a great deal on the form and design and on the performance of the ships in which they sailed. The capability of ships then was critical to navigation in the broadest sense of the term.

European navigation, like the population and the economy, underwent long-term development from the mid-tenth century to the mid-fourteenth. While population grew and production of agricultural and industrial goods increased, knowledge of what to do at sea to make shipping more efficient grew as well. It is all too easy in an effort to correct the optimism, the positive view of scientific progress shared by many historians of earlier generations, to forget that there were real improvements in knowledge about the physical world and especially about getting around at sea in the high and late Middle Ages. Greater use of classical texts offered a better theoretical grounding for discussions about navigation among scholars. Writers developed better ways of describing and explaining what geography and astronomy were about and what could be learned from the study of those fields. Technical improvements, most notably in the instruments, did make possible better measurement of a ship's position. Experience served as well. Greater knowledge about various waters, various routes, various methods of navigation improved the chances of success for captain and crew. Not incidentally, they improved the chances of making voyages profitable for investors and sailors alike.

There was in Europe by the fifteenth century more knowledge of the rest of the world in every way thanks to travel literature. Information from works like the description of the travels of Marco Polo or the agglomeration of stories produced under the name of Sir John Mandeville gave Europeans a great deal of information about the world beyond their shores. Much of the information was inaccurate and much of it taken from other earlier authorities but it did give to Europeans an expectation of finding different peoples and different cultures beyond their own continent. If nothing else it equipped them with an ability to deal with novelty, with the unknown. The travel literature, and not just that which dealt with far away places, served also to help navigators in a general way but also sometimes in a highly particular way with specific information about certain ports or stretches of water. A unique combination of the navigator's new tools and the fascination with describing the world beyond Europe came in the Catalan Atlas compiled probably on one of the Balearic Islands in 1375. It showed the shores of Europe, often highly accurately, with courses from port to port and also sets of rhumb lines. While surprisingly accurate for the Mediterranean and the Iberian peninsula, it became less good for northern and northwestern Europe. For Africa and more so for China the influence of travel literature was greater than that of the experience of navigators.

While the Catalan Atlas might bring together information from navigation and from travel literature in general the split between practical and theoretical knowledge of navigation was not broached in the Middle Ages. In 1300 there was still an impassable gulf between the navigator finding his way at sea and the geographer or astronomer or cosmographer concentrating on theories of the universe or of the location of land masses and seas. Efforts to overcome that division, to create a bridge between the two worlds was a hallmark of the fifteenth century. It was a matter of bringing the growing knowledge created by speculation to bear on practical questions of finding position at sea and finding the way to novel lands. For travel within Europe, for travel to known ports, theoreticians had little to offer. Captains had established over the years effective methods of finding their way, even if that way was to take on a pilot distinguished by his extensive experience with the waters of the region. It was more for pushing out the boundaries of maritime activity, for establishing new routes across the open sea that men of science had some contribution to make for sailors. Prince Henry in Portugal, later called the Navigator, was by no means the only one to press theoreticians to help mariners. The new monarchs, most notably in Spain and Portugal, with their new found resources, were the most prominent in developing ways of connecting ideas with practice. Fifteenth century governments supported research, for example, into establishing position north or south of the equator by use of the height of the sun above the horizon and then having tables produced

31

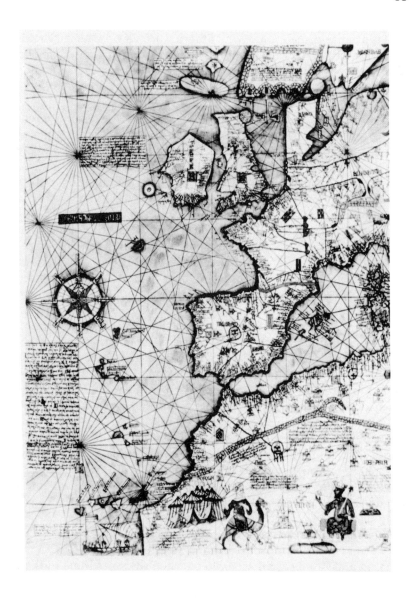

Figure V. Western Europe and northern Africa from the Catalan Atlas of 1375, constructed in the usual method for portolans, including rumb lines. The map makers had much better information about southern European waters and accuracy decreased for the northern British Isles and Scandinavia. © cliché Bilbliothèque Nationale de France, Paris.

which could in turn be used by their captains. Once written down and reproduced such tables and others, such as tide tables, could be and were improved in subsequent editions. In this promotion of the application of scientific and geographical theory to practical navigation Europeans appear to have been different from others in the rest of the world.

The drive to use new knowledge in navigation was generated in part by pressing problems created by the long-distance trips promoted by governments. Voyages to the Atlantic Islands and then down the coast of Africa by Spanish but especially Portuguese sailors had uncovered new problems about establishing position. Sailors did not have the experience of anyone to fall back on so had to find some way of thinking about navigation which would help them in dealing with the unknown. At the same time Europe and especially Italy was enjoying an intellectual ferment, a desire to create a rebirth or Renaissance of classical culture, which was in a sense an exploration as well. Study of Latin and Greek texts, finding out about a different civilization, promoted a search for knowledge on a broad front. The discovery of classical texts dealing with geography promoted interest and gave to the study of navigation a greater respectability and importance. The combination of the intellectual exploration that was the Renaissance and the practical questions governments were finding in the exploration at sea combined to promote an effort to transfer theoretical knowledge, whether derived from the classical past or newly developed, to the practice of navigation.

European navigation in the Middle Ages was not inherently superior to that in other parts of the world. In 1300 and probably even in 1500 and later navigators in the South Pacific were better than were their European counterparts in finding the way from one isolated island to another across hundreds of miles of open sea. The accomplishments of Polynesian sailors were simply beyond the comprehension of European navigators who had trouble believing that such trips could be made. Europeans were also impressed with what Muslim and Chinese sailors could do when they met them in the Indian Ocean. In order to find his way to India from the southeastern coast of Africa, Vasco da Gama took on a Muslim pilot. Portuguese sailors marveled at the ability of that man and of his fellow navigators to set courses based on the rising and setting of certain known stars. Sailing most the time near to the equator, Muslim sailors could not rely on the Pole Star or the Southern Cross as a fixed point in the sky. They had solved the problem in a practical way but one alien to what was common in Europe. Chinese sailors could and did make voyages across the Indian Ocean, but more commonly they carried on, with an efficiency surprising to Europeans, regular commercial trips from China to ports throughout southeast Asia. While Chinese and Muslim navigators impressed European sailors when they first met them and while in the earliest days of sailing in the Orient and the New World Europeans found their only avenue to success was to rely heavily on knowledgeable local sailors, Europeans did have a long-term advantage. At least theoretically they had a way to expand and extend navigation in the narrow sense, because of the theoretical basis being forced on navigation by the actions of governments. Because of governments and because of the success of the merging of science and practice over time, European sailors were better able to use celestial observations to decide on their position. Despite those advances and despite a growing literature to help, guide and educate captains and despite institutional regulations from governments and companies which forced the use of navigation based on science, it was still rare for sea captains even in the late seventeenth century to bother with the sophisticated gear and the theories of navigation. Though they knew how to use a sextant and though they could determine their position with some accuracy, it was still the case that in enclosed waters the position was of little relevance. On the open ocean, the exact position was of little more than academic interest until the vessel came close to land.

Though the widespread use of something that might be called scientific navigation was a long time in coming, still it was the case that Europeans enjoyed some advantages over their counterparts in Asia, Africa and the Americas. The advantages were in navigation in the broadest sense and not just in being able to take out an instrument, look at the sun and then find a point on a chart which reflected where the ship might be. The advantages came in the ability to sail where they wanted to go. That ability was, of course, always subject to prevailing conditions. But the combination of experience, of the application of theory to the practice of navigation and developments in ships made it possible for Europeans to overcome or at least mitigate many adverse conditions. European success at sea which became increasingly obvious at the end of the Middle Ages had a great deal to do with the ships they used. The designs developed by Europeans and the way they handled those ships proved positive assets and in combination with advances in navigation made possible the maritime accomplishments of Renaissance Europe.

3

SHIPS OF THE
LATE MIDDLE AGES
Richard W. Unger

Trying to describe European ships of the fifteenth century is difficult. Information is inadequate. There were almost no written contracts between builders and buyers. Builders almost never wrote about what they were doing. When they did it is hard to understand what they wrote. Artists that made pictures of ships relied on contemporary ships for models but they did not feel obliged to represent the vessels in precise technical detail. The few ships from the period that archaeologists have excavated are, as with all such finds, damaged and often badly. There is no way of knowing if what is found is typical of ships of the day.

If difficulties with sources of information is not enough to make the task daunting, the history of ship design in the period compounds the problem. The fifteenth century, the end of the Middle Ages and early Renaissance in general, was a time of great change in the design, construction and even in the conception of ships. In such periods of change and novelty, a variety of technologies often exist side by side, the old remaining in place next to the new along with a number of intermediate forms vying for prominence. Varying local conditions and varying needs always meant that shippers used a variety of vessel types. Those local or regional variants lasted a long time. The personal experience and idiosyncracies of captains as well as the need for repairs from time to time always meant that individual ships were subject to modification throughout their lives. Those men did make adjustments, especially to the rigging, to suit conditions of the moment or to suit their own tastes or to suit the unique nature of the specific ship. The technological advances of the late Middle Ages made this variety even greater. The innovators had to work with the raw material of designs and types developed in the early Middle Ages. Those vessels had already been subject to a number of changes and adjustment. So the origins of the superior ships which Europeans had in the sixteenth century had to be found in vessels from hundreds of years before. Any discussion which deals only with some of the principal ship types obscures the variety which always existed and runs the risk of obscuring the sources of technical advances made in one type or in one region which then could be and were borrowed for more general use. The technology which emerged at the end of the fifteenth century in shipbuilding was the basis for the maritime success of Europeans and indeed for the maritime history of much of the world in subsequent centuries. The technology of shipbuilding directed and constrained trade, travel and exploration through the Renaissance and for years afterward.

Since shipbuilders developed the raw material for late medieval innovation over a very long period it is difficult to establish a starting point for that innovation but eighth-century Scandinavia seems to be a good choice. The first explorers of medieval Europe were the Vikings. Their ships embodied some of the innovations which would form the basis for features brought together at the end of the Middle Ages to create effective ships for voyages to distant lands as well as economically efficient ships for regional and local use. Viking ships themselves developed from earlier rowing barges, vessels of German speakers who lived along the shores of the North Sea and also the Baltic. The vessels were long relative to their width and had no sails. The passengers formed the crew of rowers. These narrow rowing barges could not venture out to sea but could move a number of men speedily along the coasts and over short stretches of open water. Construction was simple. There were few planks and they overlapped one another both to give strength and to keep out water.

In the seventh and eighth centuries shipbuilders in Scandinavia made two changes which transformed the rowing barge into a seagoing vessel capable of trips across the North Atlantic. They added a mast and a square sail. They added a true keel. The ship retained the same proportions though the number of planks on the sides increased and the profile of the vessel changed somewhat with planks flaring out quickly from the keel and then turning up at the sides. They lost the rounded shape of the rowing barge but the vessel got a smooth curve which allowed the hull to ride over the top of the water while still, with a keel, able to hold better to a course in a crosswind. Crews could take down masts and sails easily on warships with windpower quickly replaced by propulsion with oars. By the ninth century, builders came to differentiate between warships and cargo ships though both shared many features, including overlapping planks and the curve of the hull. They built cargo ships more sturdily, nailing ribs in place permanently and fixing the mast so it could not be taken down. They built cargo ships with shorter length-to-beam ratios and deeper holds. Instead of a through deck, the center of the hold was left open for storing goods. It was in such single-masted cargo ships that Vikings made their way to Iceland, brought colonists and all their goods, and then carried on regular trade to Greenland and to Canada. Scandinavians used smaller versions of the cargo ship, vessels they could carry, to make their way up and down the great rivers of Russia and Ukraine. Viking warships proved highly effective in the hit-and-run raids the Scandinavian warriors carried on in England, France and into Iberia. As raiders and also as Crusaders, Scandinavians brought those warships into the Mediterranean. The Viking ship proved highly versatile and able to make voyages of unprecedented length. Shipbuilders found ways to adapt the basic design so that Viking ships could carry out, highly efficiently, a wide variety of tasks. Their principal contributions were to show what a single-masted ship with a square sail could do and to open up new routes which could later be exploited using other types of ships. In the thirteenth century the use of vessels of the Viking type declined in northern Europe. Such ships still found a place in coastal trades and for naval work, especially amphibious operations. For long distance trade, however, vessels of the well-established Viking type were driven from many of the major trades by a different and recently dramatically improved type, the cog.

Cogs were an old Celtic type, in use in northern Europe since at least Roman times. They had flat bottoms, sharp angles between the flat bottom and the sides and sharply angled posts at both bow and stern. The planks on the bottom abutted one another but the side planking was overlapping. There was a single mast with a single square sail in the middle of the ship. Because cogs were usually only three or four times as long as they were wide and because of the sharp angle between bottom and sides they could carry a great deal of cargo for each meter of length. They were ideal for coastal trading among the sandbanks and sandbars off the coast of Frisia along the southern shore of the North Sea. Cogs, though, did make their way as far north in Sweden as the region around modern Stockholm and perhaps as far south as the Iberian Peninsula, all that before the year 1000. What changed the cog and made it an effective competitor for the trade of northern Europe was the addition of a true keel. Once introduced to the flat-bottomed cog, the vessel became a much better sailor and one able to negotiate the open waters of the North and Baltic Seas. The change was presumably in imitation of the Viking ship. Once the change was made cogs went through further modifications, most notably making them longer and taller with deeper holds. Already with an advantage because of the shape of the hull the modifications made cogs by the fourteenth century highly efficient carriers of bulk goods. They became so large that they had to stay out from land, away from the shore. That presented some problems for navigators. Cogs also became so large that they began to press the limits of the size of the single sail.Sails had to be large enough to move the weight of the ship and its cargo and as sails got bigger so did the number of crewmen needed to hoist them. The change to a sternpost rudder in place of the side rudder typical of Viking ships helped somewhat with controlling the bigger cog. The sheer size and weight of the ships though meant, as always, that it was from effective use of the sail that most control over the ship came. With only one sail and with few lines to control that sail control was difficult. Cogs were clumsy vessels but they could carry, by standards of the fourteenth century, large quantities of goods. They also found another and, in the long term, equally important use.

Because cogs rode so high in the water and because of the high sides which rose above the decks, men on cogs could look down on men in other ships from a protected position. It did not take long to discover the advantages of that higher position in battle. Fighting at sea was typically hand to hand, like a land battle, preceded by an exchange of missiles. The higher position of men in cogs gave them an absolute advantage in hurling rocks, spears, arrows and anything else at the enemy. To counteract the inherent advantage builders added raised platforms, castles, at either end of the descendants of Viking long ships. It took little time for the builders of cogs to realize that they could retain the advantage for their ships by adding castles too. Those were at first just temporary stages but relatively quickly they came to be built into the hull of the ship. The final result was to make the cog the dominant warship of northern Europe as well as the dominant cargo ship. Royal governments built cogs for use in battle and then leased them in peace time to traders. Royal governments also conscripted cogs in wartime, paying their merchant owners a rental fee which the government set.

As the cog itself was enjoying this triumph and forcing vessels of that earlier Scandinavian type into lesser roles it had to face a challenge from another type of cargo ship, a challenge which saw the cog lose ground throughout the fourteenth century. The hulk was not originally a ponderous bulk carrier as it would become in the sixteenth century. It was a boat of Celtic design like the cog, in use in Roman times and probably before. The hulk was a simple boat, shaped like half a banana with planks abutting and then made watertight by having planks fitted over the seams where the principal planks met. The planks had to be brought together at the bow and stern, brought up to a point and then held together in some way since there was no keel. The hull shape made hulks ideal for use on rivers and in estuaries. They may have been pulled along rivers but by the eleventh century they were certainly sailing ships, capable of making short voyages across the North Sea. They carried a single square sail on a single mast just as did other northern European ships. In the course of the thirteenth but especially the fourteenth century the average size of the hulk grew. Increasingly builders were able to solve the problem of how to retain that rounded hull form on larger ships. One thing they did was to make the planking overlapping like cogs and Viking ships so that for them too the strength came from the exterior shell of the ship with internal ribs added later only to give some greater stability.

At the end of the fourteenth century the distinction between cogs and hulks became blurred. The same ship was called a hulk in one port, a cog in another. The reason for the confusion was that shipbuilders, presumably in the Baltic, found ways to combine the best features of both designs to create a new, composite vessel. This new type had the keel, sharp posts and sternpost rudder of the cog but also the curved cross-section of the hulk and overlapping planking throughout including near the keel. Propulsion came from a single large sail on a single mast but now with a number of different lines to help in controlling that sail. The composite type lost none of the carrying capacity of the cog but was easier to handle, more seaworthy and better in getting in and out of port. It was this improved bulk carrier which came to dominate northern waters in the fifteenth century as a cargo ship as well as a warship. It was that ship which northern builders had as a model, as a source for ideas when they confronted an entirely new type of ship with entirely different ways of construction which turned up in the North and Baltic Seas in the fifteenth century from the Mediterranean.

In southern Europe the basis for ship design in the Middle Ages was established in the days of the Roman Empire. Ships in the first centuries of the Christian era fell into two large categories: relatively long-oared galleys and shorter, tubbier sailing ships. Both types carried a mast in the middle of the ship with a single square sail. There was also a small square sail at the bow, an artemon, to aid in controlling the vessel. There were two rudders typically, one on each side. Hulls, decks, all parts of the ships were built with mortise and tenon joints. The strength came from the hull as with northern ships using overlapping planking but the quality of workmanship and the quality of the ships was much greater in the Mediterranean. As the Roman Empire declined, as population decreased and the economy deteriorated shipbuilders no longer had the skill to produce vessels of such quality. They evolved a new method of construction where they put together the internal framework first and then tacked the hull planks to the internal ribs. The resulting vessel was lighter, easier to build and more easily subject to variation and adaptation. It was also less watertight and required more and more frequent repairs and maintenance. By the end of the first millennium of the Christian era that skeleton-first form of construction was commonplace in the Mediterranean. Also commonplace was a different type of sail plan. Ships now typically carried not square but lateen or triangular sails. While fine for small vessels in the Roman era, during the early Middle Ages lateen sails came to be used on vessels of all sizes and types. They had the advantage of making it possible to sail closer to the wind than with a square sail. Lateen sails were somewhat harder to handle requiring more crew for a given size of sail and also requiring more work when coming about into a different direction. In trying to sail close to the wind sailors followed a zig-zag course tacking back and forth to make some way toward their goal even when the wind was against them. With a square sail the angle to the wind was rarely less than 90 degrees. At that angle no forward progress could be made but with a lateen sail and an ability to sail at angles somewhat under a right angle to the wind tacks were productive. On small vessels the additional work to handle a lateen sail mattered little but as the sails and yards became larger on galleys and on cargo ships, the extra work entailed greater care and more effort on the part of a larger crew. Lateen sails could not be shortened so in strong winds the sails had to be changed to smaller ones. Ships carried sets of lateen sails of different sizes and crews large enough to make the shift when needed. It was the skeleton-first ship powered by lateen sails that dominated the Mediterranean Sea for both Christian and Muslim sailors through the high Middle Ages.

The Roman differentiation between cargo ships and galleys continued. Galleys went through experiments with different configurations of rowers. By the end of the thirteenth century Mediterranean galleys had one level of oarsmen sitting three to a bench with the benches angled so that each rower could pull his oar without interfering with the others on the bench. The galleys were light, rode high in the water, and carried a small number of marines. The principal offensive weapon was a ram at the bow, soon to be supplemented and then supplanted by cannon which appeared on ships in the fourteenth century. The galleys were so shallow and had such large crews that they were of no practical value as cargo ships. While earlier versions in the tenth and eleventh centuries might have served to carry some cargo the modified medieval galley was purely for fighting. Those warships had to be produced at government-owned shipyards, such as the arsenals at Venice and Barcelona, since no private individual would undertake the task. There was no potential reward to shippers.

One option tried at the Arsenal in Venice at the end of the thirteenth century was to build a vessel more in the shape of a cargo ship but with oars. The great galley proved a decent sailing ship, capable of voyages from Italy to the Holy Land, the north shore of the Black Sea and even to England and the Low Countries. The rowers increased the cost of operating the vessels so the ships proved useful only for the most valuable to cargoes such as high quality textiles, the best wools and people, that is pilgrims. The rowers did also mean that the great galleys were not as much subject to wind and weather. They could make their way in and out of port much more easily because they could generate their own propulsion. The work of moving such ships under oars was hard and so the crew tried to avoid rowing as much as possible. Even so great galleys did find a place for a limited range of commercial ventures in the late Middle Ages and through the sixteenth century. Being around and in use they, along with the smaller and lower war galleys, offered an example of an alternate form of ship design which could and did serve as a source of ideas for the construction of other types.

The sailing cargo ship of the high Middle Ages in the Mediterranean grew larger while retaining most features of its Roman predecessor. The length-to-breadth ratio was generally around three. The keel and with it the hull was curved, swept up at the stern. There were rudders on either side with the tillers passing to a point at the middle of a raised deck at the stern where the helmsmen could handle both of them. These cargo ships rode high in the water, given their capacity, so captains had to ensure that deck cargo was light to avoid difficulties in handling. On the larger vessels there was not just one but two masts, each with its own lateen sail. The masts were raked forward to improve the performance of the sails. The addition of a second mast did much more than simply increase the potential sail area and thus the potential size of the ship. With two sails captains had much more control over their ships. Once on a course, by making small adjustments in the position of the sails the captain could direct the ship by balancing the wind forces on the two separate sails. The lateen sail was better for sailing close to the wind than its square counterpart but with two lateen sails, and the greater control involved, going to windward was much easier. Two-masted ships, both galleys and cargo ships, appeared in the Mediterranean already in the twelfth century and probably before. Improved over time, they proved capable of carrying a variety of cargo and in increasing quantities, including carrying Crusaders and all their equipment and horses to the Holy Land on those major expeditions of the twelfth and thirteenth centuries.

The Crusades brought new types of ships to the Mediterranean. Viking ships came from Norway and large cargo vessels, cogs, came from England and the Low Countries. It was not until early in the fourteenth century though that the cog and the entire northern tradition of shipbuilding had an effect in the Mediterranean. The cog could carry more cargo than its southern European counterpart for each meter of length. It had disadvantages though and southern shipbuilders tried to overcome those by adapting the northern type to what they knew. The first step was to change construction to skeleton-first, dropping the overlapping planking of the North. Builders also modified the stepping of the mast and the rigging. They retained the sternpost rudder and castles at bow and stern. The modified cog proved a valuable bulk carrier for certain Italian and Iberian towns. But what made it even more effective was another modification builders made some time in the course of the fourteenth century.

If two-masted galleys and cargo ships were superior to single-masted vessels then, presumably so southern European shipbuilders thought, would be a two-masted cog. Instead of adding another square sail on the new mast at the stern, though, they put the typical Mediterranean lateen sail there, creating the carrack. The combination gave the carrack an ability to sail closer to the wind because of the lateen sail while retaining its greater size because of the square sail. Two-masted carracks were in use by the closing years of the fourteenth century, making trips throughout the Mediterranean but also into the Atlantic and the English Channel.

They would remain bulk carriers at least through the fifteenth century although they increasingly faced competition from an even more efficient, versatile and effective type: the full-rigged ship.

With two sails captains were able to balance one with another. In the two-masted carrack the sails were of different types and the mainsail was large being the principal driving sail. In a following wind a captain would find his ship falling off in one direction and it did not take long before a captain or shipbuilder hit on the idea of balancing the lateen sail at the stern with a sail at the bow. That way as the ship fell off the sail on a foremast would catch the wind and bring the ship back on course. The foresail in the beginning was not large but greatly added to control over the ship. All the essential features of the three-masted ship then had come into place, probably already by the first years of the fifteenth century. The three-masted ship was easier to handle than its predecessors. With a lateen sail it could get closer to the wind than a vessel with only square sails. With square sails it took less crew to handle the sails and less skilled crew for the jobs on board. Vessels could be built larger without a proportionate increase in crew or in risk of loss of the ship. Skeleton construction made it possible to adjust hull shape and also, once the ship was in service, to make repairs more easily. The three-masted ship was superior to any European ship which came before. It formed the basis for European ship design for the next four hundred years and more. It was the basis for the superiority of Europeans at sea.

In the case of the full-rigged ship, as with all others, captains and shipbuilders found ways to improve them over time. Mariners added more sails, diversifying the sail plan. A small sail slung under the bowsprit gave greater control, supplementing the foresail. A sail above the mainsail on the mainmast supplemented the main driving sail and made it possible to make that mainsail smaller. With a greater number of sails the number of crew could be decreased. The largest sail was smaller so fewer men were needed to handle that sail. They could deal with each sail in turn which also gave the captain greater flexibility in handling changing wind conditions. Brought back to northern Europe in the new form local shipbuilders there had difficulty in changing over to producing the new three-masted carrack. They typically retained some features or construction methods from the old cog. That created local variants of the ship though the differences were often subtle. The hull shape proved highly versatile, able to sustain a broad range of different relative lengths and shapes so that adjustments for shallow harbors or

Figure VI. In 1520, when King Henry VIII of England embarked at Dover for a meeting with his French counterpart, Francis I, Henry mustered as an escort to symbolize the strength of his monarchy, the ships of his newly constituted navy, including two massive four-masted vessels. The artist's rendering of the event is more devoted to showing the vessels as symbols of royal power than to depicting what actually happened. *Reproduced by permission of Her Majesty Queen Elizabeth II.*

especially stormy conditions were possible with little or no loss in sailing qualities.

Three-masted ships proved capable of carrying more cargo per crew member than earlier types. That made them not only economically more efficient in Europe but also effective vessels for exploration. In the fourteenth century Iberian explorers used barks, descendants of Viking ships. They then turned to caravels, low slung ships from the Mediterranean with two masts, each with a lateen sail. The ship itself caught little wind and so was good at tacking, necessary given the contrary winds Portuguese explorers found as they explored the African coast. Shipbuilders modified that simple coastal vessel so that caravels appeared in various forms. The most durable was a relatively large cargo ship mounting four masts with lateen sails on all but the square-rigged foremast. Caravels like that enjoyed a long career in trade between Iberia and the Atlantic Islands. Caravels were exceptional among vessels of exploration, though. Once the Portuguese found out about the prevailing winds and currents of the Atlantic off West Africa they too, like all other explorers, turned to forms of the full-rigged ship.

Voyages into unknown waters created much greater demands on ships. They had to be maneuverable, reliable and durable. They also had to be efficient carriers of cargo. In Europe ships carried enough food for four months and water for one month for each crewman. That was 500 kilograms of cargo space for each man on board. For his voyages Columbus carried about 15 months worth of food and six months of water or about 1300 kilograms per crewman. Vasco da Gama on his voyage to India took almost 36 months worth of food and six months worth of water or about 2600 kilograms per crewman. On voyages of discovery the crew was usually, for all kinds of good reasons, about twice the normal size of crews in familiar European waters. That meant that in Europe with a vessel of 30 tons if there were 2 tons per crewman then 15 men would need 7.5 tons of cargo space set aside for their needs which would leave 22.5 tons for payload. But on a voyage of discovery in unknown waters a 30-man crew in that same 30-ton vessel would need 39 tons of cargo space for their needs. The ship simply could not make the voyage. Until the design of the full-rigged ship, modified and improved, came into widespread use many voyages of exploration were logistically impossible. The critical parameters in such voyages were the amount of food and water needed per man and the tons served per crew member. It was hard to force down the needs of the crew, so the tons served per crew member had to rise before distant voyages could become first practical and then economically viable. European ships of the Middle Ages could make impressive voyages over long distance. But getting somewhere is less than half the battle. Much more important was the ability to get back to the starting point.

The vessels explorers used might vary in size and in the precise configuration of the rigging but they were almost invariably full-rigged ships. Columbus's *Santa María* and most other ships traveling to the New World had three masts with a lateen sail on the mizzenmast at the stern. The Portuguese carracks which made the longer and more dangerous voyages around the Cape of Good Hope, up the east coast of Africa and then across the Arabian Sea to India were larger than the full-rigged ships of the Atlantic. They carried more sail and were built much higher in the water. That made them much more defensible but also clumsier. By the end of the sixteenth century they were approaching 2,000 tons, among the largest of wooden ships ever built. The rig was so well balanced though that in the open ocean with regular winds even a handful of men could sail them. They were just large modifications of the full-rigged ship.

Guns on board ship were known well before the voyages of exploration. They began as light, anti-personnel weapons used to hurl projectiles at those on the decks of opposing ships. Toward the end of the fifteenth century though governments began to put heavy siege cannon on either side of sailing ships. Those big guns could, if they ever fired properly, sink an enemy ship. Such guns created the opportunity for battles at sea which were not like land battles but instead artillery duels with boarding only a final and often unnecessary action. It would be more than a century before guns became reliable enough or accurate enough or inexpensive enough for that to be true. But already in the early sixteenth century, the presence of guns and especially big guns had implications for the design of sailing ships. Guns were heavy so they had to be carried low in the ship and balanced with equal numbers on either side. There had to be gunports so that the holes in the hull through which the guns could pass did not become gaps for water to pour in when the guns were at rest. Space had to be cleared away for the operation of the guns and cargo space had to be found for the powder and shot of various sorts used in the guns. If captains were going to stand off from enemy ships and fire at them then the speed and maneuverability of warships became more important to them. Through the sixteenth century the distinction between the design of warships, armed with guns, and cargo ships became greater until cargo ships became helpless in battle and warships were only built and used by governments since the vessels had no commercial use at all. Guns made certain ship types more valuable and forced adjustments in the design of ships. The new waters visited by European ships, new routes followed also put pressure on European shipbuilders to make adjustments in the design of the full-rigged ship. Changes in cargoes carried within Europe also gave reason to modify existing designs. The basic form of the full-rigged ship might continue but European builders produced a vast array of variants in the sixteenth and seventeenth centuries to meet the growing range of needs of Europeans shippers and governments. Those different types with their typically longer and lower hulls, their more diversified and divided sail plans made possible not just the voyages of exploration and colonization of the Renaissance and later. They also served to expand the scope of the European trading network, both in Europe and beyond. They played a large and probably immeasurable part in giving Europeans a superiority in navigation throughout the world.

Already by the end of the fifteenth century there was a variety of ships in use in Europe for various purposes. The variety provided a store of tools for many different jobs. Perhaps the most important feature of Columbus's flagship, the *Santa María,* was that she was not unique. She was just an ordinary vessel of the day as were many of the ships used on voyages of exploration and colonization. Iberians were able to take advantage of newly discovered routes to the Far East and the New World very quickly because of the variety of technically sophisticated vessels which they had immediately available and in, for the day, large numbers. The technical advances in ship design which had been the norm in Europe in the fourteenth and fifteenth centuries made long-distance voyages economically viable. In the hands of a skilled captain three-masted ships could weather violent storms, make their way through narrow waters and take effective advantage of favorable winds. Navigation, in the broadest sense, at the end of the fifteenth century could be and was raised to a higher level than ever before in Europe, and a higher level by any measure.

The limitations to oceanic sailing were not just technological. In the broad range of advance in knowledge about astronomy and geography, in the exploration of ideas and new lands, in the developments in the cut of sails and rudders it is all too easy to overlook the very real economic constraints on navigation. It is just as wrong to overlook naval considerations in the actions of sailors. Mariners always knew the importance of security, of defense against attack. They also always knew that if the returns from a voyage were less than expenditure the voyage was a failure. Surprising is the level of technical progress achieved under the conditions that prevailed. Gains were made slowly. Technical information was passed on in rather primitive fashion. Shipbuilders and mariners somehow understood the technical limitations and economic needs, articulated those needs one to the other, and found solutions to the problems as they understood them and within boundaries that they could not explain. Shipbuilding with the breakthrough of around 1400, the introduction of multimasted ships with skeleton-first construction, became a leader in technology in Europe. That sector demonstrated signs of continued technological changes, of continued advance through the following two centuries and more. The superior and improving ships which came from European yards in the fifteenth and sixteenth centuries tipped the balance between land and sea in the lives of Europeans more toward maritime activity. The technical changes created new opportunities for Europeans and laid the basis for a changed definition of the role of the sea and seaborne commerce in daily life. The technical changes also created opportunities for an expansion in the role of the state—and for the Renaissance that meant monarchies—in the search for knowledge, in the use of the sea and in the daily lives of subjects. The distinguished maritime historian, John H. Parry, called the navigational accomplishments of Europeans of the fifteenth and sixteenth centuries "the discovery of the sea" but it would be just as correct to call it a conquest with Europeans and peoples throughout the world in their train better able to use the sea to satisfy their own needs, desires and even pleasures.

SUGGESTIONS FOR FURTHER READING

Cipolla, Carlo. *European Culture and Overseas Expansion*. (Harmondsworth, Middlesex: Penguin Books, 1970).

Denoix, L. "Charactéristiques des Navires de l'Époque des Grandes Découvertes," in *Actes du Cinquième Colloque International d'Historie Martime (1960)*. (Michel Mollat, ed., Paris: S. E. V. P. E. N., 1966, 137–147).

Harland, John. *Seamanship in the Age of Sail*. (London: Conway Maritime Press, 1984).

Magnusson, Magnus, and Hermann Palsson, trans. *The Vinland Sagas The Norse Discovery of America*. (Harmondsworth, Middlesex: Penguin Books, 1965).

Miskimin, Harry A. *The Economy of Early Renaissance Europe.* (Englewood Cliffs, New Jersey: Prentice-Hall, Inc., 1969).

Miskimin, Harry A. *The Economy of Late Renaissance Europe, 1460–1600.* (Cambridge: Cambridge University Press, 1977).

Needham, Joseph. *The Shorter Science and Civilization in China.* (Cambridge: Cambridge University Press, 1981).

Oakley, Francis. *The Western Church in the Later Middle Ages.* (Ithaca, New York: Cornell University Press, 1979).

Parry, J. H. *Discovery of the Sea.* (London: Weidenfeld and Nicolson, 1975).

Parry, J. H. *Europe and a Wider World 1415–1715.* (London: Hutchinson University Library, 1949).

Phillips, J. R. S. *The Medieval Expansion of Europe.* (Oxford: Oxford University Press, 1988).

Phillips, William D. and Carla Rahn. *The Worlds of Christopher Columbus.* (Cambridge: Cambridge University Press, 1992).

Polo, Marco. *The Travels,* R. Latham, trans. (Harmondsworth, Middlesex: Penguin Books, 1958).

Pryor, John H. *Geography, technology, and war Studies in the maritime history of the Mediterranean 649–1571.* (Cambridge: Cambridge University Press, 1988).

Scammell, G. V. *The World Encompassed.* (Berkeley: University of California Press, 1981).

Unger, Richard W. *The Ship in the Medieval Economy, 600–1600.* (Montreal: McGill-Queen's University Press, 1980).

Part II
Portuguese Expansion

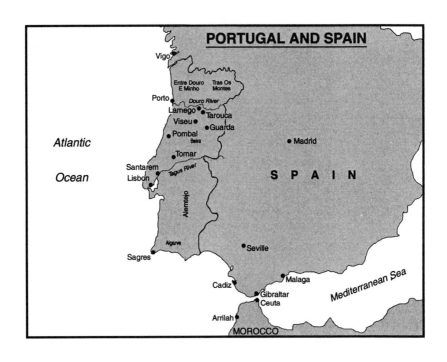

4

BACKGROUND AND BEGINNINGS OF PORTUGUESE MARITIME EXPANSION

Charles Verlinden

The maritime expansion of Portugal was no miracle that began with a sudden wave of Henry the Navigator's wand. Henry, who navigated so little, has been, as often as not, the subject of pseudoscientific hagiography. His common label, "the navigator," seems to date only from 1868, when the English writer R. H. Major published his *Life of Prince Henry surnamed the Navigator*. The book was a best-seller for many years, because of its romantic interpretation. Its primary source was the *Cronica dos feitos notaveis que se passaram na conquista da Guine por mandado do Infante D. Henrique,* written by Gomes Eanes de Zurara during the lifetime of the prince, with the flattery that a courtier, who was at the same time a chronicler, was prone to manifest towards a prince who protected and paid him. Following Major, Raymond Beazley used this same romantic biographical material in his 1890 book, *Prince Henry the Navigator,* using the same surname Major had used 20 years earlier and with the same interpretation of Zurara, who surprisingly enough had never used the now famous surname in his yet very flattering *Cronica*. For Beazley, too, Henry was a saintly character who spent all his days in work, building up his wonderful knowledge, often passing the night without sleep.

Nevertheless, our subject requires that we try to find out how long-distance navigation started in Portugal long before Prince Henry's time. The standard sources tell us very little and emphasize the agrarian character of Portugal rather than the beginnings of navigation.[1] In fact, it is under the great King Dinis who ruled between 1279 and 1325 that Portuguese maritime enterprise began on

an international level. Even before that, under Dinis's father, King
Alfonso III (1248–79), there were connections with northwestern
Europe. Alfonso's law of 26 December 1253 fixed prices for a long series of commodities, imported from Flanders, northern France and
England.[2] The law mentions cloth coming from eight towns in Flanders, against only one in England, and then without any name of a
city. As early as 1253, there were certainly closer relations with
Flanders than with England. The Portuguese law applied to the region of Entre Douro e Minho, whose principal port is Porto at the
mouth of the Douro river. Probably most of the northern types of
cloth arrived there. Unfortunately, we do not know whether it came
on board Portuguese or foreign ships, but since the king was also
count of Boulogne, close to Flanders, it is very possible that Portuguese ships frequently went that far north during his reign.

Under King Dinis, the traffic was organized and the first permanent Portuguese trading center in northwestern Europe was established at Harfleur on the estuary of the Seine River in Normandy,
as we know through a very detailed privilege given by King Philip
the Fair of France in January 1310.[3] This Latin privilege was meant
for all *"mercatoribus portus Portugallie et Lexibone"* who were at
Harfleur. Through this document, we learn that Harfleur was a
relay-station for Portuguese trade with Flanders, both by ship and
by cart over land from Normandy to Bruges, then the most important port of northern Europe. In 1341, Philip VI of France confirmed
the Portuguese entrepôt at Harfleur as a permanent establishment
in three different privileges. In addition, he extended permission to
merchants and mariners from southern Portugal or Algarve[4] to stay
and to trade there. The initial base for this commercial development
had begun under King Dinis in 1310 and, in 1317, Dinis took an even
more important decision. He appointed a rich Genoese merchant
and mariner as admiral of the Portuguese fleet.[5] Like many of his
compatriots since the end of the thirteenth century, this man had
specialized in trade with Flanders. The Genoese ships generally
stopped over in Portuguese ports, and there were many more Genoese to be seen in Lisbon. Among them, King Dinis chose Manuel
Pessagno (Peçanha in Portuguese), made him a vassal of the Crown,
giving him in fee the royal estate of Pedreira in Lisbon. Pessagno's
oath of allegiance as a new vassal and admiral implied his service to
the King with *"viinte homeens de Genua sabedores de mar, taaes que
seiam convenhaiis para alcaydes de galees e para arrayzes."* This
means that from 20 Genoese, the commanding officers of the galleys
were to be chosen, and also of the *navios,* the sailing ships which

were very different from the rowed galleys. The royal deed of appointment shows that all Portuguese mariners were to obey "*Miser Manuel Genoes, meu vassalo.*" And this went on under the descendants of Admiral Peçanha and the successors of King Dinis, Alfonso IV, Fernando, and even João I, founder of the new dynasty of Aviz and father of Henry the Navigator. Three sons of Manuel Peçanha were successively admirals of the Portuguese fleet like their father, and after them, two other members of the same great Genoese merchant family. All had received the same privileges, holding at the disposal of the Portuguese kings their staffs of Genoese experts in navigation. We know some of these men: one, through cartographical evidence complete with written documents; another one, only through written, and afterwards printed material.

It is well known that the Canary Islands, known in Antiquity as *Insulae Fortunatae,* were forgotten in the Middle Ages, but were rediscovered by the Genoese Lanzarotto Malocello. The date of their rediscovery is wildly different from one author to another.[6] The first mention of the rediscovery is found on the Majorcan chart made by Angelino Dulcert in 1339. Among the four Canary Islands that appear on it for the first time on a chart, there is an "*insula de Lanzarotus Marocelus.*" On this island the cross of Genoa is drawn, while later charts like that of the Genoese Bartolomeo Pareto, add after "*Marocelus*" or "*Malocelus,*" the word for Genoese, "*Genuensis.*" This means that a Genoese made the discovery, but it was not a discovery for Genoa, since Genoa never claimed any of the Canaries.

On the contrary, Portugal claimed the archipelago. In a letter from King Alfonso IV to Pope Clement VI in 1345,[7] the king says that inhabitants of his realm, "*regnicole*" as the Latin text has it, made the discovery, but he adds that up to then no possession had been taken due to the war with Castile that began in 1336. Therefore, it is possible that the discovery was made slightly before that year. On the other side, we know that it was the work of a Genoese from the chart of Angelino Dulcert in 1339. The discoverer was necessarily one of the Genoese officers of Admiral Pessagno who lived in Lisbon when ashore, as we learn from the royal privileges for the Peçanhas. This man, Lanzarotto Malocello, obviously commanded a crew that was mainly Portuguese. We also know through a series of notarial deeds from Genoa that there were many current business relations and maritime collaborations existing between the Pessagnos and the Malocellos.[8]

Another Genoese in Portuguese service, Nicoloso da Recco, continued the reconnaissance of the Canaries. On June 1, 1341, two *navios* and a *navicula minuia,* which meant a Portuguese *barca,* had left Lisbon. They crossed the whole archipelago as we know from a letter of Italian merchants living in Seville who had been informed by Nicoloso himself.[9] The archipelago was reached within five days which shows that the way thither was known. Nicoloso's was the first expedition after Lanzarotto's, five years earlier, since the islands still had no collective name and were only called *"eas insulas quas vulgo repertas dicimus,"* i.e., the islands found recently to wit— by Lanzarotto, a colleague of Nicoloso.

In the cartography of the fourteenth century, the increasing geographical knowledge of the Portuguese can be followed and understood much better than in the Portuguese chronicles written by courtiers sometimes a century, or even more, after the actual discovery or reconnaissance. The fact that the cartography is Italian or Majorcan is not surprising since the information easily reached Italy or Majorca through the Genoese Peçagna admirals. For Majorca, we have already seen that this occurred with the Dulcert chart of 1339. Another example is to be found in The Medicean Atlas of the Biblioteca Laurenziana in Florence, made by Genoese, probably in 1351. For the first time, the archipelago of the Madeiras appears in it. Here one can find the *Iso la de Legname,* which is the Italian name used before the later Portuguese Madeira. Both words mean "wood," referring to the very dense cover of trees and arborescent shrub before the Portuguese colonization and deforestation in the following century from Henry the Navigator's time onwards. Also, the other important island of the archipelago, Porto Santo, appears in the 1351 Atlas. This means that crews whose officers spoke Italian first sighted the archipelago of the Madeiras, since the names obviously come from them. One thinks immediately of the Genoese who served the Portuguese kings.

The nomenclature is still Italian on the magnificent 1375 chart of the Majorcan Abraham Cresques in the Bibliothèque Nationale in Paris. Some of the Azores also appear here. There is also Italian nomenclature in the *"Libro delconscimiento de todos los reynos e tierras e señorios que son por elmundo"* by an anonymous Aragonese Franciscan, who relates imaginary voyages he could have made up himself, just like Sir John Mandeville did about the same time. The friar uses charts to determine his itineraries and enumerates all three archipelagoes of the Canaries, the Madeiras and the Azores with 25 islands. This is nearly correct and comes right down from the 1385 chart by the Majorcan Soler. All that Italian nomenclature goes on in other Majorcan charts until the end of the fourteenth century and the beginning of the fifteenth, when the Azores become still more detailed and accurate.

How was all this possible? After the discovery of the Canary Islands by Lanzarotto Malocello and the voyage of Nicoloso da Recco, there had been, just the year after Nicoloso's reconnaissance, two Majorcan voyages to the "*Ylles noveylament trobades a les parts de ponent,*" which means the islands newly discovered in those places. This was in 1342, but just like the two previous Genoese-commanded Portuguese voyages, the Majorcan voyages had no political consequence. Moreover during the next year, Aragon absorbed the ephemeral Majorcan kingdom. However, everyone holding political power in southwestern Europe became interested in the newly discovered archipelago and Pope Clement VI, who by then had his seat not in Rome but in Avignon, granted the archipelago to the Castilian pretender Luis de la Cerda in 1344. The Castilian King Alfonso XI protested, as did the Aragonese Peter IV. Alfonso IV of Portugal in the letter of 1345 that we have utilized previously, claimed the islands, but admitted that Portugal had not yet taken possession of them. It was not until 1370 that the Portuguese took possession of the Canary Islands, and it was at that moment that they started their first, but ephemeral, colonial expansion, exactly 24 years before the birth of Henry the Navigator.

It is worthwhile to examine these events more closely. We know from a kind of diary written by the two priests who went to the Canaries in 1402 with the French adventurers, Jean de Béthencourt and Gadifer de la Salle, that these men found on the island of Lanzarote "*ung viel chastel que Lancelot Maloesel avait jadis fait faire quand il conquist la pays,*" i.e., an old castle that Lanzaroto Malocello had already had made when he conquered the country. The Spanish historian Serra Rafols, who edited the text, thought that Lanzarotto Malocello had occupied the island under the Genoese flag for many years, during the first two decades of the fourteenth century. We have seen, however, that neither Lanzarote nor any other of the Canary islands have ever been Genoese. We also know, from Angelino Dulcert's 1339 chart, that Lanzarote was only sighted a short time before that date, and from the letter of King Alfonso IV of Portugal, that "*regnicole*" of his kingdom had been there, namely Lanzarotto and Nicoloso both of whom were Genoese residing in Portugal and in Portuguese service.

We know that the Portuguese took possession of the islands in 1370, from a deed of King Fernando, the predecessor of Henry the Navigator's father. A deed of João I written in 1385 tells us that

Lanzarotto was killed that year on the island of Lanzarote by the natives. This is confirmed by the *Libro del Conoscimiento,* of an Aragonese Franciscan, dating from the same time. In the royal Portuguese charters, Lanzarotto is called de Framqua instead of Malocelo, because he had, in the meantime, been in French service, like several other members of his family and had become an admiral there. All this shows that the island of Lanzarote in the Canary archipelago had been Portuguese between King Fernando's deed of 1370 and that of King João I in 1385. Henry the Navigator remembered this much later and several times claimed the archipelago in vain, after it had been conquered by the Castilians.[10]

Some problems in navigation are involved in all this. First of all, there was the transformation of the Portuguese caravel. From a small ship for coastal fishery in the twelfth century, it became, by crossing with Italian and northern European ship types, the ship of the great discoveries. The caravel-planking came from northern Europe and the lateen or triangular sail from the Mediterranean. Combined with the light and rather small shape of the coastal fishery ship, this resulted in an ideal type of reconnaissance ship that lasted until after the discovery of America and the southeastern sea route to India. This improved ship type allowed a much swifter return from the Canaries. All the more so that it has more masts than previous ships and that it stood out more easily to sea, so that it could go far enough to the West in the Atlantic to catch the trade winds blowing from the West towards Europe. As a consequence, seamen sighted and reconnoitered first the Madeiras, and then the Azores, during the fourteenth century as shown in the contemporaneous cartography. All this was a question of winds, not of sophisticated instruments. Dead reckoning and primitive astronomical navigation were enough. In the northern hemisphere, where the eastern Atlantic archipelagoes and central America lie, the altitude of the pole-star corresponds approximately with the latitude. When the horizon is unclouded, which happens frequently when the trade-winds blow, there is enough time to take the altitude when the stars are already visible and the horizon is still clear enough. When the angular distance from the horizon does not exceed 15 degrees, and such is the case in the area of the eastern Atlantic archipelagoes, a mariner, who is accustomed to it, can estimate the angle by the naked eye within one degree, sailing by dead reckoning and without instruments. Such a mariner knows how to find the pole-star and other stars that help him as reference marks. All this was accomplished in the time of the Genoese admirals of the Peçanha family, and their largely Portuguese crews, as the king reconfirmed their privileges in 1372 and again in 1383.

Meanwhile, during the time of Henry the Navigator, the Canaries were passing more and more under Castilian control, explaining why the Portuguese concentrated on the Madeiras and the Azores.

Prince Henry the Navigator was born on 4 March 1394 in Porto. Properly known as Dom Henrique, he was the third son of King João I, the founder of the new dynasty of Aviz. Henrique actually became a prince of some importance in 1408, when his father asked the Cortes or Parliament to grant him 5 *contos* a year to keep up his household. The eldest of the three brothers and the future king, Duarte, got 8 *contos,* while Pedro, the future regent, got 5, like Henry. This allowed the princes to maintain their royal standing, *as suas honras e estados.* With what the Cortes added to buy *terras e herdamentos,* land and properties, Henry controlled, at the age of 14, 10 contos a year.[11] By the age 17, he had concentrated his possessions around Viseu, Lamego and Guarda in the Beira.[12] When he was 20, he gave great feasts at Viseu. Zurara, in his *Cronica de Ceuta,* said that Henry's passion for luxury and bursts of showing off was *de guisa que parecia a alguns extrangeiros que por alli passaron que aquelle ajutamento nom era senom de corte de rey.* Thus, it was clear that he already learned how to promote his image and that he intended to play a role that placed him at the same height as his elder brothers.

In 1415, at the assault of Ceuta in Morocco, just opposite Gibraltar, he behaved as a knight, indeed he was dubbed there by his father, but he held no important command. This did not prevent him, in 1416 at the age of 22, from getting the title of duke of Viseu, a town that he already possessed.[13] In 1420, he became *"regedor e governador do Mestrado da Ordem de Cristo."* As Master of the Order of Christ, he found means that he would use, as we shall see. He now controlled Tomar, the capital city of the Order, which he called *"minha vila,"* showing how much he considered the possessions of the Order of Christ as his own. He organized the fairs that were held there and let houses and shops to merchants. Seeing how much this yielded, he did the same at his ducal town of Viseu, and later at two of his other estates in Beira, Pombal and Tarouca. He followed this policy with remarkable continuity, showing foresight when his economic advantage was concerned. He was a very successful entrepreneur.

In 1421, he acquired rights to a fishery in the Tagus River and, even better in 1433, the monopoly of tuna fishing along the coast of Algarve, allowing him either to operate with his own ships or to let permission to others. Later on when his ships followed the Atlantic coast of northwestern Africa, he instructed his crews to hunt seals, since their oil could be utilized in his soapworks, of which he enjoyed the monopoly in Portugal itself as well as in his island of Madeira. Coral, too, interested him and he acquired the monopoly on it in 1450, at the end of the contract held by the Italian, Bartolomeo Florentin, and the Frenchman, Jean Forbin of Marseilles. The saintly knight of the chronicle appears here as a successful capitalist and, like capitalists of other times, he invested what came from business in real estate and in new industrial activities, such as dyeing and producing textiles at Batalha and Lagos.[14]

Zurara in his "Cronica dos feitos notaveis que se passaram na conquista de Guine," presents the biography of Henry as if the exploration of the northern parts of the Atlantic coast of Africa were by far the most spectacular aspect of the Infante's activity, but it is worthwhile briefly to examine whether the proportion of the Infante's achievements in the islands, on the one hand, and along the African coast, on the other, actually matched what traditional historiography tells, under the influence of the magnificently written chronicle of Henry's panegyrist.

The Madeiras and the Azores had been reconnoitred in the fourteenth century, but taking possession of them and the beginning of their colonization were achievements of Henry the Navigator.

In 1425, the Portuguese, João Gonçalves Zarco and Tristão Vaz Teixeira, two noblemen of the retinue of Prince Henry, occupied the uninhabited archipelago of the Madeiras. As a consequence, King Duarte gave the island in fee to Henry, by a royal deed of 26 September 1433, immediately after his accession to the throne. The real colonization and settlement now started. A document of the same date from the Order of Christ says that the settlement was "novamente," i.e. newly undertaken, showing that it is really Prince Henry who made it possible and that the first occupation of 1425 was of little consequence. Next, Henry used his own financial and economic means, as well as those of the Order of Christ, to further the settlement. The Infante realized that more naval and human resources were needed than just two noblemen with their crews, as in 1425.

On 8 May 1440, the Infante, as lord of the islands, granted to Tristão, "cavaleiro da minha casa," a deed to part of Madeira. Although Tristão was one of the men who had taken possession of the island in 1425, he had now to administer his hereditary fee *"em justiça e em direito."* He received the monopoly of the grain mills, as feudal lords generally enjoyed, and this shows, by the way, that the population had already increased. Estates were granted to newcomers who had to till their land and make it productive within five years. This required, first, the heavy work of deforesting the island, and afterwards, introducing new plants, among which sugarcane rapidly became the most important. There was obviously a flow of people that came in the ships of the *Infante,* lord of the islands. Livestock had to be imported, too, and as deforestation progressed, more were needed. After a while, the land had to be fenced in order to protect the new fields from the livestock, showing both the development of agriculture and of the population. All this implied active navigation for the *Infante*'s ships. Meanwhile, Prince Henry granted the second largest island of the archipelago, Porto Santo, in 1446 to Bartolomeo Perestrello, a second generation Italian immigrant, who was already one of the prince's *"cavaleiros da casa."* Henry granted him the whole island, *"minha hilha,"* as he says in the document of appointment. We know through the Venetian Cà da Mosto that in 1455, some nine years later, Porto Santo was really productive and that the population enjoyed the island's productivity with much grain and that it was *"abbondante di carne di manzi."* The oxen and cows had, of course, been imported by sea and, in 1458, we learn that there were herds of them, further proof of intense navigation by the prince's men.

The beginning of sugar production on Madeira was equally an achievement of Dom Henrique. In 1452, he concluded an agreement with his *"escudeiro,"* Diogo de Teyve, whom he granted the right to have a machine, or *engenho,* constructed to produce sugar. This is the beginning of an industry that would make Madeira, for a series of decades, the biggest producer of sugar in the world. The agreement says that one third of the production has to be delivered to the *Infante,* who completed the outfit by supplying a sugar press. This was a real business association, and all the details of the production were regulated in the deed of agreement. Other sugar producers soon arrived, among them foreigners, such as the German nobleman whom the prince allowed to come with eight compatriots and who got permission, in 1457, to plant vines and canes.

To the Madeiras, Henry added the Azores. On 2 July 1439, King Alfonso V, then seven years old, permitted Henry to populate and colonize seven islands of this second Portuguese archipelago. A short time before, the *Infante* had sent ships with livestock to feed colonists on the uninhabited islands. The regent, Dom Pedro, Henry's elder brother, was also interested in one of the Azores, but Pedro's death at the battle of Alfarrobeira in 1449 left the whole archipelago to Dom Henrique. This, too, implied intense activity for the *Infante*'s ships. In this sense, he deserves the label of navigator, but actually he made others navigate for him.

The same pattern of events occurred along the Atlantic coast of northwestern Africa, but with fewer ships and men than in the navigation to the islands, where for a while he dreamed of making a kingdom for himself, as shown, for instance, in a document of 1450 in which he speaks of *"minha real authoridade como senhor das ilhas."*[15]

Zurara's *Chronicle* concentrates on the African coast and there he shows Henrique not as an economic entrepreneur, but as a heroic knight who conquered Guinea. Of the 97 chapters of his *Chronicle,* only seven treat, and then very superficially, of the islands. The others describe with infinite detail the individual voyages of the Navigator's men along the African coast, detailing the capture of Moorish and Negro slaves. Between 1441 till 1448, they amounted to 927.[16]

The events are as follows. In 1434, Gil Eannes went further than the insignificant Cape of Bojador, where Portuguese navigation along the African coast had stopped up to that time, although we know that some Genoese and some Catalans had earlier gone further. In 1435, another of Prince Henry's ships went 200 miles more to the south. Each time, there was only one ship, and not even a caravel: the first time, a *barca*; the second, a *barinel,* both smaller than the caravel. In 1436, ships cleared the desert-belt and reached Cape Blanco, another 200 miles to the South. For the next five years, there were no other voyages until 1441, but in that year, Antão Gonçalves and Nuno Tristão reached Rio de Oro, where they captured a few Moorish villagers and enslaved them. Zurara presents this episode and a series of similar events in his most brilliant heroic and chivalrous style. What he calls the conquest of Guinea is a series of similar stories. In 1448, Henry's ships reached the bay of Arguim, where a fort was built on a small island as a base for the slave trade. A year later, the Portuguese civil war began between the followers of the regent Dom Pedro and part of the nobility around the bastard line of Bragança. The result was Dom Pedro's death at Alfarrobeira and the triumph of the Braganças. They now dominated the 15-year-old king, Alfonso V. In this conflict, Dom Henrique had not supported his brother, but nevertheless, for the victorious party, he was more

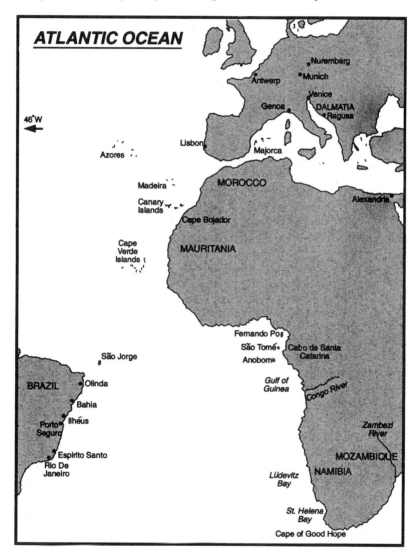

or less suspect. The king therefore suggested that Zurara, who was the official chronicler, should write Prince Henry's biography to show him as a hero of the struggle against the heathens and Moslems in Africa, a hero who was dreaming chivalrous, not political, dreams. Zurara achieved this purpose, and his image of Henry, drawn with such accomplished literary talent, impressed most of his contemporaries, as it has impressed so many ill-documented historians in later centuries.

In Portugal, a few decades ago, some historians saw the civil war of 1449 as a conflict between social classes: commoners interested in navigation and colonization around Dom Pedro, against nobles around the Braganças. Because there is no evidence to support such a view, it is now abandoned. Actually, the civil war was just a conflict between two groups of noblemen, one headed by a legitimate son of João I, namely Dom Pedro, the other by a bastard, the duke of Bragança.

Surprisingly enough, although he outlived the *Infante,* Zurara did not continue his biography until his hero's death in 1460. That year, Pedro de Sintra reached present-day Sierra Leone and Liberia, but it was too late for Henry to hear of it.[17] He had remained interested in Africa's coast, for it had allowed slave trade and had produced still more trading advantages, and sometimes even gold dust. But even so, these voyages had gone on with only one or two ships each time. This, together with the earlier long interruptions in the years between 1436 to 1441 and from 1447 to 1455, proves that the great majority of the crews and ships of the prince were bound for the Madeiras and the Azores, where Portuguese colonization was progressing so well under his direction. The real image is just the opposite of the picture Zurara paints for his readers.

A bull of Pope Nicolas V, dated 8 January 1455, has raised a problem for historians. The last sentences of this bull show clearly its real purpose: papal confirmation of the monopoly that Henry had secured in 1443 from the then 11-year-old King Alfonso V to grant licenses for navigation to the islands and to the African coast. During the years preceding 1455, non-Portuguese vessels had appeared in African waters,[18] and the bull provided that they were to be repelled also by papal excommunication against intruders. The bull's long and rhetorical *arenga* or introduction was obviously inspired by Henry's envoys. It said that, during the past 25 years, the Portuguese army had conquered Africa as far as Guinea, but no such army had gone any further south then Ceuta and northern Morocco. It also mentions the *"polum antarticum"* and Indians (*Indos*) who were Christians. That was enough for the Portuguese historian, or more exactly essayist, Joaquim Bensaude,[19] to describe Henry as a crusader against the Turks through an alliance with the supposedly Christian people of India. This was, of course, as silly as if one were to insinuate that Henry intended to explore the Antarctic because of the phrase *"polum antarticum"* in the *arenga* of the bull. In Henry's time, the Gulf of Guinea was not reached, so that it was impossible to understand the real southward extent of Africa. Nevertheless, some people still see Henry as thinking of circumnavigation and crusade, although even Zurara's panegyric does not go that far.

In conclusion, one can make out the real significance of Henry in the history of Portuguese navigation and expansion. Henry was not the romantic knight and hero that appears in Zurara's *Chronicle*. He was a pragmatic entrepreneur, who nevertheless did not forget that he was a royal prince surrounded by noblemen, who respected knights much more than successful entrepreneurs. Therefore, he certainly enjoyed the manner in which Zurara painted his image, but he utilized the noblemen of his own retinue in his island-world of the Atlantic, and along the African coast, from whence came slaves, seal oil and possibly gold dust. Most of his endeavor was towards the islands: the Madeiras, the Azores, and even the Canaries, where the Castilians outstripped him. Before his time, Portuguese navigation was coastal, even towards the northwestern Europe ports in England and Flanders. In the fourteenth century only the seamen of the Peçanhas, the Genoese admirals of Portugal, reconnoitred the archipelagoes, that later would interest the *Infante* so much. What was really the most important fact in his achievement was that, as a consequence of his enterprise in the archipelagoes, the Portuguese got used to sailing the high Atlantic. At that time, following the African coast was not the real problem. In that direction, the great problems would start after him and mainly under the great King João II, (1481–95), who would make it possible for his country to round the Cape of Good Hope, find the sea route to India and, even later, take possession of Brazil. João was the man who laid the foundation of what has been called the Portuguese Empire. What Henry did was to start ocean-going navigation, although he himself never crossed more than the strait of Gibraltar, and begin the Portuguese colonization of the islands. Uncritical and ill-documented historians have credited Henry with what came later, as if he had consciously foreseen and prepared it, but such attributions belong to the realm of imagination, not of scientific historical investigation.

NOTES

1. If one opens H. V. Livermore's standard *History of Portugal*, even in its second edition of 1966, one finds a chapter with the title "The agrarian monarchy." It has only a very short paragraph on the reign of King Dinis (1279–1325). The reader learns virtually nothing about the commercial and

maritime aspects of his reign, since the author considers everything merely "agrarian." The same is true for Charles Nowell's *History of Portugal* (New York, 1952). Both the Englishman and the American have taken their overemphasis on the agrarian monarchy from J. Lucio de Azevedo, *Epocas de Portugal economico* (1928). In 1960, Baily W. Diffie in his very superficial booklet, *Prelude to Empire: Portugal overseas before Henry the Navigator*, brings very few new insights and often inaccurate information. What he has written about the same period in *Foundations of the Portuguese Empire* (1977) is not better, but fortunately the second part of that book by George Winius is of a much higher quality.

2. *Portugaliae Monumenta Historica. Leges et Consuetudines* I (Lisbon, 1886), p. 192. See Charles Verlinden, "Contribution à l'etude de l'expansion de la draperie flamande dans la péninsule ibérique au XIIIe siècle," *Revue du Nord*, XXII (1936), pp. 5–20.

3. E. de Laurière, *Ordonnances des rois de France* II (1729), pp. 159 seq.

4. All this evidence was published anew and studied in detail in my article, "Deux aspects de l'expansion commerciale du Portugal au moyan âge: Harfleur au XIVe siècle, Middelbourg aux XIVe et XVe," *Revista Portuguesa de Historia,* IV (1947), pp. 5–45.

5. J. Martis da Silva Marques, *Descobrimentos Portugueses* (Lisbon, 1944), I, p. 28.

6. D'Avezac in 1848 preferred 1275, but called it himself a "*chiffre conjectural.*" Beazley in 1901 rounded it to 1270 without giving any reason, which did not prevent Prestage to take it over in his *Portuguese Pioneers* in 1933 without any proof. La Roncière in his *La découverte de l'Afrique* in 1925 selected, more or less haphazardly, 1312 and Hennig in *Terrae Incognitae* III (1953) followed suit with others after him. All that is rather sad as far as seriousness of scientific historical research is concerned.

7. A. J. Dias Dinis, *Monumenta Henricina* (Coimbra, 1960), I, p. 231.

8. C. Verlinden, "Lanzarotto Malocello et la dècouverte portugaise des Canaries," *Revue belge de Philologie et d'Histoire* (1958), pp. 1173–1209. C. Verlinden, "La découverte des archipels de la Mediterranée atlantique (Canaries, Madères, Açores) et la navigation astronomique primitive," *Revista Potuguesa de Historia,* (1976), pp. 105–131.

9. Silva Marques, *op. cit.,* I, pp. 77 seq., and Dias Dinis, *op. cit.,* I, pp. 202 seq.

10. C. Verlinden, "Henri le Navigateur et les iles Canaries," in *Vice Almirante A. Teixeira da Mota: In Memoriam* (Lisbon, 1987) I, pp. 43–55.

11. A. J. Dias Dinis, *Estudos Henriquinos* (Coimbra, 1960), I, pp. 381–384: Document of 7 April 1408.

12. *Ibid.,* pp. 386–390: Document of 27 April 1411.

13. *Ibid.,* pp. 392–393.

14. For all this, see the very accurate study in Dias Dinis, *Estudos Henriquinos,* pp. 1–107.

15. On Henry's activities in the islands, see C. Verlinden, "Formes féodales et domaniales de la colonisation portugaise spécialement sous Henri le Navigateur," *Revista Portuguesa de Historia,* IX (1960), pp. 1–44 and C. Verlinden, "Henri le Navigateur songea-t-il à crèer un 'Etat' insulaire," *Revista Portuguesa de Historia,* XII (1969), pp. 281–292.

16. Zurara, Chapter 96.

17. Dias Dinis, *Estudos Henriquinos,* pp. 317–369.

18. J. W. Blake, *Europeans in West Africa 1450–1560,* (London, 1942). Two volumes.

19. In a very superficial, excited chauvinistic book, *A cruzada do Infante Dom Henrique* (1942).

5

THE BIG LEAP UNDER DOM JOÃO II: FROM THE ATLANTIC TO THE INDIAN OCEAN

Charles Verlinden

The great king, Dom João II, eldest son of the insignificant, and later unbalanced, Alfonso V, was born in Lisbon on 5 May 1455. When he was 16, he participated in the conquest of Arzila on the Atlantic coast of Morocco. In the same year, he became a very rich and important prince, when he was granted six towns, including Lagos, the naval base in Algarve. In 1475, his father made him regent of the realm, in order to allow himself to travel to France and to fight a losing war against Castile. Two years later, Alfonso declared that he intended to join a religious order and that João should be proclaimed king. But in the same year, Alfonso changed his mind and remained king until his death in 1481. Actually, João had held power since about 1474 and, where maritime questions were concerned, even earlier. It is possible that at the age of 14, he was already influential enough to suggest to his father, who was only casually interested in Morocco, that the king conclude an agreement in November 1469 with the rich Lisbon merchant Fernão Gomes for commerce and exploration along the coast of Guinea. One of his pilots,[1] Rui de Sequeira, followed the coastline as far as 2° South of the equator, at Cape St. Catharina, after Gomes's contract was prolonged in 1473. Even the too often absent-minded king, in a document dated 4 May 1481, just a short time before his death, declared that João had held *"mui boa ordem a navegaçao destes trautos e os governava mui bem [held excellent order during the navigation to those parts and administered very well]."* The prince had also played an important part in concluding the treaties of Alcaçovas in 1479 and of Toledo in 1480. These agreements stipulated that Castile and Portugal would divide the eastern Atlantic, leaving Portugal to control, in addition to the Madeiras and the Azores, the whole area of the Atlantic south of the Canaries.

When he became king, João II severely punished the nobles of the duke of Bragança's party, who were still trying to dominate the political scene, executing some of them for conspiracy. The king's brother-in-law, the *Infante* Diogo, was involved. He was a son of Dom Fernando, successor of Henry the Navigator as lord of the islands, where colonization had progressed remarkably under his rule. At first, the king pardoned Dom Diogo, who was one of the ringleaders, but when he plotted again, King João, himself, stabbed Diogo to death in the castle of Palmela. From then on, there were no further plots and João focused on his foreign policy aimed at maintaining peace with other states in order to concentrate on maritime expansion.

Right from the beginning of the reign important events tread on each other's heels. Already before the end of 1481, the very efficient Diogo de Azambuja was sent to the Gold Coast to build the castle of São Jorge da Mina. This was done very rapidly, but also so well that the fort still stands.[2]

São Jorge da Mina, which had been reached 10 years before the construction of the castle, became not only the principal base for the gold and slave trade, but for voyages southward along the west African coast. The progressive voyages southward were planned with the very clear idea of reaching the southernmost extremity of the African continent. Up to this time, they had failed in reaching this objective, not realizing that it lay very far to the south. But at this time, the idea of circumnavigating Africa first became concrete and was no longer the vague rhetoric such as that found in the papal bull of 1455.

The first voyage of Diogo Cão in 1482–84 made this obvious. Beyond the points reached by the captains and pilots of Fernão Gomes, inspired wholly or partly by the crown prince, the royal explorer Cão penetrated into the completely unknown, not only geographically, but, much more important, nautically. Up to the time of Prince Henry and of Fernão Gomes, voyagers sailing south along the coast of Africa had found that ocean currents had made their passage easy. From the Portuguese coast downward a favorable current carries to the northern part of the coast of West Africa. Alongside the Moroccan and Mauritanian coastline, the Canarian current leads southward to Cape Verde and the beginning of the Gulf of Guinea, presenting no difficult navigational problems. The seamen who reconnoitered the west coast of northern Africa under Henry the Navigator faced no other problems than those resulting from the increasing distance from the base of departure in Portugal. The return, or *volta* was quickened from the Canaries northward by the trade winds that had, already in the fourteenth century, facilitated the reconnaissance of the Madeiras and the Azores. Also along the coast of the Gulf of Guinea, a west-east current helped navigation, while on high sea an opposite current made return easier.

South of the Gulf of Guinea, the situation was different, raising more complicated problems of navigation. There, the Benguela current pushes northward along the coast, opposing a southward passage. A north-south current does lie in the open sea, but it had yet to be found. In addition, the Doldrums played an important part.[3]

Cão's first achievement on the first of his voyages was to discover the mouth of the Congo River where, probably on 23 April 1483, he erected a commemorative monument or *padrão*. Farther to the south, he followed the coast of Angola nearly to the place where Mossamedes now stands, reaching it in August. Cão wrongly interpreted an eastward curve of the coast as indicating the southernmost extremity of the continent and thought that he was close to having access to the east coast of Africa. For that reason, he decided to return to Portugal prematurely. Nevertheless in spite of this error, the leap toward the south in a single voyage had been enormous. With voyages such as these, the rhythm of discovery under João II became much more rapid than it had been under Henry the Navigator, or even under Fernão Gomes, notwithstanding the problems of navigation and distance. In the presence of Pope Innocent VIII on 11 December 1485, the Portuguese envoy Vasco Fernandez de Lucena delivered the *Oração de Obediencia* showing that Lisbon now thought that the Portuguese seamen had reached Ptolemy's *Promontorium Prassum,* the separation between the Indian Ocean and the Atlantic. Meanwhile, in order to pass beyond the supposed *Promontorium,* Cão organized a second voyage, during which that great seafarer reached a point somewhat to the South of Lüderitz Bay in Namibia, as shown on the 1489 chart of Henricus Martellus Germanus. A cartouche on this chart says that Cão died at that place.

Once again cartography affords the best information. The chronicles of Rui de Pina and Garcia de Resende are useless for the chronology of Cão's voyages. João de Barros's *Asia,* though written 50 years after the events, is somewhat better, since it allows us to date the inscription on the rocks of Ielala in Zaire. The inscription itself bears no date. Barros tells us that Cão sent members of the first expedition to the king or *Mani* of Congo and placed some *padrãos*. Today, three rocks with inscriptions stand about 170 km. inland from the mouth of the Congo River, but the dates on those commemorative monuments are partly destroyed. This occurred sometime before April 1484, because during that month King João granted two royal deeds for a rent and a coat of arms to Cão, who had just come back from his first voyage. In addition, there is further evidence in the oldest preserved Portuguese map, made by Pedro Reinel in 1484, showing part of the toponymy that resulted from the first voyage. The toponymy of the second voyage, which went as far as Namibia, is completed by the 1489 map of Henricus Martellus Germanus and by the so called "Soligo chart" of the same year in the British Library's Egerton Manuscripts.[4]

Cão sailed on his second expedition during the second half of 1484, but his squadron returned to Portugal in the first half of 1486, without having achieved his chief end. Disappointed by the failure of Cão's second voyage, King João adopted the first of a series of measures that were to make the following year, 1487, the most decisive in the history of Portuguese discovery.

João II adopted the first measure in a royal deed of 24 July 1486.[5] By this privilege, the king confirmed an agreement concluded 12 days before between one Fernão d'Ulmo and Alfonso do Estreito, a rich sugar planter on Madeira.[6] He was also a seaman, as was more than often the case with the most important planters. Fernão d'Ulmo was a Fleming, called Ferdinand van Olmen in his own language. He was one of the *captains-donatorios,* that is one of the tenants-in-chief at Terceira in the Azores. Several of his compatriots, whom we know very well through a series of Portuguese deeds, held similar functions in that archipelago at about the same time and, like d'Ulmo, were also mariners. In the document of July 1486, the king says "*Elle* [i.e., d'Ulmo] *nos quiria dar achada huna grande ylha ou ylhas ou terrafirme per costa que se presume ser a ylha das Sete Cidades e este todo a sua propria costa e despesa* [He intended to find a great island or islands or the coast of a continent that is considered to be the Island of the Seven Cities, and all that at his own expense]." What this had to do with the general policy of the Portuguese discoveries has to be explained. The island of the Seven Cities was sometimes called Antilia, and it had played a part in the proposals Columbus made at the beginning of 1485 to the Portuguese court to find the way to India by sailing westward. He had made his proposal just at a time when Diogo Cão was on his second voyage, and when the Portuguese court still expected him to bring back definitive information on the passage across the Indian Ocean to India. Meanwhile, Columbus had gone to Spain, but when King João II found that Cão's second voyage had not achieved its expected purpose, he became interested once again in the western itinerary to India that Columbus had proposed. However, because Columbus had gone to Spain after his unsuccessful attempt to get a Portuguese appointment and ships, João had to find a substitute. According to the deed of July 1486, van Olmen was to go *"Per capitam a descobrir a ilha das Sete Cidades por mandado del Rey nosso senhor* [as captain for the discovery of the Island of the Seven Cities on behalf of the king our lord]." Clearly, he was the man whom the king selected to substitute for Columbus. According to the agreement between João do Estreito and van Olmen, Estreito was to hire two caravels in Madeira and to pay for them, but van Olmen would be in command.

According to their mutual agreement, d'Ulmo and Estreito's voyage to the West was to start from Terceira before March 1487. Their contemporary, Bartolomeo de Las Casas, reports in his *Historia de las Indias* that they really undertook the voyage, but that it failed, like so many preceding and subsequent voyages to the West starting from the Azores. Las Casas reports that Columbus had known that d'Ulmo had failed and that was one reason, added to the fact that Columbus had meanwhile transferred to Spanish service, why he started his voyage in 1492 from the more southerly position of the Canaries.[7]

When King João discovered that d'Ulmo had failed he called Columbus back from Spain, where he had not yet been successful. Columbus returned to Portugal, but he arrived there in December 1488, precisely when Bartolomeu Dias returned from discovering the Cape of Good Hope and finding the access to the Indian Ocean that would lead later to India. With this discovery, the king of Portugal was not longer interested in a supposed western route to India, and there was no chance left in Portugal for Columbus. He returned to Spain and finally, as everybody knows, discovered America for her in 1492 without knowing it, continuing to think until his death in 1506 that he had reached Asia, or at least some islands close to it. Perhaps if d'Ulmo had succeeded in doing what he had proposed and what King João had ordered him to do, Brazil would not have been the only Portuguese-speaking country in America, as it later became. Currents, winds and chance are powerful factors in maritime history.[8]

For Portugal, the voyages of Pero da Covilhão, also in 1487 like the voyages of d'Ulmo and Dias, were of the utmost importance. What we know about Pero da Covilhão comes from the account by Father Francisco Alvares about the Portuguese embassy to Abyssinia or Ethiopia in 1520–27.[9] Covhilhão had been held as a kind of hostage by the *negus* or emperor of Ethiopia, whom he had visited after his voyages to India and East Africa at King João's command. Covilhão had lived in Ethiopia for nearly 30 years, when he told his adventures to Father Alvares, a member of the Portuguese embassy. The Ethiopian emperor had treated Covilhão very well and had granted him land on which he had lived comfortably, although he had not been allowed to return to his own country. He even had become a government officer of the *negus*.

In his youth, Covilhão had been a page at the court of Alfonso V and, later, had served João II as a kind of envoy in North Africa. The king had sent him on missions to Tlemcen and Fez in Muslim North Africa, where he learned Arabic very well. Together with Alfonso de Paiva, João II charged him with localizing the areas from which the different kinds of spices came and finding out whether the so called Prester John, that is the emperor of Ethiopia, could be helpful in organizing Portuguese navigation in direction of India, the land of spices. In Europe, there was a long medieval tradition about a Christian ruler called Prester John, now identified as the Christian, but schismatic, emperor of Ethiopia. It was not then known whether his country touched the Eastern or Indian Ocean.

On 7 May in that all important year of 1487, Covilhão and Paiva left Santarem in Portugal. In August of the same year, Bartolomeu Dias left Lisbon on the voyage that revealed the Cape of Good Hope and penetrated into the Indian Ocean, albeit for only a short distance. Covilhão and Paiva had obtained a chart, probably of the type by the Venetian Fra Mauro of 1459–60, that bore some indications about Ethiopia, eastern Africa and part of the Indian Ocean.[10] A Portuguese ship brought Covilhão and Paiva to Egypt, where they first met trouble with the customs administration in Alexandria. Actually, after having changed clothes and adopted Arab styles, they joined a caravan traveling to Arabia. With it they reached the Sinai peninsula and, then by ship, Aden in southern Arabia. Then, Paiva set out for Ethiopia, but died before reaching it. Meanwhile, Covilhão sailed to India on an Arab ship. There, 10 years before Vasco da Gama arrived, he visited Calicut, Cannanore and even Goa, the future capital of the Portuguese in Asia. From Aden, he had reached Cannanore, on the Malabar coast of India, in one month. Clearly, he had learned about the monsoon winds and their pattern. From India, he crossed the Indian Ocean a second time, reaching Africa at the latitude of Sofala in Mozambique. At that time, the southernmost point of Arab navigation on Africa's east coast ended some 800 miles from the Cape of Good Hope, a few hundred miles north of the northernmost point reached by Bartolomeu Dias.

Still on Arab ships, Covilhão continued to follow the African coast of the Indian Ocean, and then sailed up the Red Sea. From the present location of Suez, he went to Cairo, where he met José of Lamego and Abraham, rabbi of Beja, two Portuguese Jews who knew Arabic. They brought instructions from King João, asking Covilhão for the results of his voyages and telling him to go to Ethiopia which his companion, Paiva, had failed to reach. In response, Covilhão wrote a relation for the king and gave the first copy to José of Lamego, who carried it back to Portugal from Cairo. With Rabbi Abraham, Covilhão went to Ormuz, an important port on the Arabian Gulf where a maritime route from India intersected with an overland route to several eastern Mediterranean ports in the Levant. From there, Abraham was to bring a second copy of Covilhão's relation to the king.

Thus, Covilhão had visited nearly all the places that would later become bases of Portuguese economic and maritime power in the Indian Ocean. In his relation, Covilhão told the king, according to our informant, Father Alvares, that cinnamon could be bought at Calicut, but that cloves came from farther away. He also said that Portuguese vessels would have to sail along the whole western coast of Africa, as the Arab mariners who had brought him to Sofala had explained. From either Sofala or from the island of the Moon, i.e., Madagascar, one could reach Calicut by directly crossing the Indian Ocean, as he himself had done in opposite direction.[11]

Now, the Portuguese had to work out a plan. Bartolomeu Dias's work was to circumnavigate Africa, and he hoped he could also reach India. In August of that decisive year 1487, Dias left Lisbon with two caravels and a transport ship with food, suggesting that he planned for a long absence. With their nautical knowledge, the Portuguese could now sail directly from Cape Palmas, near Cabo Verde, straight to the mouth of the Congo River, without following the coastline. Diogo Cão had first acquired the knowledge of these currents and winds during his voyages, and they were now being put to good use. Dias reached Lüderitz Bay, but somewhere beyond it, stormy weather drove the great explorer past the Cape of Good Hope, without sighting it. He went ashore at the mouth of the Great Fish River on the coast of Natal, after having realized that he now was progressing northward and, thus, had completed the first segment in

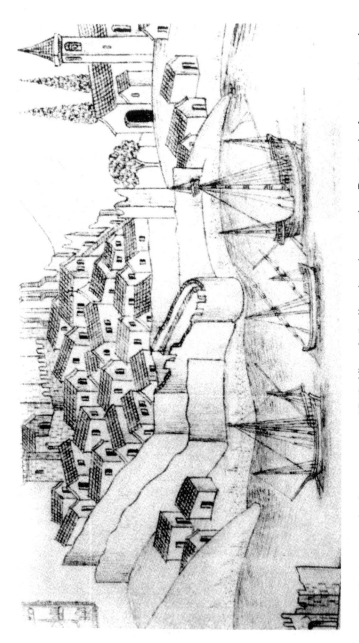

Figure IX. Portuguese harbor scene, c. 1510. King João II ordered a courtier, Duarte do Armas, to travel around the peripheri of Portugal to sketch its defences and border towns. The work was completed after the King's death, about 1510 and compiled in a manuscript, *Livro das Fortalezas*, from which this illustration is taken. *Courtesy of the Arquivo Nacional da Torre do Tombo.*

the circumnavigation of Africa. Somewhat farther to the north, the crews refused to go on and Dias had to turn back. This time, he saw the Cape and called it Storm Cape, but on his return to Lisbon at the end of 1488, King João renamed it the Cape of Good Hope. At that moment, he had probably already received Covilhão's relation, otherwise he would not have fostered "good hope," and would have been only disappointed by the fact that Dias had not sailed as far as he had hoped. In fact, the King granted no special privileges to Dias, as he had to Cão after his first voyage.

While it seems logical that a final voyage to India should have been organized immediately, the Portuguese waited nearly nine years before Vasco da Gama's squadron left Lisbon on 8 July 1497. This long delay needs to be explained.

The first seven years of King João II's reign had brought enormous progress in Portuguese maritime exploration, far more remarkable than everything achieved until then. The last seven years of the reign were full of problems in which the king needed all his strength. Relations with Castile became tense after Columbus's discoveries in 1492. He had acted for Castile and he was now admiral of the Ocean Sea. In addition, the new Pope Alexander VI Borja—or italianized, Borgia—was a Spaniard. By a series of bulls, and according to the tradition, or at least pretension, of medieval papal power, Alexander granted to the Catholic sovereigns, Ferdinand and Isabella of Spain, all the islands that were and would be discovered, except those islands that already belonged to a Christian prince, that is to the king of Portugal, who held the Madeiras, the Azores, the Cape Verde archipelago, and the islands of the Gulf of Guinea. King João protested. By a bull dated 4 May 1493, the pope specified that the grant to Castile applied to all lands that would be discovered west of a line from pole to pole, one hundred leagues west of the Cape Verdes and the Azores. João continued to protest and he began direct negotiations between Portugal and Spain in the spring of 1493, first at Barcelona, then in the spring of 1494, at Medina del Campo. However, the Spanish kings had just conquered Granada, the last Moorish kingdom in Spain, expelled the Jews, and were faced with the rush toward the newly discovered islands. The threat of war with Portugal, if João II did not get what he wanted, was too much for Ferdinand and Isabella. They agreed to replace the pope's dividing line with another one, much more favorable to Portugal at 370 leagues west of Cape Verde. This was done by the treaty of Tordesillas on 7 June 1494. Later, this agreement allowed the unoccupied coast of Brazil to come to Portugal, entirely changing the history of

South America, since Brazil became lusitanized, while the other regions were hispanized. In addition, the treaty of Tordesillas repeatedly mentioned in its text the treaties of Alcaçovas and Toledo of 1479 and 1480, negotiated many years before under influence of the then still crown-prince João. Together, this series of treaties enabled Portugal to control not only the whole southern Atlantic, from the Canaries southward, but also the central South Atlantic as far as the Brazilian coastline.

How King João knew where to choose the new dividing line is only explained by the fact that Portuguese voyages continued after the discovery of the Cape of Good Hope in 1488, and that attempts were made to follow new routes, contrary to traditional opinion. Those attempts implied navigation still farther to the west in the southern Atlantic and still closer to the Brazilian coast. It was as a consequence of this Portuguese navigational method that Cabral reached Brazil in 1500, sailing to India in the expedition that followed the more celebrated one of Vasco da Gama in 1497–98.

There is both Portuguese and Arab evidence[12] that, in the last years of King João II's reign, Portuguese seamen attempted to sail beyond the point reached by Dias on the east coast of Africa. In Fernão Lopes de Castanheda's exceptionally well documented *Historia do descobrimento e conquista da India pelos Portugueses,*[13] he wrote that, after Dias's voyage, King João decided *"proseguir este descobrimento* [to continue the discovery]" and that he had ships specially built to follow up these discoveries. Damião de Góis, in his *Chronica do Serenissimo Senhor Rei Dom Emmanuel,*[14] speaks of several voyages at the end of the reign of João *"correndo hos nossos muito mas allem do Cabo da Boa Esperança atte chegarem a hos limites e terras de Sofala e Moçambique* [our people going very much farther than the Cape of Good Hope until they reached the territory of Sofala and Mozambique]." That is precisely the region where Pero da Covilhão had been.

These two Portuguese chronicles were written in the mid-sixteenth century, but archival material was destroyed in Portugal for the period after 1489 until the end of the reign in 1495. Therefore, we need to look at a contemporary arab source.

The *As-Sufaliyya,* a rutter in verse by the famous nautical expert Ahmad Ibn Madjid, author of a series of *urdjuzas* or nautical poems that are preserved in the libraries of Paris, St. Petersburg and Damascus, will help us. There is a mention of Portuguese trying to navigate in the region of Sofala in the years 1493–94.[15] The pilots of the Portuguese ships did not know how the monsoons blew in that area, and were destroyed at the beginning of October, precisely the moment when the monsoon starts blowing from the east, against the route from Africa to India.[16] The As-Sufaliyya was written a few years after the voyage of Vasco da Gama, whom Ibn Madjid knew very well as we shall see. Another arabic source written somewhat later, the chronicle of Kutb ad-Din an-Nahrawalī also mentions the destruction of Portuguese ships before the voyage of Vasco da Gama on the southern part of the east African coast.

Probably not all the Portuguese ships that went to the region of Sofala during the last years of João II were destroyed and it is very possible that Vasco da Gama was on one of these, since he easily passed the difficult zone of Sofala in 1497. That famous expedition, in the second year of King Manuel's reign, appears as the continuation of the great leap under João II.[17]

Gama's squadron left Lisbon on 3 July 1497, on the voyage that finally reached India. En route, it did what all preceding expeditions had done, it went very far out to the west in the Atlantic. The pilots were among the best collaborators of Cão and Dias. They were men who had learned their job under João II and they showed what Portuguese nautical technique now allowed. In four months, from 3 August until 4 November, they sailed without sighting land, until they dropped anchor, only some 130 miles north of the Cape of Good Hope, in the Bay of St. Helena in the land of the Hottentots. After clearing the Cape, they reached the mouth of the Zambezi River and took a month of repose. They had successfully avoided the Sofala area. Bypassing it, they had then followed the coastline northward, as Pero de Covilhão had done 10 years earlier in an Arab ship. Gama was at Mozambique on 2 March 1498 and at Malindi on 15 April.[18]

According to Fernão Lopes de Castanheda, after seven days at Malindi, Vasco da Gama concluded an arrangement with a pilot, called Canaqua, from Gujarat in India. The squadron left for Calicut two days later, on 24 April.[19] During Vasco da Gama's stay at Malindi, merchants from the realm of Cambay in Gujarat went on board the Portuguese flagship. The Portuguese crew thought they were St. Thomas Christians, because they bowed before a picture of the Virgin, that they had mistaken for the image of one of their own Indian goddesses. Among the merchants was a Gujarati Muslim called Malemo Cana, who agreed to sail with the Portuguese. This man showed the admiral nautical instruments and a chart of the Indian Ocean, explaining the whole system of navigation, winds and currents in the ocean, in such a way that the admiral realized he was in contact with a great expert. Thanks to him, the Portuguese made

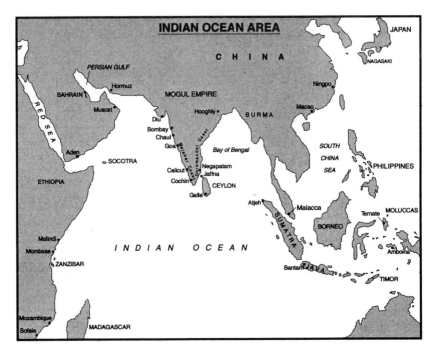

the journey from Malindi to Calicut in 22 days, without any difficulties.

Who was this man? In his *Chronica de Dom Manuel,* Damião de Góis calls him Malemo Canaqua.[20] Leopold de Saussure[21] has shown that Malemo is the Portuguese transcription of the Arabic word mu'allim, master of navigation or pilot, and Canaqua is the Sanskrit word used in India to designate a pilot who was able to navigate as an astronomer, by the stars. So it is clear that we have here a designation, not a name. We learn the name from an Arabic chronicle, the history of Yemen by Kutb ad-Din an-Nahrawalī, who says that it was Ahmad-ibn Madjid, the author of *As-Sufaliyya,* and no less than 35 other nautical poems, or *Urdjuzas.* So, Vasco da Gama had been lucky enough to find the best Muslim expert in navigation of the area, who, in his poems, also calls himself a Mu'allim, a master of navigation, the Arabic word that the Portuguese chroniclers took for his name.

On 18 May 1498, Vasco da Gama sighted India, and two days later, dropped anchor at Calicut. Now, diplomatic and commercial problems arose. The first people with whom the Portuguese came into contact were Muslims of North Africa, who were also there for trade. They spoke to them in Spanish. The local population itself seemed poor to the newcomers, but nevertheless, some had precious stones as ornaments, causing the Portuguese to look on them with a mixture of greed and contempt. From the port, Gama was brought by boat to the palace of the local ruler or *Samorin*. On the way there, the men who accompanied their admiral saw Hindu temples, which they first took for Christian churches. At the entrance of the palace, the crowd was so enormous that some Portuguese were wounded. They were very impressed by the luxury and the jewels the *Samorin* wore, but the Portuguese were not admitted to an audience. The next day, Gama brought very inadequate presents for the Indian ruler. Rejected by the Indian courtiers, the admiral once more failed to obtain an audience with the head of the state. A day later, he was finally received, but with very little respect. During their return from the palace to the ships, there were incidents, and things went from bad to worse. Finally, the Portuguese offered a small quantity of goods brought from Europe, for which they got in exchange an equally small quantity of cloves, cinnamon and a few precious stones to show King Manuel in Portugal that they had really been to the country of spices and wealth.

Three months passed. Muslim merchants, well connected to the palace, dominated the export trade and intrigued against the Portuguese. On 19 August, a few Hindu noblemen came on board, and the Portuguese took them prisoner, in order to exchange them for Portuguese who had been put in a similar condition ashore. Then, a letter came from the *Samorin* for King Manuel, in which the Indian ruler said that, next time, ginger, pepper, cinnamon, cloves, and perhaps precious stones, could be had for silver, gold, cloth, and above all, scarlet and coral. This, at least, was useful for the next voyage, but it showed how badly the Portuguese had calculated their presents and their trade goods. On 30 August, after a short struggle with some local ships, Gama left the country where he had been given such a bad reception.

This time he had no Ibn Madjid to bring him back to Africa. He stopped over at the Angediva islands, awaiting favorable winds until 5 October. There, food and water was scarce and scurvy menacing. Already 60 of the crew members had died. There was a mutiny and some wanted to return to India, but finally, the easterly monsoon blew and Gama was able to sail. He reached Africa on 2 January 1499, then uneasily followed the coastline down to Malindi, where they arrived not earlier than 7 February. The pilots learned much that would be useful in later journeys. They had done in 90-

some days what they had done under the guidance of Ibn Madjid in 22 days. It was evident that they would have to avoid the same mistakes in future voyages.

Because they had found they could no longer man all their ships, they burned one. After five days at Malindi, Gama sailed with only two ships. They stopped at Mozambique, went on to the Cape, and from there, they reached the Cape Verde archipelago in 27 days, as they had learned in the time of King João II. Although the expedition's journal ends here, we know that Gama went to the Azores, where his brother, who had been one of his captains, died. The other captain reached the Tagus on 10 July 1499, and Vasco da Gama himself at the end of August.

On receiving the news, King Manuel sent a trimphal letter to Ferdinand and Isabella of Spain, for whom Columbus had merely discovered several islands. But the great Florentine merchant, Sernigi, wrote from Lisbon that the ships back from India had brought only a few things, without real value. Nevertheless, such skepticism did not prevent King Manuel from adding to his titles. He now became "lord of the conquest, navigation and commerce of Ethiopia, Arabia, Persia and India." In fact, all this had still to be made, at least partly, true.

NOTES

1. Gomes's pilots were João de Santarem, Pero de Escobar, Pedro de Sintra, Soeiro da Costa, Lopo Gonçalves, Fernão do Po and Rui de Sequeira.

2. J. Vogt, *Portuguese Rule on the Gold Coast,* (Athens, Georgia: 1979); J. W. Blake, "O castello de São Jorge da Mina or Elmina Castle,—Reflections on its history under the Portuguese arising from some recent advances in knowledge," *Vice-Almirante A. Teixeira da Mota in Memoriam* (Lisbon, 1987), I, pp. 391–404).

3. G. Schott, *Geographie des Atlantischen Oceans,* (Hamburg, 1926).

4. G. Hamann, *Der Eintritt der südlichen Hemisphäre in die Europäische Geschichte* (Vienna, 1968).

5. J. Ramos Coelho, *Alguns documentos do archivo nacional da Torre do Tombo* (Lisbon, 1892), p. 58.

6. His position is proved by the *Livro do almojarifado dos Açuquares* of the island established in 1494, where he is mentioned as having been dead for several years.

7. C. Verlinden, "Un precurseur de Colomb: le Flamand Ferdinand van Olmen (1487)," *Revista Portuguesa de Historia. Homenagem ao Prof. Dr. D. Peres,* (1962), pp. 453–466.

8. C. Verlinden, "Christophe Colomb et Barthélemy Dias," *Academia das Ciencias de Lisboa. Instituto de altos estudos.* Nova Serie, VI (1979).

9. We have also the excellent book of the Conde de Ficalho, *Viagens de Pedro de Covilhan* (Lisbon, 1898) and a useful, revised English translation

of Padre Alvares: C. F. Beckingham and C. W. Huntingford eds., *The Prester John of the Indies: Narrative of the Portuguese Embassy to Abyssinia (1520–1527),* (Hakluyt Society, vols. 114–115, 1961).

10. G. Crone, "Fra Mauro's representation of the Indian Ocean and the eastern islands," *Studi Colombiani,* III (Genoa, 1952), pp. 57–64.

11. On Covilhão, see also C.F. Beckingham, "The travels of Pero da Covilhão and their significance," *Congresso Internacional de historia dos descobrimentos,* III (Lisbon, 1961), pp. 7–14.

12. On these and other Arab matters see J.R. Tibbets, *Arab Navigation in the Indian Ocean before the coming of the Portuguese* (London, 1971 and 1980).

13. book I, chapter I.

14. chapter XXVIII.

15. On folio 94, the manuscript of St. Petersburg, published by the Russian scholar T. A. Chumovsky in 1957, mentions a voyage that took place two years before 900 of the *Hegira,* that is the year 1495–96 of our own era; thus the voyage took place in 1493–94, still during the reign of João II.

16. *Ibid.,* folio 92.

17. Garcia De Resende, in his chronicle of João II, chapter 206, says that Gama had already been appointed under João II as commander of the fleet going to India. King Manuel should have only confirmed this.

18. We know all this from Antonio Baião, *Diario da viagem de Vasco da Gama* (Porto, 1945), 2 volumes.

19. Book I, at the end of chapter XII and beginning of chapter XIII. Barros in his *Asia,* Decade I, book IV, chapter VI, has another version that now follows.

20. (Coimbra, 1926) I, p. 81.

21. In Gabriel Ferrand, *Introduction à l'astronomie nautique* (Paris, 1928), p. 196.

6

SPICES OR EMPIRE IN AFRICA, ASIA, AND BRAZIL

Charles Verlinden

That prevalent spice, pepper, appears in Portugal in the law on prices of 1253. It is sold by *arrobas* of 16 kilos, at the price of 15 pounds, showing that it was already abundant in the thirteenth century. Since it is mentioned together with saffron, one may think that it came from Italy, where saffron by then was produced. Italy got pepper from the ports of the Levant and from Egypt, where it was brought by Muslim traders.

Under Henry the Navigator, certain dye stuffs came from the Madeiras and the Azores, but Portuguese ships had to wait for spices, first from Africa, and later from Asia. *Malagueta* or Guinea pepper was to be found on the European market since the thirteenth century under the name of "grains of paradise." It came by caravans across the Sahara to the ports of Barbary in North Africa. There, it was picked up by Italian ships, and sometimes, at least in the fifteenth century, when a caravan had gone to Morocco, it was picked up by an isolated Portuguese ship as well. *Malagueta* was used together with ginger to prepare hypocras, a valued wine drink. As the reconnaissance of Africa's western coast progressed, the Portuguese came closer to areas of production, up to then unknown to Europe. The Genoese Antoniotto Uso di Mare, who was in Portuguese service a few years before the death of Henry the Navigator, first mentioned Malagueta in Gambia. But it was not very abundant there. Somewhat later, the region of present day Liberia got the name of the Malagueta Coast. In 1482, the foundation of São Jorge da Mina on the Gold Coast made this fort and port, under King João II, the center of the malagueta trade as well as the gold dust and slave trade. The whole region of Benin and Cameroon then produced malagueta and the trade in this spice developed further production. Soon the natives brought basketfuls of it to the ships. Later, at the beginning of the sixteenth century, malagueta came also from the island of São Tome in the Gulf of Guinea. Even after the arrival of much better pepper from India that traffic went on. More surprising, the prices doubled, as more pepper was requested from everywhere. Already at the end of the reign of King João II, it was sold in huge quantities by the royal Portuguese factor in Antwerp, together with another African pepper, called *pimenta de rabo* in Portuguese documents, and elephant tusks. When pepper began to reach Portugal regularly from India, the king no longer kept malagueta under the control of his factor, but farmed it out, first to a Portuguese and, then, to the great Florentine merchant Bartolomeo Marchione, who was also interested in slave trade on the African west coast, and somewhat later, in the trade with India. That was the beginning of a tendency that would become harmful to Portuguese monarchical capitalism.[1] At the end of the reign of King Manuel in 1521, the great period for malagueta had passed, although it went on playing some part in European markets.

Portugal's destiny on the route to Indian spices was decided 10 years before Vasco da Gama, during the voyage of Pero da Covilhão, who reached Calicut on an Arab ship in 1487. In his relation to King João II, he explained how Portuguese vessels could get to Calicut, along the two coasts of Africa and by crossing the Indian Ocean, and that cinnamon and cloves could be bought there. It was only under King Manuel the Fortunate that Portuguese vessels reached India under Vasco da Gama. It was a wonderful performance, with little financial consequence at first, but with high loss in human lives. Of a 170 men crew, only 55 came back.

The second voyage, under the command of Pedro Alvares Cabral, left Lisbon on 9 March 1500, with 13 well-armed vessels, realizing that to smash Arab influence in India, force was indispensable. Cabral took the open sea, far to the west, and touched the Brazilian coast. On 13 September, he reached Calicut. He set up a factory, but its members were slaughtered. Cabral answered by shelling the town, seizing 10 Arab vessels and killing the crews. He then left for Cochin, where the rajah, of course, received him well. There, he loaded five ships with spices and had another stopover in Cannanore, to complete his freight. He was back in Lisbon on 23 June 1501. This time, the profit for the Crown was conspicuous. The spices could now be sold by the newly established royal *Casa da India,* appearing now beside the *Casa da Guine e Mina,* created previously for the African trade in slaves and malagueta. At the same time, the Portuguese realized that the risks were very high and that there was tribute to pay to the dangers of the sea, on the long route to and from India.

Before Cabral's return, King Manuel sent four vessels to India, under the command of João da Nova, who was very well received at Cannanore, from where the departed for Cochin, where the factor left by Cabral with an interpreter and two assistants had raised a good cargo. Da Nova returned, with all his ships, on 11 September 1502. The regular navigation to and from India, the *Carreira da India,* was beginning to materialize.

The king now thought of eliminating, as completely as possible, all Muslim competition, while also securing new bases along the usual route. To this end, Vasco da Gama sailed a second time to India, with not less than 20 vessels. Leaving Lisbon in February 1502, the admiral was already at Sofala on 14 June. The knowledge of the winds and currents had progressed immensely in a few years; clearing the Cape of Good Hope was no longer a problem, nor even navigation along the eastern coast of Africa. In sailing up, Gama forced the *emir* of Kilwa, in present-day Tanzania, to accept Portuguese protection. In that way, Portugal secured an important relay station. In India, Gama called to Goa, the future Portuguese capital. He captured an Arab ship close to Cannanore, setting fire to it, with between 200 to 400 passengers onboard, in order to terrorize the Muslims. At Calicut, he ordered a bombardment to persuade the *samorin* to banish the Arab merchants and another massacre occurred. After leaving four ships in India to patrol the Malabar coast, Gama's return voyage lasted eight months. Despite the long voyage, this time the cargo he had loaded at Cannanore and Cochin brought a favorable profit when it was sold in Portugal.

On 28 March 1505, Francisco de Almeida sailed for India with an even more impressive fleet than Gama's. He carried 2,500 men, of whom 1,500 were to stay in India and Africa to help establish and to protect fortified Portuguese factories. Along the east African coast, they established factories at Sofala, Kilwa, Mombasa, Malindi, and Mozambique. In India, they established them at Cochin, Cannanore and Quilon. At the three last places, where Portuguese agents had previously been left and had been very active, Almeida was able to load a few ships with spices and to sent them directly home to Portugal. Establishing himself in Cochin, he planned further trading voyages. He had been instructed to penetrate as far as the Malayan peninsula, where cloves, nutmeg and mace were found, and also to go to Ceylon, the cinnamon island. In November 1505, Almeida sent his son, Laurence, to Ceylon, where he stayed for some time at Galle, in the south of the island. The local Muslims called for help to the Egyptian mamluk sultan, who, in response, sent a fleet at the beginning of 1508. They destroyed Laurence and his ships, but Francisco, the father, in his turn destroyed the Egyptian fleet close to the island of Diu in the Gulf of Cambay. Thus, the only naval power, at that time, that could have opposed the Portuguese in the Indian Ocean was driven out of it.

While Francisco de Almeida was still in India, King Manuel appointed his successor, Afonso de Albuquerque. The new governor left Lisbon in March 1506, together with the squadron commanded by Tristão da Cunha. The king ordered Albuquerque to blockade the exits from the Red Sea and the Persian Gulf to the Indian Ocean. For this purpose, Albuquerque used six vessels. With them, he first established a fort in the island of Socotra, close to Cape Guardafui at the exit of the Red Sea, then he forced the sultan of Hormuz (Hormuz is an island on the Persian Gulf,) to pay tribute. In this way, Albuquerque evidently intended to blockade the junction of the maritime and land routes at the end of the Persian Gulf, so as to deprive Venetian, Genoese and Catalan merchants of the supply of spices that had obtained through the ports of the Mediterranean Levant.

When Albuquerque arrived in India, communication between Lisbon and the Portuguese factories was difficult and slow. At first, Almeida did not understand the basis for Albuquerque's authority. Seeing him only as a competitor Almeida had him jailed. Eventually, Albuquerque was able to relieve Almeida and begin the work he had been ordered to do. As soon as Almeida had left for Europe, Albuquerque began to put into effect the plan for an end to Muslim activity in Calicut. As Albuquerque began his effort, Almeida perished on the African coast, before reaching Portugal.

On 2 January 1510, the new governor went to the capital of the Samorin, who was still hostile to the Portuguese. At this point, he had 30 ships at his disposal and 1,500 men, among whom were native auxiliaries who opposed the Samorin. Despite these strong forces, the Samorin repulsed them. Albuquerque then tried to establish Portuguese authority on the island of Goa, in the middle of the Malabar coast to the north of Calicut. Just at the moment that Albuquerque arrived at Goa, the sultan of Bidjapur, to whom it belonged, died. Taking advantage of the succession troubles that followed as well as of the hostility of the Hindi inhabitants against their Muslim master, who resided far away inland, Albuquerque took Goa at the end of November 1510 and made it his capital.

Following this, Albuquerque decided to follow up an order that the king had given earlier to Almeida and to capture Malacca on the Malayan peninsula. He left Cochin in May 1511, arrived in the Malacca area in July and was able to take it on 8 August. From Hormuz to Malacca and Sofala to Socotra, Portugal now dominated a series of strategic positions, giving her control of the Indian Ocean. In Lisbon, it was hoped that this would be enough to monopolize the spice trade. Nevertheless, it seemed that holding Socotra was not sufficient to control the Red Sea route to Alexandria and the Mediterranean. In order to do this, the governor prepared an expedition at the end of March 1512, to seize Aden, but it failed. Albuquerque tried to palliate this failure by entering the Red Sea, but he got no farther than the desert island of Kamaran. After his return to India in August 1513, he was able to reinforce the Portuguese position at Hormuz in order to cut the caravan connection from the Persian Gulf to the Levant in the Mediterranean. On his return from this expedition, Albuquerque died in 1515 in the roads of Goa, his capital. While governor, Albuquerque had not only established Portuguese positions at Hormuz and Goa, but it should be remembered that he also had been able to make the first contact with the Moluccas, through his captain Antonio de Abreu in 1511, while in 1514 Jorge Alvares had pushed eastward as far as the vicinity of Canton in China. Under Albuquerque, the Portuguese had taken what could be called the measurement of the Indian Ocean and had even prepared for penetration into the Java and China Seas. Everywhere, spices were now within direct reach of the Portuguese.[2]

During this entire period which witnessed the ever increasing hold of the representatives of Manuel the Fortunate on the Indian Ocean, from the time of the first return of Vasco da Gama in 1499 until the death of Albuquerque in 1515, the spice fever did not let up in Portugal. In fact, from Portugal, it spread and reached a large part of Europe. As a consequence of the discovery of the route to India by the Cape of Good Hope, and of its increasing control by Portugal, the major axis of European trade shifted from the Mediterranean to the Atlantic. Lisbon became the center of dispersion, at least for a while, with Antwerp as its main subsidiary distribution point for the ports and river systems of northern and central Europe.

It was pepper that now dominated and even determined economic and political life in Portugal. From 1502, the Portuguese royal factor in Antwerp sold Indian pepper. From there, part of it went to Augsburg and Nürnberg, where it was portioned out over Central Europe. From that area, the Portuguese received metalware via

Antwerp and used it for their trade in Africa and India. After a while, German merchants wanted to participate in that trade. Foremost among them, the Fugger and the Welser sent representatives to Lisbon and others followed.[3] As a result, the famous Fondaco dei Tedeschi in Venice lost much of its trade to the benefit of Lisbon and Antwerp. At the same time, the Venetian satellite Alexandria in Egypt, lost its previous importance for the spice trade. The diminished quantities of pepper that now reached it cost much more than what the caravels brought to Lisbon, directly from India by the *Carreira da India,* now fully organized.

In the beginning, foreign investors brought capital to Portugal and were associated with commissioning Portuguese for the Indian Ocean trade, since the means of the Crown were insufficient. Bartolomeo Marchione and Girolamo Sernigi of Florence, the Affaitadi from Cremona and many other Italians sent ships to India with the Portuguese squadrons and sold, with great profit, all kinds of spices to other merchants, who again sold them all over Europe. This practice obviously opened a breach in royal control of the spice trade. It is all the more remarkable that royal representatives, such as Albuquerque who was actually as much a capitalist businessman as a conqueror, appreciated these investors and their factors so highly. Some of the foreigners were active in making some of the first contacts. For example, among the Italians, Sernigi commanded one of the ships that went to Malacca in the time of Albuquerque and Francisco Corbinelli was even royal factor at Goa until 1526. Among the Germans, the Hirschvogel of Nürnberg played an important part in the spice trade as well as in that of precious stones; their agents acted in India until 1529. The royal monopoly maintained in Lisbon was not tight in India.[4]

Initially, these developments seemed irremediably to jeopardize Venetian trade. Nevertheless, it soon reappeared along side that of Lisbon. Albuquerque's failure to take Aden in 1512 meant the Red Sea remained open and the spice trade via Alexandria was able to resume its former habits. At first, rather bashfully, as a matter of fact. In 1527, Venice proposed to King João III that Venice take over, at a fixed price, all the pepper that reached Lisbon. The Venetians, of course, would not have proposed this, if they had been able to provide themselves in the Levant as easily as they had done before. Little by little, Arab and Indian merchants learned how to pass through the mesh of Portuguese control and to supply anew the traditional caravan trails that the Portuguese garrison in Hormuz could not block. In India, foreign merchants could use opportunities to bribe

Portuguese officials. Furthermore, Portugal only occupied a series of relay stations along the coast.

There was never a compact Portuguese empire, comparable with the empire that the English established in India in the mid-nineteenth century, after the London government took over the affairs of the East India Company. The only empire that existed in the Indian subcontinent during the Portuguese period was that of the Great Moghul, founded and developed by Babur from 1526. The other great Muslim power was the Turkish sultan, who dominated, on the one hand, Syria and Lebanon, and, on the other, Egypt and the Red Sea: the terminal points of the caravan roads.

Aleppo and Beyruth, Cairo and Alexandria thrived again. In the Orient, a kind of compromise had been reached between foreign merchants, often Muslims, on the one hand, with Portuguese officials and mariners on the other. The government in Lisbon ultimately was obliged to allow the crews of the *Carreira da India* to participate in the trade towards Europe with quotas on spices that varied according to rank. That meant that noblemen were always favored since they held all important offices. In the metropolis of Lisbon, extravagance reached fantastic proportions. The kings suffered from oriental dizziness, and built architectural masterpieces. By 1544, bankruptcy menaced, but the pepper fascination maintained credit with the merchant bankers. Nevertheless, one should not exaggerate the effect of the revival in Mediterranean trade, as some historians have done. The truth is that the traditional spice routes played their part beside the new. The merchants of Ragusa, presently Dubrovnik, on the Dalmatian coast, and the Armenians across Russia had been able to use diverse opportunities.[5] The greatest merchants and bankers of the sixteenth century, namely the Fugger of Augsburg, made no mistakes. They had their representatives in Lisbon, the new outcome, and also in the Dalmatian and Levantine ports of the Mediterranean. There, the traditional arrivals of spices continued, as they had in the medieval period.

João III managed the resources of his realm badly, but it was worse under King Sebastian (1557–78), who wasted the resources of India in a hopeless war in Morocco where he was killed. In 1580, Philip II of Spain, who was connected with the Portuguese dynasty, added Portugal and its colonial possessions to his immense empire, stretching from the Iberian Peninsula to the Philippines, South America and Mexico. While Portuguese India and its trade had been previously disorganized, Sebastian inaugurated a policy of freedom of trade in place of the royal monopoly that had never been fully successful. Later, his chimerical mind handed over everything to foreign capitalists. At first, it was to the German Rott, then, to the Italian Rovelasco. In India, dissension prevailed between the town administration of Goa and the governor-general, who soon took the title of viceroy. High officials ransacked the treasury. Decadence was rampant. The fault, however, was not Philip II's. It came from the bad administration that had become a tradition since the end of the reign of João III.[6]

In 1588, England's destruction of the Armada stripped the Iberians of their exclusive domination in the Atlantic, the key to the Indian Ocean as the Portuguese had proved from the time of Diogo Cão to that of Albuquerque. Now, the way was open for the Dutch, who were struggling with Philip, and therefore with Portugal, one of his other possessions. Dutch companies in which emigrants from the Spanish Netherlands, i.e., present-day Belgium, played an important part, organizing for war in the Indian Ocean even before they were brought together in an United East India Company that would progressively take over from the Portuguese. The English followed, although their East India Company was two years older. The English succeeded, no more than the Dutch, in really dominating India, where they only occupied relay stations as the Portuguese had done. It was only after the first industrial revolution that they established their Indian Empire, and it was only in the reign of Queen Victoria that Disraeli presented her with the Indian imperial crown. Similarly, the Dutch dominated Indonesia, only after the middle of the nineteenth century.

The Portuguese prepared and made possible the dream of all this, through the late medieval myth of the spices. That dream animated João II as it did Covilhão and Albuquerque. For several decades, that myth made Lisbon and, with her, Antwerp, the commercial capitals of Europe. In China in 1553, the Portuguese created Macao as the predecessor of Hong Kong. They, too, made possible the work of Saint Francis Xavier, the great missionary, (although a Spaniard and not a Portuguese) who laid the first foundation in connecting Japan with the West, connections amplified later through regular navigation between Macao and Nagasaki. Without the hypnosis of spices, the world would not have been what it became, neither in Asia nor in Europe, where the hypnosis was born and where it stimulated covetousness. Europe diffused her material civilization in return for the resources and wealth that she gathered through the colonial expansion that began along the Portuguese spice routes. She developed and maintained her hold until her colonies reached independence, generally in the course of our own century. Portugal was the last to concede the independence, both in Africa and in Goa.

By way of a summary, it is useful to outline the Portuguese political position in the Indian Ocean, during the fifteenth and sixteenth centuries.[7] In Africa, the most important, more or less islamized, Swahili states on the east coast were Kilwa, Mombasa and Malindi. They were commercially prosperous and they were coastal city-states whose friendship was useful for the Portuguese or upon which they imposed their protectorate.

The Arabian peninsula, too, had a fringe of coastal towns that, in theory, had submitted to the authority of the sultan or shah of Hormuz in the Persian Gulf, whose coins, above all the golden *ashrafi,* or *serafim* as the Portuguese called it, was current in all the ports as far as Malacca. Persia, present-day Iran, was Shiite Muslim, while, more to the west, the Turks in Anatolia were Sunnites. The Portuguese could and did use them against each other.

In India, the northern principalities of Gujarat, Delhi and Bengal had Mohammedan rulers, but most of the population was Hindu. In the center of the subcontinent, there were five Mahommedan sultanates with a similar religious outlook. In the southern part of this area, called Deccan, there was a great Hindu state called Vijayanagar or Bisnaga. It had no access to the sea, although the Muslim king of the Deccan kingdom of Bidjapur dominated Goa until it was conquered by Albuquerque. The Malabar coast was divided among a series of small Hindu states with rajas. One of them was the often mentioned Samorin of Calicut. All the states had Muslim trading communities that enjoyed a great economic influence. In Ceylon, the Singhalese were in the majority and were Buddhist, while in the North, the Tamil of Jaffna, nowadays still in conflict with the Singhalese, were Hindu. There were also Arab and Indian Muslim merchant communities on the coast. The Mughals, who were central-Asian Turks whose power was first established by Babur (1526–1530), had conquered most of continental India in Portuguese times.

In southeast Asia, present-day Burma, Thailand and Vietnam had a number of small states generally at war with each other. In the Malayan Peninsula, there was also much political division, but Malacca, under Muslim rule, was the richest state, and attracted shipping that came from the whole area between Arabia and Japan.

In Indonesia, the island of Sumatra was the source of pepper and some gold. It was divided into petty Muslim states, but in the second half of the sixteenth century, the kingdom of Atjeh spread through the big island. On Java, the old Hindu empire of Madjapahit was declining while Islam extended its influence. The island of Timor produced sandalwood and had no political power, while the sultans of Ternate and Tidore competed for the suzerainty of the Moluccas, the clove islands. On Borneo, there was a sultanate at Brunei and, further North, Islam was beginning to spread into the Philippines. Some Chinese merchants from the coastal provinces of Fukien and Kwantung traded in the Philippines and sometimes went to Indonesia or even as far as Malacca. In Japan, the Daimyos, that is the feudal nobility, dominated political life.

All these states, whether small or large, had neither artillery nor war fleets to oppose the armed Portuguese squadrons. The local merchant ships were mostly those of the Indian-born Muslims, who lived in coastal areas of which the most important was Gujarat.

In East Africa, a similar situation prevailed in the islamized city-states of the Swahili group. Everywhere, the Portuguese utilized brute force, but they were only able to establish coastal relay stations, failing to make inland conquests and to create a real empire.

These developments in the Indian Ocean area were quite different from those in the Atlantic area. There, the Portuguese had first populated the uninhabited archipelagoes of the Madeiras and the Azores, organizing them according to the semifeudal system of the *capitanias*. They also adopted this same system on the opposite side of the Atlantic in Brazil. Later, they applied it in the African colonies of Angola and Mozambique.[8]

In 1504, King Manuel the Fortunate gave the island of São Jorge, 50 leagues off the coast of Brazil, to Fernão de Noronha, *cavaleiro* of the royal household, with the "*direitos e jurisdiçao que com a dita capitania a de ter*." Confirmed in 1522 by João III, this led to the introduction of the *capitania* system in Brazil. The system reached the continent on March 10, 1534, with the grant of the *capitania* of Pernambuco to Duarte Coelho. Quite large a concession, it stretched over 60 leagues, i.e., 240 kilometers, along the coast. The limits were described with precision: the Rio S. Francisco to the north and the Rio Santa Cruz to the south. Inland (*Sertão e terra fyrme*), the capitania stretched "*tanto quanto poder entrar e for da minha conquista*," meaning that progressively it could stretch as far as Spanish possessions, i.e., very far inland indeed. Coelho dispensed both justice and administration for Portuguese as well as the natives. Justice was in the hands of the *ouvidor* appointed by the *capitão-donatario*. Under the *ouvidor,* there were *meirinhos* and *escrivaes,* in other words, a whole administration. There could also be more than

Figure XI. Woodcut map of Brazil. Illustration from Hans Staden, *War-haftige Historia und Bescreibung einer Landschaft der wilden nacketen Grimmigen Menschenfresser Leuthen in der Newunwelt America gele-gen* (Hamburg, 1557). *Courtesy of the John Carter Brown Library at Brown University.*

one *ouvidor* when the population and the settlement were increasing. The captain was allowed to found cities or villages, under the same laws as in Portugal. These settlements had to be separated by at least six leagues from each other. The area around them was called a *termo*. The officials of these subdivisions owed feudal homage to the captain, as was common in all fees in Europe, but here sugar mills, or *engenhos,* were added. The Portuguese settlers owed military service, under the command of the captain. Moreover, the captain could send native slaves to Portugal or use them in his ships. In addition, he had rights on mills and salt pans. The captains could trade directly with Portugal, but foreigners who imported commodities into the *capitania* had to pay a tithe and also when they exported colonial produce. Foreigners were not allowed to buy from the natives; they had to buy from the captain or from other Portuguese settlers. Among the native commodities, spices and drugs were controlled as a royal monopoly. Brazilwood was also a royal monopoly as an important material for dyeing, and sometimes used for furniture. If precious stones, pearls, gold, silver, copper, tin, lead or other metal ores were found, the king claimed a fifth of its value.

Coelho came to Brazil with all his property and with a number of Portuguese followers. He named his *capitania* "Nova Lusitania" and had his capital, first, at Igaraçu, then at Olinda, a short distance from the present city of Recife in Pernambuco state. Under his guidance, sugarcane plantations developed rapidly.

A number of other *capitanias* were created in Brazil. Martin Afonso de Souza held one around São Vicente, near present day São Paulo and he had another one in the area of Rio de Janeiro. Between those two, there was the *capitania* of Santo Amaro, belonging to Pero Lopez de Souza, who also possessed Santa Ana, South of São Vicente. He also had Itamaracá, North of Duarte Coelho's *capitania.* This practice of giving more than one *capitania* to an individual implied that they were represented by agents in some areas.

There were also *capitanias* in the farthest north regions of Parà, Piauhy as well as more to the south in Bahia, Ilheus, Porto Seguro, Espiritu Santo and São Tomé. Most of these became the origins of the present-day states in the Brazilian union. Settlers and stores arrived rapidly in these areas as foreign merchants like the Schetz of Antwerp, the Adorno and Doria of Genoa invested in sugar plantations in certain *capitanias.* In São Vicente and inland Piratininga, present-day São Paulo, there were already 600 settlers and 3,000 slaves by 1543.

After a time, the government in Lisbon felt that there should be more central authority in Brazil. In 1549, a governor-general, Tomé De Souza, was appointed. Some former Portuguese officers in India preferred to establish themselves in Brazil, using what they had earned in India. Even some foreign capitalists bought a *capitania* in Brazil, after having earned a fortune in India as Luca Giraldi from Florence did in 1551.

By 1536, the *capitania* of Bahia was already producing cotton and sugar. In 1549, the governor-general moved his capital to Bahia and, from that time forward, the captains were governors of provinces under the central colonial government. The *capitania,* both before and after the creation of the central colonial administration at Bahia, was the basis by which the Portuguese penetrated into the *Sertão,* the interior of the country. The same was true in Africa, first in the islands of the Gulf of Guinea, and later in Angola and Mozambique.

This administrative structure provided an enormous difference in contrast to the Portuguese enterprise in India. In Brazil and in southern Africa, there developed a real colonial empire, persisting, in the case of Brazil, until the independence at the beginning of the nineteenth century and then under a Portuguese emperor. In Africa, the colonies existed until only a few decades ago. Brazil, an enormous state with a population of more than a hundred million in our own day, retains its entirely Portuguese language and cultural tradition, as the result of what had been the real Portuguese empire. That empire was located in Brazil, not in India where the Portuguese never penetrated farther inland than the coast. Today, India has a series of languages, but not Portuguese. There are remnants of Portuguese architecture in a few places in India, Ceylon and Malaysia, but there is no Portuguese cultural tradition as in Brazil. Therefore, Brazil is the great achievement of Portuguese expansion, not India.

NOTES

1. M. Nunes Dias, *O capitalismo monarquico portugaes (1415–1549)* (Coimbra, 1963–64) 2 volumes.
2. For more detail, see J. Lucio de Azevedo, *Epocas de Portugal Economico* (Lisbon, 1947), particularly the chapter "A India e o ciclo da pimenta," pp. 89–184.
3. H. Kellenbenz, *Die Fugger in Spanien und Portugal bis 1560. Großunternehmen des 16. Jahrhunderts* (Munich, 1990). 3 volumes.
4. H. Kellenbenz, "The Portuguese Discoveries and the Italian and German initiatives in the Indian Trade in the first two decades of the 16th century," *Congresso Internacional Bartolomeu Dias e a sua epo ca, Actas, III.* (Porto, 1989), pp. 600–623.

5. M. Malowist, "Le commerce du Levant avec l'Europe de l'Est au XVIe siècle," Mèlanges Braudel (Paris, 1972), I, pp. 349–357.

6. See Lucio de Azevedo, op. cit. and C. R. Boxer, The Portuguese Seaborne Empire (London, 1969).

7. Boxer, op. cit., pp. 39–47.

8. C. Verlinden, "Formes fèodales et domaniales de la colonisation portugaise au Brèsil au XVIe Siècle," Homenaje al Doctor Ceferino Garzon Maceda (Cordoba-Argentine, 1973), pp. 115–132); B. Henze, "Die portugiesische Besiedlung und Wirtschaftspolitik in Angola (1570–1607)," Portugiesische Forschungen der Goerresgesellschaft, 17 (1982), pp. 200–219.

7

PORTUGUESE DISCOVERIES AND INTERNATIONAL CARTOGRAPHY

Charles Verlinden

During the period of the great discoveries, maps were on the one hand manuscript and drawn, and on the other, printed. The first type grew out of the medieval portolan chart, i.e., a map of the coast and islands for the practical use of mariners, the accuracy and extension were continually kept up to date according to the information received from mariners and discoverers. In contrast, printed maps were learned products by scholars. They partly followed the rather unrealistic, medieval manuscript *mapae mundi* and, for another part, the tradition of the ancient geography that came down from Ptolemy. He was the Alexandrian scholar of the second century A.D. who had taken over from Poseidonius (first century B.C.) a much too short length of the equator, which, by the way, swayed Columbus into seeking Asia where he unknowingly found America. Nevertheless, Ptolemy transmitted to the time of the great discoveries the division of the great circle of 360 degrees and the habit of calculation by parallels and meridians. Ptolemy's atlas, attributed to the perhaps legendary Agathodaemon, was generally inaccurate because of wrong latitudes and longitudes. His astronomy was translated from the original Greek to Arabic, and then from Arabic to Latin. It was summarized in the thirteenth century by the Englishman John of Holywood or Sacrobosco, under the title *Sphaera Mundi,* and became the nautical handbook of Renaissance mariners. The charts of the atlas were progressively improved, according to observation by mariners and discoverers. This resulted in bringing closer together the direct observations on the portolans with the learned tradition, at least for the coastal zones, as may be noted already in the first editions of the Atlas, made at Ulm from

1483 onward, where the Mediterranean and the Baltic are more accurately drawn than they had been before.

Turning to the cartographic record of the first Portuguese discoveries, we know that the Canary islands archipelago was discovered by the Genoese Lanzarotto Malocello. The chronology of the discovery is known through the Majorcan chart of Angelino Dulcert dated 1339. Malocello was a Genoese in Portuguese service, as was the great Genoese merchant Manuel Pessagno, who had been appointed admiral of the Portuguese fleet by King Dinis in 1317 and kept the office until 1342, when the eldest of his three sons succeeded him. The other two sons also became Portuguese admirals. This is a good example of the typical international collaboration of the day, as was also the fact that the chart that first portrayed the newly discovered Canary Islands was not Portuguese, but Majorcan.

This chart combined the type of the portulan for the coasts and islands with the tradition of the medieval *mappae mundi* for the hinterland. It is very clearly dated and signed: "*Hoc opus fecit Angelino Dulcert anno M°CCC°XXX°IX° de mense augusti in civitate Maioricharum* [This work was done by A.Dulcert in 1339 in August at Palma on Majorca.]" It exhibits a great similarity with a chart of 1330 that shows none of the Canary Islands and is signed and dated: "*Hoc opus fecit Angelinus de Dalorto. Anno Domini M CCC XXX de mense martii composuit hoc.*" This chart is generally considered as Genoese, but the name of the cartographer is the same as in 1339. The surname, Dalorto, is an Italian adaptation of the Majorcan or Catalan name, Dulcert. This is shown by the fact that "*de Dalorto*" is bad Italian, since it has a double and useless genitive "*de*" and "*Dal*", a mistake that an Italian would not have made. Therefore, it appears that Dulcert and Dalorto are the same cartographer and that the Majorcan cartographer Dulcert had learned his art in Genoa, where the chart of 1330 that obviously belongs to the Genoese school was made. This school began about 1300 with the so called *Carta Pisana* that, despite its label, is Genoese work. It is followed by the 1306 map of Giovanni da Carignano that bore a date at Genoa before its destruction during World War II. It contained inscriptions concerning Ethiopia that Dulcert took over in 1339, another proof of his Genoese connection. There is also a series of maps by a Genoese, Pietro Vesconte, made between 1311 and 1320. One of this series is dated at Venice, showing a cartographical connection between Genoa and Venice, as Dulcert's does for Genoa and Marjorca. Through these examples, one can see how international cartographic connections and schools developed, in Venice as well as on Majorca, from Genoese models.

Another work by the Genoese school is the so called *Medicean Atlas* of 1351.[1] This atlas shows, for the first time, the Madeira archipelago with the Isola de Legname. This is the Italian name, used before the latter-day Portuguese name, Madeira, both words meaning "wood" from the dense cover of trees and arborescent shrub so common before the Portuguese deforested the islands in the fifteenth century from the era of Henry the Navigator onward. Porto Santo, the other important island of the Madeira archipelago, also appears in the 1351 atlas. These Italian names show that the archipelago was first sighted by crews whose officers spoke Italian, and were the direct or indirect informants of the cartographer. One thinks immediately of the Genoese men who served under the Peçanha admirals of the Portuguese kings from Dinis onward. One of these men was Lanzarotto Malocello, the discoverer of the Canary archipelago in the 1330s, followed in 1341 by another Genoese, Nicoloso da Recco, and then by Majorcan mariners. In this period, new ship types with caravel planking and lateen or triangular sail allowed the use of the west-east trade winds blowing toward the Iberian peninsula, coming back from the Canaries. In these years, diplomatic activity and correspondence concerning the Canaries following Pope Clement VI's grant of the archipelago to the Castillian pretender Luis de la Cerda show that Italian-commanded Portuguese crews and that Majorcan-Aragonese ships frequented this route. All this took place in the middle of the fourteenth century, precisely the period of the *Medicean Atlas* of 1351, which again illustrates the international character of both navigation and cartography.

To the north of the Madeira archipelago lies that of the Azores, which first appeared on the 1375 *mappa mundi* by the Majorcan Jewish cartographer Abraham Cresques.[2] This map shows the islands, to the north of the Madeiras and grouped together, with the names Insula de Corvi marini and Li Conigi. Also, equally clustered, it identifies San Zorzo, Insula de la Ventura, Li Columbi, and Insula de Brasil. Except for the last legendary island of Brasil, the rest of the nomenclature on this Majorcan chart is Italian. The position of the whole group obviously suggests the Azores.[3] Konrad Kretschmer identified several of the names on the map, relating Li Conigi with the modern island of Flores, Ventura with Fayal, Li Columbi with Pico and Brazil with Terceira, i.e., the entire western and central part of the archipelago that had been initially reconnoitered by ships coming from the southwest, pushed by the trade wind on their way back to Portugal from the Canaries. The Italian nomenclature is of Genoese origin, as shown by the form of certain names. At the date of the Cresques atlas, the Portuguese admiral was the third son of Manuel Peçanha, Lançarote Peçanha, who in 1371 received royal confirmation of possessions in Odemira in Alemtejo with the motivation: "*esguardando como Mice Lançarote Peçanha, nosso vasallo et nosso almirante a nosso padre et a nos et a nosa casa de Portugal fez sempre muitos e muy grandes serviços e obras de muy grandes merecimentos* [considering that Lord Lançarote Peçanha, our vassal and admiral, did great and meritorious service to my father, to me and to the dynasty of Portugal.]" Among these great achievements was certainly the reconnaissance of the Azores, with their Italian names of 1375.

By analogy, the Italian names of the Madeiras on the 1351 chart come from the time of admirals Carlos or Bartolomeu Peçanha. We know that, although their crews were Portuguese, some or all of their officers were Genoese, as the appointments of the admirals still mention the compulsory presence of twenty Genoese "*sabedores de mar* [knowing the seas.]"

The Italian nomenclature persists on the Majorcan charts of Guillermus Soler of 1385[4] as well as one two Catalan maps,[5] both from the end of the fourteenth century. This nomenclautre is also found in the famous *Libro del Conoscimiento de todos los reynos e tierras e señorios que son por el mundo,* written by an anonymous Aragonese Franciscan, who used maps[6] to write his very successful story of imaginary voyages, just like Sir John Mandeville did at about the same time. Furthermore, the *Libro* mentions the death of the Genoese Lanzarotto on the island of the same name, and we know through a deed of King João I, the father of Henry the Navigator, that Lanzarotte died in 1385. All this forms a complex set of reasons for establishing the date of the *Libro* at 1385 or shortly afterwards.

The Italian nomenclature of the different islands disappears precisely at the moment when the Genoese admirals of the king of Portugal loose their importance under the new dynasty of Aviz. At that time, the Peçanhas become Portuguese noblemen just like the Boccanegras, another Genoese family who had been admirals of the Castillian kings, did in the neighboring kingdom of Castile. We can see this transformation clearly in an Italian map by Nicolo de Pasqualin, drawn in Venice in 1408.[7] There, Madeira is called by its Portuguese name and no longer named Legname, in Italian. At about this same time, the Portuguese began to be interested in the colonization and settlement of that island. The 1424 Venetian map by Zuane Pizzigano[8] shows that the return west-east navigation from the Canary Islands, that had initially brought about the first reconnaissance of the Madeiras and the Azores in the fourteenth century, continued more to the west in the first decades of the fifteenth century. In the maps of that time two big islands appear, one called Antilia with two smaller neighboring islands. This entire cluster could possibly be a first, very hesitating and inaccurate, picture of the island-world of Central America. To identify those islands with the Azores, as has been done, makes little sense, since the latter archipelago already appeared on the charts by Abraham Cresques and Guillermus Soler. More important is the fact that royal deeds concerning Portuguese voyages to the westward of the Azores and the Madeiras only appear from 1462 onward. The first of them, a charter of King Alfonso V, dated 29 October 1462, mentions a voyage of Conçallo Fernamdes of Tavira. Other such deeds date from 1473, 1474, 1475, and 1484. All mention islands, "nas partes do Mar Ouciano."

In 1475, there is a charter which mentions the island, "das Sete Cidades," which is the general name for islands or even a continent to the west. King João II's 1487 appointment document for Fernão d'Ulmo, alias the Fleming Ferdinand van Olmen who was to sail to the West from Terceira in the Azores, refers to them at about that time. Thus, there remains a gap of half a century between the "Antilia" of Pizzigano's 1424 map and the first of the documents about the "Sete Cidades." Nevertheless, it is extremely curious to see on the Baptista Becario[9] map of 1435 that the Antilia group appears again with the startling note, "insulle de novo reperte [recently discovered islands.]" It is unnecessary to suppose that this implies that the cartographer used some lost Portuguese maps, as some historians have done, as there were no Portuguese maps for this period. Because cartographic information about Portuguese discovery was shared internationally since the fourteenth century, it is unlikely that the information could have been completely lost. One can conclude that, perhaps around 1424 and 1435, Portuguese navigators had seen some of the Antilles, but that written administrative documents about voyages to the western Atlantic appear only several decades later.

A striking feature of fourteenth-century cartography is the absence of Portuguese and Spanish charts, although Portuguese and Spaniards played an important part in the first contacts with the archipelagoes of the eastern Atlantic. The absence persists, even into the fifteenth century.

Of course, Portuguese cartography derives from preceding achievements in other countries. Like Spanish cartography, it has no independent or separate origins. The link between them is both Genoese and Majorcan. This double connection is personified by Jafuda Cresques, son of Abraham, the maker of the 1375 Majorcan chart. In 1403, and the following years, this man first appears under his Christian name, Jacme Ribes, in a series of charts he made with the Genoese, Francesco Becario. In fact, he had collaborated with Becario as early as 1399. Some decades later, he passed into Portuguese service as a cartographer, during the time of Henry the Navigator.

Contemporary Portuguese sources document the fact that Ribes was the founder of Portuguese cartography, although nineteenth and even twentieth century, chauvinistic Portuguese historians have denied it. Duarte Pacheco Pereira (c. 1450–1533), in his well-documented, *Esmeraldo de Situ Orbis* (1505–1508), says that Henry the Navigator "*mandou à ilha de Malhorca por um mestre Jacome* [i.e., our Jafuda [Jacme Cresques] *mestre de cartas de marear na qual ilha primeiramente se fezeram as ditas cartas, e com muitas dadivas e merces ho ouve nestos reynos, ho qual as ensinou a fazer àquelles de que os que em nosso tempo vivem aprenderam* [he sent people to Majorca for Jacome, a master in maritime charts in that island. With many gifts and advantages, he attracted him to this land to make the charts from which those who live in our time learned their job."] From this, his role is quite clear. In addition, we know through a deed of the prince regent, Dom Pedro, dated 22 October 1443 that the first map or portulan establishing the African coast south of Morocco was drawn about that year, completing earlier Italian or Majorcan charts for coastal navigation.[10] Jafuda Cresques started Portuguese portulan cartography between 1443 and 1453, the year in which Zurara stops writing his *Cronica*.[11]

Nevertheless the chart that best shows the southward progress of Prince Henry's ships along the African coast in those years is the 1448 chart by the Italian Andrea Bianco.[12] It is signed "*Andrea Bianco, Venecian, comito di galia me fexe a Londra M CCC XXXX VIII.* [Andrea Bianco, a Venetian officer on a galley, made me in London in 1448.]" This officer of a Venetian galley sailing to England in a convoy or *muda* stopped over, as usual, in Lisbon and obtained his information there, but he drew his chart during the time he spent in London, before his return voyage.[13] Like several of his compatriots in those and later times, Bianco was a cartographer who remained a mariner.

The discovery of the Cape Verde archipelago took place at the very end of Henry the Navigator's life, through the endeavor of two Italians in his service, the Venetian Alvise Cà da Mosto and the Genoese Antonio da Noli. The discovery was completed by Diogo Afonso, *escudeiro* or squire of Don Fernãndo, the *Infante*'s adopted son and heir. The *mappa mundi* of the Venetian friar Fra Mauro[14] utilizes the narrative of his discoveries left by Alvise Cà da Mosto, a fellow Venetian. Cà da Mosto had sailed on a new caravel of 45 tons belonging to a Vicente Dias from Lagos, in the south of Portugal, that Dom Henrique had ordered for him. Fra Mauro had read the *Prima Navigazione* of Cà da Mosto and used it as a source.[15] However, the friar died in 1459, before Cà da Mosto published the *Seconda Navigazione* and, for that reason, he did not show on the *mappa mundi* the Cape Verde archipelago that da Mosto had found during his second voyage.

This archipelago did appear, however, on the charts of Grazioso Benincasa of Ancona, on the Adriatic coast of Italy. This great cartographer drew a long series of maps between 1461 and 1482. On his oldest chart,[16] made in Genoa in 1461, the west coast of Africa is only shown as far as Cape Bojador, the insignificant cape where earlier Portuguese navigation had stopped. From 1463, Benincasa worked at Venice and his chart of 1468[17] utilizes the *Seconda Navigazione* of Cà da Mosto, who had just returned to Portugal from the Cape Verde archipelago. Together with it, he utilized the report of Pedro de Sintra's voyage, edited by Alvise Cà da Mosto.

In 1483, the first entirely Portuguese map appeared. This is the map by Pedro Reinel.[18] Like the first printers in Portugal, this founder of grand Portuguese cartography was of German origin, making one more example of international collaboration at the time of the great discoveries. On his map, Reinel shows the coast of Africa as far as the mouth of the Congo River, discovered by Diogo Cão just before the chart was drawn. It shows the complete Cape Verde Islands as well as the islands of the Gulf of Guinea discovered by the men of Fernão Gomes, the rich merchant of Lisbon to whom the commerce and exploitation of the gulf had been granted from 1469 until 1474 under the influence of the then crown prince, João II. This chart also shows for the first time the development of colonization in the Azores. On São Miguel Island, Reinel labels *"a gram povoraçam* [the great town]" at Ponta-Delgada, the actual capital of the archipelago. On Madeira, he also shows Funchal, the capital. It was long thought that one of the islands of the Gulf of Guinea, Annobom, was not discovered at the time of Fernão Gomes, appearing for the first time in cartography on the Cantino map of 1502.[19] However, a careful examination of the Reinel map shows that the whole archipelago of islands in the Gulf of Guinea was already known by 1483.

The discoveries of Diego Cão and Bartolomeu Dias along the entire western coast of Africa and the southernmost part of its eastern coast are reflected in the maps of Cristofalo Soligo and Henricus Martellus Germanus. Soligo's map,[20] which dates from 1489, retraces the African coast as far as Angola, which Diogo Cão reached during his first voyage. We know nothing of Soligo, but he seems to have been a Venetian, because the manuscript atlas in which the map is included is mostly composed of maps of Venetian cartographers made for the Corner family, members of the Venetian nobility. The map of Henricus Martellus, a German called Hammer, who worked in Florence, exists in different forms. The oldest is probably from 1489 and the latest from 1491.[21] The 1489 map shows the portion of the western coast of Africa reached by Diogo Cão during his second voyage as well as the part of the eastern coast reached by Bartolomeu Dias. In addition, it also has an inscription mentioning the death of Cão off the coast of Namibia. The latest version of 1491,[22] is printed or engraved. A merchant, Martin Behaim, very probably brought a copy of it to Nürnberg in southern Germany, and supplied it to the group of humanists, who inspired, and the artisans, who made the globe of 1492.[23] This globe is of very little value for the history of Portuguese discoveries, since it is full of errors.[24]

For evidence of exploration on the coast of East Africa, India and Southeast Asia, the first really important map we have is the Cantino planisphere, a Portuguese map of 1502.[25] This map was bought in Lisbon by Cantino, a diplomat of Ercole d'Este, duke of Ferrara and Modena, which explains its name and location in Modena. On this map, the whole of Africa was drawn according to the intelligence gathered from the voyage of Vasco da Gama. It also reflects improved knowledge about Southeast Asia, since there is now a single Malay peninsula, where the Ptolemaic tradition had two of them. Although Sri Lanka, Sumatra and Madagascar are somewhat badly located, they are also shown.

Some two years or so later, the Caneiro map appeared. It seems that it is a work by a Genoese living in Portugal.[26] India is now drawn better than previously. Although this map served as a model for the printed Ptolemy Atlas of 1513, the manuscript *mappae mundi* developed further, as shown by the 1508 chart of the Genoese

Vesconte Maggiolo.[27] Continued progress in geographical knowledge about India and Southeast Asia is evident. For instance, Sumatra now appears under its own name, not as one of the two Javas of the preceding charts.

In the times of Albuquerque and his captain, Abreu, the progression of Portuguese voyages to the East is reflected in cartographical evidence, namely in the charts of the Portuguese Pedro and Jorge Reinel made at Munich and London in 1517–1519. Malaya is shown much more accurately now, and even Indo-China and southeastern China are indicated. After the Reinels came the Homems: Lopo, the father and his son Diogo, who made many very beautiful atlases among which Diogo made one for Philip II of Spain in 1558.[28]

The most splendid works of Portuguese cartography are the atlases of Fernão Vaz Dourado, a colonial cartographer who was born and lived most of his life in Goa. The works of this wonderful master, both of color and accuracy, are found today in Lisbon and London and dated 1568, 1571 and 1573. Jan Huyghen van Linschoten used them in his *Itinerario,* the 1595–96 book that prepared the Dutch for their role in India and Indonesia.

The really interesting cartography of Brazil belongs to the second half of the sixteenth century. It is mostly Portuguese, and only to a lesser degree international with the Italian Gastaldi in 1562 and the Flemings Mercator and Ortelius in 1569 and 1570. The work of the latter were quickly printed and there is much less direct information for documenting the course of exploration to be found from them than from the older manuscript charts. Nevertheless in their later printed atlases of northwestern Europe, Mercator and Ortelius did utilize the work of the most important cartographer of the Dieppe school in France, Pierre Desceliers, who left manuscript *mappae mundi* of 1546 and 1550.

In general, early printed maps are of little value for documenting the history of the Portuguese discoveries. As demonstrated in this essay, the best information can often be found through evidence made directly from the contemporary reports of Portuguese mariners and explorers, passed through the international exchange of cartographical infcrmation, and found on Italian, Majorcan, Portuguese and German manuscript maps.

NOTES

1. In the Biblioteca Laurenziana in Florence.
2. Now in the Bibliothèque nationale in Paris.

3. As the great German historian of cartography, Konrad Kretschmer, very clearly demonstrated as early as 1901 in his *Die italienische Portolane des Mittalalters.*

4. One in the Archivio di Stato in Florence, the other in the Bibliothèque Nationale in Paris.

5. One in Paris, the other in the Biblioteca Nazionale in Naples.

6. In 1877, the Spanish editor of this wonderful text, Marcos Jimenez de la Espada, thought that it should be dated about 1350. Actually, the more or less Aragonised nomenclature is the same as the neatly Italian one of the map of Soler in 1385.

7. Preserved in the National Library of Austria in Vienna.

8. In the James Ford Bell Library at the University of Minnesota.

9. In the Biblioteca Palatina in Parma.

10. See chapters 76 and 78 of Zurara's chronicle.

11. Charles Verlinden, "Quand commença la cartographie portugaise?," (Lisbon: Centro de Estudos de Cartografia antiga, 1979)

12. Preserved in the Biblioteca Ambrosiana in Milan.

13. Andrea Bianco's portulans of 1443–53 are lost.

14. A 1460 copy exists in the Biblioteca Marciana in Venice.

15. As shown by two inscriptions on the map from the chapters XII and XXXIX of the *Prima Navigazione.*

16. Preserved in the Archivio di Stato at Florence.

17. In the British Library.

18. Preserved in the Archives départementales de la Gironde in Bordeaux, France.

19. In the Biblioteca Estense in Moderna, Italy.

20. British Library, Egerton manuscript 73, fo. 63v°.

21. Copies of the oldest one can be found in several places: the British Library, the University Library of Leiden, the Musée Condé at Chantilly France, and in the Biblioteca Laurenziana in Florence.

22. In the Library of Yale University.

23. Preserved in the Germanisches Museum of Nürenberg and wrongly attributed to Martin Behaim.

24. As shown by E. G. Ravenstein in his book, *Martin Behaim and his Globe,* (London, 1908).

25. Preserved in the Biblioteca Estense in Modena, Italy.

26. It is in the Bibliothèque Nationale in Paris.

27. British Library, Egerton Atlas 2803.

28. British Library.

Suggestions for Further Reading

Cortesão, A. *History of Portuguese cartography,* 2 volumes. (Coimbra, 1971).

Fernández-Armesto, Felipe. "Atlantic exploration before Columbus. The evidence of maps," *Renaissance and Modern Studies,* 30 (1986), pp. 12–34.

Kamal, Youssouf. *Monumenta Cartographica.* (Cairo, 1926–1951).

Nordenskiöld, N. *Periplus*. (Stockholm, 1897).

Penrose, B. *Travel and Discovery in the Renaissance*. (Cambridge: Harvard University Press, 1952).

Verlinden, Charles. "Dècouverte et cartografie: Canaries, Madères, Açores, Cape Vert, Iles du Golfe du Guinée," in *V. Coloquio de Historia Canario-Americana, 1982. Coloquio internacional de Historia Maritima.* (Las Palmas, 1985), vol. 4, pp. 7–23.

Figure XII. Some Portuguese ships, c. 1510, illustrations from Duarte do Armas's manuscript, *Livro das Fortalezas. Courtesy of the Arquivo Nacional da Torre do Tombo.*

8

THE MARITIME "EMPIRE" OF PORTUGAL STRIKES ROOT IN ASIA

George Winius

From both a naval and a geopolitical standpoint, once the Portuguese had passed the Cape of Good Hope into the Indian Ocean, the norms they had established for their Atlantic operations quickly changed from exploration, colonization and discovery to contact and connection with existing governments and trading networks—from nao and caravel to galley, dhow and junk and to navigation rather by pilot and monsoon than by observation of sun, stars and wind patterns. In other words, the Europeans began to adhere to Asian norms when it came alike to travel and to the equipment they used for their operations. But the way they set their goals and executed their strategy, both military and commercial, was purely European, though it is doubtful that this was dictated by anything save improvisation.

To call the Portuguese presence in Asian an "empire," as in the current common usage, is to create a misleading mental picture. One hardly ever comes across the word in the sixteenth or seventeenth centuries, except when some humanist, steeped in Roman history fancies that his countrymen resembled Alexander the Great or fatuously compares the governor, Afonso de Albuquerque, with Julius Caesar; instead the Portuguese usually spoke of their *Estado da India Oriental,* their eastern estate. It consisted in a number of enclaves, the largest only a few dozen square miles in area, and the smallest no larger than the foundations upon which its fort rested. From these, they attempted to control the sea lanes of the Arabian Sea and its commerce; their success was variable, but their overall significance was great: they survived and even throve, for a century and more, and the connections they forged in the long run have changed Asia and Europe forever. For had the Portuguese been driven from Asia during the sixteenth century, it is unlikely that in the seventeenth, the other European presences, namely the Dutch and English East India Companies, would have been conceived, let alone have been able to raise their venture capital.

Historians and intellectuals often err in looking backward and attributing far more plan and predesign to the building of colonies and empires than they actually involved. In the Portuguese case, everything seems to have been ad hoc; in fact, King Manuel and Vasco da Gama, not to speak of Pedro Alvares Cabral, who arrived in India two years afterwards, all were seeking friendly contacts with fellow Christians. Even Gama, when he rendered a report of his visit to his king, does not seem to have realized that the local ruler, the Samorin, or sea lord, of Calicut was a Hindu. I cite this as evidence that the Portuguese were not seeking any independent political role, but simply wished to enter the spice trade, with enormous profits to themselves.

The design appeared near fruition in 1500 when Pedro Alvares Cabral, the discoverer of Brazil and second task force commander dispatched to India, successfully negotiated with the Samorin for establishment of a *feitoria,* or on-shore warehouse-headquarters at Calicut. Probably, at that moment, neither Cabral nor his masters had thought much further than this purely trading operation. But, suddenly, riots incited by members of the Moslem trading communities engulfed the new Portuguese headquarters. These merchants of the old system understood immediately that they would be the victims of impending Portuguese competition for the Asian spice markets, a trade which they had enjoyed unchallenged for centuries. The new Portuguese *feitor,* or factor, was killed along with 40 of his men, and the horrified Cabral hastily attached blame to the Samorin, who seems to have had nothing at all to do with the attack. No matter: Cabral determined Portugal's future course by ordering the bombardment of Calicut itself. The act gratuitously destroyed any chance for good relations between Portugal and a ruler who had tried to be friendly enough and was almost certainly not involved in the bloodshed. (It would doubtlessly be asking too much of Portuguese perceptions at the time to expect them to distinguish their real enemies in such an unknown environment!) On the other hand, that Cabral and his successors were to make war upon the entire Moslem network extending from the Red Sea to Malacca does not seem so gratuitous, because keeping peace with them for any length of time was obviously impossible. The only path left for the Portuguese was to make the seas their own and stifle future Moslem participation in the spice trade.

The Portuguese, ridiculously far from their homeland, could only hope to succeed because Asians did not know the use of navies and did not possess round ships conceived as floating artillery platforms. Moreover, the Red Sea passage, though it might appear to have afforded a much shorter and better route to Europe, was not so handy as it might appear on a map; it was too full of reefs and rocks to afford easy passage and was subject to a variant of the same monsoon winds that limited passages between Europe and Asia to one round trip per year. But this is to get ahead of the story. Before the Portuguese could hope to establish themselves in the Indian Ocean at all, they required an Indian *pied-á-terre,* a base of operations, to replace their transient and abortive one at Calicut. One was unexpectedly presented to them when the Kolathiri raja of Cochin, down the Malabar coast from Calicut, extended Cabral an invitation to operate from his magnificent harbor. It seems that the Samorin was both his rival and his suzerain and that he longed to escape Calicut's influence; when the Portuguese successfully carried out their bombardment of Calicut, that was sign enough for him. The raja invited them in as his new protector—a happy enough relationship that lasted 161 years. The only liability remaining from Cabral's bombardment in Calicut was that the Portuguese and the Samorin were now implacable enemies.

The Portuguese had arrived in the Arabian Sea with their sturdy round ships bristling with guns, slow, but devastating. They encountered dhows and boums of various sizes, some larger baghlas, and some galleys, none of which were well armed. The dhows and the boums possessed all the superior sailing qualities of the lateen-rigged caravel, or even better, for they used the lateen sail and were more lightly built; in fact their planks were thin and exquisitely lashed together with cord rather than nailed to heavy ribwork, as were European vessels. The galleys of the Indian Ocean, on the other hand were smaller merchant vessels, ones which could be sailed as well as rowed. Until the Samorin belatedly tried to hire some Italians who had deserted the Portuguese to cast him some cannon, none of these types mounted guns or was capable of challenging a round vessel. Hence, when the Portuguese could catch enemy trading vessels riding at anchor or in a harbor from which they could not escape, they destroyed them routinely. On the other hand, they do not seem to have been swift enough to catch them in flight, which is undoubtedly the reason for the Portuguese to acquire vessels of native design, particularly galleys.

For there is evidence that almost as soon as the Europeans arrived, they began to arm and use these types themselves, if because only these were so useful for pursuit. D. Lourenço de Almeida, son of the first viceroy, D. Francisco de Almeida, used a small fleet of these in his sweeps up and down the Indian west coast and during his visit to Ceylon in 1505; in fact, when he was decoyed into Chaul harbor and ambushed in 1508, he was commanding one. Thereafter, the Portuguese employed native vessels for all their convoying and patrolling activities and only brought heavy vessels into play when they had suitable work for them to do.

The first and most decisive example of the damage these heavy vessels could accomplish occurred in the following year, 1509. Of all the parties injured by the Portuguese establishment in India over the preceding decade, the Mameluke sultans of Egypt were the most powerful—and the most desperate. This was because their chief source of income lay in the harbor and passage tolls they levied at Suez and at Alexandria on cargoes of spices and silks bound for sale to the Venetians and Turkish merchants. After their arrival in India, the Portuguese confiscated and sank wholesale the Gujarati and Omani dhows which brought this merchandise to Aden, whence it was freighted in other vessels up the Red Sea. Desperately, the Mamelukes commissioned and built their first and last navy, purchasing the lumber in Dalmatia, bringing it to Cairo and having it portaged across the desert to Suez, where it was built into large war galleys. Disastrously for them, however, a patrol of the Knights of Malta helpfully, but unknowingly, intercepted the fleet bearing the lumber to Egypt and sank several of its vessels, thereby reducing the amount of lumber suitable for shipbuilding in treeless Egypt. As it developed, only enough remained to build eight large galleys in Suez, and it was these which Egyptian crews, probably hired or impressed from the idle merchant fleets, sailed down the Red Sea to seek battle with the Europeans and clear them from the Indian coast.

Weakened as they were by the lack of enough vessels, the Egyptians apparently felt that they dared go no further without a firm alliance with the Gujarati *sidis,* or admiralties, of northwest India. With the Omani Arabs, the merchants of Gujarat had formed the backbone of the trading fleets in the Arabian Sea before arrival of the hated Portuguese *ferenghi* ("Franks," as the Moslems called them). But Gujarat appears not to have been governed by those sensitive to the maritime commercial interests of its traders; rather, its shahi were landlubbers schooled in the cavalry warfare of the uplands and hardly conscious of the sea. As a result, the *sidis* of its maritime coasts apparently did not command sufficient influence with their rulers to side openly with their natural allies when the opportunity to damage the Portuguese newcomers was actually at hand. Perhaps the revealing statistic was supplied by the Indologist, M. N. Pearson of the University of New South Wales, when he estimated that only about 6% of the revenue of the Gujarati state was attributable to the (obviously undertaxed) sea traders and their activities.[1] In other words, probably the *sidis* could not move without the support of their sultan, who probably found the oceans uninteresting.

While negotiations were thus stalled, the Portuguese viceroy had located the Egyptian fleet, which was anchored in the Gujarati harbor at Diu Island, off the southern tip of the Kathiawar peninsula. If the Gujaratis and the Egyptians were immobilized, Almeida was ready for action; he was also keen to avenge the death of his son, D. Lourenço at Chaul: he sailed boldly into the anchorage and poured gunfire into the immobilized enemy, who could offer no effective resistance. The waters were reputedly reddened with the blood of the Egyptians; the only ones to escape were those who ran their vessels aground. The battle at Diu must be classified as one of the world's most decisive naval engagements, though in reality it seems more closely to have resembled shooting ducks in a bathtub. The Portuguese thereupon continued to scourge competition from the Indian seas, and seven years later, the now bankrupt Mamelukes succumbed to an Ottoman invasion.

The vessels employed by Almeida must have been those built in Europe and not primarily those acquired in India, because they were so well supplied with firepower. But once the great battle was won, the Portuguese seem to have adopted galleys carrying armed soldiers and mounting perhaps only a naval gun or two at bow or stern to enforce their will. In other words, when it came to shipping, they "went native." they could easily afford to because they encountered so little organized resistance among the Indians until their northern European enemies, the Dutch and the English, appeared in Asia at the very end of the sixteenth century.

Viceroy Almeida was relieved of command soon after his great victory at Diu and succeeded by a rival, but one even more able than himself, the great Afonso de Albuquerque. This old soldier, veteran of many North African campaigns against the Moors, believed that more fortified harbors were needed at points near important straits in order to allow Portugal to command them. This was a bold step for such a minuscule nation so far from home, but Albuquerque knew what he was doing. He first captured Goa (1510) in order to have a suitable base of operations and then took Malacca (1511) to give him control of the straits between the China seas and the Indian Ocean, attacked Aden unsuccessfully (1512), hoping to seal off the Red Sea, and in the year of his death (1515) secured Ormuz, giving him control of the Persian Gulf. Although Aden was never captured and its substitute, Socotra, was too far away for effective control, it does not seem to have mattered much at first, if because the new masters of Egypt, the Ottomans, did little to restore the trade for several decades.

If the Portuguese did not plan their Indian administration in advance, they at least were able on short notice to piece one together which served their interests for nearly a century-and-a-half. Far from being a monolith, it had many facets designed to accommodate the largest interest groups therein participating. First, there were those of the crown. The Portuguese monarchs had paid for the whole extension into India in the first place, with the object of capturing the spice trade, and the royal legislation and representatives were engaged to procure the crown a monopoly on purchasing, storage and transport to Europe of all the prime spices, silks, and other commodities of recognized intercontinental value. The profits therefrom went directly into the royal treasury.

Another feature of the Portuguese Asian administration was its pass-and-toll system. It was created because the crown did not intend to finance its Eastern operations out of these profits, but sought other sources of revenue. The pattern seems to have been copied from the system of tolls levied by Indian rulers on the merchants passing their lands. The Portuguese officials simply adapted the practice to the sea lanes; as a first step, they sold passports, called *cartazes,* to Indian merchant vessels plying up and down the west coast of the subcontinent. The *cartazes* then required their bearers to call in Portuguese-controlled ports and pay customs duties whether or not these were their ultimate destinations. To make sure the merchants actually did so and to prevent piratical attacks on them, the Portuguese fleet commanders herded them into convoys, delivering them to the royal *alfândegas,* or customs houses. The revenues therefrom were not transmitted to the king, but used to defer the costs of the Portuguese Indian administrations.

Still another facet of the Portuguese presence in Asia was that of

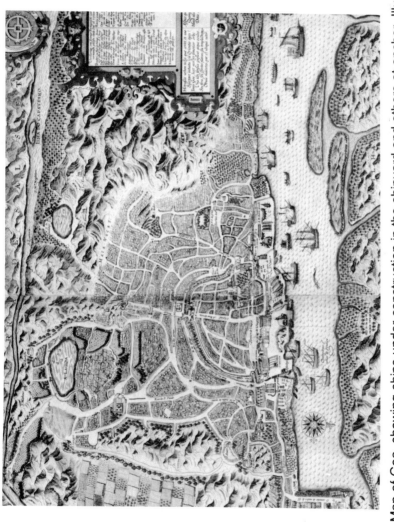

Figure XIII. Map of Goa, showing ships under construction in the shipyard and others at anchor. Illustration from Jan Huygen van Linschoten, *Itinerario* (1596). *Courtesy of the John Carter Brown Library at Brown University.*

private intra-Asian trade. Perhaps because the governor, Afonso de Albuquerque, had promoted marriage between Portuguese men and Asian women as the one way to insure a stable colony in the Orient, the government made provision to excuse those soldiers from active military service who took wives. They were known as *casados*. Some of these became shopkeepers or farmers, but many chose to go into private trade, dealing in non-royal monopoly goods and sailing their dhows and junks between Asian ports. So successful were the traders, in fact, that they wandered far beyond the Portuguese enclaves and settled in areas under indigenous rule from Nagapattinam, on the Indian east, or Coromandel coast, and São Thomé de Meliapor, now part of metropolitan Madras, to Bengal, Burma, Siam, China and Japan. Their numbers grew over the years until both the English and the Dutch concerned themselves with their presence in the seventeenth century—the Dutch of the V.O.C. sought to destroy them because they constituted a dangerous competition in Asia to that company's pretensions to control the intra-Asian trade, while the English company's traders, to whom moonlighting was a principal activity, eagerly enlisted them as partners.

How well the king's part of the Portuguese Asian system worked in the long run is open to question. One famous historian of Venice, the late Franklin C. Lane, pointed out 50 years ago that Portugal's failure to capture Aden by mid-century had allowed the Red Sea-Mediterranean routes to make a comeback; as a consequence, prices fell and the crown had to be satisfied with far lower prices than it wished.[2] In fact, the crown's whole European marketing system at Antwerp, which could only work when a monopoly was in force, had to be discarded. Soon, the king had to borrow moneys from the European spice merchants with which to outfit his next years' fleets. The happy years of D. Manuel I and the early reign of D. João III were definitely over by the regency of D. Sebastião, which began in 1557.

Portuguese Asia, however, did not collapse; only the crown suffered. The other facets of the *Estado da India* continued in force and even prospered. The private traders continued to do their own thing with great success, while the administration in Asia continued to collect its port duties and convoy fees. Had it not been for wars and military operations which flared up at intervals—most notably in the sieges of Diu in the thirties and forties and the attacks on Goa, Malacca and Chaul around 1570—the crown would not have had to contribute moneys to the *Estado* from its monopoly trade at all. But wars are expensive, even if the Portuguese Asian defense system was both simple and stable: fortresses were always built at water's edge, and save in 1570, no more than one at a time was beleaguered. Though all were chronically undermanned, garrisons could be shunted about by ship to the hot spots, all of which were capable of holding out for a time until help arrived. Meanwhile, since armies in India were mostly feudal or mercenary, or both, the fortresses could not be besieged indefinitely; sooner or later, the feudatories would look at their calendars and go home when their obligation to serve was up, or else the mercenaries would be dismissed as too costly.

Meanwhile, the administrators, all on three-year appointments, took their traditional liberties with the crown's revenue—something which later ages would call corruption—and recycled it into the *casado* trading networks. In fact, everyone but the king was solvent and happy. From Lisbon, he could do little or nothing to improve the efficiency and stop the "deviations" from his treasury: otherwise, no future official might be induced to risk life and limb to sail from Portugal unless he could help himself to certain (and royally tolerated) "extras." For after all, the little Portuguese world, strung out as it was over half the earth, displayed the characteristics of an extended clan, and the *pater familias,* the king, was both used to being exploited, and uncommonly indulgent. Portuguese Asia, as wedded to the sea as ever Venice was, might have thrived forever, at some sacrifice to the crown, had not Philip II taken over the metropolis and its throne in 1580, thereby making his enemies into Portugal's enemies. Less than a generation had passed before the Dutch and the English appeared and attacked the forts one by one, from their vulnerable water sides. After 1600, the days of colorful and peculiar *Estado da India Oriental* were numbered. By 1661, little save Goa, Diu and Daman, Bassein (which fell to the Marathas in 1738) and, of course, Macao, remained. But the Portuguese have at least one satisfaction. In 1999, Macao, the world's last European colony and the final vestige of the *Estado,* is scheduled to devolve to China, whose Cantonese governor quietly allowed the Portuguese *casados* to settle there in 1556.

Suggestions for Further Reading

The most recent work on Portuguese Asia is the best: Sanjay Subrahmanyam's *The Portuguese Empire in Asia, 1500–1700* (New York and London: Longman's 1993. This superseded the still useful and narrative work by Bailey W. Diffie and George D. Winius, *Founda-*

tions of the Portuguese Empire, 1415–1600 (Minneapolis: University of Minnesota Press, 1977). A new work with up-to-date interpretive essays on various aspects of the Portuguese presence in Asia, Brazil and the Americas is George D. Winius (ed.), *Portugal, the Pathfinder; Journeys from the Medieval towards the Modern World, 1300–1600* (Madison, Wisconsin: The Hispanic Seminary of Medieval Studies, 1995). This contains Winius's article "Portugal's Shadow Empire in the Bay of Bengal as well as excellent summaries on the Portuguese in China and Japan by Roderich Ptak and Derek Massarella. In addition, the volume contains a long bibliographical essay with mention made of all generally available printed primary sources. C. R. Boxer's *The Portuguese Seaborne Empire, 1415–1800* (New York, Alfred A. Knopf, 1969) is well written, but not to be advised for beginners as an introduction to the subject because it is thematic rather than chronological. Two more useful books by Boxer are: *Fidalgos in the Far East; Fact and Fancy in the History of Macao, 1550–1770* (The Hague: Martinus Nijhoff, 1948) and *The Great Ship from Amacon* (Lisbon: C.E.H.U., 1959). A new and suggestive book on Portuguese trade during part of the period under review is James C. Boyajian's *Portuguese Trade under the Hapsburgs, 1580–1640* (Baltimore: The Johns Hopkins Press, 1993). And Finally, if it can be located, there was a special issue of the *RC; Revista de Cultura* (of Macao) called *The Asian Seas, 1500–1800,* with well-illustrated articles on different aspects, political, nautical, economic and artistic, of the Portuguese presence in Asia. All of the above books contain useful bibliographies.

NOTES

1. Michael Naylor Pearson, *Merchants and Rulers in Gujarat* (Berkeley and London: University of California Press, 1977), *passim.*
2. F. Lane, "The Mediterranean Spice Trade: Further Evidence of its Revival in the 16th Century," *American Historical Review,* 45 (1939–40), pp. 581–90.

Part III
Spain and the Conquest
of the Atlantic

9

THE SEA AND CHIVALRY IN LATE MEDIEVAL SPAIN

Felipe Fernández-Armesto

"See America First." The old tourist slogan made it sound easy. Yet the most famous moment in maritime history is also one of the most obscure. It happened early on 12 October, 1492, when a lookout, straining through the darkness from the rigging of the *Pinta* caught the first recorded glimpse of the New World. Despite the importance of the occasion, the most elementary facts about it, in some of the earliest sources, were enveloped in uncertainty. The name of the lookout was given in irreconcilably different forms; and even the priority of his achievement was disputed by a fellow-traveler called Christopher Columbus.

Columbus's insistence that he saw America first has been variously explained by historians: as a characteristically mean and greedy pretext for grabbing the reward; as a slightly less ignoble ploy to monopolize the credit; as a genuine misunderstanding; or as a valid claim based on a flickering sighting the previous night. It becomes easier to understand, however, when we realize that Columbus's voyage, though unprecedented in history, had a precedent in literature. In the *Libro de Alixandre,* a Spanish version of the Alexander Romance, composed in the mid-thirteenth century, the Macedonian hero makes his conquest of Asia by sea. The poet tells us with particular emphasis that it was Alexander who made the first discovery of the land with his own eyes:

Dixoles Alixandre de todos más primero
Antes lo vió el que ningunt marinero

[Said Alexander to his men,
   the foremost of the crew,
That he had seen the land ahead
   ere any seaman knew.]

Is it possible that Columbus, who later called his discoveries a land that Alexander had labored to conquer, should have insisted on his own prior sighting because he saw himself as a sort of new Alexander or, at least, because he wished to emulate the hero? In the context of this chapter, which is about the influence exerted on late medieval navigators by maritime themes in Spanish chivalric literature, it may appear not only possible, but likely.

Columbus, who read Plutarch and referred to Caesar's *Commentaries* had access to a classical, humanist's image of Alexander; the dominant tradition in his day, however, was that of the medieval Alexander, the hero of metrical, romanticized versions of the story, in which the conqueror was a model of chivalric behavior and in which Achilles, without comic effect, could be enrolled in a monastery and Aristotle dignified with a cardinal's hat. In this medieval guise, Alexander was a character in the most popular and influential type of literature current in the circles in which Columbus moved and to which many—indeed most—Iberian explorers and long-range navigators of the fifteenth century belonged: men literate in the vernacular, with a taste for swashbuckling fiction and admiration for its heroes. Like pre-incarnations of Don Quixote, they fashioned their self-perceptions from this sort of reading and drew from it inspiration for their deeds. Without awareness of this background, neither the career of Columbus nor, more generally, the foundation from the Iberian peninsula of great worldwide maritime empires can be fully understood.

From the time of the emergence of the genre, the sea was seen in chivalric literature as a suitable environment for deeds of knightly endeavor. In the thirteenth century, one of the great spokesmen of the chivalric ethos in the Iberian peninsula was Jaume I, King of Aragon and Count of Barcelona, who has left us that rare thing—the autobiography of a medieval king, reasonably authentic, reflecting royal inspiration and probably, in large part, royal composition. At the very least, it captures the self-image which the king wished to project. It resounds with the chivalry which was, it seems, Jaume's dearest source of values. When he described his conquest of Majorca, the arguments which moved him to undertake it and the experience of crossing the sea to carry it out, the king revealed that he saw maritime war as a means of chivalric adventure par excellence. There was "more honor" in conquering a single kingdom "in the midst of the sea, where God has been pleased to put it" than three on dry land. The voyage was lingeringly and lovingly described; the numbers of ships, the sailing orders of the fleet, the location of the guid-

ing lanterns, the waiting for a wind, the cries of the watches exchanged when the ships made contact, the changes of breeze, the
shortenings of sail, the heaving of the sea in a storm and the resolution and faith in God it called forth. No moment matched the moment of making sail. "And it made a fine sight for those who stayed
on shore, and for us, for all the sea seemed white with sails, so great
a fleet it was."

Jaume's enthusiasm for seafaring was already shared by many of
his Catalan subjects. Now it infected the warriors of his realm and
helped to inspire a series of seaborne conquests. "The best thing man
has done for a hundred years past," the king later wrote, "God willed
that I should do when I took Majorca." He meant that it was the
"best" by the standards of chivalry, the deed of most daring and
renown. A metaphor quickly established itself, which was to become
a commonplace for the rest of the Middle Ages: the ship, in the words
of King Alfonso X of Castile, was "the horse of them that fight by
sea." By the time of Columbus, the poet Gil Vicente could liken a ship
at once to a warhorse and a lovely woman without incongruity, for
all three were images of almost equivalent importance in the regional chivalric tradition. Anyone who contemplates late medieval
pictures of fighting ships, caparisoned with pennants as gaily as any
warhorse, can grasp how, in the imagination of the time, the sea
could be a knightly battlefield and the waves ridden like jennets.

Though the knight-errant's natural medium was dry land, a
seaborne setting could add tang to his adventures, especially as the
knight's life, considered from one point of view, was a secular version or imitation—some might say a parody— of the religious life.
Two well known models had established the sea as a favored place
of exile for wandering hermits. The first was the legend of the navigations of St. Brendan, a text originally of the tenth or eleventh century, with earlier antecedents, which recounted the Irish saint's
peregrinations in search of the earthly paradise. Sometimes thought
even by critical scholars to be an account of a genuine voyage, the
Navigation of Brendan has a genuine basis in the devotional prac-
tices of early medieval Irish hermits, who took to seaborne exile in
leather boats in expiation of their sins. They ranged surprisingly far
and wide across the Atlantic, leaving traces of their settlements, for
example, in Iceland and, perhaps, Greenland. The *Navigation* was
one of the most popular hagiographical works of the Middle Ages,
surviving in 116 Latin manuscripts and in translations into most
western European languages. Its popularity with seafarers, which
might be assumed, is exemplified in cartography: there are refer-

ences to the legend in every surviving late medieval Atlantic map.
St. Brendan had direct imitators in the fifteenth century—Valen-
cian hermits who envisaged a wasteland-retreat for themselves in
the uninhabited island of Madeira in 1436. Columbus's own allu-
sions are so close to the text as to suggest strongly that he must have
read it.

The second legend to connect the sea with the religious connotations of chivalry was that of St. Eustace, the Roman *eques* or
"knight" supposed to have been converted to Christianity while
hunting by a vision of the Cross between the antlers of a stag. His
faith was tested by separation from his family in a shipwreck, followed by a long seaborne search, amid many calamities and afflic-
tions. Reunited at last, after humanly unbearable sufferings, they
were all martyred together by roasting in a brazen bull. The dramatic possibilities of this story made it a favorite with romanticiz-
ers and it hard to say whether some of the many works written in
the Eustace tradition belong more properly to the genre of hagiography or that of chivalric romance. Though its relationship to the
Eustace tradition is disputed among scholars, a fourteenth-century
Spanish work, the *Historia del cavallero Zifar,* tells a similar tale of
the hero's search for his lost wife and sons. The transformation of
the Roman archetype from knight to saint and back to knight re-
minds us of the double lives of some of the heroes of early European
maritime expansion: of Henry the Navigator, for instance, the explorer's patron who took pride in his chastity and his hair shirt, or
of Columbus himself, who affected almost simultaneously the roles
or "a captain of cavaliers and conquests" and of a prophetic, almost
priestly figure, clad in a friar's habit.

Despite overlaps with religious ideals and hagiographical literature, chivalry was essentially a secular ethos, espoused by the
knightly class and those who wished to join it. In purely secular
Spanish chivalric texts of the late Middle Ages, the sea is even more
prominent than in works with a hagiographical bent or flavor. No
text better represents this tradition than the chronicle of the deeds
of Count Pero Niño, written by his standard-bearer in the second
quarter of the fifteenth century. A treatise of chivalry, as well as an
account of campaigns, *El vitorial* celebrates a knight never vanquished in joust or war or love, whose greatest battles were fought
at sea; and "to win a battle is the greatest good and the greatest glory
of life." When the author discourses on the mutability of life, his in-
terlocutors are Fortune and the Wind, whose "mother" is the sea
"and therein is my chief office." This helps to explain an important

empire the world had ever seen and incomparably the greatest ever created with preindustrial technology. In the sixteenth and seventeenth centuries, the Atlantic and Pacific Oceans were Spanish "lakes," in which Spanish shipping controlled and virtually monopolized the best transoceanic routes. It is tempting to try to explain the apparent paradox psychologically, by analogy—say—with a colleague at the Maritime History Institute where this book took shape, whose interest in the sea was unaroused until he moved to Kansas. Awareness of the prominence of the sea in Spanish imagination helps (see Chapter 9). The scale and extent of Spanish penetration of the Atlantic in the late Middle Ages, which are the subjects of this chapter, form a background against which the problem, at least, can be understood.

When the continuous history of the recorded exploration of the Atlantic began, in the late thirteenth century, none of Europe's Atlantic seaboard peoples took part in it. The European 'discovery' of the Atlantic was an enterprise launched from deep in the Mediterranean, chiefly by Genoese and Majorcan navigators, who "unstoppered" their sea by forcing their way, against the race of the adverse current, through the Strait of Gibraltar. From there, some turned north to exploit the commerce of the north, as far as England and the Netherlands, and others south into waters unsailed—as far as we know—for centuries, toward the African Atlantic and the islands of the Madeira group and the Canaries. Along this route, for instance, the Vivaldi brothers of Genoa—the earliest participants known by name—departed in 1291 to seek "the regions of India by way of the ocean," thus anticipating, by two centuries, the very terms of Columbus's project. They were never heard of again but helped to inspire voyages in their wake which made the Canary Islands "as well known" to Petrarch—so he claimed—in the 1330s "as France."

The excitement aroused by the African Atlantic can be glimpsed in a remarkable series of surviving documents from April 1342. In that single month, at least four voyages were licensed from Majorca bound for the Canary Islands. That at least one license related to an actual voyage is shown by the chance survival of a mariner's claim for wages. A detailed account of what may be a fifth expedition of about this time survives in a corrupt version in a printed book of the next century, which describes a fortuitous landfall in the islands by pirates pursuing a galley or fleet of the King of Aragon. The ships named in the licenses were specifically "cogs" ("cocas" or "coques" in the original texts); probably round-hulled merchants' ships, poor advantage of a maritime milieu for the teller of chivalric tales: it is on the sea, with its rapid cycles of storm and calm, that the wheel of Fortune revolves most briskly.

Into the factual elements of his tale, Count Pero's squire weaves episodes from fiction, giving us unequivocal evidence of the interpenetration of the worlds of real and imaginary knights. In his pages we encounter sea monsters, dragons and enchanted fleets. We hear the story of the daughter of the Duke of the mythical land of Guiana, set adrift for defying her evil father's incestuous embraces, before rescue by a prince of England leads to marriage and a happy fadeout. The author's purpose is blatant: he exalts his real-life hero by buoying him up on a sea of romance. For Count Pero, the biographer and his readers, the type of virtue to which a sea dog should aspire— the role-model, as we say nowadays—is drawn from the pages of romantic fiction.

Typical elements of works of fiction of this type include a hero down on his luck—usually an exiled prince—who ventures his life upon the sea in an attempt to repair his fortunes. The attraction of the sea is evoked early in most of the stories and ships are often invested with an allure of their own. Sometimes this amounts to a magical enchantment, like that of the silk-sailèd singing ship in which the Infante Arnaldos is carried off in the verse romance which bears his name, or the enchanted vessel in which an invisible empress abducts the desirable Count Partinuples—a story which was to enjoy exceptional popularity in Spain's American colonies in the sixteenth century. After the hero has been visited by a maritime vocation, in most of the stories an episodic series of encounters follows, in the course of which he generally discovers or conquers an island-realm, becomes its ruler and marries a princess. There are often enchantments to be overcome and always feats of valor and endurance to be performed. This is the kind of plot satirized by Cervantes in *Don Quixote* when he makes Sancho Panza weary the Don with requests to be made "governor of some island" with, if possible, "a small portion of the sky" above it. A subtler satire occurs in the work recommended by Don Quixote as "the best in the world," *Tirant lo blanc,* where a "King of Canary, a hardy youth whose virile and restless soul was stirred by dreams of conquest," launches a counter-invasion of England from his Atlantic kingdom in a neat inversion of the usual model. The hero often has to face much or most of his time of trials alone, reminding us of Columbus's lonely self-image. The first illustrated edition of Columbus's report of his first voyage, usually known as the *Letter to Santángel,* shows an image which might have been used to embellish a seaborne chivalric tale, with a solitary figure manipulating the rigging of a ship against a backdrop of fabulous islands.

The bones of the standard plot—the sea voyage, the island destination, the elevation of the hero's status and the romantic dénouement—are all present in the legend which was probably the starting point and perhaps the archetype of the chivalric genre in Spain. The Brutus myth was known in a metrical Spanish version, the *Historia troyana polimétrica,* by a date early in the second half of the . thirteenth century. It became part of the subject of a prose fiction, the *Sumas de historia troyana,* early in the fourteenth century and recurred in "Trojan histories" which were among the most popular works in the genre for the rest of the Middle Ages. Transmuted into a chivalric hero by the alchemy of medieval adaptors, the dispossessed and exiled Trojan prince sailed from the "seas of Spain" via the dukedom of Guiana to Albion, where, after victory over giants, he married a princess and founded a kingdom. The Trojan origins of Rome and the high status of Trojan stories in classical literature heightened the appeal of Brutus as a late-medieval hero and enhanced his glamour both as a literary type and an adventurer's role-model.

The themes of his tale or others like them occur in all the texts which form part of the tradition. In Spain, one of the earliest works to develop seaborne chivalry as a motif was the mid-thirteenth century *Libro de Apolonio,* based on the story of Apollonius, Prince of Tyre, who was forced into exile on discovering the incestuous love of the King of Antioch and his daughter. Apolonio cheerfully takes to sea and, after various adventures, becomes the victim of a providential shipwreck in a land where he finds love. On his journey home, he is parted, like Eustace, from wife and daughter; but the sea which has sundered them eventually brings them together again and the tale ends with a happy family reunion. Although, for linguistic reasons, the surviving version must be the work of an Aragonese writer, from an inland part of Spain, it is so saturated in brine that the author might have shared his hero's declaration, "I was born upon the sea, where are born the fishes."

Apolonio prefers the moral environment of the sea, with all its dangers, to the wickedness of the landlubbers' world he abandons; it is part of God's territory, almost explicitly contrasted with the kingdom of this world left behind in Tyre. At sea, God intervenes with greater freedom than on land, through storms and shipwrecks; He guides the writer's characters by means of the wind, which in the

Latin Middle Ages as in many periods and cultures, was considered a phenomenon of Nature peculiarly close to God. Parallels with Columbus again suggest themselves: his life was always best-regulated when he was at sea; his enemies were mostly shoredwellers and armchair navigators; and his perceptions of himself as an instrument of Providence, divinely selected to fulfill part of God's purpose on earth, was no doubt enhanced by the predicament he shared with Apolonio, voluntarily adrift at the mercy of the wind.

Though the surviving version is in verse, there may have been a Spanish prose story of Apolonio. In what can genuinely be called novels of chivalric romance of the following three centuries many of its narrative features are renewed in prose fictions which have every quality of the modern novel except realism. For example, in the *Historia del rey Canamor y del infante Turián su hijo,* the royal hero is attracted to an enchanted ship by the lure of battle with the lions who form its crew. In this case, the enchantment proceeds from a righteous source and leads him to his future wife. His son Turián takes to the sea more capriciously, "thinking to find his fortune aboard a ship" embarks on the now familiar sequence of love found, sundered and restored. *Triant lo blanc* is not a determinedly maritime novel like *Canamor,* but its hero is a typical swashbuckling figure, a conquering privateer, of a sort familiar from the real history of Catalan maritime expansion in the late Middle Ages. By the standards of the genre it is a fairly late work (written entirely in the second half of the fifteenth century and printed, first of all chivalric romances in Spain, in 1490). The authors were able to build on the previous achievements of the tradition and their book, with its relatively sophisticated plotting and characterization, is one of the most original and innovative in its genre. Yet it does not fail to include the common amorous fade-outs: the hero anticipates the usual marriage—in this case with the daughter of the emperor of Constantinople—by raping his future bride but Tirant's son, Hipòlit, who eventually inherits the empire, marries a princess of England with due dynastic decorum.

Of all the protagonists of this type of fiction, the most popular in Spain was Amadis of Gaul. Though the original version of his story ended with his tragic death, mistakenly inflicted in a joust by his own son, the best-known text transformed him into a once-and-future hero, like Arthur, Alexander and Charlemagne. His story inspired numerous imitators and continuators and at least eight sequels, by a variety of hands, got into print in sixteenth-century Spain. *Los cuatro libros del virtuoso cavallero Amadis de Gaula* in its surviving version is a work of about 1492 but the story was known from the early fourteenth century. Amadis is the person- ification of every chivalric viture—a sort of Lancelot with the human weaknesses left out. He does not have to embark on seaborne ad- ventures to find a wife—his Oriana is a princess of the court he serves; but he does have to undertake an Odyssey and endure a demanding series of them before he can be united with her. In a sense, the sea is his proper element, for he was cast adrift at birth to spare his royal but unwed parents from the shame of an illegiti- mate child. A great part of his adventures takes the form of island- hopping between isles whose names are strongly reminiscent of the Atlantic toponymy of contemporary charts. On Isola Firme, No Fallada, Triste, Santa Mariá, Isola del Diablo and on the island of Giant Balán, he struggles with enchantment or contends with mon- sters.

Behind and beyond these examples it must be remembered that the sea was an important part of the background of literature in a particular tradition within the Arthurian cycles of tales, which were universally known and loved in late medieval Latin Christendom. A lost but much-mentioned version of the *Gesta Arthuri,* well known in the fifteenth century, dealt with Arthur's supposed seaborne ad- ventures and attributed to him the conquests of six western islands as well as of Iceland, Greenland, Norway, Lapland, Russia and the North Pole. (The last claim should not be treated with derision: the belief that a clear-water route led to the Pole was common at the time and a fourteenth-century English friar claimed to have been there at least five times). In a Spanish text of a little before 1476, the *Libro de bienandanzas e fortunas* of Lope García de Sálazar, it was suggested that the enchanted isle where Arthur's body lay might be the island of Brasil, frequently included in maps and ac- tively sought, towards the end of the century, by explorers. In a Spanish version of the Tristram legend, the hero takes to sea when humiliated in combat "to seek his fortune at sea where he might re- cover" and meets Isolde on the island of Ireland.

This chivalric literature was part of the common culture of the time. Its function resembled—though its influence transcended— that of the "pulp" fiction and "station bookstall" fiction of our own day. It is no exaggeration to say that it was read by everyone who could read—saints and sinners, noble and humble. St. Teresa of Avila wrote a continuation of *Amadis* with her brother. Cardinal Cisneros published saints' lives and an agricultural handbook in the hope of weaning knights and peasants from literary tastes he found unedifying. According to Cervantes, the novels of chivalry were the favorite reading of innkeepers and reapers. King Charles V collected the tales as did Columbus's son, Fernando Colón, who was the foremost bibliophile of the age. The Spanish Protestant humanist, Juan de Valdés, lamented the years of his life he had wasted in thrall to chivalric fiction.

In particular, however, chivalric romances or, more exactly, chivalric romances of the sea, were the proper reading-matter of the real seaborne adventurers of the Iberian Middle Ages. Some were predisposed to chivalric careers from baptism. The Genoese adventurer of the fourteenth century who attempted the first recorded colonization in the Canary Islands, probably in Portuguese service, was called Lancelot; his Poitevin successor of the early fifteenth century bore the storybook name of Gadifer. Sometimes suitable names not bestowed at christening were arrogated later. A cut-throat desperado who ruled part of Madeira in the mid-fifteenth century called himself "Tristram of the Island." This sort of transformation was consciously aimed at by many participants or would-be participants in overseas enterprises. In 1344, a dispossessed scion of the Castilian royal house called Luis de la Cerda was proclaimed "Prince of Fortune" by the pope and invested with an island principality in the Canaries. In 1412, a Norman conqueror in Castilian service had himself proclaimed "King of the Canary Islands" in the streets of Seville. When Spanish monarchs took the title "King and Queen of the Canary Islands" or were styled by Columbus as "King and Queen of the Islands of the Ocean Sea," they were appropriating a tradition from chivalric romance which various real life adventurers had already exploited.

The strongest indications of the seaward pull of chivalric values in the fifteenth century occurred in the circle of the Portuguese prince whom we usually call Henry the Navigator. In chronicles written under his patronage around the middle of the century, Henry projected what has become the traditional image of himself as the *beau idéal* of romance: an Arthurian figure, surrounded by Merlinesque cosmographers and adventurous knights and squires, riding the waves on missions of knightly and Christian virtue, doing battle with swart paynims, discovering exotic lands, braving supernatural terrors in seas of darkness and fighting for the faith. Henry certainly shared this sort of self-perception. Little survives of any writing of his own, but the two probably authentic memoranda attributed to his pen, recommending expeditions against the Moors in Tangier and Málaga respectively, are replete with chivalric images.

Their concern is not with the practicalities of warfare but with the glamor of great deeds—*grandes fectos*. Battle with the infidel is commended as "more honorable" than war against Christians. Similarly, Henry's correspondence with the popes—not, of course, direct from his hand but reflecting ideas current in his milieu—while addressing the specific priorities of its intended audience and stressing the evangelistic possibilities of Henry's proposed conquests, is always heavily colored by chivalric influences. The prince's pagan, primitive opponents in the Canary Islands or on the African coast, are either elevated to the status of "Saracens"—fit targets for the sword-stroke of a crusader—or derogated to the ranks of the wild men of the woods, the *homines silvestri,* who, commonly in the art of the time, figured as the symbolic adversaries of knights. The death on La Palma in the Canaries of one of Henry's Castilian rivals was celebrated in richly chivalric language:

> Weep, ladies, weep, if God give you grace,
> For Guillén Peraza, who left in that place,
> The flower, now withered, that bloomed in his face.
>
> Guillén Peraza, Guillén Peraza,
> Where is your shield and where is your lance?
> All is undone by fatal Mischance.

The quiver full of chivalric imagery—the invocation of ladies, the allusion to God, the mention of shield and lance, the brooding presence of Misfortune—makes La Palma resemble an island of romance. In reality, the wars of the Peraza were squalid affairs waged against neolithic savages who were scarcely appropriate opponents for a knight.

The "knights and squires" who captained the voyages commissioned by Henry the Navigator, and who obtained fiefs or commands on the islands or coasts of the African Atlantic, seem to have shared their master's world of values and to have sought to transform their own fortunes by imitating the heroes of fiction. An example of special significance was that of Bartolomeu Perestrello. He was the son of an Italian merchant who set up in business in Portugal in the very late fourteenth century and did well enough to be able to board his children at the royal court. Bartolomeu's brother rose to be head of a fashionable monastery; his sisters became concubines of the Archbishop of Lisbon. He was brought up in the household of the heir to the throne and transferred to Prince Henry's entourage when his first master died. He was employed in the colonization of the islands

of the Madeira group and in 1446 was granted the hereditary captaincy of Porto Santo—a tiny, barely viable Atlantic fief. It was as if
Don Quixote had conceded Sancho Panza's request. Bartolomeu had
followed in his life story the trajectory of a hero of a romance of the
sea; the usual connubial dénouement could not be supplied in the
uninhabited island of his day but he provided his own by marrying
successively two wives of noble birth.

Examples like his were before the eyes of the young Columbus,
who set out to make his own fame and fortune on the late fifteenth-
century Atlantic. The particular example of Bartolomeu Perestrello
is uniquely significant because it was more prominently before
Columbus's eyes than any other. For some 20 years or more after Perestrello's death Columbus married his daughter, Felipa Moniz. To
the Genoese weaver's son, union with a nobleman's daughter—albeit
from the poorest and remotest fief in the kingdom—was a dramatic
social coup, comparable, *mutatis mutandis,* with the love-interest of
a chivalric tale. According to an early tradition, the couple met in Lisbon; Columbus, however, certainly knew his lady's home island of
Porto Santo, so that the resemblances between Dona Filipa and a
chivalric heroine were compounded by an insular setting. Whether
or not Columbus himself read the chivalric fiction of the sea, its influence was certainly transmitted to him via his father-in-law's example.

In some respects, the influence of the chivalric tradition in the
making of the Spanish empire has always been acknowledged. The
names of California, Guiana and Patagonia were among those borrowed from novels. When the conquistadores first beheld the city of
the Aztecs, it resembled—according to the recollections of one of
them—the enchanted cities of Amadis. One of the first historians of
the New World, Gonzalo Fernández de Oviedo, was also a writer of
chivalric romance and borrowed models from the genre for some of
his embellishments of the deeds of conquistadores. The books were
carried by conquistadores and exported in their wake for the delec-
tation of their heirs. Everywhere they encouraged empire-builders
to dare to aspire to the social transformations—the ascents through
the ranks of society—which they so often craved and which, indeed,
were often the most powerful source of their motivation. An unsuccessful colonial projector in 1522 proposed the creation of an order
of "Knights of the Golden Spur" for Spanish settlers willing to work
the land themselves. A few years after the publication of *Don
Quixote,* when Pedro de Quirós, the self-styled "new Columbus,"
thought he had discovered the unknown "Southern Continent," he

celebrated by founding a city which he called "New Jerusalem" and knighting his cooks.

The influence of chivalric literature in inspiring and guiding Spanish conquerors in and beyond the Atlantic seems—we can now say with some confidence—to have been preceded and exceeded by similar influence on the explorers who were their precursors. Material determinants are insufficient to explain the foundation of the Spanish seaborne empire from such a poor and underpopulated mother-country. Ideology has often been said to have supplied the deficiency of resources: the ideology of crusade or of reconquest. But ideology commonly influences rhetoric more than deeds and the whole trend of modern research on the Spanish Middle Ages has been to limit or even eliminate the importance of these traditionally overemphasized themes. Ethos is more powerful than ideology in shaping behavior because it supplies individuals with standards by which to adjust and appraise their actions. Not only was chivalry the great unifying aristocratic ethos of the western Middle Ages; it has continued as a powerful and enduring spur to western actions and self-perceptions ever since. In the nineteenth century, it could still cram Victorian gentlemen creaking into their reproduction armor. In the twentieth, it could still compensate the "knights of the air" of the Battle of Britain for their generally modest social origins. Not far from the scene of the maritime history institute at which this book originated, in a stained glass window in one of America's most socially acceptable churches, it clads the image of Cornelius Vanderbilt, with unconscious self-mockery, in Lancelot's garb.[1] In the late Middle Ages, it was still strong enough to inspire the vanguard of Iberian overseas expansion, as characters in search of the dénouements of their romance penetrated the Atlantic and reached its further shores.

NOTE

1. Trinity Church, Newport, Rhode Island. Memorial window to Cornelius Vanderbilt II by Louis Comfort Tiffany, 1899.

Suggestions for Further Reading

Amezuca, J. *Libros de caballería hispánicos.* (Barcelona, 1973).

Balaguer, P. Bohigas. "Origenes de los libros de cabellería," in G. Díaz-Plaja, ed., *Historia general de las literaturas hispanicas.* (Barcelona, 1949), 521–41.

Bonilla y San Martin, A. *Libros de caballería.* (Madrid, 1907).

Cary, G. *The Medieval Alexander.* (Cambridge, 1967).

Delehaye, H. "La Légende de saint Eustache," *Mélanges d'hagiographie grècque et latine: Subsidia Hagiographica,* xlii (1966), 212–39.

Entwhistle, W. E. *The Arthurian Legend in the Literatures of the Spanish Peninsula.* (London, 1925).

Fernández-Armesto, F. *Before Columbus: Exploration and Colonization from the Mediterranean to the Atlantic, 1229–1492.* (London and Philadelphia, 1987).

Fletcher, R. A. "Reconquest and Crusade in Spain, c. 1050–1150," *Transactions of the Royal Historical Society,* 5th s., xxxvii, 31–38.

Ife, B. W. "Alexander in the New World," *Renaissance and Modern Studies,* xxx (1986), 35–44.

Keen, M. H. *Chivalry.* (New Haven, 1991).

Leonard, L. A. *Books of the Brave.* (Cambridge, Mass., 1949).

Loomis, R. S. (ed.). *Arthurian Literature in the Middle Ages.* (Oxford, 1959).

Menéndez y Pelayo, M. *Orígenes de la novela española,* i. (Madrid, 1911).

González, A. Navarro. *El mar en la literatura medieval castellana.* (La Laguna, 1962).

Phillips, W. D. and C. R. *The Worlds of Christopher Columbus.* (Cambridge and New York, 1992).

Severin, T. *The Brendan Voyage.* (London, 1981).

Thomas, H. *Las novelas de caballerías españolas y portuguesas.* (Barcelona, 1952).

10

SPANISH ATLANTIC VOYAGES
AND CONQUESTS
BEFORE COLUMBUS

Felipe Fernández-Armesto

Madrid is as far from the sea as you can get in the Iberian peninsula; yet it is full of seafood restaurants. The Castilian passion for the sea is a curious feature of the history and culture of a people whose heartlands are deep inland and who have been almost cut off from the coasts for formative periods of their past. Most of the Atlantic seaboard of the peninsula, with the mouths of the greatest rivers, belongs to the Portuguese, who have maintained an independent state, often hostile to Castile, since the twelfth century. Most of the Mediterranean coast is occupied by speakers of Catalan or cognate languages, who were not fully incorporated into the Spanish state until long after Castile's worldwide seaborne empire was founded. The northern margins, which, behind their wall of mountains, look out over the Cantabrian sea, have, for most of the last thousand years, belonged to the same political entity as Castile; yet the peoples who occupy most of their shore, with most of the best harbors, are not Castilians but Galicians and Basques—communities which contributed a disproportionate share of manpower to the overseas enterprises of the Castilian crown. In the south, Castile's direct outlets to the Atlantic, via the river Guadalquivir, and to the Mediterranean, across the virtual wastelands of Murcia, were not acquired until about the middle of the thirteenth century. Until then, the economy of Castile was sustained by the laborious treks of mule-trains to and fro across the mountains between the productive pastures of Castile and the northern ports.

Astonishingly, from this unpromising starting-point, late medieval Castile pursued a sort of collective maritime vocation with a zeal that produced, in the early modern period, the most extensive

performers against the wind, intended to sail with the Canary current and return in October, sweeping the sea for a favourable wind.

A gap in the Majorcan archives conceals the next few years' activity, though it seems unlikely that the hectic pace of the early 1340s can have been long sustained. The wage claim of Guillem Joffre indicates the commercial failure of the voyage on which he was employed and the death of its leader. This may have been a disincentive to other potential explorers, but continued activity during the sparsely documented years is indicated by an allusion in a late fourteenth-century atlas to Jaume Ferrer's voyage of 1346, wrecked on the coast of Africa in search of the "River of Gold"—perhaps, that is, the Wad Draa, alchemically transmuted, or even the Senegal. It was formerly thought that Atlantic exploration suffered a "check" in the mid-fourteenth century because of the effects of the Black Death and the technical insufficiency of ships and nautical aids. Certainly, when archival records become available again from 1351, there is little evidence to suggest this. It may be, however, that some of the commercial impetus of the early voyages was lost, as most of the Majorcan expeditions of the next generation appear, from surviving records, to have been the work of missionaries.

Majorca's precocity in Atlantic exploration is not surprising, though Majorcans' role as early leaders in the late medieval space race in the Atlantic is too often forgotten or ignored. Majorca was itself something of a "colonial society" and "frontier zone" reconquered from the Moors only a century previously; it was briefly (1276–1343) the center of an independent island-kingdom which lived by trade and, therefore, from the sea. It was a center, too, for the technical developments in shipping and cartography which helped to make Atlantic navigation practicable on a large scale. Majorca's mapmakers, the most renowned in Europe, were assiduous gatherers of geographical information, aided by the large Jewish community, from whom many of them were drawn. Exploration of the Canaries was, in a sense, a natural extension of existing Majorcan interests in Africa and the Atlantic: Majorcan shipping carried Catalan trade to northern Europe in the late thirteenth and early fourteenth centuries; and the dispensations Majorcans enjoyed to trade with the Moors peculiarly fitted them to take part in navigation along the African coast. The island, moreover, had long been a staging post for Genoese westward navigation and the home of a school of missionaries.

More surprising than the early Majorcan initiatives is the late start made by the Atlantic-side kingdoms of Portugal and Castile in the exploration of Atlantic islands. The earliest expedition of which a really detailed account survives (copied, apparently, by Boccaccio and dated, perhaps unreliably, 1341) was in part, at least, a Portuguese enterprise, guided by Italian pilots, and including, at a lower level, Castilian personnel and mariners "from other parts of Spain." It was via Italian merchants in Seville that the surviving account was transmitted to Florence and to Boccaccio's hand. However, the first recorded flash of official interest in Atlantic exploration by the Castilian crown came in March, 1345, prompted by the pope's attempt to invest Luis de la Cerda, an exiled scion of the Castilian crown, with the right of conquest of an island-realm. It was to be called the "Principality of Fortunia" and to comprise the Canaries and the Mediterranean islet of Jalita—perhaps intended by the pope as a launch-pad for a crusade into North Africa. Replying to the pope's request for aid with the project, King Alfonso XI of a Castile asserted a prior claim to the Canary Islands, which, he declared, had formed part of the perquisites of his predecessors in Visigothic times, while "the kingdoms of Africa are of our conquest."

These words were not, at first, backed up by deeds. Aragonese and Portuguese attempts to make conquests in the Canaries are strongly suggested by evidence relating to the 1360s and 1370s, but no better evidence than tradition links Castilian voyages with the African Atlantic until the 1390s, when a consortium began to coalesce in Seville of parties concerned to prosecute rights in the region. In 1390, Gonzalo Pérez de Martel sought royal permission for an attempted conquest. According to a tradition recorded in the sixteenth century, Enrique III in that year made a grant of the conquest to a Sevillan gentleman, Fernán Peraza. The interest of the Peraza family was joined in 1393 with that of the Guzmán, counts of Niebla, in an expedition (in effect, a slave-raid, representative, no doubt of others in about the same period) which wrought much destruction and captured many slaves. According to the account of the *Crónica de Enrique III*, Sevillan and Basque mariners shipped on this voyage, which seized a native chief and his consort on the island of Lanzarote and reported to the king "how those islands were easy to conquer, if such were his grace, and at small cost." This was the sort of glib prediction which lured many conquistadors to a terrible fate in the course of Castilain overseas expansion.

From that time onwards, there was no activity in the Canaries without some Castilian, and indeed Sevillan, dimension. Of the first conquest to establish a lasting European colony in the archipelago, the leaders and much of the personnel came from France—from Normandy, Poitou and Gascony. Jean de Béthencourt and Gadifer de la

Salle, adventurers attracted by the legend of the "River of Gold," seem at least at first to have envisaged their enterprise under the French crown. But the exigencies of logistics soon drove them into reliance on Castilian support and patronage. Part of the inspiration and some of the funds for their venture came from Robert de Braquemont, Béthencourt's cousin, who was connected, through his sister's marriage, to leading families of Castile, including the Guzmán and Peraza lineages. Seville became the base of the French adventurers' operations; Béthencourt did homage to the King of Castile and his conquests—the islands of Lanzarote, Fuerteventura and Hierro, became a fief of the Castilian crown. It was one of those epoch-making accidents that history sometimes throws up. As an undesigned result, Castile had Europe's first Atlantic colony and—more significantly for the future course of events—a base almost athwart the Atlantic trade winds. Castile was therefore placed to control access to the Atlantic wind system when the era of transoceanic navigation began later in the century. To adapt a famous phrase, without Béthencourt, Columbus would have been unthinkable. And without the curtain raiser in the Canaries, the drama of Castile's transatlantic empire could never have opened.

The pull of Seville's undertow was confirmed by the terms of an agreement of 15 November 1418, in which Béthencourt's heir renounced most of his rights in the islands to the Count of Niebla, who promised to continue the founder's work and subjugate the unconquered islands. There is no evidence that the new master complied, but members of the Peraza family, who acquired rights in the islands, both from Niebla and directly from the king, in the next decade, were active in promoting settlement and attempting to extend the conquest. By the time of the first surviving records from the island-colonies in the mid-fifteenth century, the language was Castilian and the institutions thoroughly, unmistakably, Castilian.

Between the end of Béthencourt's conquest ad the last quarter of the fifteenth century, Gomera was the only island to fall to Castilian arms. The Peraza family disputed the right of conquest with numerous other contenders, especially with the Prince Henry of Portugal, who, in the 1430s and 1440s, strove vigorously to build up an Atlantic fief or kingdom for himself. Not until the late 1440s did the then head of the house, Fernán Peraza, feel strong enough in the possession of Lanzarote, Fuerteventura and Hierro to give undivided attention to the extension of the conquest. His efforts, successful only in Gomera, were said to have cost him 10,000 ducats and the life of his son (see above, p. 132). The tenacity with which the native defenders, armed

only with sticks and stones, fought off European armies, is a remarkable and ill understood aspect of the story. The aboriginal Canary Islanders disappeared so completely in colonial times—exported in slavery, massacred or assimilated into the immigrant
population—that it is hard now to recover any idea of what they were
like. Probably, they were descendants of the pre-Berber population
of North Africa, not dissimilar from the fishing peoples like the Im-
raguen and the Znaga, who survive in small numbers, clinging to the
rim of the Sahara to this day. Their valor contributed two vital consequences to the story: first, they beat off Portuguese attacks, en-
suring that Castile would not have to share the archipelago with another European power; second, their resistance to the private efforts
of Fernán Peraza and his heirs ensured that the Castilian crown
would eventually commit official resources to the conquest.

The conditions which made possible this further and final phase
came together in the 1470s. Castilian interlopers in the African
trade had attracted Portuguese complaints in the previous three
decades, but the war of 1474–79, in which Afonso V of Portugal challenged Ferdinand and Isabella for the crown of Castile, acted as a
catalyst for Castilian activity. The monarchs were openhanded with
licenses for voyages of piracy or carriage of contraband; the Genoese
of Seville and Cadiz were keen to invest in these enterprises, and
Andalusian mariners, including many who were to ship with Columbus or who made transatlantic journeys after him, were schooled in
Atlantic navigation. The main action of the war took place on land
in northern Castile but was accompanied by a "small war" at sea in
the latitudes of the Canaries. Castilian privateers were licensed by
their monarchs to break into Portugal's monopoly of Guinea trade
by force; the Genoese governor who ruled the Cape Verde Islands for
Portugal deserted to Castile; Portuguese ships made numerous attacks on Castilian settlers in Lanzarote. The royal courts of the peninsula became impressed with the potential strategic importance of
the unconquered islands of the archipelago—precisely the largest
and richest, Gran Canaria, La Palma and Tenerife—and the fragil-
ity of the Castilian hold on Gomera, which remained at the mercy of
its rebellious native inhabitants. When Ferdinand and Isabella sent
a force to Gran Canaria to resume the conquest in 1478, a Portuguese expedition in seven caravels was already on its way. Castilian
royal intervention thus has the character of a preemptive strike
against the Portuguese.

Other, longer-maturing reasons also influenced the royal decision.
First, the monarchs had other rivals than the Portuguese: the Per-

aza lordship had effectively descended, by marriage with Inés Peraza, to Diego de Herrera, a minor nobleman of Seville, who fancied himself as a conquistador. His claim to have made vassals of nine "kings," or native chiefs, of Tenerife and two of Gran Canaria was, to say the least, exaggerated. He had raided those islands in the hope of exacting tribute by terror, and had attempted in the manner of previous conquistadors, to dominate them by erecting intimidating stone turrets. But such large, populous and indomitable islands could not be conquered by the private enterprise of a provincial hidalgo. Effective conquest and systematic exploitation demanded concentrated resources and heavy investment, such as could be organized with greater readiness at court. And even had Herrera been capable of completing the conquest, it would have been unwise to permit him to do so. He was not above intrigue with the Portuguese; he might have become a turncoat, like Antonio da Noli in the Cape Verde Islands. He was typical of the sort of truculent paladin whose power in a peripheral region was an affront to the crown. Profiting from a local rebellion—one of many against seigneurial authority in 1475–6—the monarchs determined to enforce their suzerainty and, in particular, the most important element in it, the right to be the final court of appeal throughout the colonies of the archipelago. In November, 1476, they initiated an inquiry into the juridical basis of the lordships of the Canaries. Its findings were embodied in an agreed settlement with Herrera of October, 1477: that Herrera's rights were unimpeachable, saving the superior lordship of the crown, but that "for certain just and reasonable causes," which were never specified, the right of conquest should revert to the crown.

Beyond the political motives for royal intervention in the Canaries were economic ones. As always in the history of Latin involvement in the African Atlantic, gold was the spur. According to a highly privileged observer, King Ferdinand's interest in the Canaries was aroused by a desire to open communications with "the mines of Ethiopia" (that is, Africa generally). The conquest was also worth pursuing for the islands' own sake, especially for their dyestuffs and for the potential sugar lands of the unconquered islands. Both these commodities had rapidly growing markets in Europe.

It proved almost as hard to advance the conquest under royal auspices as under those of Herrera. It took six years of campaigns to reduce Gran Canaria to submission. The conquests of La Palma and Tenerife were not considered complete until 1492 and 1496 respectively. The ferocity of native resistance was responsible in part; but finance and manpower proved almost equally hard to command.

Though royal intervention had begun as an attempt to bring the conquest out of private hands and into the "public" domain, as the conquest wore on private sources of money and means of recruiting tended increasingly to displace royal ones. Instead of wages, the conquistadors were promised plots of conquered land. Instead of the yield from the sale of indulgences or the direct use of the crown's share of booty to meet the costs of the war, booty yet uncollected was pledged as rewards to conquerors who could raise the necessary finance elsewhere. By the end of the process, in La Palma and Tenerife, the conquest was being financed by ad hoc companies, in which financiers and conquistadors were to share the proceeds.

At the nerve-center of the monarchs' war effort, scraping contingents together, assembling groups of financial backers, was Alonso de Quintanilla, a treasury official who was one of the most influential architects of policy in the reign of Ferdinand and Isabella. He seems to have been given responsibility for the organization of the conquest from 1480, when dwindling returns from the sale of indulgences caused a crisis of finance. He devised a wide range of expedients, including the mortgaging of royal booty and recourse to Italian, chiefly Genoese, capitalists. In doing so he adumbrated the circle that would later contribute to the financing of Columbus. Quintanilla himself was instrumental in arranging the backing for the "Enterprise of the Indies," as for that of the Canaries. In both cases he was helped by key figures, the Genoese merchants of Seville, Francesco Pinelli and Francesco da Rivarolo. Pinelli had been involved in Canarian finance for as long as Quintanilla, as he had administered the receipts from the sale of indulgences on the monarchs' behalf from March, 1480; Quintanilla's first personal subvention was made in April of that year. Pinelli went on to acquire the first sugar mill on Gran Canaria and make loans to the conquerors of La Palma and Tenerife. For his part as a backer of Columbus, the monarchs made him one of first administrators of the Indies trade when it was organized as a royal monopoly in 1493.

Francesco da Rivarolo may have done even better out of the whole affair. There is no evidence that he contributed personally to the conquest of Gran Canaria, but his son-in-law was one of the biggest investors, and the Rivarolo family was a close-knit business partnership carefully managed by the patriarchal Francesco. He took part in the financing of the conquests of La Palma and Tenerife in his own right and became the richest merchant of the archipelago with interests essentially, but not exclusively, concentrated in sugar and dyestuffs. He was a mainstay of Columbus, whose fourth voyage he helped to finance and who, at one time, dwelt in his house. Some non-Genoese of Seville from the fringes of Columbus's world also took a hand in paying for the conquest of the Canaries: the Duke of Medina Sidonia, head of the house of Guzmán, whom Columbus saw as a possible patron; and Gianotto Berardi, one of Columbus's biggest creditors, a Florentine (according to most sources) who had a share of the New World trade in its earliest years. The balance, however, was strongly Genoese. The same is broadly true of the financial circle that sustained Columbus or advanced money for his voyages. There seems to have been sufficient overlap for the conquest of the Canaries and the discovery of America to be seen, to some extent, as the work of the same group of men. The Genoese played, for Castile in the Atlantic, a role similar to that of the Florentines of Lisbon in the impulsion of Portugal into the Indian Ocean a few years later.

The Canaries were a vital part of the context of Columbus in a further sense: they provided him with his starting point. The port of San Sebastián de la Gomera, from which he set sail on 6th September, 1492, was uniquely suited to his purpose: no suitable deep-water harbor was further west, none closer to the path of the northeast trade winds that would provide the power to carry him across the Atlantic. When Columbus made use of it, its security had only recently been established. The Peraza lords of the island had never had more than a tenuous hold over the inhabitants. They shut themselves up in their crude and comfortless keep of stone, which stands to this day, and sustained with their "vassals" a relationship of mutual fear. The natives had rebelled in 1478, taking the opportunity of the Luso-Castilian war allegedly to "procure favours from Portugal." A further rebellion in 1484 can be inferred from the monarchs' warning that the inhabitants should obey their lords and pay their tribute. By 1488 they were again in revolt. In 1488 and 1489, royal forces from Gran Canaria made two brutal incursions, between which Hernán Peraza, who ruled the island on his family's behalf, was put to death by the insurgents. In revenge, the rebels were executed or enslaved in droves, with dubious legality, as "rebels against their natural lord," and the island permanently garrisoned from Gran Canaria. The treatment of the natives touched tender consciences in Castile; the monarchs established an inquiry by a committee of jurists and theologians into the properties of the case; the release of the enslaved Gomerans was recommended and many of them eventually returned to the archipelago to help colonize other conquests. Their native land, however, was now ripe for transformation by European settlers and exploitation by transatlantic voyages. The crushing of the rebels left the island in the hands of the ex-mistress of the king and widow of Gomera's administrator, Doña Beatriz de Bobadilla; she had probably met Columbus in Cordova in 1486 and, according to a shipmate of his, stirred his affections.

Castile had been preceded in the Atlantic by Genoa and Majorca; until Columbus, the range of her penetration of the ocean had been exceeded by Portugal's. But by concentrating her efforts on the Canaries she had secured a prize of incomparable value. Throughout the age of sail, the islands' central position in the Atlantic wind system gave Spain privileged access to the circum-Caribbean region of America, where the wealth of the New World was concentrated—including, in central America and Mexico, the Pacific-side ports of departure to the riches of Peru and the harbors of return for transpacific missions. The Canaries, in the estimation of a seventeenth-century Spanish king "are the most important of my possessions, for they are the straight way and approach to the Indies." The fate of Columbus's enterprise, compared with the projects of other would-be Atlantic explorers of the period, shows how crucial was this consequence of late medieval Castile's maritime history.

For Columbus was not the only projector of Atlantic exploration in his day. Between 1452, when the westernmost islands of the Azores were discovered, and 1487, when the Fleming Ferdinand van Olmen was commissioned to seek, like Columbus, "islands and mainlands" in the ocean sea, at least eight surviving commissions for voyages into the recesses of the Atlantic were issued in Portugal; and from 1481, at the latest, Bristolian seafarers were urgently engaged in their search for the legendary isle of Brasil. Attempts from the Azores, like van Olmen's, were doomed to be turned back by the prevailing winds; those from Bristol had to succeed, if at all, within a perilously short favorable spring season, and, given the conditions of navigation on the far side of the ocean, would find it hard to get beyond Newfoundland. Columbus succeeded where others failed because, sailing under Castilian auspices, he had access to the best route, via the islands which unlocked the secret of the wind system, along a wind-course which led to enticing and exploitable lands.

The Spanish achievement in the late-medieval Atlantic before Columbus was the fruit of the modest miracles of high-medieval technology: the compass, the portolan chart, the cog, the caravel and primitive celestial navigation. The navigators based their judgments of relative latitudes on glimpsed appraisals of the height of the sun or the Pole Star above the horizon, with the unaided eye.

Most were "unknown pilots"; many known by name are recorded only in stray documents or cartographers' jottings. They often had crusading experience, like Gadifer de la Salle or Joan de Mora, an Aragonese captain in Canarian waters in 1366. They were sometimes penurious noblemen escaping from a society of restricted opportunity at home. They sought "routes of gold," like Jaume Ferrer, or "routes of spices," like the Vivaldi brothers, or slaves like the Peraza; increasingly, like the Guzmán, they were genuine colonial entrepreneurs looking for cheap land to grow cash crops.

They strove to embody chivalric fable, to win fiefs or create kingdoms, like Luis de la Cerda, the would-be "Prince of Fortunia" or Jean de Béthencourt who had himself proclaimed "King of the Canaries" in the streets of Seville. Or else they were missionaries, like the Franciscans of the Canarian bishopric of Telde—established by Majorcans early in the second half of the fourteenth century—who sailed to and from for some 40 years until they were massacred in 1393. They came from a world steeped in the idealization of adventure (above, pp. 123–134). They aspired to fame and most have been forgotten; but the impulse and direction they gave to Castilian overseas expansion had enormous and enduring effects.

Suggestions for Further Reading

P. Adam, "Navigation Primitive et navigation astronomique." *VIe Colloque International d'Historie Maritime.* (Paris, 1966), pp. 91–110.

E. Aznar Vallejo, *La incorporación de las Islas Canaries en la corona de Castilla.* (Seville, 1983).

F. Fernández-Armesto, *Before Columbus.* (London and Philadelphia, 1987), *Columbus.* (Oxford and New York, 1991).

R. Pike, *Enterprise and Adventure: the Genoese of Seville and the Opening of the New World.* (Ithaca, N.Y., 1966).

L. de la Rosa Olivera, "Francisco de Riberol y la colonia genovesa en Canarias," *Annuario de estudios atlánticos,* xviii (1972), 61–198.

A. Rumeu de Armas, *Espana en el Africa Atlántica,* 2 vols (Madrid, 1955), *La conquista de Tenerife.* (Santa Cruz, 1975), *El obispado de Telde.* (Madrid, 1986).

C. Verlinden, *Les Origines de la civilisation atlantique.* (Paris, 1966), *The Beginnings of Modern Colonization.* (Ithaca, N.Y., 1970), "La découverte des archipels de la Méditerranée Atlantique." (Canaries, Madères, Azores) et la navigation astronomique primitive," *Revista portuguesa de história,* xvi (1978), 124–39.

Figure XIV. Christopher Columbus at the Royal Court of Spain. Lithograph by Mast, Crowell & Kirkpatrick, 1892. *Courtesy of the Library of Congress, Washington, D.C.*

11

COLUMBUS AND THE EUROPEAN BACKGROUND: THE FIRST VOYAGE

William D. Phillips, Jr., and Carla Rahn Phillips

During his lifetime, Christopher Columbus inhabited many worlds, both physically and in his imagination. Before 1492 those worlds included Genoa where he as born, Portugal where he prepared for his ventures, and Castile where he received backing for his transatlantic voyages. Every verifiable historical document clearly indicates that Columbus was born in the independent Italian republic of Genoa, probably in late summer or early fall of 1451.[1] His father Domenico had trained as an apprentice weaver and made his living as a weaver during the late 1430s and into the late 1440s. He opened a shop in Genoa and took on an apprentice of his own in 1439. Domenico began to buy income-producing real estate and became active on the local political scene as a supporter of the Fregoso faction, one of the political groups that controlled Genoese life. His political loyalty and connections led to an appointment as the warder or gatekeeper of the Porta dell'Olivella in 1447–48 and again around 1450.

What education Columbus received would have begun at home; there is no direct evidence that he had formal schooling, though he may have attended a grammar school for weavers' sons. We can assume that the religious instruction Christopher received was Roman Catholic. Both his father and grandfather owned land, a privilege restricted to Catholics in Genoa. Moreover, his father could not have engaged in politics or become the warder of a city gate unless he was a practicing Catholic. The persistent notion that Columbus's family was secretly Jewish or had converted from Judaism has no credible basis in the historical record.

By 1472, when Christopher Columbus was about 21 years old, he
described himself as a *lanerius,* or wool worker. Some writers question whether he could have been a wool worker, a mariner, a merchant, a bookseller, and perhaps a mapmaker, all before he was 30.
Such a varied career is hardly surprising in the context of the late
fifteenth century, however. Columbus's own father, in addition to
being a weaver and a political appointee, also had his hand in a number of other ventures. There is nothing mysterious in his son
Christopher's propensity to turn his hand to several different occu-
pations. He was following a tradition of social advancement common
in his city of origin and in his own family.

Columbus wrote of himself in 1501: *"from a very early age I went
to sea sailing and I have continued it until now."*[2] Genoese merchants had created a number of commercial enclaves on the
Mediterranean and Atlantic coasts, and it was not difficult for a
young Genoese to ship out on one of the many trading voyages they
sponsored. Columbus's father could have arranged it easily. At first,
the young man probably sailed on short voyages close to Genoa. He
also went on a longer voyage to Chios, an island in the Aegean then
held by the Genoese. At the time of his first voyage across the Atlantic, Columbus claimed that he had previously seen "all the east
and west," and most historians assume that his voyage to Chios lay
behind this extravagant claim.[3] Chios could be considered the east
or the Levant, especially given its connections to Constantinople and
Asia Minor.

Other adventures from Columbus's early days at sea have even
more exotic connotations. At one point, Columbus claimed to have
sailed for King René of Anjou, in command of a war vessel. René
of Anjou, as a claimant to the kingdom of Naples, was an enemy
of the King of Aragon and the leading foreign supporter of the
Fregoso faction in Genoa, to which Columbus's father Domenico
belonged.

> It happened to me that King René (whom God has taken) sent me to Tu-
> nis to capture the galleass *Fernandina*; and when I was off the island of
> San Pietro, near Sardinia, a vessel informed me there were two ships and
> a carrack with the said galleass, which frightened my people, and they
> resolved to go no further but to return to Marseilles to pick up another
> ship and more men. I, seeing that I could do nothing against their wills
> without some ruse, agreed to their demand, and, changing the point of
> the compass, made sail at nightfall; and at sunrise the next day we found
> ourselves off Cape Carthage, while all aboard were certain we were bound
> for Marseilles.[4]

Whatever the truth of this story, by his middle twenties Columbus had acquired considerable sailing experience in the Mediterranean and had begun to venture into the Atlantic. Around 1475 or 1476 Columbus moved to Portugal and lived there for about a decade, arguably the most formative period of his life. He learned enough in those years to believe in the possibility of sailing westward toward Asia. As important as Columbus's Portuguese sojourn was to his intellectual formation, however, we know only the broadest outlines and a few basic facts about his life during those years.

The scanty documentary evidence that remains suggests that Columbus continued to make his living from maritime and commercial activities while he lived in Portugal. He expanded his network of personal contacts, sailed on Portuguese and Spanish commercial voyages to Italy, and continued his close association with Italian merchant companies based in Iberia. He testified in a court case in Genoa in 1479 that he was acting as an agent of the Genoese merchant Paolo di Negro for a shipment of sugar from Madeira. Many years later, his writing demonstrated a thorough familiarity with the sugar business on that island.

During his years in Portugal, Columbus's knowledge of spoken Portuguese helped him assimilate into local society, just as his Genoese identity bound him to the Italian immigrant community established in Portugal and enhanced his fortunes. Presumably through his personal and business connections in the Italian-Portuguese community, he was able to contract a very favorable marriage alliance. Sometime in the mid-to-late 1470s Columbus married Felipa Moniz, a noblewoman descended from an Italian couple who had moved to Portugal sometime around 1385. Filippo (or Filipone) Pallastrelli and his wife Catalina (or Caterina) had emigrated from Piacenza, and Filippo made a fortune from commerce in Lisbon and the northern city of Oporto. In 1399 he received recognition as a Portuguese noble. His youngest child was Bartolomeu, whose daughter Columbus would later marry. Filippo arranged for Bartolomeu to be raised in the household of Prince João, son of King João II and grandfather of the future queen Isabel of Castile. Such a position testifies to the distinction that Filippo had attained in his adopted homeland. After Prince João died, Bartolomeu went to live in the household of Prince Henrique, another son of João I and commonly known in modern times as Henry the Navigator.

Bartolomeu's chance at distinction came with the Portuguese settlement of the Madeira islands. In 1466 the king granted him the island of Porto Santo as a heritable captaincy. Bartolomeu Perestrelo married twice. His first wife Brites Futado de Mendonza bore three daughters before she died. Bartolomeu married a second time about 1449 to 1450 to Isabel Moniz, who belonged to an important noble family with interests in both southern Portugal and Madeira. Bartolomeu Perestrelo and his second wife lived in Porto Santo and had three children: a son, also named Bartolomeu Perestrelo, an elder daughter named Felipa Moniz, and a younger daughter named Violante Moniz. Bartolomeu Perestrelo died in 1457, leaving his minor son and namesake the rights to Porto Santo. When Columbus married Felipa Moniz in 1478 or 1479, he gained ties with two families that enjoyed access to the Portuguese court and had broad experience in the business of overseas exploration and colonization.

During his years in Portugal, Columbus gradually developed his ideas about the size of the earth and the array of land masses on its surface, necessary prerequisites for his plan of a voyage westward from Europe to Asia. He based those plans on what he had learned from his own sailing experiences, from rumors he heard, and from his reading in geographical texts.

While a resident in Portugal, Columbus embarked on many voyages into the Atlantic, gaining valuable first-hand knowledge about the currents and winds, islands and shorelines of that vast ocean sea. His travels toward the north and northwest probably included visits to Ireland, England, Flanders, and Iceland. His travels toward the west and south were arguably more important to his evolving scheme. In his writings, Columbus unambiguously described his experiences in Africa and the Atlantic islands, leaving no doubt that he knew those areas well. He traveled as far south as the fortress of São Jorge da Mina, built on the Gold Coast. He may have commanded vessels during those African voyages, or he may have been a merchant-passenger. During his later travels in American waters, Columbus wrote down explicit comparisons between the flora and fauna of the new lands he found and their equivalents in the Old World. Many of these comparisons revealed his familiarity with Africa. Moreover, Columbus often used Portuguese words describing Africa when writing about plants, animals, and aspects of native culture in the Caribbean,[5] additional supporting evidence that he had visited Africa during his years in Portugal.

In that same period, Columbus traveled frequently to the Madeiras—both the main island and Porto Santo—and at least once he returned to Genoa. On those voyages, we can assume that he carefully observed the winds and seas, storing the knowledge away with his prior experience. The wealth of real knowledge and sea lore that Columbus accumulated during his years in Portugal contributed valuable ingredients to his grand design.

By the early 1480s, Columbus had acquired the skills, knowledge, and experience that helped to shape his notions about the possibility of a westward voyage to Asia. He had learned to command a ship, which meant that he knew about practical navigation and geography. He had sailed to Portuguese trading stations in parts of the world unknown a generation before. Beyond his own experience, the most important early sources of his ideas were probably simple stories, rumors, and physical evidence. He knew that wealth had been made in new discoveries in Africa and the Atlantic islands, and he knew the honors that the discoverers and governors had received from grateful monarchs. He had read about the potential riches that Asia offered. As he heard stories that merchants and sailors told of faraway riches and strange peoples and things from the west, we can assume that he fitted them into a gradually developing explanation of the world.

One group of stories featured strange and portentious physical objects drifting in from the western seas. A Portuguese ship's pilot named Martín Vicente told Columbus that, 50 leagues west of Portugal's Cape St. Vincent, he had pulled from the sea a piece of wood that had been carved, but not with iron tools. Vicente assumed that the wood came from unknown islands far out in the ocean sea. Pedro Correa da Cunha, his wife's brother-in-law, told how he had found a strangely carved piece of wood driven ashore on Porto Santo, while he served as the island's governor. He had also found pieces of thick canes unlike any others known to the Portuguese. Cunha took the strange canes to the Portuguese court, showing them to the king and speculating that they had come from nearby islands or perhaps even from India. Obviously, both Vicente and Cunha believed there were inhabited lands to the west, close enough that a piece of carved wood might float into Portugal's orbit under certain circumstances.

Taken together, these stories suggested that hitherto unknown islands lay fairly close to European shores. Even more intriguing, some inhabitants of the Azores and the Madeiras asserted that they regularly saw more islands to the west; a few mariners actually claimed to have sailed out to find them. Ferdinand Columbus's biography tells us that his father dismissed those stories, because their authors had sailed less than one hundred leagues to the west, and because he thought they had mistaken reefs for islands. Nonetheless, Columbus was clearly fascinated by the possibilities such stories suggested, and he was not the only one who thought seriously that the ocean barrier might be breached. However fanciful the stories of western islands might have been, they coincided with medieval tales of islands in the ocean sea: St. Brendan's Isle and Antilia, among others. The Canaries, the Madeiras, the Cape Verdes, and the Azores had all been discovered relatively recently. Actual discoveries in the fourteenth and fifteenth centuries naturally led to speculation that there were more islands yet to find.

Columbus was still collecting stories on the very eve of his first voyage. A pilot from Palos named Pedro de Velasco had participated in the voyage of the Portuguese Diogo de Teive in the 1450s. Long afterward in 1492, he told Columbus of their long trajectory southwest from the Azores and their subsequent northward loop to the latitude of Ireland. Because of the land birds they sighted, and the condition of the seas, they assumed that land lay fairly close to the west, but the approach of autumn persuaded them to return home instead of searching father. The stories known to Columbus were also known to countless others, and many were as intrigued as he was by the prospect of lands to the west between Europe and Asia. In this atmosphere of restless voyaging and speculation, it was only a matter of time before someone put together the evidence from all the tales and conceived of a westward attempt to reach Asia. As far as we know, Columbus was the first—if not to conceive the plan—to persevere until he found backing for it.

In addition to practical experience and the inspiration of others, Columbus drew on his own reading and geographical speculations. The late fifteenth century was the early age of the printed book, when newly invented typesetting techniques made a variety of books available much more cheaply than before. Columbus had access to a wide range of notions about the size and configuration of the known world and its peoples, as well as the cosmos beyond, from ancient writers recently printed, and from recent writers commenting upon them. From that range of scholarly opinion, Columbus bolstered his notions about the feasibility of sailing west to reach Asia, trying to impress his would-be patrons with the support of scholarly opinions. Unfortunately, Columbus did not write about his own geographical ideas in detail until his third voyage across the Atlantic, so we cannot date their evolution with any precision. It seems reasonable to suppose, however, that his geographical hypotheses grew incrementally, beginning with a fairly simple idea of sailing west to reach the Indies, and later adding evidence from academic geographers to buttress his case.

The principal scholarly geographical texts available in the fifteenth century did not offer European mariners much practical assistance. Over the centuries, however, scholars had developed enough information to suggest that ocean routes to Asia were possible. In 1264 Roger Bacon had published his *Opus Majus,* which summarized ancient geographical knowledge and integrated contributions from Muslim geographers in the Middle Ages. Bacon accepted the view that the habitable portion of the world was composed of three parts—Asia, Africa, and Europe—and that the rest of the globe was covered by oceans. In a crucial break with tradition, however, Bacon rejected the common notion that seas and lands near the equator were too hot for human beings to survive. Instead, he believed that Asia and Africa extended downward beyond the equator and could be inhabited. Once scholars began to doubt the existence of a Torrid Zone, the possibility of southerly voyages lost their fearsome quality.

Bacon's work was only one of many speculating about the shape and character of the world and questioning the wisdom of ancient and medieval authors. The geography of Ptolemy, greatest of the ancients, was translated into Latin in the early fifteenth century, providing a convenient framework for depicting the terrestrial globe in graphic form. Among his other contributions, Ptolemy divided the earth into 360 degrees, which became the basis for subsequent western maps. Unfortunately, he made two fundamental errors, estimating the size of the earth as about one-fifth too small, and describing Africa and Asia as being joined at their tips. This configuration would have made the rich trading network of the Indian Ocean inaccessible to ships sailing from Europe. Academic geographers in Columbus's times did not always agree with ancient authorities or with one another, but their speculations stimulated discussion and controversy. Enea Silvio Piccolomini (later Pope Pius II) published a work in the early fifteenth century summarizing much of Ptolemy's geography but rejecting the idea that the Indian Ocean was an enclosed sea. As Columbus assembled academic support for his grand scheme in the late fifteenth century, he undoubtedly read Piccolomini's work and probably found it appealing.

Pierre d'Ailly, an early fifteenth-century cardinal, published a geographical work called *Imago Mundi* that was to have a great influence upon many European scholars, merchants, and mariners, among them Columbus. The cardinal relied heavily on geographical treatises by classical and Muslim scholars, and, to increase the accuracy of his work, he disregarded the accounts of mere travelers such as Marco Polo. Nonetheless, he made several fundamental errors, exaggerating the size of Asia and underestimating the extent of oceans on the face of the earth. He was thus able to conclude that a westward voyage from Europe to Asia was eminently possible. Other geographers at the same time estimated the size and shape of the earth much more accurately than d'Ailly. He remains important, however, because Columbus enthusiastically adopted his calculations and used them as a basis for his grand scheme.

By the late fifteenth century, merchants, popes, princes, and other members of the intellectual elite could pick and choose among the available theories, selecting interpretations that were the most persuasive or the most agreeable to their own opinions. In Columbus's writings, especially in his *Book of Prophecies,* he cited numerous authorities, but it seems that most of them came from the citations and quotations contained in Pierre d'Ailly. Columbus also read and annotated Marco Polo's account of Asia. From Polo, Columbus derived an exaggerated idea of the wealth of Japan and the erroneous notion that it lay 1,500 miles off the coast of China. Columbus almost certainly used Polo's description of the gold-encrusted temples and palaces of Japan as a selling point to gain support for his scheme. Pierre d'Ailly may have been the more trustworthy as a geographer, but, for Columbus, Polo the merchant was undoubtedly more persuasive.

European geographical ideas of the late fifteenth century were depicted most strikingly on a globe by Martin Behaim in 1492, which presented a view of the world almost identical to that of Columbus. Behaim placed Japan far distant from the mainland of Asia and showed the ocean between Europe and Asia strewn with islands. The Americas were totally missing, of course. As far as we know, Columbus and Behaim had no contact with one another, even though they were both in Lisbon at about the same time. Their conceptions of the world agreed almost entirely, however, being based on the academic geography available at the end of the fifteenth century.

Columbus's access to the Portuguese court presumably increased the store of knowledge he had accumulated from his own personal experiences and from the experiences of others. Even if Columbus himself was not in regular attendance at court, his wife's relatives were. Along with other information from the court, Columbus found inspiration in a letter sent to the king of Portugal by the Florentine geographer and merchant Paolo dal Pozzo Toscanelli. Toscanelli wrote to the Portuguese king in 1474 that one could reach Quinsay (Hangchow) in China by sailing west for five thousand miles, breaking the trip with stops at the islands of Antilia and Cipango (Japan). Toscanelli's letter was discussed in Lisbon and was commonly known to those who frequented the court. Columbus supposedly wrote to Toscanelli himself in 1481, receiving in return encouragement and a copy of the letter and map that had been sent to the king of Portugal in 1474. Whether or not any correspondence really occurred between Columbus and Toscanelli—and some doubt it— Columbus clearly knew about Toscanelli and his theories.

In developing his notion that a westward voyage to Asia was not only possible but practical, Columbus adopted the same erroneous assumptions from his readings that had influenced Toscanelli and others. Following those premises, the open ocean between Europe and Asia shrank to a manageable size, with hospitable islands along the way. On the basis of his sources, Columbus calculated a distance of only 2,400 nautical miles from the Canaries to Japan, whereas the real distance is 10,600 nautical miles. In other words, Columbus chose a set of figures that made his enterprise plausible. Convinced that he was right, Columbus tried first to interest King João II of Portugal in his scheme for a westward passage to Asia. After consultation with his advisers, however, João refused to support Columbus. Their rejection is hardly surprising, given the disagreement among experts at the time. Many contemporary scholars used the evidence to arrive at estimates very different from Columbus's for the size and character of the earth's ocean and lands.

After being rejected in Portugal, Columbus traveled to Spain sometime about 1485. He would spend the next seven years to secure the backing of Spain's monarchs. Those seven years are better documented than the years Columbus spent in Portugal, but the documents do not permit us to trace his movements and actions at every stage. We have information about the highlights of what he did, but not always precisely when he acted, or why. We can surmise, however, that Spain was the logical second choice for his enterprise. Next to Portugal, Spain had the most extensive experience in Europe of Atlantic exploration. Castile also controlled the Canary Islands, and Columbus may well have determined that the Canaries were the perfect starting place for an Atlantic crossing. Of the four voyages he made, the first, second, and fourth began in the Canaries, though on the third he went as far south as the Cape Verdes before heading west. Spain also challenged Portugal's lead in Atlantic exploration. If the Portuguese would not back him, perhaps their Spanish rivals would. Columbus probably went first to the region of the lower Tinto River valley, to the towns of Palos, Moguer, and Huelva. He had relatives living in Huelva, his late wife's sister Violante Moniz and her husband Miguel Moliart. It is likely that Columbus visited them directly after his arrival in Spain and left his young son Diego with them while he pursued his quest at court.

Through personal contacts, Columbus was introduced to the royal court; he met Fernando and Isabel for the first time early in 1486, probably while the court resided in Alcalá de Henares. The monarchs took an interest in Columbus's idea and appointed a commission to investigate its feasibility. Although the learned commissioners knew perfectly well that the earth was round, they seem to have found Columbus's scheme unconvincing for other reasons. From our twentieth-century perspective, it is easy to condemn the clerics and professors who resisted Columbus's charm and powers of persuasion; with hindsight, we know that Columbus's erroneous calculations about the size of the world did not matter in the long run. Nonetheless, they mattered at the time. Columbus thought Asia lay within easy sailing distance of Europe, but any hardheaded analysis of his reasoning would have revealed the highly speculative nature of his calculations. It is not surprising that the royal commission of experts advised against supporting him. It is more surprising that the monarchs did not reject his proposal out of hand but instead encouraged him to believe they might support him once they had finished their long war of conquest against Muslim Granada. They even provided him with subsidies as the war dragged on.

The long delay must have been galling for Columbus, but he seems to have recognized that Fernando and Isabel represented his best hope. At some point he discussed his venture with the Duke of Medina Sidonia and the Duke of Medinaceli. Either of these powerful aristocrats could have underwritten a small venture such as his; both had maritime interests and investments. Yet neither of them could grant Columbus the social advancement, especially noble status, that he persistently sought; only monarchs could confer nobility. In pursuit of alternative royal backing, Bartolomeo Columbus spent years in England and France unsuccessfully trying to sell his brother's scheme, while Columbus waited in Spain. At one point Columbus received an invitation to return to Lisbon and met with João II, but his visit seems to have coincided with the return of Bartolomeu Dias from the Cape of Good Hope, bringing with him knowledge that the Indian Ocean lay open to the next Portuguese expedition. Columbus could do nothing more than wait for the end of the Granadan war and the possibility of Spanish funding.

During those years, Columbus lived principally in southern

Spain, in the cities of Seville and Córdoba. In Córdoba he met Beatriz de Arana, a poor orphan, and had an illegitimate child by her, named Ferdinand. Although Columbus never married Beatriz, he did legitimize their son, to whom he left an impressive fortune. Columbus seems not to have gone to sea during the years he spent in Spain before 1492. Instead he supported himself from periodic subsistence grants from the crown and from the income of business ventures, possibly including work as a bookseller or as a maker and seller of maritime charts.

By the early fall of 1491, he seems to have decided that the Spanish monarchs would never support him—either that, or he was hoping to increase the pressure on Fernando and Isabel by threatening to leave. He went to the monastery of La Rábida near Palos in 1491 with the expressed intention of embarking for France. Columbus explained the disappointing royal reception of his plans to Juan Pérez, who was the current warden (*guardián*) of La Rábida and a former official of Queen Isabel. Intrigued, Pérez asked a physician of Palos, a man of some scientific knowledge, to question Columbus about his theories. Demonstrating his skills as a master salesman, Columbus won over both Pérez and the physician to his cause. Pérez proved to be a powerful intermediary. He wrote to Queen Isabel requesting further consideration of Columbus's proposal and an audience for himself. She responded within two weeks, granting official permission for Pérez to come to court at Real de Santa Fe, the royal military encampment outside the city of Granada. There he made a forceful argument in Columbus's favor. Luckily for Columbus, Pérez's visit came at an opportune time. The Muslims had just signed agreements promising to turn Granada over to the Catholic Monarchs in 1492. With the end of the long Granadan campaign in sight, Isabel ordered Columbus to return to court.

Once Columbus reached Santa Fe, his proposal underwent a new inquiry, conducted by royal councilors and outside experts. Disastrously for Columbus, the council confirmed the judgment of the earlier commission; apparently his figures were too far off the mark. The well-founded decision of the council was the final blow for Columbus. He set out on the road for Córdoba, his first planned stop on a journey to France. After seven weary years he had abandoned hope of securing support in Spain and was heading off to find it elsewhere.

Then King Fernando stepped in. Up to that point, Queen Isabel had been in charge of the negotiation with Columbus, with her confessor Hernando de Talavera coordinating most of the staff-work necessary. For reasons unstated in the documents, the king ordered Talavera and Diego de Deza to see if something could be arranged with Columbus after all. Years later Fernando would remember his crucial action when he asserted in 1508, "*It was I (who was) the principal cause why those islands were discovered.*"[6] The queen was finally persuaded by Luis de Santángel, an Aragonese who served as the king's manager of household accounts. His argument was eminently practical: backing Columbus would be an inexpensive gamble, with comparatively little risk for a potentially great reward. The opportunity should be seized; if not, Columbus would go to a foreign power, which would reap all the potential benefits if the gamble paid off. Isabel agreed, and sent out a royal guard to find Columbus and escort him back to court. He was two leagues north at the bridge of Pinos, on his way to Córdoba, when the rider reached him. He turned back to Granada and into the pages of history.

Meanwhile at court, talk turned to the question of where to find funds to outfit the voyage. The royal treasury was dangerously drained and promised into the future. In 1492 the monarchs would have to pay a massive sum to the Muslims for relinquishing Granada. The biography of Columbus attributed to his son Ferdinand reported that Isabel offered to pawn her jewels to pay for the voyage. If she actually made such an offer, it would not have been the first time she had raised money in that way. In 1491 some of her jewels had been in pawn for two years. She still had others available, but their use was unnecessary. Luis de Santángel offered to find the money, not by advancing his own but by shifting royal funds among various governmental bodies. The money in the first instance came from the treasury of the Santa Hermandad, the national organization of rural militias in Castile. Talavera was a joint treasurer of the Hermandad, and, as its income passed into his control, he used it for the expenses of preparing Columbus's small fleet. Later the Hermandad was reimbursed from other governmental funds. Deficit financing and fiscal maneuvering were not invented in the twentieth century.

With finances secured, other details could be negotiated. The final agreements negotiated between the crown and Columbus, the *Capitulaciones de Santa Fe,* followed a standard form of agreement or contract in fifteenth-century Castile, with specific points arranged in separate paragraphs or chapters (*capítulos*). By their terms Columbus secured noble status, together with the offices of admiral, viceroy, and governor in all the islands and mainlands that he might claim for Castile in the Atlantic. These royal gifts would become effective only after the discoveries and the claims were made.

The total cost of the voyage was projected at two million *mara-vedís,* but it is impossible to reconstruct all parts of the financial arrangements. Columbus apparently contributed 500,000 *mara-vedís* to the venture, but it is not altogether clear where he might have obtained that sum. Recent research suggests that he borrowed from Italian merchants, including the Florentine Juanoto Berardi, a slave trader since at least 1486, and a man who remained closely linked to Columbus until Berardi's death in 1495. The Catholic Monarchs contributed 1,140,000, from the funds Santángel shifted from the Santa Hermandad. One million was to go toward the general expenses of the voyage, and 140,000 comprised Columbus's salary as captain-general (*capitán mayor*) of the fleet. The town of Palos was obliged to put up the rest of the funding, because a group of local mariners had broken royal law by illegally trading in African waters reserved to the Portuguese. With the agreements duly signed and the finances settled, Columbus was ready to begin preparations for the long-awaited voyage.

The monarchs ordered Palos to provide Columbus with the use of two caravels; they supplied the *Pinta* and the *Niña.* Columbus also chartered a larger ship (a *nao*) called the *Santa María.* All three vessels were small but typical of the merchant vessels of the time. The *Santa María* would have carried square sails on a foremast and a mainmast, with topsails for each one, and a triangular lateen sail on a mizzen mast at the rear of the ship. Given an estimate of its size at just over 100 *toneladas,* it was probably no more than 19.2 feet in maximum width or beam, no longer than 38.5 feet on the keel, and 57.7 feet on the lower of its two decks. The depth in the hold, measured from the lower deck down to the floor laid on top of the keel, would have been no more than 9.6 feet. These are all gross estimates, based on the general shape of merchant *naos* of the time, but they would have resulted in a ship measuring about 108 *toneladas.*[7] The caravels *Pinta* and *Niña* were somewhat smaller, at about 75 and under 60 *toneladas* respectively. We estimate the *Pinta's* dimensions at a maximum of 17.6 feet wide, 42.2 feet on the keel, 55.1 feet in length, and 7.6 feet in depth of the hold beneath its one deck. The *Niña's* measurements would have been similar, at no more than 15.9 feet wide, 38.5 feet on the keel, 49.8 feet long, and 6.8 feet deep. The *Pinta* was rigged like the *Santa María*; the *Niña* would begin the voyage rigged with two lateen sails. Once they were fully crewed, the *Santa María* carried 40 men, the *Pinta* 26, and the *Niña* 24, including officers and seamen of all ranks.

At first Columbus had trouble raising the crew for his venture, largely because the sailors were suspicious of such a speculative voyage and feared they might not find land and would be unable to return home. Finally, with the help of Martín Alonso Pinzón, a prominent local mariner, Columbus gathered a crew of around ninety men, including four from the local jail. The three ships sailed from the Palos before dawn on 3 August 1492. An important religious holiday for the region on 2 August was the feast of Nuestra Señora de los Angeles, the patroness of the monastery of La Rábida. There could be no question of missing the event, given the importance of La Rábida and its Franciscans to the region and to all on board the three ships. Tradition has it that on the same morning Columbus's small fleet left Palos, a group of ships carrying the last of Spain's Jews into exile sailed from the same port. The monarchs had set early August 1492 as the deadline for Spanish Jews who refused to covert to Christianity to leave the country. Similar expulsions had occurred in England in 1295 and in France in 1306. Thus 1492 marked the last medieval expulsion of Jews from western Europe and the end of the last Muslim possession of western European territory, even as it marked Columbus's voyage into the unknown.

Columbus chose the Canaries as the real starting point for his first Atlantic crossing, believing that Japan lay directly west of the Canaries, and knowing that the fall and winter winds usually blew from east to west in that latitude. He gambled on his assumption that the prevailing winds would carry him across the ocean to Japan at the latitude of the Canaries. On the voyage to the Canaries, the *Pinta* handled badly and twice suffered damage to her rudder. Columbus left the *Pinta* under its captain Martín Alonso Pinzón off the island of Gran Canaria while he took the other two ships to the island of Gomera to top off their provisions. After the *Pinta's* repairs were completed, she joined the others at Gomera. The *Niña* had not been handling well either, so she was re-rigged at Gomera from a two-masted lateen to a three-masted combination of square and lateen sails, like the other two ships. With last-minute preparations made, water barrels filled, and firewood and fresh meat loaded on, the fleet was ready to set sail. A little over a month after having left Palos, the fleet began its voyage into the unknown on 6 September 1492, from the island of Gomera.

After losing sight of Hierro, the last island in the Canaries, on 9 September, they sailed along the northern edge of the belt of northeast trade winds. Columbus and the ships' pilots navigated by dead reckoning, using direction, time, and speed to plot their course and position. That meant determining direction by compass, time by a

Figure XV. Departure of Columbus from the port of Palos. Painting by Joaquín Sorolla y Bastida, 1910–1911. *Courtesy of the Mariner's Museum, Newport News, Virginia.*

sand clock marking the half hours, and speed by eye and feel. Columbus kept a diary of each day's events, carefully marking down his estimates of the distance traveled. In the prologue of the diary he kept, he also promised to keep a maritime chart indicating the lands the expedition encountered.

Bartolomé de las Casas, whose summarized diary of the first voyage is the only version that remains, produced a document flawed in many ways. It should be used cautiously by modern historians.[8] One example concerns a "false log" of the voyage that Columbus supposedly manufactured to fool his crew. According to Las Casas, Columbus made two sets of calculations for the distance traveled, to deceive the crew into thinking that they had sailed less far than his real calculations indicated. This notion of a "false log" has passed into the mythology of Columbus and is mentioned in virtually every discussion of the 1492 voyage. Nonetheless, the theory makes little sense. Columbus would have had to fool not only the sailors on his own ship, but also the captains, masters, and pilots on the other two ships, all of whom were presumably experienced navigators. On several occasions during the voyage, the pilots of all three vessels compared their calculations, and there is no hint that Columbus had to persuade them to accept his figures. A much more likely explanation for the dual calculations is simply that Las Casas misunderstood the diary. Instead of making a false log for the crew, Columbus first calculated the distance traveled by a method he had learned as a young mariner; then he calculated the equivalent in terms the crew understood. Much the same thing happens when modern travelers deal with miles and kilometers. In figuring distance or speed, travelers tend to start with the system they knew better, and then calculate the equivalent in the other system if need be. The mysterious and slightly sinister "false log" that Las Casas postulated may be no more mysterious than that, and not sinister at all.[9] We cannot know for sure until and unless the original version of the diary is found.

The voyage was rather short—just 33 days from the Canaries to the Caribbean—and mainly uneventful. The little fleet encountered good weather, mainly calm seas, and remarkably little dissension. From 16 September on, Columbus said, they encountered fair weather akin to April in Seville, an evocative phrase for anyone who has ever experienced the warm, soft days of spring in Andalusia. Also in mid-September they first encountered the weeds of the Sargasso Sea, which they had been warned not to fear by an old mariner back in Palos. Instead of fear, they felt hope, believing the Sargasso weeds to be plants torn from nearby land. During such a quiet and uneventful voyage, there was time to watch the sea and sky carefully for signs and portents. Officers and crew alike closely noted each sighting of birds, identifying them and indicating whether they were sea birds or land birds, for they believed that land birds would not be far from land. They were also aware that the Portuguese had followed flights of birds to locate previously unknown islands. Journal entries from 16 September onward record a steady stream of signs that the men on board interpreted as indicating nearby land, including—in addition to the birds—whales, dolphins, and crabs on the surface of the Sargasso weed. Nevertheless, Columbus believed the mainland to lie due west and was unwilling to lose time beating around looking for islands.

Life on board ship cannot have been very pleasant by modern standards.[10] On the *Santa María,* 40 men lived and worked together in a very cramped space, and conditions were similar on the two caravels. Only the top officers would have had enclosed quarters for sleeping and stowing their belongings. The rest of the men would have simply staked out some corner as their own, trying to stay out of the way of lines and tackle for the working of the ship. Sanitary facilities barely existed. For bathing, a bucket of water could be hauled out of the sea, if anyone were so inclined. For toilet facilities, a seat suspended over the edge of the ship sufficed. Presumably, fastidious passengers might prefer the privacy of a bucket, but lifelong sailors probably did without such niceties. The abstracted diary of the voyage says nothing about living conditions on board, but there is no reason that Columbus would have mentioned them, even in his original diary.

For over two weeks, until about 22 of September, the winds were so regular and the seas so calm that the crew began to complain. They feared that those conditions meant there would never be favorable or sufficient winds to take them back to Spain. On the twenty-second, Martín Alonso Pinzón on the *Pinta* asked for Columbus's chart, which indicated certain islands. After studying the chart for several days, Pinzón was convinced that they were in the vicinity of the islands. He shared his conclusions with Columbus on the twenty-fifth and returned the chart to him by means of a line stretched between their two ships. Columbus also calculated their position on the chart, with the help of his pilot and other sailors on the *Santa María.*

On 25 September, Martín Alonso Pinzón called out from the poop of the *Pinta* that he saw land, to the great excitement of all three crews. In thanks and relief, the crews said the "Gloria in excelsis deo," probably adding it to the regular prayers that they said every day at nightfall. Several men climbed the masts and rigging and confirmed the sighting. Columbus believed the land to lie about 25 leagues off to the southwest, and the fleet changed course to approach it. The next day, with breezes sweet and soft, and with the sea as calm as a river, they had to admit disappointment. The men and their leaders had seen a mirage, and in their eagerness to find land they had persuaded themselves that it was real.

Resuming their westward course, the ships sailed for several more days, until, on 3 October, Columbus believed they had gone beyond the place where he had charted islands. Nonetheless he was determined to press on westward toward what he considered to be the mainland of Asia. He probably did this in large part to maintain his authority over the captains and their crews. He had told them to expect land due west of the Canaries. Allowing side excursions in search of islands would diminish the aura of certainty that he had been at pains to project.

On 6 October Martín Alonso Pinzón asked Columbus to change course to the southwest. On that same day, Columbus faced his first near mutiny when the men of the *Santa María* began demanding a return to Spain. In response to the complaints of his crew. Columbus decided to consult the other captains and ordered a cannon fired to signal the other ships to close up with his. When they had assembled, Columbus told the other captains about his crew's desires to return and asked them for their opinions. Their responses, as recalled by witnesses in legal cases years later, were wholly supportive of continued exploration.

On 7 October, the crew of the *Niña* believed they had seen land, but again the sighting proved illusory. When the ships came together that evening at sunset, no one had been able to verify a landfall. As the ships approached their sunset rendezvous, however, all present noted multitudes of birds flying from north to southwest. They interpreted this phenomenon in two ways, both of which reinforced the idea that land was near. Either the birds were flying home to sleep for the night, or they were migrating in anticipation of the approaching winter in the north. The latter interpretation may have been correct. Early October is the height of the autumn migration of birds from North America southward to the Caribbean and South America.

Impressed by the huge flocks, and mindful of Portuguese discoveries made by following birds, Columbus agreed to deviate from his westward course and sail west-southwest for two days. From the evening of the seventh, they followed that course, with calm seas and favorable winds. All along, they kept monitoring the kinds and numbers of birds they saw, and carefully watched where the birds were heading. On the evening of the ninth, they were still on the same course without sighting land. The wind shifted and they changed course toward the west once again. In the spare but evocative words of the abstracted diary, "*All night they heard birds pass.*"

On 10 October, serious grumbling swept the crew. The masters of all three ships, plus Martin Alonso Pinzón, who captained the *Pinta,* and his brother Vicente Yáñez Pinzón, who captained the *Niña,* now turned against Columbus, though they had supported him until a few days before. No doubt reflecting the rising anxiety of their crews, they expressed fear that the nearly continuous winds blowing from east to west might make it impossible to return home at that latitude. Columbus could only answer that God had given them the weather to take them this far and he would give them proper weather to get back home. That rather lame defense suggests that he did not fully understand the North Atlantic wind patterns, though he had unerringly chosen an ideal trajectory westward. Mutinous crewmen began to rattle their weapons, but Columbus urged them to reconsider and proposed a compromise. They would continue on their westward course for two more days (or three or four; accounts vary). If they still had not found land at the end of that period, they would turn back. The Pinzones and the other officers accepted the compromise easily, returning to their ships and persuading their crews to continue the voyage.

After their near mutiny of the day before, on 11 October the crew needed surprisingly little encouragement. All day they seized on everything they saw as a portent of an imminent landfall. They identified land birds. They eagerly scrutinized the flotsam in the ocean: a cane, a stick, a plank, another stick seemingly worked by iron, and still another covered with barnacles. At the evening rendezvous Columbus set the course again to the west. From all the signs, he was convinced they were approaching land. Two hours after midnight, on the twelfth, with the *Pinta* sailing ahead, the weather cleared. In the moonlight, one of the sailors on the *Pinta,* Juan Rodríguez Bermejo, saw a white sand beach and land beyond it. After his shout of "*Land! Land!*" the *Pinta's* crew raised a flag on its highest mast and fired a cannon. As Columbus later told the story, however, he had sighted land before the sailor on the *Pinta,* when he saw a faint light late in the evening of 11 October. Based on his recollections of the events of 11 October, he claimed for himself the reward promised to the first man to sight land. His conscience may have troubled him, however, for he later assigned the reward to Beatriz de Arana, rather than keep it for himself.

When the three ships drew together before dawn on 12 October, land was clearly visible, but wind blowing them toward the island made the officers wary of approaching more closely until daylight. Fearing unseen rocks and shallows, the three ships tacked back and forth offshore until the eagerly-awaited dawn. They had found land and proven that there were more islands in the ocean sea. They also believed they were on the verge of establishing direct contact with Asia, its rich spice markets and is houses roofed with gold. Instead, they were a few short hours from one of the most fateful human encounters in all of history, a meeting between peoples previously unknown to one another. Columbus and the Pinzones believed they were somewhere close to the legendary Cipango. Instead, they were off an island in the Bahamas and Japan was still half a world away.

On the morning of 12 October 1492, Europeans made their first verified contact with peoples in the Western Hemisphere since the time of the Vikings, five centuries before. As their ships approached the island, they could see naked people on the beach, watching their progress. Columbus assembled a landing party, which rowed to the beach in the *Santa María's* launch, with Columbus carrying the royal banner. The Pinzón brothers, as captains of the two caravels, carried the expedition's flags that Columbus had ordered for all three ships: they bore a green cross in the center, and on either side the letters F and Y, each surmounted by a crown, to signify King Fernando and Queen Isabel (sometimes spelled Ysabel in those days). When they reached the shore, Columbus spoke the standard proclamation for taking possession of lands for the crown, and named the island San Salvador, in honor of Jesus Christ, the Holy Savior of the Catholic faith. By these acts, Columbus fulfilled the conditions necessary for him to become Admiral of the Ocean Sea. He had found land and claimed it for his sponsors. What the local inhabitants thought of all this is not recorded. If they had been able to understand the language, they would probably have been somewhat puzzled by the proceedings. The island, which they called Guanahaní, was presumably already under the lordship of their own chieftains.

The location of the island where Columbus first landed has been vigorously debated over the past century, with most scholars agreeing that it was the Bahamian island currently named San Salvador, and formerly named Watling. In the 1980s, the controversy was revived by several amateurs and a few professional scholars who offered alternatives to the San Salvador thesis, many of them based on the sailing directions and descriptions of islands in Las Casas's abstract of Columbus's diary. The flawed abstract offers no conclusive proof of the landing site, however. Moreover, the hundreds of islands in the Bahamas and its neighboring chains that resemble descriptions in the diary make the matter an intellectual dead-end for most serious scholars. Without Columbus's original diary, the issue cannot even be addressed adequately, let alone resolved. The controversy will no doubt persist, but it has little importance, even if it is someday sorted out. The real significance of the voyage lies elsewhere, in the first encounter of Europeans and inhabitants of the Western Hemisphere since Viking times, and in the far-reaching consequences of that encounter. For these more general matters, rather than the specific details required to reconstruct Columbus's navigational course, Las Casas's abstract of the diary can be useful.

The landfall marked the last moment of the voyage that corresponded to Columbus's plan, although he had no way of knowing that. Until the landing, everything he had predicted and every hope he had held were coming to pass. The fleet had reached land in approximately the location predicted. Columbus believed they had landed on an island off the coast of the Asian mainland, having inadvertently bypassed Cipango. There was no reason at first for him or anyone else to doubt the underlying assumptions of the expedition.

Still, nothing they observed about the island matched their mental image of Asia as described by Marco Polo and Toscanelli. No great ships had appeared. They did not see populous and prosperous cities with houses and temples roofed with gold. Their first reaction was to continue the search. In the history of the expedition, and especially in Columbus's actions, we can trace several processes at work as exploration of the islands proceeded. Because the figure of Columbus dominates the documentary record, we know less about the other men on the voyage, but his observations, as summarized by Las Casas and bolstered by other evidence, can stand as a general description of their experiences. On one level, Columbus and his colleagues acted as geographers, naturalists, ethnographers, and anthropologists. They observed and remarked upon the natural beauty of the islands they found. They also tried to understand the people they encountered, to observe their society, and to find ways to communicate and trade with them.

On another level, Columbus and his colleagues pursued their entrepreneurial agenda, driven to find wealth one way or another. In search of wealth, Columbus simultaneously followed two avenues of approach, which he mentioned repeatedly in his diary. Until fairly late in his reconnoitering of the Caribbean on the first voyage, he believed he would soon come upon the rich Asian ports that he had set out to find. At the same time, he constantly looked for gold, natural products, and other commodities that could be traded profitably. As time passed and he failed to find golden-roofed temples, or anything else resembling Marco Polo's Asia, this latter approach came to occupy the center of his attention. Columbus's model for seeking out local commodities was the experience of Portuguese expansion in Africa. Like the Portuguese, he hoped to establish contact with centers of trade and set up "factories" or fortified trading posts. That approach had worked well for the Portuguese, given coastal West Africa's decentralized kingdoms and fairly simply trading networks. Columbus well knew from reading Marco Polo that the scale and complexity of trade in Asia was a quantum leap from the African situation. He had expected to find Asian trade in the islands he reached; instead he found a situation more akin to the African variety, but much less developed.

That discouraging realization did not come to him immediately, however. In sailing around the Caribbean in search of Asia, Columbus followed Portuguese precedents, contacting local inhabitants and their leaders, and trying to gain their confidence and learn the locations of their trading centers. Columbus had brought along trade goods that had been popular in Africa: glass beads, small bells, and so on. He also saw to it that the fleet carried samples of Asian spices, so that they could be compared with native plants in the lands they visited. His ultimate goal was to locate the great Asian trading centers that Marco Polo had made famous in Europe.

Eventually Columbus was forced to admit that large-scale commerce did not exist on the islands he had found. Although there was an extensive inter-island trade among local peoples, it was not large enough for European merchants to tap into profitably. Even worse, Columbus had to face the fact that the great commercial cities of Asia were not in the immediate vicinity. He had to revise his plans accordingly. Faced with the reality of the Caribbean islands, his thoughts would ultimately turn to colonization as a way to make the islands profitable. The Castilians and the Portuguese had created prosperous colonies in the Atlantic islands. Columbus had personal knowledge of how he might accomplish the same result. He had, after all, married into the family that governed the Portuguese colony of Porto Santo, and he had lived in the Madeiras and visited the Canaries. He knew that European settlement, and the introduction of commercial plants and livestock, could turn new-found islands into profitable enterprises. And profits were certainly needed. Columbus had sold his scheme to financial backers eager for a return on their investment. In many ways, they were the "venture capitalists" of the fifteenth century. The evolution in Columbus's model from Asian trade to African trade to island colonization would occur gradually over the course of three months, marking the partial triumph of experience over expectations. Yet as disappointed as he might be, his diary continued to portray the lands, peoples, and products he found in highly positive manner, if Las Casas's abstract can be trusted. Just as he had sold the notion that Asia could be reached easily by sailing west, he tried to sell the notion that the lands he had claimed for Spain were infinitely beautiful and bountiful. He had to persuade his backers that his venture would bear fruit and that they should continue and expand their support. Readers of the abstracted diary must keep this context in mind.

Just as the islands were nothing like Asia, the people Columbus met bore no relation to the Asians he had read about in Marco Polo. Their nakedness suggested to him people living in a state of nature, and his writings referred to their simple nature, their innocence, and their malleability. Even what he took to be their lack of religion was presented in a positive light: without the vices of a bad religion to overcome, European missionaries could easily convert the people to Christianity. Columbus's depiction of the islanders as noble savages became a motif that colored the European imagination from his time forward, and it still has seductive power in the modern world. Some of the most earnest detractors of Columbus in the late twentieth century accept without question the naive descriptions of the islanders in Columbus's diary. Only at the end of his first voyage did reality begin to intrude on his descriptions, and even then, the overall thrust of the language was optimistic.

Columbus's ideas evolved as he progressed through the Bahamas, to Cuba, and on to Española. In the first days on Guanahaní-San Salvador, he mentioned an exchange of goods, noting the friendliness of the local people and their desire to communicate with the newcomers and exchange goods with them. Columbus viewed these transactions as the start of a fruitful commerce, though his pleasure was tempered by the suspicion that the inhabitants were not the wealthy Asians he had sought. His disappointment seems obvious when he described them as *people poor in everything.* Their most striking characteristic was their nakedness. Next was their hair, described as straight and coarse as a horse's tail, and short, except for a long piece in the back which was left uncut. Columbus noted that they painted themselves in black, red, or white; some painted their whole bodies, others just portions, and some just their noses. Columbus was also struck by the skin color of the islanders. Assuming he was near India, he called them Indians, noting that they were not black like Africans, but rather the color of the Canary Islanders. He added, "*Nor should anything else be expected since this island is on an east-west line with the island of Hierro in the Canaries.*"[11] Like many of his contemporaries, Columbus seems to have believed that skin color varied according to distance from the equator; the close to the equator, the darker the skin tone, and the farther north toward the pole, the lighter the skin tone. After describing the people, Columbus described the boats they made of hollowed logs and tree trunks.

These anthropological observations quickly gave way to the search for Asia and its fabled wealth. Columbus noted that some of the islanders had pierced noses in which they wore small pieces of gold. It was not much, but it might be a clue leading toward the golden roofs of Cipango. He asked the Indians about the source of their gold, and interpreted their response to mean that gold lay toward the south. Before leaving Guanahaní-San Salvador, Columbus he found a reef-enclosed harbor which he grandly claimed could hold "*as many ships are there are in the whole of Christendom.*"[12] He continued to comment on harbors and good defensive sites throughout the voyage, perhaps to emphasize the superiority of the lands he had claimed to the inhospitable coastline of Africa explored by Portugal. The Portuguese had found very few good harbors on the African coast, and they —like Columbus—were well aware that harbors and fortresses were the keys to successfully establishing trade in remote outposts.

Columbus intended to take back to Spain samples of everything he found that could be traded or otherwise turned to profit. Unfortunately, that included people. The men he encountered on Guanahaní-San Salvador were not very warlike, he noted. They had no metal weapons and were so ignorant of swords that they grabbed them by the blade and cut themselves. Fifty Europeans could dominate the island, Columbus asserted, and although not apt warriors, the islanders would nonetheless make good servants. He expressed his intention to take islanders with him from Guanahaní to Spain, where they would be converted to Christianity, learn the Castilian language, and return with subsequent expeditions as interpreters.

He clearly intended to treat his captives well, but he never seemed to doubt that he had the right to hold them against their will. This would gain him the dubious distinction of being the first European slaver in the Western Hemisphere.

Before sailing from Guanahaní-San Salvador on 14 October, Columbus asked his Indian informants about nearby islands. They named over a hundred for him and said the islands were in fact numberless. Soon the Europeans gained some idea of the local trading networks. As they progressed through the Bahamas, they overtook a lone Indian in a canoe making the same journey. Columbus brought him aboard the *Santa María* and learned a bit more from him about the inter-island trade. Astonishingly, he was carrying a small basket with Castilian trade goods: a string of small glass beads and some small Castilian coins, which had obviously been inserted into the local trading network as soon as Columbus's men had bartered them. Local inhabitants were not only spreading European goods, but also the knowledge of an alien presence in their islands and a new source of trade goods. The man in the canoe had not met the Europeans before, but only their goods, and yet he was able to communicate with them when he came on board the *Santa María*. In the four days since Columbus's landing on 12 October, communication and trade had been established between the inhabitants of the old and the new worlds, but the fruitful encounter was still very different from what Columbus had hoped.

Nevertheless, he was impressed with what the Indians had told him about the size and wealth of Cuba, and he assumed it had to be Cipango. Columbus's descriptions of Cuba began on 28 October with phrasing so similar to earlier diary entries that it was a cliché: *"that island is the most beautiful that eyes have ever seen: full of good harbors and deep rivers. . . ."* His guides from Guanahaní-San Salvador told him there were gold mines and pearl beds on the island. In his ignorance and enthusiasm, Columbus also believed the natives were telling him that ships from the Great Khan visited Cuba and that a powerful local king maintained his seat nearby. He therefore sailed northwest along the Cuban coast in search of the river that would lead to the king's court. In planning his approach to the king, Columbus followed precedent from the Portuguese in Africa. He would send emissaries with presents for the king and a copy of a letter from the Spanish monarchs. To lead the expedition he selected a sailor who had participated in the same sort of mission in Africa.[13] The embassy carried strings of beads to exchange for food during the six days allotted for the journey. They also carried samples of spices to compare with what they might find, and Columbus instructed them carefully on what to say to the king once they arrived. On the night of 5 November, the embassy returned from the interior. They had found a village of around fifty houses but no sign of a large city anywhere nearby, or any king. Nonetheless, when the villagers were shown samples of pepper and cinnamon, they had replied that large amounts could be found to the southeast. With a careening of the vessels completed, Columbus planned to sail off to the southeast toward what he envisioned as the center of the Asian trade.

The entry in Columbus's diary for 12 November reflected a boundless optimism, regardless of the somewhat disappointing results of the expedition inland. In words addressed to Fernando and Isabel, Columbus first expressed his attitudes and beliefs regarding missionary activity. Las Casas quoted Columbus as saying,

> These people have no religious beliefs, nor are they idolaters. They are very gentle and do not know what evil is; nor do they kill others, nor steal; and they are without weapons and so timid that a hundred of them flee from one of our men even if our men are teasing them. And they are credulous and aware that there is a God in heaven and convinced that we come from the heavens; and they say very quickly any prayer that we tell them to say, and they make the sign of the cross,+. So that Your Highnesses ought to resolve to make them Christians: for I believe that if you begin, in a short time you will end up having converted to our Holy Faith a multitude of peoples and acquiring large dominions and great riches and all of their peoples for Spain.

Once again, Columbus's will to succeed led him to color reality in the rosiest possible hues, failing to see that the peoples he had met were human beings, presumably with as much variety in their behavior as any other group of human beings.

He went on to offer wholly exaggerated accounts of the financial opportunities in the islands. He assured Fernando and Isabel that gold was to be found in "*a very great quantity,*" and precious stones, and pearls and infinite spiceries, despite the fact that he had seen only small amounts of personal jewelry worn by the islanders, no precious stones, no pearls, and no spices. He also announced that he had found mastic—a case of mistaken identity, as it turned out. Cotton he had certainly seen, and throughout the islands. In his optimistic boosterism, he asserted that profits could be made from cotton without even having to transport it to Spain. It could be sold in "*the big cities belonging to the Grand Khan, which doubtless will be discovered. . . .*" More was at stake than mere profits. Columbus had to justify the support the sovereigns had given him. He had to find the riches of Asia and the multitudes of potential Christian converts, because he had promised to find them. When asked about gold and Great Khans, the local inhabitants almost always had responded in terms the Europeans took as indicating they lay south or southeast. Columbus and his men understood that southeast of Cuba lay rich islands, and the richest was named Baneque. On the evening of 21 November, Martín Alonson Pinzón took the caravel *Pinta* and headed east toward Baneque, without Columbus's permission. Thereafter Martín Alonso and his crew were on their own, and Columbus had no indication of when, or if, they would ever return.

Meanwhile, Columbus had decisions to make. On 25 November a new tone appeared in the diary, with the first entry admitting that European enterprise, and not trade alone, would be necessary to produce wealth from the islands Columbus had found. In eastern Cuba he came upon a grove of magnificent pines, tall and straight. Columbus deemed them suitable to provide masts and planking for the ships of Spain, and noted that they were located where a water-powered sawmill could easily be constructed. Slowly but inevitably, Columbus's approach to the islands was shifting from the trading post model of African exploration to the settlement and colonization model of the Atlantic islands.

Although his own attitudes were changing, and although he was distressed by Pinzón's departure, he still described everything he saw in glowing terms. In the words of Las Casas's summary, *"He kept telling the men who were in his company that, in order to report to the sovereigns the things they were seeing, a thousand tongues would not suffice to tell it or his hand to write it; for it seemed to him that it was enchanted."* Columbus reinforced the imagery of an enchanted land with the assertion that no one had been sick or even had a headache on all three ships, except for one old man who had long suffered with kidney stone.

But this demi-paradise still had to yield a profit. The region should be settled extensively, Columbus advised, because of the variety of products available to be traded in Europe. Once settlements and trade had been established, Spain could do a profitable business in the islands. To leave no doubt that piety and profit went hand in hand, Columbus also recommended that only Catholic Christians be allowed to trade with or settle in the Indies, writing that *"the beginning and the end of the enterprise was the increase and glory of the Christian religion."* Once again, Columbus discussed the religious future of those he had dubbed Indians, emphasizing that they had no false religion, and predicting their quick and easy conversion to Christianity, once missionaries knew the local language.

By the fifth of December, the expedition had reached the eastern tip of Cuba. Sailing east the next day they reached a large island that Columbus called La Española. On Española, Columbus eagerly catalogued the items that might make for profitable commerce. Nonetheless, for the short term he eagerly sought gold, hoping to find enough before his return voyage to please his royal sponsors. Writing on 16 December, he reported that the people of Española were naked like the others and the most handsome people yet encountered. They were also *very white, for if they went about clothed and protected themselves from the sun and wind they would be almost as white as people in Spain.* Just as he described Española as the most fertile and the most beautiful of the islands he had visited, adding hyperbole to hyperbole, Columbus described its inhabitants as *plump and brave and not weak like the others.*

At this point in his explorations, Columbus abandoned his insistence on finding the trade of the Grand Khan, and also abandoned the Portuguese model of the factory system. Instead, on 16 December he outlined what he considered a suitable colonial policy for the islands he had discovered, invoking the policies that had succeeded in the Atlantic islands. Yet he had had not abandoned his hopes for a gold trade, trusting that God would lead him to its source.

As Christmas approached, the men of the *Santa María* and the *Niña* explored the northwest coast of Española. In his descriptions of the islanders and their leaders, Columbus anticipated all the noble savage mythology of the New World that would color European attitudes well beyond the eighteenth century. On 18 December, he described the arrival of a young king who ruled about five leagues away from the fleet's anchorage. The Spanish monarchs, he said, would have approved of these people and their bearing, *even though everyone went about naked.* The king came aboard ship and met Columbus in the sterncastle, where he was eating. Columbus offered the king food, and then exchanged gifts with him. Columbus then showed the king a Castilian coin with the likenesses of Fernando and Isabel. Always eager to embellish, Columbus put a speech into the mouth of the young king praising the Spanish sovereigns. Unfortunately, he spoiled the effect in the next sentence by confessing that he had actually understood very little of what the king said.

On Christmas eve, the *Santa María* went aground on a bank off the north coast of the island. Although this was the moment of greatest drama in the entire trip, Columbus reported it laconically in the diary, arguably because it represented an unadorned loss for the expedition, and one that could have been prevented by greater vigilance on his part. Several routine precautions in caring for the ship had been relaxed, perhaps because of the holiday, setting the stage for the tragedy. Efforts to save the ship proved too late: the tide was running out, and as the ship stood higher and higher out of the water, her planking opened up. In what must have been a bitter moment, Columbus then abandoned his flagship and took his crew to the *Niña*. There was nothing to be done but salvage what they could from the wreck, but they lacked the manpower to do it on their own. In response to Columbus's plea, King Guacanagarí, a local ruler whose town was a league and a half away, immediately sent his people in large canoes to help in the unloading and donated some houses to the Europeans for the storage of their goods and equipment. Columbus's attitude toward the local people displayed a curious but understandable ambivalence. He placed armed guards around the clock to guard the storage houses, but in his words to the Catholic Monarchs, he called the Indians a loving people, docile, and without greed.

There was no choice but to leave a portion of the fleet's crew on Española, because they could not all travel home on the *Niña*. On the day after Christmas, preparations began to provide for the men left behind. Guacanagarí, their impromptu host, arrived at dawn. He had his people help unload the stricken *Santa María* and gave the Europeans permission to erect a fort on shore.

As preparations proceeded, Columbus's diary entries combined practicality with religious speculations. In the unquestionably disturbing aftermath of the loss of his flagship, many of Columbus's deepest emotional and intellectual traits came to the fore. He saw the will of God behind his predicament and interpreted the wreck as a sign that he should further explore the area and found a settlement. Once a trade in gold had been developed, its profits could be used for the conquest of Jerusalem, the time-honored goal of Christian crusaders and millenarians alike.

Columbus was leaving 39 men behind an Española, in the improvised settlement he called "La Navidad"—Christmas. The men seemed to be relatively secure. They had their fortress, built with timbers from the wreck. They believed they had the friendship and support of King Guacanagarí. Nonetheless, to reinforce earlier lessons, Columbus had the departing crew and the remaining settlers stage a mock battle, designed to impress the locals with the power of European weapons and fighting skills. However much he might praise the docile nature of the Indians in his reports to his sovereigns, apparently he was fully aware of their warlike side and took pains to protect his men.

On 4 January, Columbus left shore with a favorable wind and worked the *Niña* eastward along the north coast of Española. On 6 January, a lookout saw the *Pinta* sailing toward them. The caravels approached one another and anchored together for the night. Martín Alonso Pinzón came aboard the *Niña* and offered a series of excuses for having left the company, all of them unpersuasive. Though Columbus seethed inside, the diary tells us, he nonetheless hid his anger so as not to endanger the return voyage. Pinzón told Columbus that the *Pinta* had first sailed to the island the natives called Baneque (now called Great Inagua), but they had failed to find gold there. They had also gone to Española and had been conducting a lively gold trade before they rejoined the *Niña*.

A few days later, Columbus took advantage of the wind and decided to set a course straight for Spain, northeast by east. The return voyage presented a sharp contrast to everything the expedition had experienced thus far. The idyllic weather, the favorable winds, the exciting discoveries, and the good health that had sustained the spirits of Columbus and his crews until then was replaced by increasing difficulties. They could not find a favorable wind for days, and Columbus at first persisted on a direct course toward Spain, although he was bucking the northeast tradewinds in so doing. Only when he finally took the ships farther north did they find the winds to take them eastward without resistance. Columbus probably knew the easterly wind patterns before he left Spain, but he found the westerlies in the Atlantic only by trial and error.

During the storm-plagued return, the *Pinta* and the *Niña* became separated. Columbus and the crew of the *Niña* had to anchor in the Azores and then in Lisbon because of violent storms. They reached Palos only on the fifteenth of March. Later that same day, Martín Alonso Pinzón brought the *Pinta* into Palos as well, after first landing at Bayona in Galicia on the northwest coast. The first voyage was over, having brought the eastern and western hemispheres inextricably together, and having raised Columbus to the height of his career.

NOTES

1. He would have been known in the Genoese dialect as Cristoforo Colombo, but his name is almost always rendered into whatever language an author is using. In English he is Christopher Columbus, in Spanish Cristóbal Colón, in Portuguese Christovão Colom, in French Christophe Colomb, and so on. His father Domenico Colombo and his wife had four

other children after Christopher: three boys—Bartolomeo, Giovanni-Pellegrino, and Giacomo—and a girl named Bianchineta. The two brothers who would join Christopher in Spain and the New World are usually known by the Spanish or English equivalents of their names: Bartolomé or Bartholomew for Bartolomeo, and Diego or James for Giacomo.

For an up-to-date biography of Columbus, see William D. Phillips, Jr., and Carla Rahn Phillips, *The Worlds of Christopher Columbus.* (Cambridge: Cambridge University Press, 1992). For a summary of his early years, see William D. Phillips, Jr., *Before 1492: Christopher Columbus's Formative Years* (Washington, D.C.: American Historical Association, 1992).

2. Cristóbal Colón, *Textos y documentos completos,* ed. Consuelo Varela (Madrid: Alianza Universidad, 1982), p. 252.

3. Oliver Dunn and James E. Kelley, Jr., eds. *The Diario of Christopher Columbus's First Voyage to America 1492–1493, Abstracted by Bartolomé de las Casas* (Norman, OK: University of Oklahoma Press, 1989), pp. 252–53.

4. Ferdinand Columbus, *Life of the Admiral Christopher Columbus by his Son Ferdinand,* trans. by Benjamin Keen (New Brunswick, N.J.: Rutgers University Press, 1959), p. 11.

5. Colón, *Textos y documentos,* ed. Varela, pp. xxxii–xl.

6. Juan Manzano Manzano, *Cristóbal Colón: Siete años decisivos de su vida, 1485–1492,* 2d ed. (Madrid: Ediciones de Cultura Hispánica, 1989), p. 366.

7. Scholars' estimates differ widely, but the ones generally accepted are much larger than this. The distinguished Spanish naval historian José María Martínez-Hidalgo Terán used his own method to estimate the size of Columbus's ships, rather than the official Spanish formula for calculting tonnage from a ship's dimensions. *Columbus's Ships,* ed. Howard I. Chapelle (Barre, Mass: Barre Publishing Co., 1966), pp. 40–42, 96–100. However, applying the official tonnage formula to Martínez-Hidalgo's figures gives an estimated size of 250.4 *toneladas* for the *Santa María,* which we consider unacceptable. For the official tonnage formula, see *Recopilación de leyes de Indias,* libro 9, título 28, ley 25, 3 pp. 363–69. See also, Carla Rahn Phillips, "Sizes and configurations of Spanish Ships in the Age of Discovery," *Proceedings of the First San Salvador Conference, Columbus and His World, Held October30–November 3, 1986* (Ft. Lauderdale: CCFL Bahamian Field Station, 1987), pp. 69–98.

8. David Henige, *In Search of Columbus. The Sources for the First Voyage* (Tucson: The University of Arizona Press, 1991)

9. Dunn and Kelley, *Diario,* p. 29, suggest this eminently logical possibility. See also the discussion by James E. Kelley, Jr., "In the Wake of Columbus on a Portolan Chart," *Terra Incognitae,* 15 (1983):77–111, particularly pp. 91–92 and appendixes B and C.

10. See Carla Rahn Phillips, *Six Galleons for the King of Spain: Imperial Defense in the Early Seventeenth Century* (Baltimore: Johns Hopkins University Press, 1986), pp. 152–80.

11. *Diario,* entry for October 13. His latitudes were incorrect. Hierro lies at about 28 degrees north, whereas the central Bahamas lie at about 25 degrees north.

12. *Diario,* entry for 14 October.

13. *Diario,* entry for 30 October.

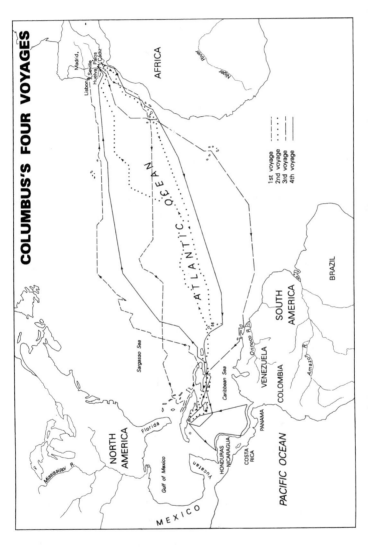

Figure XVI. The four voyages of Christopher Columbus across the Atlantic Ocean. Columbus's approximate routes are marked in both directions for the first, second, and fourth voyages. Only his outbound route is marked for the third voyage, because he returned to Spain under arrest, rather than in command of the voyage. *Map prepared by the Cartography Laboratory, Department of Geography, University of Minnesota.*

12
THE LATER VOYAGES
OF COLUMBUS
William D. Phillips, Jr. and
Carla Rahn Phillips

When Columbus returned to Spain in the spring of 1493, he believed he had accomplished his dream of reaching Asia by sailing westward from Europe. Columbus's efforts at manipulating opinion in Spain about his triumph began even before he reached Barcelona, with a letter to Luis de Santángel. A version of that letter, altered by royal officials, formed the basis for numerous printed editions that circulated throughout Europe. Even if Columbus was not its sole author, the letter still sketches the general outlines of his first glimpse of lands in the western ocean, and continues the optimistic tone of the diary of the voyage. Columbus presented the islands as a combination of a terrestrial paradise and a secular wonderland of untapped wealth. All of the islands, the letter said, were inhabited by peaceful and gentle people, who were as naked as the day they were born and had no skill with weapons. Willing to trade anything they had for European trifles, they could easily be put to work and converted to Christianity. Presumably, they would accept their new masters peaceably and thus be protected against enslavement, according to European law. But there were other native tribes, known as fierce fighters and cannibals, who would have to be conquered and could then be enslaved for profit. Presumably commenting on European legends about part-human monsters who inhabited far-away places, Columbus's letter confided that he had encountered no monstrous races across the ocean, but had heard stories about them.

Columbus exaggerated the economic potential of the lands he had claimed for Spain, knowing that his reputation and his future success would depend on their profitability. The islands were *"fertile to a limitless degree,"* he announced, blessed with harbors *"beyond comparison with others with I know in Christendom.*" Cuba was larger than England and Scotland and had eastern mountains higher than those in the Canaries. Neither statement was true, of course. Española, whose coastline he described as longer than that of the Iberian Peninsula (another exaggeration), was described as well-endowed with woods and arable fields. The human population was numberless, the land afforded vast amounts of spices, and the interior possessed *"great mines of gold and other metals."* On this marvelous island, Columbus announced that he had founded a large town, La Navidad, *"in the most convenient place for the gold mines and for trade with the mainland . . . belonging to the Great Khan, where there will be great trade and profit."* He said nothing of the shipwreck that had forced him to establish the colony, nor about the low-lying position of the site that made it unsuitable for long-term settlement. The letter concluded with a litany of profitable commodities available in the islands.

The letter to Santángel is obviously a tissue of exaggerations, misconceptions, and outright lies. Columbus had found no gold mines. He was mistaken when he identified mastic and aloe, rhubarb and cinnamon. The only local items that had real commercial potential were cotton and the Indians themselves, and fifteenth-century Europe had little demand for cotton and slaves. The summary of the on-board diary suggests that Columbus had given up on finding the Great Khan and rich Asian commerce in the immediate vicinity of the islands, yet the letter to Santángel reported that La Navidad was perfectly placed to benefit from that commerce.

Obviously, Columbus had inflated the evidence to support his main contention—that he had found new lands of boundless wealth and numerous peoples apt for Christian conversion. He emphasized and exaggerated positive features of the lands and the inhabitants, minimized or omitted negative features, and exuded energy and optimism. Whether or not he really believed what he wrote, he proved once again that he was one of the greatest salesmen of his time. Columbus repeatedly proved that he could inspire a wide range of people to want what he had to sell. But in selling his vision of the Indies, he promised too much and implied that success would come quickly. His glorious descriptions of the islands, which he may sincerely have believed to be near the terrestrial paradise, embellished reality in powerfully evocative terms. He created an image of the Americas before contact with Europeans that still glows five hundred years later. Like Columbus's audience, sophisticated humanity continues to long for a terrestrial paradise, unspoiled and endlessly bountiful. Ironically, many modern readers still believe the idyllic verbal portrait Columbus sketched, though his contemporaries soon realized that the portrait needed revision. Columbus's arcadian imagery would betray him when it became apparent that treasures were not to be gained for the asking and that extracting profits across the ocean would be extraordinarily difficult.

When reality intervened, Columbus needed the practical skills of a manager and administrator; not only did he lack those skills, but he seemed to lack the temperament to develop them. For the rest of his life, Columbus would find himself torn by the multiple responsibilities thrust upon him by the needs for colonization and administration of Spanish settlements in the Caribbean. Columbus was always more interested in continued exploration than in the more prosaic satisfactions of careful administration, and the new tasks constituted a challenge that he was unwilling or unable to meet. Although at first his inadequacies were masked by the competence of royal bureaucrats working with him, they became increasingly apparent as time passed. Columbus's enterprise of the Indies, so long in the planning, quickly outgrew his abilities. Over his protests, the Spanish monarchs would eventually remove him from control, in part because he shamelessly oversold what he had discovered.

But that was in the future. In 1493 Columbus and his seven Taino companions were the toast of the continent. Even before he made his way to the royal court, versions of his letter were coming off printing presses all over Europe, spreading his fame and aiding the Spanish effort to secure papal recognition for Castilian control of the islands in the western ocean. Just as Columbus crafted his report to his own advantage, the monarchs and their advisers tailored it to suit their interests. Both a papal bull of 1481 and diplomatic agreements of 1479–80 recognized Portuguese interests in the Atlantic south of the Canaries and west of Africa. Similarly, by treaty and papal bull, Spain had sovereignty over the islands of "the Canaries already discovered and yet to be discovered." Several small but significant fictions form part of the Santángel letter as we know it, apparently designed to show that the islands Columbus had discovered were near the Canaries and in fact part of the same chain. If these alterations aided the Spanish campaign at the papal court, all to the good. If they helped to disguise the true locations and sailing directions from the Portuguese, even better.

The altered Santángel letter was part of the shrewd diplomacy of the Spanish monarchs, designed to ensure that the lands Columbus had claimed for them would stay in their possession. Fernando and

Isabel turned to the pope to support their claims to the lands discovered by Colu' ibus. Luckily for Spain's interests, the pope at the time was Alexander VI, a member of the Borja (spelled Borgia in Italy) family of Valencia in the Crown of Aragon. Because Spain was too valuable an ally of the papacy to alienate, Alexander VI issued four bulls in 1493 advancing Castilian claims in the Atlantic. João II of Portugal, whose kingdom's efforts at overseas exploration were focused on India, protested. Well aware of where his interests lay, the pope would not rescind his support for Spain, so João approached Fernando and Isabel directly. After due deliberation, Portugal and Castile agreed to the Treaty of Tordesillas, signed in 1494. This crucial document drew a dividing line at 370 leagues west of the Azores and the Cape Verdes. Thus the Portuguese gained ratification of their African claims and the African route to India (plus Brazil, as it would turn out). Castile gained an undiluted claim to what would become is empire in the Western Hemisphere.

When Columbus received a royal invitation in spring of 1493 to attend Fernando and Isabel at court, he headed across Spain for Barcelona, accompanied by Taino Indians and green parrots from the exotic lands he had discovered. The trip was a public relations bonanza. People crowded into the towns he passed, attracted by the novelty of his accomplishments. Nothing could have spread the news more effectively about the Indies and their reported riches. Together with the printing of his report, Columbus's stately progress from one corner of Spain to the other created a tidal wave of excitement about the lands and peoples across the ocean.

Columbus must have been very satisfied with the reception he received on his overland journey, and he was surely pleased with the response from Fernando and Isabel. Even before he reached court, their letter of welcome indicated that they were disposed to confirm the promises made to him in the agreements of Santa Fe. Columbus's arrival in Barcelona in mid-April was tumultuous. Through thronged streets he proceeded to the royal court, where Fernando and Isabel had arranged to receive him in the impressive Gothic throne room of the counts of Barcelona. There he told them about his voyage and introduced the seven Indians he had brought with him. A solemn mass of thanksgiving concluded the welcoming ceremony.

In the weeks following that initial interview, public processions and private banquets in Barcelona continued to honor Columbus. The Indians who accompanied him were all baptized, with the king and his heir Prince Juan acting as godfathers. As an extraordinary sign of royal favor, beyond what was contained in written agreements, the monarchs allowed Columbus to place the lion of León and the castle of Castile—part of the royal insignia—on his own coat of arms. His brothers benefited as well. Bartolomeo (Bartolomé) and Giacomo (Diego), both became members of the hereditary nobility of Castile, with the right to use the term "Don" before their names.

In Barcelona Columbus reached the pinnacle of his fame, if not of his fortune. Yet, ever since losing his flagship at Christmas time and being forced to leave 39 men on Española, Columbus had been anxious to embark on a second voyage, to relieve those he had left, to settle Española on a more secure basis, and to continue his explorations. The monarchs were in full agreement with the need for a second voyage. While Columbus was still in Barcelona, they appointed a team in Seville to make the preparations. Fernando and Isabel were vitally concerned for the welfare and conversion of their new subjects across the ocean. On 29 May 1493, they issued a set of instructions for the operation of the new settlement in the Indies that began with a statement urging good treatment of the Indians and their religious education and conversion to Christianity.

The royal instructions called on Columbus to secure the best caravels and crews available in Andalusia for the voyage, and continued with an outline of how they expected the enterprise to be run— as a royal monopoly. All goods coming or going across the ocean were to be registered in a customs house in Cádiz. Everyone going to the Indies had to swear homage to Fernando and Isabel. All private trade was forbidden. The only trade permitted would be royal trade orchestrated by Columbus. The settlers were to be salaried employees who would be given their wages at regular musters. Fernando and Isabel seemed determined to keep a very tight rein on their colonial enterprise, obviously attempting to create a modified version of the Portuguese model of overseas trade. News of Columbus's first voyage had spread so quickly and made the Indies seem so alluring that he had no difficulty in finding about 1,200 men to go on the second voyage. The settlers included artisans and farmers, in addition to soldiers and gentlemen volunteers. They carried with them plants and animals for establishing agriculture and husbandry in the Indies on a European model: horses and cows, goats and sheep, wheat for planting, and seeds for garden vegetables and citrus and apple trees.

In Cádiz a large fleet of seventeen vessels was assembled, including three *naos: Colina, La Gallega,* and the flagship *Santa María,* nicknamed *Marigalante* (not, of course, the *Santa María* wrecked off Española on the first voyage). The owner and master of Columbus's flagship was Antonio de Torres, a man with connections at court who also enjoyed Columbus's confidence. There were also 10 *carabelas redondas* (caravels with both square and lateen sails), two lateen caravels, and other smaller vessels. On 25 September 1493, the expedition departed from Cádiz for the Canaries. The fleet reached Gran Canaria on October second and stayed in port for a day to repair a leaking ship. By the fifth they were anchored at Gomera, where they topped off their provisions before beginning the Atlantic crossing. A prolonged calm kept the fleet from leaving the Canaries until 13 October, however, a year and a day after the first expedition's landfall on Guanahaní. The ocean crossing, on a course west by south, was even quicker than on the first voyage, and on 3 November, they sighted two islands. The first Columbus named Dominica after the Latin word for the Lord God, and the second he called Santa María la Galante for his flagship.

No diary by Columbus remains for the second voyage, but we have a letter he wrote to the Spanish monarchs, as well as vivid accounts left by other members of the expedition. The first-hand, straightforward testimony of witnesses other than Columbus provide sharp contrasts to the admiral's own sentimental hyperbole. One comes down to us from Diego Alvarez Chanca, a physician from Seville who sailed with a royal commission as the fleet's doctor. Dr. Chanca wrote an extensive letter to the members of the municipal council of Seville recounting the events of the voyage. The other important account comes from Michele de Cuneo, a gentleman from Savona on the Ligurian coast near Genoa. Both letters were valuable correctives to the admiral's overblown descriptions. Unlike Columbus, neither writer had any reason to embellish his descriptions. They were charmed by the scenery, but their accounts of the people of the islands and their customs frequently contradicted Columbus's glowing accounts.

Chanca's first description of a deserted village on the island named Santa María la Galante reported the discovery of human arm and leg bones in the houses, presumably the remains of a cannibal feast. Later, on Guadalupe, Dr. Chanca reported the seizure of a number of Caribs and their captives, who fled to the Europeans for deliverance from their captors. The women captives were especially grateful to be rescued and secretly told the Europeans which of the islanders were Caribs and which were not. After this incident, Chanca and the other commentators began drawing a distinction between the Caribs or cannibals, and the "Indians," who were not cannibals and feared the Caribs. From then on, some of the complexity

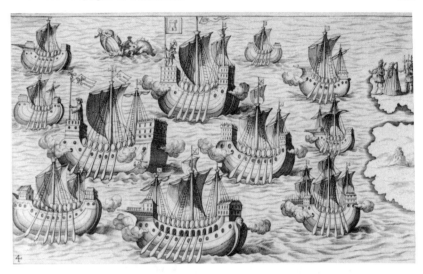

Figure XVII. Columbus's departure for the second voyage with a fleet of seventeen ships. The engraving is from Caspar Plautius, *Nova Typis transacta navigatio* (1621). The right hand portion, showing Fernando and Isabel in Spain and the three ships nearest to them, is often used erroneously to illustrate the departure of the first voyage. *Courtesy of the James Ford Bell Library, University of Minnesota.*

of New World societies began to color their narratives. Chanca was horrified by what he and his colleagues learned from the women they rescued. He described the Caribs as "*bestial*" and indicated their treatment of conquered peoples.

> These people raid the other islands and carry off the women whom they can take, especially the young and handsome. They keep them in service and have them as concubines, and they carry off so many that in fifty houses no males were found, and of the captives more than twenty were girls. These women also say that they are treated with a cruelty which appears to be incredible, for they eat the male children whom they have from them and only rear those whom they have from their own women. As for the men whom they are able to take, they bring such as are alive to their houses to cut up for meat, and those who are dead they eat at once. They say that the flesh of a man is so good that there is nothing like it in the world, and it certainly seems to be so for, from the bones which we found in their houses, they had gnawed everything that could be gnawed, so that nothing was left on them except what was too tough to be eaten. In one house there a neck of a man was found cooking in a pot.

They castrate the boys whom they capture and employ them as servants until they are fully grown, and when they wish to make a feast, they kill and eat them, for they say that the flesh of boys and of women is not good to eat. Of these boys, three came fleeing to us, and all three had been castrated.[1]

Chanca's matter-of-fact reporting of these horrors leaves little doubt of the authenticity.[2]

After leaving Guadalupe, the fleet sailed north, west of the Leeward Islands. On the 14 November, the expedition anchored on the island Columbus named Santa Cruz (now known as St. Croix), where an encounter with the local Caribs developed into a bitter fight. The Europeans saw a canoe approaching, with a party of three or four Carib men and two Carib women. They had two Indian captives aboard, and had recently castrated them, the Europeans later learned. The Europeans gave chase in a ship's boat, and the Caribs met them with arrow shots, wounding several men, including one who later died. The Europeans captured or killed everyone in the canoe.

That was the first recorded skirmish between Americans and Europeans since the Skraelings and the Vikings had clashed five centuries earlier. It foreshadowed the shape of things to come. In the aftermath of the engagement, Michele de Cuneo related a sordid tale of his own, emblematic of the age-old relations between conquering men and conquered women. Cuneo had been in the ship's boat and participated in the skirmish.

When I was in the boat I took a most beautiful cannibal woman, whom the lord Admiral made a gift of to me; and having her in my berth, with her being nude according to her customs, the desire to enjoy myself with her came over me; and wishing to put my desire to work, she resisting, she scratched me with her fingernails to such a degree that I would not have wished then that I had begun; but with that seen, to tell you the end, I grabbed a leather strap and gave her a good chastisement of lashes, so that she hurled such unheard of shouts that you could not believe. Finally, we reached an agreement in such a manner that I can tell you that in fact she seemed to have been taught in the school for whores.[3]

These two incidences in the same day interjected a harsh note of reality into the admiral's sanitized version of the encounter between two very different societies. The presence of outsiders had added a new element to local politics and provoked a mixed response, depending on whether the local peoples saw the outsiders as aggressors or potential allies. When fighting broke out, the outcome of the

Figure XVIII. Battle between cannibals and Spaniards in the Caribbean. Illustration from Caspar Plautius, *Nova typis transacta navigatio* (1621). *Courtesy of the James Ford Bell Library, University of Minnesota.*

struggle depended on which side had the most power. Women, treated as prizes by locals and outsiders alike, and lacking power, adapted to the changing situation as best they could. Although Columbus and the rest of the expedition did not know it yet, the same drama had already been played out on Española between local inhabitants and the men left behind on the first voyage.[4] The story of clashes between newcomers and earlier arrivals was as old as human history, and it would be repeated countless times more.

Leaving Santa Cruz on 15 November, the expedition headed north for the chain of islands that Columbus named in Spanish "The Eleven Thousand Virgins" to commemorate the legend of St. Ursula; they are still called the Virgin Islands. Then the fleet coasted along the south shore of the island that Columbus named San Juan Bautista and that came to be called Puerto Rico for its earliest port city. On 22 November the fleet reached the eastern end of Española. One night, as the ships coasted toward La Navidad, canoes approached and the Indians in them asked for the admiral. When he came on deck, they asked that his face be lighted so they could recognize him. Satisfied that he was the admiral they had been seeking, they said they were emissaries of Guacanagarí. Coming on board the flagship, they presented Columbus with a golden mask.

When asked about the 39 Europeans at La Navidad, Guacanagarí's emissaries said they were all fine, except for those who had died of sickness and others who had got into quarrels. It turned out that those categories included the whole garrison. One after another, they had all been killed by the Indians. Guancanagarí was terrified that Columbus would hold him responsible. He had not been responsible for the deaths, but he had been unable to prevent other chiefs and their men from killing the Europeans. For Columbus, the news marked the realization of his worst fears.

The fate of the garrison added even greater urgency to Columbus's mandate to found a suitable settlement. Taking the fleet back east laboriously along the northern coast, in the face of the steady trade winds, he reached a location near where he believed that gold would be found and broke ground in early January 1494 for a settlement he called La Isabela in honor of the queen. Columbus chose poorly in founding La Isabela on a flat plain a mile away from the nearest fresh water. Nevertheless, he began by laying out a grand classical grid of streets. Michele de Cuneo reported the more modest reality. *"Here we made two hundred houses, which are as small as hunting cabins back home and are roofed with grass."*[5]

The European settlers soon began to fall ill, for reasons that are not hard to discern. They had been on short rations during the voyage; they had been forced to labor in the construction of La Isabela; and they had experienced a change in climate. Moreover, they seem to have been suffering from malnutrition. Little of the imported seed brought along on the voyage had been planted, and it had not had time to mature. As a short-term expedient, Columbus ordered a flour mill built and then had the remaining seed grain ground for food. Dr. Chanca noted that the local fish were good, but they had to be eaten immediately or they spoiled.

In January, Columbus sent Alonso de Hojeda (sometimes spelled Ojeda) to reconnoiter the interior of the island. He returned by the end of the month with large nuggets of gold. Even though Columbus wanted to gather more gold to send back to Fernando and Isabel, he had no choice but to send the bulk of the fleet back to Spain immediately for additional supplies. Columbus's elaborate dreams for the new colony were already going badly wrong, and he might have felt the need to present his version of the situation to Fernando and Isabel as soon as possible. He entrusted his official account of the expedition's progress and problems to Antonio de Torres, along with a detailed set of instructions on what he should say in the royal audience.

The instructions reveal what Columbus thought he had accomplished and what he judged necessary to assure the success of his plans. As usual, he took great care in presenting the best case possible to his audience. Torres was to tell the monarchs first of all that ample evidence of spices could be seen from the shore on Española, and that Ojeda had found many rivers full of gold in incredible amounts during his scouting expedition—both obvious exaggerations. He did note that the colonists would have to sink mines to extract the gold, and urged the crown to recruit miners for Española. Indirectly at least, Columbus was warning the sovereigns that they should not expect quick returns on their investment.

Not surprisingly, given the annihilation of the original garrison, he also retreated from his earlier confident reports about the gentle nature of the Indians. Even though he still called them *very simple and without malice,* he reported ordering guards on day and night duty and the construction of a wall around the Spanish settlement. He next mentioned plans to build a fort to hold the gold until it could be loaded on ships for the voyage to Spain. As long as the Europeans remained watchful, Columbus assured Fernando and Isabel, the Indians would never attempt an assault, suggesting that a lack of care had led to the destruction of the garrison at La Navidad.

Columbus also reported that his men were falling ill, which had prevented his sending more gold, but he assured the sovereigns that their maladies were nothing to worry about. The change in air and water had sickened them, and when they received the Spanish food he was requesting, they would recover. The dependence on Spain for provisioning would be only temporary in this most beautiful of lands, he confidently predicted. When the wheat and vines he had brought began to flourish, *"There will be no need of Andalucía or of Sicily,"*[6] two proverbially rich agricultural regions. At the moment, however, he acknowledged that the situation was difficult. Poor casks had allowed most of the wine to leak away, and much of the salted meat turned out to be bad. Columbus asked the monarchs to send provisions to tide the expedition over. He also requested sheep and lambs, calves and young heifers, male and female asses, and mares. Except for horses for the troopers, either domestic animals had not formed part of the original supplies, or the animals had perished or been slaughtered for food.[7] It must have been clear by then that the islands lacked domestic animals altogether, both for food and for hauling power. Like so many other things, they would have to be imported by the colonists.

Columbus presented an elaborate scheme to increase the imports of livestock to the islands by establishing a regular trade. He suggested that the funds could be raised to pay for the imports by exporting human slaves, one of the few saleable items readily available in the islands. With the Torres fleet, Columbus had sent between 20 and 30 Indians, presumably from among the cannibals. They were sold as slaves as soon as they reached Seville. Columbus claimed that their enslavement could be justified not only by their defiance of the Europeans, but also because it was for their own good. Columbus instructed Torres to tell the monarchs,

> it is thought here that to take some of the men and women and send them home to Castile would not be anything but well, for they may one day be led to abandon that inhuman custom . . . of eating men, and there in Castile, learning the language, they will more readily receive baptism and secure the welfare of their souls.[8]

Columbus also thought the capture of cannibals would make a positive impression on the Indians who were their mortal enemies. The admiral's report seems to have aroused suspicions in the minds of his royal patrons. Sickness among the colonists and the lack of domestic animals in the new colony could not be blamed on Columbus, nor had he been responsible for provisioning, but the monarchs might have suspected a lack of care in his overall management of the expedition. It had just barely arrived and already the basic requirements of life were in dangerously short supply. Moreover, Columbus had clearly neglected his duties in the loading of the royal troopers and their equipment. Columbus never inspected them as they embarked. "*I did not see to it, because I was a little indisposed.*"[9] Only when he reached Española did he realize that the troopers had sold their good horses and purchased cheap nags for the voyage, pocketing the difference in price. They and many other armed men had done the same with their weapons and armor.

It was clear from his report to the monarchs that Columbus could not control the troopers. Even when they were sick or when they refused duty, they would not allow anyone else to use their horses. Columbus proposed buying their horses, bad as they were, so that the expedition as a whole would get at least some use out of them. That must have seemed an astonishingly weak suggestion to Fernando and Isabel, skilled commanders who had quelled rebellions in Castile and Catalonia and successfully waged a five-year war against the Portuguese and a 10-year war against the Muslims. Columbus seemed unable to manage even the resources given him, and he certainly seemed unable to command anyone outside a ship's crew. His version of events almost always blamed someone else when things went wrong.

Whatever doubts they may have had, the monarchs responded generously to Columbus's requests in the spring of 1494, with a few notable exceptions. They rejected out of hand his proposal to buy the troopers' horses. Instead, Columbus was told to remind the troopers of their duty and force them to relinquish their horses when ordered to do so. The monarchs deferred comment on Columbus's scheme to enslave New World cannibals to pay for European livestock. Isabel was very concerned about the possibly unjust enslavement of her new subjects, cannibals or not. She and Fernando told Columbus that he should combat the cannibals when the need arose, and try to convert them to Christianity, but in the islands, not by bringing them to Europe.

After the Torres mission departed for Spain, Columbus himself made an expedition into the interior of the island of Española in March of 1494 to seek gold, leaving his brother Diego in charge of the settlement at La Isabela. Shortly after his return from the interior, Columbus sailed from the settlement for Cuba, which he then believed was a peninsula of the Asian mainland. Once again he left Diego in charge of Isabela. His small exploratory fleet consisted of the *Niña* from the first voyage and two smaller vessels, the *San Juan* and the *Cardera,* all three suitable for coastal exploration. On 29 April, they landed at the eastern cape of Cuba, and Columbus performed the formal ceremony that claimed the land for Castile.

Through May and into June of 1494, the fleet explored the south coast of Cuba, without finding anything resembling Asia. Acting on information the Indians provided, Columbus took a detour to the south and came upon Jamaica. He returned to Cuba after finding hostile Indians and no gold on the island. By early June, when he was about 50 miles from the western end of Cuba, Columbus believed he had reached the Gulf of Siam or the Malay Peninsula. He fantasized about completing the world's first circumnavigation by sailing on farther west to work his way back to Spain. To confirm his perceptions, Columbus had his men attest and swear in writing that Cuba was the mainland of Asia and could in no circumstance be an island. They were further required to corroborate Columbus's erroneous reckoning that they had coasted Cuba for 335 leagues. This strange exercise could not change reality, but it could prolong Columbus's claims to have discovered the westward route to Asia.

Then, because supplies were dwindling fast, Columbus headed back to Española and the colony at Isabela. The return voyage along Cuba's south shore proved difficult, because the ships had to sail in shoal waters eastward against the prevailing winds. Columbus then sailed for Jamaica, where he explored the island's southern shore, and on 19 August, the little fleet left Jamaica for Española. Arriving at the end of the month off the southern coast, they had to ride out a hurricane. Columbus became ill shortly thereafter, possibly suffering from exhaustion, overexertion, and poor food. His officers took the fleet back to Isabela. When they arrived on 29 September, Columbus had to be carried ashore.

Good news awaited them. Several months earlier, Columbus's brother Bartolomé had arrived, whom he had not seen for several years. Bartolomé had been in France at the time of the first voyage, and when he finally reached Spain early in 1494, Fernando and Isabel appointed him captain of a small relief fleet to La Isabela. Bartolomé set sail with two or three caravels and reached Española on 24 June 1494, carrying the much-needed supplies. Any good news was welcome to Columbus, because conditions had gone from bad to worse in the colony. Diego had proven to be even less effective as an administrator than Columbus, and discontent was running so high that disillusioned settlers had seized several caravels and sailed home to Spain without permission. Before the end of 1494 Antonio de Torres returned from Spain with another relief fleet and an invitation for Columbus from the Catholic Monarchs. They expressed pleasure with his work and his expertise, and asked him to return to Spain to advise them on their negotiations with Portugal.[10] Columbus declined their request at the time, but things might have gone better for him later had he accepted.

In February of 1495 Antonio Torres took a fleet back to Spain once again, and Columbus was determined to send with him proof that the colony was showing a profit. Consequently, he organized a mass round-up of Indians, intending to send many of them back to Spain to be sold. He justified his actions with the same reasoning being used to justify enslavement in the Canary Islands: the islanders were at war with the Europeans. The indigenous peoples were considered subjects of the Castilian crown in both the Canaries and the Caribbean islands, and were thus protected against enslavement in ordinary circumstances. Only if they warred against the Europeans could they be seized and enslaved, as captives in a "just war." By the time Columbus's second voyage arrived in the Indies, some of the people of Española had certainly turned hostile toward the Europeans, but that was beside the point. Fernando and Isabel wanted a moratorium on slaving until the situation could be clarified, and, unfortunately for all concerned, Columbus did not realize it. He and his men marched through the island with horses, dogs trained for warfare, and arquebuses, taking captives as they met resistance.

The native population was already declining, due to the effects of disease as well as to casualties in battle, and Columbus's slaving expedition only made the situation worse. Relations between Europeans and Indians continued to degenerate during 1495, as Columbus responded to growing hostility toward Europeans and their property. In March he fought and won a pitched battle in the interior of Española. To reward his men and protect his battlefield gains, he instituted a system of forced labor on the island, assigning natives to work for the settlers. He also ordered the construction of scattered forts to protect Spanish interests. By 1496 the island's people had been reduced to obedience. The explorers and settlers had become conquerors, and their erstwhile hosts had become enemies to be vanquished.

Back in Spain, those opposed to Columbus were spreading stories about his misdeeds, and the crown began to listen. The most vocal critics were among the disillusioned settlers returning from the second voyage. They informed the monarchs that the whole enterprise was a joke, that there was no gold on Española, and that the expenditures of the crown would never be recovered. Their main complaint seems to have been directed at the strict control Columbus and his lieutenants strove to maintain over the colonists. Spaniards were familiar with their own traditions of reconquest, in which settlers in newly acquired territories individually received grants of land and collectively received a municipal charter with rights of self-government. The system Columbus and the Spanish monarchs were trying to maintain in the Indies, with official trade conducted by salaried employees, was an alien notion that did not appeal to them.

Contemporary supporters of Columbus, as well as his modern apologists, often accuse his critics of envy or blame the mindless hostility of the Spanish colonists toward a foreigner. There was much more to it than that, however. Columbus had made himself a target of discontent by overselling the supposed virtues of the islands and their inhabitants. It took no more than a realistic view of the situation to call everything Columbus had said into question and to make the colonists feel betrayed as well as disillusioned.

There is no doubt that Fernando and Isabel were committed to making the colony self-supporting as soon as possible. Nonetheless, trying to direct a colonization plan across the ocean in a part of the world unknown to them two years before, they needed reliable administrators. At home they trusted Don Juan Rodríguez de Fonseca, a competent cleric from a well-known family. He had begun arranging the Spanish end of Columbus's ventures during the planning for the second voyage. In the Indies they had trusted Columbus, whom they knew as masterfully persuasive. As reports reached them that the Indies and their peoples were not as Columbus had presented them, however, they began to doubt his veracity. To investigate the conflicting reports they had received from Columbus and his critics, the Spanish monarchs appointed Juan Aguado with an official royal commission.

In October of 1495 Aguado arrived on Española and was appalled by what he found. In addition to alarmingly high deaths among the natives, the number of colonists had been greatly reduced by disease and desertions. Perhaps galvanized into action by Aguado's investigation, Columbus decided to return to Spain. He sailed in March of 1496, leaving his brother Bartolomé in charge of the colony, with the title of *adelantado* (frontier governor). Columbus took only two vessels with him, the faithful *Niña,* now completing her second transatlantic round trip, and the *India,* a small caravel cobbled together from the timbers of two wrecked ships. Perhaps looking for a short-cut, he tried a trajectory eastward from the Leeward Islands, considerably to the south of his first Atlantic return, a choice that forced him into a long and wearying trip, fighting headwinds all the way. This inefficient route provides further support for the idea that Columbus was still learning the winds and currents that led back to Iberia. His fleet first sighted land north of Cape St. Vincent in Portugal, and on 11 June 1496, Columbus arrived in the port of Cádiz.

As soon as Columbus landed in Cádiz, he wrote the monarchs telling them of his arrival and of his eagerness to report to them in person. At that point Fernando and Isabel were in Old Castile, preoccupied with diplomatic negotiations involving their relations with France and the marriages of two of their children. Columbus traveled northward to Burgos in late October or early November of 1496 to report on his progress and solicit further support.

Columbus had begun dressing like a Franciscan friar by this point in his life. Garbed in this modest clothing, suggesting voluntary poverty and self-abnegation, and accompanied by Indians carrying rich and exotic wares, Columbus was at his persuasive best. If he could inspire Fernando and Isabel, despite the opposition of others at the court and in the face of unsettling news from the Indies, the monarchs also knew how to handle Columbus, as they had shown in the past. He wanted to return quickly to the Indies, and they had already promised support for the voyage. They told him, however, that all their available funds were allocated elsewhere, and that his next voyage could be funded by the gold that Peralonso Niño was bringing back from the Indies. The inference was clear: continued exploration of the lands across the ocean would have to pay for itself.

When Niño arrived in Cádiz on 29 October 1496, he handled relations with the court very badly. His initial report of the gold he carried raised the monarchs' hopes that their financial straits would soon be eased, but he irritated them by his delay in reporting to court. Instead of coming immediately to Burgos, where Fernando and Isabel were awaiting the gold he carried, and where Columbus was awaiting news of the colony in the letters Niño carried, he went home to Moguer and did not travel to court until the end of December. By then, the monarchs were greatly annoyed, and Columbus was in a state of high anxiety. It only made matters worse that the gold proved to be far less than expected, and that Niño's estimate of profits from the voyage had included projected sales as slaves of the Indians he carried. The circumstances surrounding Peralonso Niño's return reflected poorly on Columbus as well, causing many at court to doubt his tales and promises of riches in the Indies. Nonetheless, despite their doubts, the monarchs were far too astute to break with him. Better to let him wait until the political situation in Europe had clarified. Charles VIII of France had invaded Italy in 1494, and Spain was involved in the initial phase of a long series of wars to thwart French ambitions.

Back on Española, the situation was drifting into anarchy under the administration of Columbus's brother Bartolomé. A schedule of tribute payments from the Indian communities had been instituted before Columbus sailed for Spain. Indians with access to gold were to provide a certain amount periodically to Columbus, as their new overlord. If a community were located away from the gold bearing streams, its inhabitants could substitute cotton or spices. Because the Indians collected gold simply by hunting for nuggets, there was almost no possibility of expanding output sufficiently to meet the quotas. Harsh punishments were meted out to those who missed their payments. Shortly before Columbus had left Española, the settlers from Isabela had found gold in another area, across the mountains in the southern part of the island. Bartolomé Columbus had a series of forts built to connect Isabela with the new gold field, and established a new port, Santo Domingo, on the southern shore of Española. It was located in a good harbor at the mouth of a river and was surrounded by fine arable lands. Moreover, the routes from Santo Domingo to the gold fields passed over moderate terrain.

Concentrating on the gold regions and Santo Domingo, Bartolomé began stripping Isabela of whatever useful equipment and supplies he could move, angering its settlers and making it more difficult to collect tribute from the Indians. This led to a revolt against the authority of the Columbus brothers, headed by Francisco Roldán, who armed the European settlers and recruited Indian allies by promising them to end the tribute system. Bartolomé failed to make the tribute system work, and he was unable to bring down Roldán. That was the situation that would face Columbus when he returned.

By early April 1497, Fernando and Isabel were ready to turn their attention back to Columbus, reconfirming his titles and rescinding the permission they had granted to other explorers. For the time being, Columbus's exclusive rights were secure, but he still had no funding for a third voyage. A set of royal orders prepared between April and July set out directives for Columbus's colonial administration. He received authority to hire enough new people to bring the total on the royal payroll up to 330. These were to include 40 mounted troopers, 100 foot soldiers, 30 sailors, 30 apprentice sailors, 20 gold workers (neither the Europeans on the island nor the Indians knew the techniques of placer mining), 50 farmers, 10 truck gardeners, 20 artisans of different skills, and 30 women. The royal orders also specified the tools and supplies that were to be carried. The millstones and other equipment on the lists would allow the settlers to construct a mill. Enough oxen, mares, and asses were to be taken to make up 20 yokes of draft animals for cultivation. Fernando and Isabel were obviously providing for a self-sustaining agrarian colony that would produce food for those in gold mining ventures, the primary aim of the colony. The monarchs also decreed that tools and experts for making gold coins be sent to the island.

Fernando and Isabel also demonstrated concern for the indigenous inhabitants of the islands whom they claimed as subjects. The first provision in their instructions for the admiral enjoined him to work for the conversion of the Indians and to arrange for clerics and priests to serve the spiritual needs of both Indians and Europeans. They also confirmed the tribute system that Columbus had instituted, even including his plan to have the Indians wear a brass or lead coin around their necks, to be marked each time they paid their tribute. The monarchs also gave Columbus authority to make land grants in the colony to those who agreed to occupy the land for a four-year period. That decree set the legal basis for the distribution of land, or *repartimiento,* in the colonies. It marked a significant shift from the modified factory system that Columbus and the crown had first attempted in the islands, with settlers as salaried employees. In response to changing circumstances, the crown was gradually formulating the policies that would define the Spanish empire in the New World. Permanent, self-sustaining colonies would be needed to develop the economic potential of the lands claimed for Castile. To attract and retain colonists, the crown abandoned the fortress and factory model used by the Portuguese in Africa. Instead, Fernando and Isabel reverted to the model of settlement that had proven successful during the reconquest of Castile and the ongoing colonization of the Canaries: land grants and a significant degree of local self-government in the form of town councils. The crown would retain overall authority, regulate trade, and provide the structure of government and the rule of law.

Royal agreements had provided for eight ships to be sent to the Indies with Columbus.[11] Two of them were readied before the others and sailed ahead of the main fleet that Columbus would command. The remaining six were divided into two contingents. The first, comprising one *nao* and two caravels, would be at Columbus's disposal to use for exploration. The other three caravels carried provisions for

Española and had authorization to carry 300 men and 30 women as additional colonists, if they could be recruited. That proved more difficult than it had been for the second voyage. To entice settlers, the crown offered pardons to all prisoners (with some major crimes excepted) if they would join the expedition. Eventually, 10 pardoned murderers signed up as the only criminals among approximately 226 participants of the third voyage.

On 30 May 1498, the fleet sailed from Sanlúcar de Barrameda, and then called in at Madeira before heading for Gomera in the Canaries. At Gomera the two contingents separated, with the three caravels bound for Española departing directly from Gomera, while Columbus took the other three ships farther to the south. He may have planned his course to test the notion that gold and other luxuries were to be found in hotter regions near the equator. Many of Columbus's contemporaries believed that metals grew and matured under certain conditions; gold was the metal that had most fully matured, and therefore it supposedly grew best under the influence of the sun.

From Gomera Columbus traveled south to the Cape Verde Islands. From there, he headed west across the ocean on 7 July, reaching an island off the northeast coast of South America on the thirty-first. Columbus named the island Trinidad, because its three distinctive mountain peaks evoked the Holy Trinity. Along the south shore of the island, the fleet anchored and sent a party ashore to reconnoiter and collect fresh water. Sailing north thereafter, they encountered the northwest tip of Trinidad and saw to the west the mountains of Venezuela, the first Columbian landfall on the continental shores of the Western Hemisphere. On further exploration, they reached the multiple mouths of the awe-inspiring Orinoco River. From the quantity of fresh water flowing from the Orinoco, Columbus deduced—not that they had reached a vast continent—but that they were near the earthly paradise. Holy Scripture, he wrote, stated that the terrestrial paradise contained the sources of the four great rivers of the world: the Ganges, the Tigris, the Euphrates, and the Nile. Columbus thought he was near that paradise, or somewhere very like it, *"for I have never read or heard of so great a quantity of fresh water so coming into and near the salt . . . and if it does not come from there, from paradise, it seems to be a still greater marvel, for I do not believe that there is known in the world a river so great and so deep."*[12]

In speculating about his discoveries, Columbus revealed some of his more eccentric geographical notions. In one famous passage, he speculated on the irregularity he thought he had noted in the supposedly spherical earth:

> I have always read that the world, land and water, was spherical, and authoritative accounts and experiments which Ptolemy and all the others have recorded concerning this matter, so describe it and hold it to be, by the eclipses of the moon and by other demonstrations made from east to west, as well as from the elevation of the pole star from north to south. Now, as I have already said, I have seen so great irregularity that, as a result, I have been led to hold this concerning the world, and I find that it is not round as they describe it, but that it is the shape of a pear which is everywhere very round except where the stalk is, for there it is very prominent, or that it is like a very round ball, and on one part of it is placed something like a woman's nipple, and that this part, where this protuberance is found, is the highest and nearest to the sky, and it is beneath the equinoctial line and in this Ocean sea at the end of the East.[13]

Columbus believed that the earthly paradise was located at the peak of the protuberance he described, and that he would come as close as possible to it by sailing south of the equator. *"Not that I believe that to the summit of the extreme point is navigable, or water, or that it is possible to ascend there, for I believe that the earthly paradise is there and to it, save by the will of God, no man can come."*[14]

This is the earliest document that has been found in which Columbus explicitly mentioned the sources for his theoretical knowledge of geography and his critique of those sources based on experience. Much of the world was still unknown to Europeans, and some of their traditional notions about the habitable parts of the world had already been challenged by the discoveries of Columbus, and of the Portuguese in Africa. Moreover, to Columbus and his contemporaries, Holy Scripture was not just a religious text but a valid source of knowledge about the world. Consequently, Columbus's speculations about the earthly paradise, and his blending of the Bible, Ptolemy, and his own experience would not have seemed as odd to his intended audience as they seem to us. Nonetheless, in Columbus's descriptions and speculations, he often allowed preconceived notions, religious and otherwise, to color his version of reality.

After briefly exploring the coast of Venezuela, where the expedition encountered pearl beds and pearl fishers, Columbus sailed on to Española. There he found chaos and crisis. Some of the colonists had mutinied, the natives were up in arms and mightily sick of tribute payments, and of the undisciplined hoard of Europeans in their midst. Neither Bartolomé nor Diego Columbus had been able to maintain order, and Columbus himself had little better luck once he arrived. The rebellion of Roldán still had not been settled, and, in addition to Roldán's supporters, a large number of disaffected settlers was ready to abandon the colony. Columbus gave them permission to leave and provided free passage home, allowing each settler to take a slave with him. In the report to the crown he sent back with the departing settlers, Columbus continued to exaggerate the promise of the colony, even as he reported on Roldán's uprising. The contradictions between Columbus's reports and the reality of rebellion and disillusionment among the settlers must have been disquieting.

One troublesome issue was slavery. The caravels that brought Columbus's letters also brought about three hundred former settlers and an equal number of slaves. That slaves were still being taken contravened the crown's evolving policy on native subjects; the queen was furious and ordered the would-be slaves freed. One of Columbus's letters proposed to send many more slaves, in obvious disregard of royal policy. Adding insult to injury, he pointedly reminded the monarchs of his devoted service. Self-assured as ever, Columbus blamed his opponents for any small failures that might be observed in his conduct. After complaining that those who doubted him *"talk about me worse than a Muslim without giving any reason for it,"* he boasted that *"Our Lord, who knows my intention and the truth of everything, will save me as he has done until now, because until today there has not been a person opposed to me with malice whom He has not punished. . . ."*[15]

He concluded another letter with a typically Columbian piece of hyperbole. In describing Española, where Indians were being killed and enslaved, where Europeans were starving or giving up as settlers, and where no one had yet made a profit, he still used the same exaggerated sales pitch, this time with overtones of religious fanaticism. He boasted about

the land, which it is obvious that Our Lord gave miraculously and which is the most beautiful and the most fertile under heaven, in which there is gold and copper and many kinds of spices and a quantity of brazil wood. . . . And I believe from the needs of Castile and the abundance of Española, a large population will have to come from there to here, and the capital will be in Isabela, where the beginning was, because it is the most ideal spot and better than any other in the land, as should be believed because Our Lord took me there miraculously, for it was impossible to go on or go back with the ships. . . .[16]

The monarchs had enough information from other sources to recognize that their admiral's reports were largely fantasy. It was commonly known at court that Columbus had chosen a disastrously unsuitable site for the town of Isabela, and that Bartolomé Columbus had moved the settlement to Santo Domingo, taking everything from Isabela that he could. Columbus did not help himself by going on to say that tales told against him at the court originated from his enemies, *"for envy, as to a poor foreigner; but in everything He who is eternal has helped and is helping me. . . ."*[17]

Fernando and Isabel decided to launch an investigation into the state of the colony and designated Francisco de Bobadilla as their agent, granting him extraordinary measures to restore authority. Bobadilla brought years of military and executive experience to his post in the Indies. As a further demonstration of their loss of faith in Columbus, Fernando and Isabel resumed licensing other voyages of exploration, effectively rescinding their concession of exclusive rights to Columbus.

Ironically, by then Columbus had finally been able to solve many of the problems facing the colony, although not on terms that were likely to please the crown. Roldán and his supporters had ended their rebellion in exchange for the rights to form their own communities and to requisition the use of labor services from Indian communities. According to his instructions from the queen, Columbus could make land grants to individual Europeans according to their merits, if the grantees would live on their grant, build a house, and farm the land. In settling with Roldán and rewarding his own followers, however, Columbus exceeded his authority by making a very different sort of concession—granting the labor services of a chief and his people. The grantee could move the people wherever he wished and make them do whatever he wished. In other words, the system of *repartimiento,* which had originated as a land grant in medieval Castile, was coupled in the Indies with a grant of labor services, forerunner of the *encomienda* system, in which Indian laborers were commended to a landholder, who had the right to part of their labor. In settling his differences with Roldán, Columbus created the foundations for a damaging pattern of European overlordship and Indian labor service in the Indies. Combined with European diseases and warfare, the systems of *repartimiento* and *encomienda* would cause great disruption in the early sixteenth century, contributing to the disintegration of many native communities.

Besides Roldán's rebellion, additional challenges had arisen to Columbus's government by the time Bobadilla arrived in the harbor of Santo Domingo on 23 August 1500. As he approached the harbor, Bobadilla had his first view of the situation from the deck of his vessel. He could easily see the corpses of seven rebels hanging from prominent gallows, and he soon learned that five more were awaiting execution. This shocking news must have seemed proof of a government gone badly wrong, and Bobadilla acted decisively to restore order. He seized control of Santo Domingo, confiscated Columbus's goods, arrested Diego Columbus, and demanded that the admiral and his brother Bartolomé the *adelantado* also surrender to him. In October 1500 he sent them all home ignominiously, in chains.

The captain of the vessel offered to remove the chains, but Columbus, with stubborn pride, refused, perhaps visualizing the impact such as spectacle would have in Spain. The hero disgraced by changeable fortune formed one of the standard vignettes of classical and Renaissance drama, and the image of Columbus in chains has continued to excite the imagination of poets, artists, and writers even to our own day. Columbus used the enforced idleness of the voyage to write a letter of lament to Doña Juana de Torres, the sister of his friend Antonio de Torres and the former nurse of Prince Juan. By writing to her, Columbus knew that the contents of his letter would reach the king and queen, without risking royal displeasure by directly questioning their authority. This was the opening salvo in Columbus's campaign for restitution, and he asked for inquiries to be made so that justice might be done. Similar complaints of ingratitude and injustice would color his writings for the rest of his life. Taken by themselves, without allowing for the great wealth he was accumulating for himself and his heirs, his complaints have led to the persistent view that Columbus died impoverished, neglected, forgotten, and bitter. In fact, he was only bitter. Amid the complaints, Columbus did make one effective point in his favor:

> At home they judge me as a governor sent to Sicily or to a city or two under settled government, and where the laws can be fully maintained, without fear of all being lost; and at this I am greatly aggrieved. I ought to be judged as a captain who went from Spain to the Indies to conquer a people, warlike and numerous, and with customs and beliefs very different from ours, a people, living in highlands and mountains, having no settled dwellings, and apart from us; and where, by the will of God, I have brought under the domination of the king and queen, our sovereigns, another world, whereby Spain, which was called poor, is now most rich.[18]

By the time he wrote this letter, he had a vastly altered view of the native inhabitants of the Indies and was not reluctant to share it.

In the same letter, Columbus mentioned more than once that the lands he had found constituted "*a new heaven and a new earth,*" echoing the apocalypse of the biblical Book of Revelation.[19] Some writers have used this phrase as evidence that Columbus realized he had not reached Asia, but a new continent instead. It seems clear from his other writings, however, that he thought this new heaven and earth were located in a hitherto-unknown part of Asia. For example, in the draft of a letter to Pope Alexander VI in February 1502, which he may or may not have actually sent, Columbus repeated his assertion that Cuba was the mainland of Asia.[20] Besides, when he wrote to Fernando and Isabel in preparation for his fourth voyage, he asked permission to take two or three Arabic translators with him, as Las Casas reported, "*because he always held the opinion that having passed this our mainland, if a sea passage were found, he had to come across people of the Great Khan or others who spoke that language or a bit of it.*"[21]

Columbus arrived in Cádiz in November 1500. Fernando and Isabel immediately ordered him released from custody and summoned him to court in Granada. Despite all that had happened, they received him warmly, assuring him that his imprisonment had been ordered without their knowledge or consent, and promising him that all would be settled to his satisfaction. Eventually they allowed Columbus to keep all of his property and some of his titles, but the titles would henceforth be empty of authority. Never again would the monarchs let him serve as viceroy or governor. They also delayed in granting him permission for another voyage. Although the pathetic spectacle of Columbus in chains had touched their hearts, they were well aware of the charges of maladministration that had led to his arrest by Bobadilla.

During the period between Columbus's third voyage and the fourth, as he sought to regain royal favor, he worked on two important compilations of documents. He would use both of them to justify his actions and sustain his legal and moral claims to primacy in the developments of the Indies. The first was his *Book of Privileges,* a notarized collection of royal agreements, orders, and letters bearing on his relations with the crown. The other was the *Book of Prophecies,* in which Columbus assembled a collection of biblical passages, writings of church fathers, and the work of modern writers such as Pierre d'Ailly. The passages were selected for their presumed relevance to Columbus's discoveries, the need to take Christianity to all parts of the world, and the reconquest of Jerusalem. The *Book of Prophecies* reveals Columbus's increasing preoccupation with apocalyptical speculation, which had already begun to color his official communications with the monarchs.[22]

While Columbus waited in Spain, the king and queen appointed a new governor for Española, Nicolás de Ovando, who sailed for the Caribbean in February 1502 with a large fleet of thirty-two ships, commanded by Antonio de Torres. The ships carried 2,500 sailors, soldiers, and settlers, enough for a fresh start at the colonization venture botched by the Columbus brothers. A month after Ovando's fleet sailed, Fernando and Isabel finally agreed to grant Columbus permission for a new expedition under his command.

It was no coincidence that they gave Ovando plenty of time to establish his authority in the colony before letting Columbus return. Fernando and Isabel realized that a large bureaucratic structure would be needed to govern the territories properly. Such a government could not rely on talented entrepreneurs such as Columbus. It had to be staffed by trained officials loyal to and dependent upon the crown. Over the course of the year 1501, the colonial administration of the Catholic Monarchs began to take shape. Already they had appointed Ovando as their new governor. In September they appointed additional royal officials. They also negotiated contracts with Antonio de Ojeda, Vicente Yánez Pinzón, and Diego de Lepe for new voyages of discovery. They secured papal approval to collect church tithes in the Indies. They issued orders prohibiting their Indian subjects from having European weapons. The Spanish empire was gradually coming into being, following well-established patterns dating from the reconquest and reaffirmed in the Canaries. In the evolution of Spain's American empire, Columbus had become only one among many.

Once he received the monarchs' approval and support for a fourth voyage, Columbus began preparing a fleet in Seville. He assembled the ships by buying four small shallow-draft vessels, suitable for exploring bays and rivers: two caravels of 70 toneladas, the *Santa María* and the *Santiago de Palos,* and two *navíos,* the *Gallega* and the *Vizcaíno,* of 50 toneladas each. Recalling earlier triumphs, the flagship that would carry Columbus and his 13-year-old son Ferdinand was named the *Santa María,* but Columbus was no longer able to attract the best seamen in southern Spain nor to secure the best ships. Altogether the expedition carried only 135 persons, underscoring its primary mission as an exploratory expedition rather than a colonizing venture.

The fleet sailed from Cádiz on 9 May and cleared the harbor two days later. On the way to the Canaries they stopped at the Moroccan port of Arzila, held by the Portuguese, before sailing for Las Palmas on the island of Gran Canaria, where they arrived on 20 May. Departing five days later, they crossed the Atlantic, "*without having to touch the sails,*" as Ferdinand Columbus would later write. The fleet reached Matininó (now Martinique) on 15 June. After sailing through the Antilles, the ships arrived at Española on 29 June, although Columbus had been expressly forbidden to go there. To emphasize the fact that he lacked all authority on the island, Fernando and Isabel had ordered him to avoid Española on his outbound voyage.

His visit to Española turned out to be more dramatic than he had planned, for a hurricane was brewing. Having experienced one hurricane in the Caribbean on his second voyage, and having sailed on the fringes of another, Columbus wanted to tell Ovando of the approaching storm and also to use the harbor at Santo Domingo as a haven for his own ships. Ovando refused to believe him and refused permission for Columbus to land. He also ordered his own fleet to sail for Spain. The hurricane struck, just as Columbus had predicted, sinking 25 ships in the fleet dispatched by Ovando. The one ship that made it back to Spain, ironically, was the *Aguja,* which carried 4,000 pesos of gold belonging to Columbus. If Columbus had ever entertained doubts that God was on his side, the hurricane and its aftermath laid them to rest.

Thereafter, Columbus and his men spent most of the remainder of the voyage along the coast of Central America. Approaching the mainland, they spotted a huge canoe coming from the north. Though made of a single tree trunk like other Caribbean canoes, this was the biggest any European had yet seen. With 25 paddlers, it was eight feet wide and "*long as a galley,*" With a pavilion in its center roofed with palm fronds. The covered pavilion sheltered women and children, plus baggage and trade goods, comprising the most sophisticated native manufactures the Europeans had yet seen. The canoe had been coming from the north, very likely from Yucatan, but even the impressive vessel and its cargo did not divert the admiral from his southward quest along the continent in search of an ocean passage to the west.

Reaching the mainland, Columbus and his companions made good time down to Panamá, where they had been led to believe a strait existed. Not finding one, they explored the region and decided to establish a small settlement on the river they christened Río Belén. Columbus planned to leave his brother Bartolomé in charge of the settlement. The *Gallega* would be left with him to be broken up for

Figure XIX. Indians constructing a typical dug-out canoe. Illustration from Theodore de Bry, *Reisen in Occidentalischen Indien* (Frankfurt, 1590–1630). *Courtesy of the James Ford Bell Library, University of Minnesota.*

building materials, since its sailing days were over. The local Indians had other ideas, however. Their attacks succeeded in making it so unpleasant for the would-be settlers that they abandoned the effort. Leaving the worn-out hulk of the *Gallega,* Columbus decided to return to Española with the remnants of his fleet. Another of the caravels, the *Vizcaína,* had been fatally damaged by the shipworms that flourished in the warm Caribbean waters, and had to be abandoned. Finally, on 1 May 1503, Columbus turned his two remaining vessels toward the north to set a course for Española. By the twelfth they had reached the numerous islands of the Jardín de la Reina south of Cuba.

The ships were so full of worm holes by then that three pumps had to be worked constantly on each vessel to keep them afloat. The added labor severely strained the crews, who were already on short rations because supplies were running out. To make matters worse, one night during a storm the ships collided, damaging both of them and rendering them barely seaworthy. After reprovisioning at a

Cuban Indian village, they made for Jamaica, because Española, the only island with Spanish settlements, lay up wind and therefore out of reach. By continual pumping, they were able to reach Jamaica, arriving with water almost up to the decks. Columbus had the caravels brought up close together and sailed straight toward land to ground them. Once grounded, they were lashed together and shored up so they would remain upright. The men built cabins on the decks and castles fore and aft, designed to be a safe home until rescue could be arranged. This makeshift wooden fortress, a crossbow shot from shore, in water that rose nearly up to the deck with each high tide, would be home to Columbus and his men for nearly a year before they could be rescued.

Early in his Jamaica stay Columbus wrote to Fernando and Isabel. Composed in the depths of despair, much of the letter was rambling, filled with stories of religious visions and grandiose plans for the reconquest of Jerusalem. Complaining bitterly of poverty and ill treatment at the hands of his enemies, Columbus beseeched his royal patrons for restitution of all his titles and honors. In recalling events at the Río de Belén, he described waiting at sea without a ship's boat, helplessly watching while his brother beat off an Indian attack on shore. Under these conditions of extreme stress, he reported having a dream-vision. Nowhere are his delusions of grandeur and his self-definition as God's chosen instrument more clear.

> I toiled up to the highest point of the ship, calling in a trembling voice, with fast-falling tears, to the war captains of your highnesses, at every point of the compass, for succor, but never did they answer me. Exhausted, I fell asleep, groaning. I heard a very compassionate voice, saying: "o fool and slow to believe and to serve thy God, the God of all! What more did He for Moses or for His servant David? Since thou wast born, ever has He had thee in his most watchful care. When He saw thee of an age with which He was content, He caused thy name to sound marvellously in the land. The Indies, which are so rich a part of the world, He gave thee for thine own; thou hast divided them as it pleased thee, and He enabled thee to do this. Of the barriers of the Ocean sea, which were closed with such mighty chains, He gave thee the keys; and thou wast obeyed in many lands and among Christians thou hast gained an honorable fame.[23]

The voice went on to compare Columbus to the heroes of the Bible, suggesting that his trials were only a preparation for greater things to come. With disingenuous modesty, Columbus concluded the passage by writing that he did not know whose voice he had heard. He then added a long dissertation on gold and suggested that the mines in Panamá were the same as the mines of Aurea, which provided King Solomon in the Bible with the means to build the original Temple of Jerusalem.

Then Columbus returned to his recurring theme of the reconquest of Jerusalem, which was prophesied to precede the end of the world, and pledged himself to lead that reconquest. Although he had previously held millenarian opinions, by 1501 he had come to see himself as an instrument in God's hands, as the Christ-bearer.

> Jerusalem and Mount Sion are to be rebuilt by the hand of a Christian; who this is to be, God declares by the mouth of His prophet in the fourteenth psalm. Abbot Joachim said that he was to come from Spain. St. Jerome showed the way of it to the holy lady. The emperor of Cathay, some time since, sent for wise men to instruct him in the faith of Christ. Who will offer himself for this work? If Our Lord bring me back to Spain, I pledge myself, in the name of God, to bring him there in safety.[24]

Columbus was suffering from increasingly poor health, with ailments that had begun to plague him from the time of the second voyage. He underwent bouts of extreme pain in his lower extremities, sometimes accompanied by inflammation of the eyes that made it impossible for him to read. These symptoms were ascribed at the time to gout, and by modern scholars to arthritis or Reiter's syndrome. Whatever his maladies, it is possible that physical torments contributed to his increasingly bleak mental outlook.

In such circumstances, the letter he wrote to his royal patrons would not have inspired them to place Columbus in charge of an empire. There is no question of the devotion of the Catholic Monarchs to Christianity; Isabel in particular was famous for her piety, which had undoubtedly helped draw her to Columbus. Nonetheless, both monarchs were also shrewd politicians and administrators. It is hardly surprisingly that they refused to reinstate Columbus to any official position in the Indies that he had claimed for them. Columbus's disturbed rantings on the fourth voyage would guarantee his continued exclusion from power, if not from wealth.

After Columbus and his crew were finally rescued from Jamaica, he returned to Spain, reaching Sanlúcar de Barrameda on 7 November 1504, the date that marked the end of his career at sea. Defying reality, as he had often done, Columbus spent the rest of his life lobbying vigorously to have all his grants and titles restored. Even without them, he was a wealthy man, but he felt betrayed and

Figure XX. Lateen caravel with two sails and a large carrack with three sails. Facsimile of the Pîrî Reis portolan chart of 1513. *Courtesy of the James Ford Bell Library, University of Minnesota.*

slighted, which left him unable to enjoy his achievements. That the Spanish crown was unwilling to grant Columbus all he wished cannot be blamed on royal ingratitude or on Castilian resentment of Columbus's Genoese ancestry. Columbus had forfeited his claim to royal preferment by badly mismanaging the Española settlement and by breaking his agreements with the crown on numerous occasions.

In a larger sense, the business of discovery and colonial settlement had quickly grown too large for any one man to manage, regardless of his administrative skills. During Columbus's later years, many other voyages set out for the new-found lands, most of them sponsored by the Castilian crown, but some sailing without any official support or even sanction. Swiftly as the crown moved to establish control over the new colonies, it never altogether succeeded. The powerful lure of trade and plunder in the Caribbean drew men across the Atlantic in increasing numbers, with and without permission. It took the most experienced and loyal administrators that Castile could muster to assert royal control under those circumstances.

Columbus died in Valladolid in 1506, surrounded by his loving family, a rich but dissatisfied man. With the perspective of nearly five centuries, we can appreciate his great accomplishments more than most of his contemporaries could, and, ironically, more than he did himself. Still believing that he was close to Asia, Columbus had discovered a New World unknown to Europeans, exploring many of the larger islands of the Caribbean and long stretches of mainland in Central and South America. And he had set in motion a chain of events that, even in his lifetime, had begun to alter human history on both sides of the Atlantic. Eventually, their effects would spread throughout the world.

NOTES

1. Chanca in Cecil Jane, ed. and trans, *Select Documents Illustrating the Four Voyages of Columbus,* 2 vols. (London: Hakluyt Society, 1930, 1933), 1:32.

2. Cannibalism was also described by two other participants on the second voyage. From Simón Verde, a Florentine merchant resident in Spain, fragments of a letter remain. Juan Gil, and Consuelo Varela, eds., *Cartas de particulares a Colón relaciones coetáneas* (Madrid: Alianza, 1984), pp. 208–211. See also the description by Guillermo Coma, ibid., pp. 188–91. The existence of cannibalism in pre-1492 America is accepted by many historians and social scientists. Some anthropologists and literary critics suggest

that it only existed in the minds of the Europeans. To sustain the view that cannibalism was invented, one needs to assume that a wide range of European commentators deliberately distorted their reports, which seems illogical, to say the least. See Anthony Pagden, *The Fall of Natural Man: The American Indian and the Origins of Comparative Ethnology* (Cambridge, Eng.: Cambridge University Press, 1982).

3. Cuneo in Gil and Varela, *Cartas . . . relaciones,* p. 242.

4. The strife on Española was not recorded, however.

5. Cueno, in Gil and Varela, *Cartas . . . relaciones,* p. 243. Add NYT story, fall 1990.

6. Jane, ed., *Four Voyages,* 1:84.

7. Domestic animals are not mentioned in the royal instructions, dated May 29, 1493, in Martín Fernández de Navarrete, *Colección de viajes y descubrimientos que hicieron por mar los españoles desde final del siglo XV* (Madrid, 1825–1837), modern ed. by Carlos Seco Serrano 3 vols. in *Biblioteca de Autores Españoles,* vols. 75–77 (Madrid: Atlas, 1954), 1:338–42. Las Casas, on the other hand, does mention domestic animals among the items carried on the second voyage. Bartolomé de las Casas, *Historia de las Indias,* ed. Agustín Millares Carlo. 3 vols. (Mexico City and Buenos Aires: Fondo de Cultura Económica, 1951), bk. 1, ch. 82, 1:346–49.

8. Ibid., 1:88–90.

9. Ibid., 1:98.

10. Navarrete, BAE, vol. 75, pp. 393–94.

11. The ships and their officers were: *Santa Cruz,* Pilot: Francisco Niño, Master: Juan Bermúdez; *Santa Clara* or *Niña,* Pilot: Juan de Umbria, Master: Pero Francés; *La Castilla,* 70 toneles, Master: Andrés García Galdín, Owner: Alfon Gutiérrez; *La Gorda,* 60 toneles; Master: Alfon Benítez; Owner: Andrés Martín de la Gorda; *La Rábida,* Master: Alfon García Gansino, Owner: Bartolomé de Leza; *Santa María de Guía,* 101 toneles, Master and owner: Cristóbal Quintero; *La Garza,* 70 toneles, Master and owner: Francisco García de Palos, *La Vaqueña,* Master and owner: unknown. For the ships of the third voyage, see Consuelo Varela, ed., *Cristóbal Colón: Los cuatro viajes, Testamento* (Madrid: Alianza, 1986), pp. 23–24. For the crews, see Juan Gil, "El rol del tercer viaje colombino," *Historiografía y Bibliografía Americanista,* 29 (1985):83–110. Gil's article also appears in Juan Gil and Consuelo Varela, *Temas Colombinas* (Seville: Escuela de Estudios Hispano-Americanos, 1986).

12. *Select Documents Illustrating the Four Voyages of Columbus,* Cecil Jane, trans. and ed., 2 vols. (London: Hakluyt Society, 1930, 1933), 2:38.

13. Jane, ed., *Four Voyages,* 2:26–36.

14. Jane, ed., *Four Voyages,* 2:36.

15. Cristóbal Colón, *Textos y documentos completos,* ed. by Consuelo Varela 2d ed. (Madrid: Alianza America, 1984), p. 238. Las Casas quotes the letter in *Historia de las Indias,* bk. 1, ch. 162.

16. Colón, *Textos y documentos,* p. 240.

17. Colón, *Textos y documentos,* p. 240.

18. Jane, ed., *Four Voyages,* 2:66.

19. *"And I saw a new heaven and a new earth: for the first heaven and the first earth were passed away; and there was no more sea."* Revelation 21, 1. King James version.

20. Colón, *Textos y documentos,* p. 286.

21. Las Casas, *Historia,* bk. 2, ch. 4. The mainland Las Casas had in mind was Mexico, where he served as Bishop of Chiapas.

22. The *Book of Prophesies* has recently appeared in two new translations. Delno West and August Kling, eds. and trans., *The Libro de las profecías of Christopher Columbus: An en face edition* (Gainesville: University of Florida Press, 1991); Kay Brigham, ed., and trans., *Christopher Columbus's Book of Prophesies* (Ft. Lauderdale, FL: TSelf, 1991).

23. Jane, ed., *Four Voyages,* 2:92.

24. Jane, ed., *Four Voyages,* 2:104.

13

IBERIAN SHIPS AND SHIPBUILDING IN THE AGE OF DISCOVERY

Carla Rahn Phillips

The study of ships and shipbuilding has attracted distinguished scholars over the years, but not as many as one might expect, given the intrinsic interest of the subject. Moreover, the field is often overly technical at one extreme, or overly general at the other extreme. Although the late J. H. Parry greatly enriched our understanding of ships and navigational techniques in the Age of Discovery, as the fifteenth and sixteenth centuries are often called, few others have taken up the challenge until recently. Iberia has been particularly neglected among scholars writing in English. The result is that we know very little about one of the most inventive periods in maritime history, when European global exploration quite literally changed the world. When, how, and why did ships develop that enabled Europeans to voyage around the globe and return safely? What characteristics made those ships successful? How did they change over time? What principal types of ships can be identified and what names have they been given? And, most obvious and yet most difficult, what did those ships look like and how large were they? Embedded within each of these questions are technical problems relating to the design of hulls, sails, and rigging, and the research of historians and underwater archeologists is just beginning to find some answers.

Although the Age of Discovery eventually involved most of Europe, Portugal and Spain led the way. The ships used by Iberians in their first daring journeys into the Atlantic developed in response to specific needs, firmly rooted in a particular time and place. There is no consensus about how the famous ships of Iberian exploration and discovery developed, or even how they looked. Few wrecks have been

215

found from the fifteenth and early sixteenth centuries, and very little documentary research has been done on Iberian ship design. Even where documents exist, they often lack the kind of specific information needed to study design and its evolution, being more concerned with the outfitting and provisioning of ships for specific fleets. Much of the pictorial evidence available for ships of the period comes from paintings, illuminated manuscripts and books, town seals, and votary statues, the latter often donated to churches in supplication for a safe voyage. These images can often seem laughably out of scale to the casual observer, with human beings nearly as tall as the mainmast, and features of design schematically presented. As one historian has observed.

> Pictorial evidence is often unreliable. An artist, unless he has been a seaman himself, seldom knows what he is trying to draw when depicting a ship. He does not understand the purpose of the gear he sees and so leaves out many things of importance and exaggerates others to suit his composition. He tends to shorten all drawings of the hulls of vessels and to accentuate all curves. We therefore see many pictures of ships looking like slices of melon, surmounted with a skewer adorned with a piece of notepaper and a few bits of string.[1]

Moreover, the illustrations and models are often difficult to identify or date with precision. Art historians could provide invaluable information by taking an interest in the depictions of ships, dating and identifying them with precision. As a general rule of thumb, the date of a work of art is a better gauge of any ships represented than the date of the event commemorated by the artist. Given the difficulties of pictorial evidence and the scarcity of information from nautical archeology and documents, there can be a wide range of opinion about nearly every aspect of the history of ship design.

One major generalization finds widespread agreement: during the fourteenth and fifteenth centuries, a blending of characteristics from northern and southern European ships eventually produced the ancestors of nearly all later ocean-going vessels. Some stages in this evolution are fairly well known; others are not. In the late Middle Ages, northern and southern ships were quite different from one another. Northern ships carried one mast and a large, square sail, which was most effective in sailing with the wind. The sail could be unfurled completely or left partially furled and tied by reef lines to take advantage of varying wind conditions. Southern ships usually had two or three forward-leaning masts carrying triangular (lateen) sails, which were more maneuverable and able to sail closer to the direction of the wind, but more difficult to alter in response to wind changes. Both northern and southern ships were steered by oars fixed at the stern, the northern ones generally having one oar and the southern ships with two. Finally, the hulls of northern ships were commonly built from the outside in, with overlapping planks nailed together, and internal bracing added later (clinker built). Southern hulls commonly began with an internal skeleton of ribs, and planks were added later, usually edge to edge and caulked in the seams between the planks (carvel built). Although clinker hulls are usually stronger than carvel hulls, they require more wood, weigh more, and generally are not suitable for large ships.

At some point in the late Middle Ages, northern and southern ships came into regular contact with one another. One tradition traces the arrival of northern ships in the Mediterranean to a voyage of Basque pirates in 1303. A more plausible scenario places northern ships in the Mediterranean from the time of the Crusades between the late eleventh and late thirteenth centuries. Regular voyages between northern Europe and the Mediterranean were facilitated, if not initiated, by the reconquest of much of southern Spain from the Muslims in the mid-thirteenth century. With Christian influence expanding in the western Mediterranean, normal trade could develop between the Mediterranean and the Atlantic and Baltic coasts. Once northern and southern ships came in regular contact with one another, a hybrid style of ship gradually evolved, produced by mutual borrowing and parallel development. The quest for the origins of particular design features on European ships has long attracted scholarly interest. Such interest could probably be better focused elsewhere, however. In a time of great technological change such as the late Middle Ages, precise origins are very difficult to determine. Much more important is the incremental process that eventually led to the generalized changes that benefited all seafarers. In that process, old and new styles could and did co-exist, even on the same ship. Moreover, the introduction of a new style and its general use could be separated in time by decades, or even centuries. For example, a hinged axial rudder began to replace steering oars as early as the late twelfth century, perhaps first in northern Europe, but it did not come into general use on large ships before about the middle of the fourteenth century. There is a particularly fine illustration of a sternpost rudder in an early thirteenth century Bible from eastern Spain.

Mediterranean shipbuilders often adopted the one-masted square sail of the north, as well as a northern-style platform on the mast.

By the mid-fourteenth century, large ships often had a second, smaller mast with a square sail, or with a lateen sail on Mediterranean ships. Higher permanent castles fore and aft, thought to have originated for battle at sea, also aided sailors working the lines of the large square sails in both northern and southern versions of this ship, which was generally called by variants of the name "cog." The cog usually had a straight sternpost and a forward-raking stempost that was curved on southern ships and straight on northern ones. By the early fifteenth century a third mast and sail had been added to the cog for balance, and the southern type of hull construction had come to be used in both north and south for larger ships, although it took a while for northern builders to master the technique. Some northerners continued to use clinker techniques for the lower part of the hull, with ribs inserted afterwards and edge-to-edge planking attached the rest of the way.

The result of this combination of styles was the so-called full-rigged ship, the great technological innovation of the fourteenth and fifteenth centuries. It carried three masts, the front two (called the foremast and the mainmast) with square sails, and the mizzenmast behind them with a lateen sail. It was steered with a sternpost rudder. Just as the one or two masted square-sailed ship of the time was commonly called a cog, the full-rigged ship was commonly called a carrack. It was usually depicted in contemporary artwork as a large rounded ship with a high, protruding forecastle, a smaller aft castle, and a deeply cut waist in between. The only surviving model of a mid-fifteenth century ship is a votary model of a carrack (often called a *nao*) from the sanctuary of San Simón de Mataró in Catalonia on Spain's eastern coast. Experts generally agree that it represents real shipbuilding techniques of the fifteenth century, but they disagree on many other points. The Mataró ship has been described at one time or another as having one, two, or three masts, although it is quite similar in shape to the full-rigged carracks described above and shown in contemporary art.

Most scholars agree that the full-rigged ship first appeared sometime during the first quarter of the fifteenth century, though its origin remains obscure. Some claim it was an Italian invention. Many scholars credit the Basques, because of their experience with both Atlantic and Mediterranean navigation and their familiarity with various types of ocean-going ships. Whatever their role as inventors, Basque shipbuilders became famous for the quality and design of their vessels, and they were probably most responsible for introducing the full-rigged ship to northern Europe in the early fifteenth cen-

Figure XXI. Southern European round ship with carvel planking, constructed over a skeleton. Illustration from Bernhard von Breydenbach, *Peregrinatio in Terram Sanctam* (Mainz, 1486). *Courtesy of the James Ford Bell Library, University of Minnesota.*

tury. There is documentary evidence that full-rigged ships were imported to the Netherlands directly from Spanish shipyards during
the 1400s.

With a combination of square and lateen sails and a sternpost rudder, the full-rigged carrack was balanced and maneuverable, able to
withstand conditions on the open ocean and to enter and leave ports
with some degree of grace and efficiency. Once invented, the rigging
and sail plan on the full-rigged ship would evolve further during the
sixteenth and seventeenth centuries by increasing the number and
decreasing the size of the sails. This allowed a wide range of sail area
aloft in response to changing wind conditions. Topsails would be
added above the sails on the foremast and mainmast. A spritsail
would be added to the forward-pointing mast at the prow (the
bowsprit). The same principle was applied to the lateen sails by
adding another mast behind the mizzen (the bonaventure or coun-
termizzen) with its own lateen sail, although this was by no means
a universal feature. From its basic hull design and sail plan, the full-
rigged carrack would develop in several directions, each one suitable
for a particular set of needs and circumstances. Several of these
variants were especially suited to the needs of early exploration and
trade pioneered by Portugal and Spain.

The hulk type of full-rigged ship was developed for its cargo capacity, rather than for speed or warfare. The hulk was more characteristic of northern Europe than of the south, although the model
for the fully developed hulk of the sixteenth and seventeenth centuries was the modified carrack developed in southern Europe and
transmitted northward. Characteristic hulks were wide, shallow
vessels such as the barge, but the Dutch fluit, developed in the late
sixteenth century, would also fit this general category. Although it
could carry guns, the hulk could be dangerously unstable when
loaded with heavy artillery, given its shallow draft. Fortunately,
generally peaceful conditions in northern European waters meant
that mariners and merchants could forego hull reinforcement and
artillery and specialize in ships that were cheap to build and sail,
and very efficient as cargo carriers.

Quite different from the hulk was the caravel, generally a long,
narrow, and agile ship, useful for coastal exploration and messenger
service. Strictly speaking, the caravel was not always a full-rigged
ship, because its earliest versions probably featured a two-masted
lateen rig. Such lateen caravels were developed and widely used
from about 1436 on by the Portuguese, following their own seafaring experience as well as the general evolution of southern sailing

ships. The word *caravela* appears in a Portuguese document of Alfonso III in 1255, referring to ships, but it is not clear what characteristics they had. The word caravel denoted a hull type in southern Europe, but it was often used in northern Europe to refer to any hull constructed of edge-to-edge (carvel; caravel) planking over a skeletal frame. This has led to a certain confusion in terminology in the scholarly literature. The first mention of caravels in Spain appears in a royal chronicle of 1434, describing a flood in Seville. Shipwrights in southern Spain most likely added square sails to the lateen caravel's rigging, making it more suitable for ocean voyages. It was this full-rigged caravel, or *carabela redonda* as the Spanish called it, that represented one branch of the development of the full-rigged ship. The fine handling qualities of both types of caravel were well-known, but the *redonda* performed better on the open sea. Perhaps the most famous caravels of the Age of Discovery were the *Niña* and the *Pinta* that accompanied Christopher Columbus on his pioneering voyage across the Atlantic in 1492. Columbus's *Pinta* was full-rigged from the beginning of his voyage, and the *Niña* was re-rigged in the Canary Islands from a two-masted lateen rig to a full rig. Both caravels were quite small, though scholars disagree on their likely measurements. Two well-known modern estimates come from Carlos Etayo Elizondo and José María Martínez-Hidalgo Terán, who each revised calculations generated from the late nineteenth century onward. In a 1963 book, Etayo claimed there were two different *Niñas* on Columbus's first two voyages. He also calculated the measure of all three ships on the first voyage as considerably smaller than previous authors had argued, based on a close and careful reading of contemporary sources. In a 1575 treatise on nautical matters, Juan Escalante de Mendoza had noted that the largest of Columbus's ships, the *nao Santa María,* was "very little larger than 100 *toneladas*"—the only specific mention of the size of the *Santa María* available.[2]

There has been considerable controversy over the definition of the Spanish *tonelada,* but, according to official regulations in 1590, it was worth 8 cubic *codos* (a linear *codo* being 22 inches), equal to what is sometimes called the *tonel macho* of Vizcaya, and to the old French *tonneau de mer* (about 1.4 cubic meters). Tonnage measures had their roots in the wine trade and the ability of a ship to carry a certain number of wine barrels of more or less known weight, and Spanish tonnage continued to refer to both volume and weight.

The *tonel macho,* which might be called a ship *tonelada,* was 1.2 times larger than the merchandise *tonelada* used for the Indies

Figure XXII. This woodcut of c. 1505 shows a typical Spanish *nao*, probably very similar to the *Santa María* of Columbus's 1492 voyage. The scene represents Amerigo Vespucci exploring the River Plate. *Courtesy of the James Ford Bell Library, University of Minnesota.*

trade in Seville, so that 12 merchandise *toneladas* equalled 10 ship *toneladas*. Many historians have assumed that sixteenth-century writers such as Juan Escalante de Mendoza and Diego García de Palacio used the merchandise *tonelada,* whether describing ships or their capacity in merchandise. This seems to be mistaken. García clearly had the larger *tonel macho* or ship *tonelada* in mind when describing ships. Escalante also seems to have used the *tonel* macho when referring to ships. One passage in his 1575 manuscript has given rise to much confusion, because he mentions both sorts of *tonelada* together, but he differentiates their use for ships and for merchandise capacity.

Etayo based his estimates of Columbus's ships on the assumption that both Juan Escalante and Diego García de Palacio had used merchandise *toneladas* rather than *toneles machos.* Etayo believed so strongly in his estimates that he sailed the Atlantic in a reconstruction of the presumed second *Niña* he envisioned. The verdict thus far, however, is that there was only one *Niña* and that Etayo's estimates were too small, for a variety of reasons. Martínez-Hidalgo's reconstructions have generally been preferred, though they seem to have been based on several faulty assumptions. His final estimates for the configuration of the *Santa María* fall well within the range for *naos* of Columbus's time, and supposedly produced a vessel measuring 105.9 *toneladas.* Martínez-Hidalgo had in mind what he called "light displacement tons," however, a concept quite alien to the fifteenth and sixteenth centuries. Moreover, he argued that the merchandise *tonelada* measured about 1.4 cubic meters, and the *tonel macho* measured about 1.7 cubic meters, neither of which is accepted by most scholars. Surprisingly, neither Etayo nor Martínez-Hidalgo made use of the Spanish tonnage formula codified in 1590 and undoubtedly in use much earlier, which gauged ships in the *tonel macho* of Vizcaya. By that formula, Martínez-Hidalgo's figures yield a *Santa María* of 239 *toneladas,* and the 1992 replica based on a modification of his figures defined a ship of 224 *toneladas,* both unacceptably large.

Spaniards used simple mathematical formulas for calculating tonnages, based on a ship's official dimensions. All measurements were in linear *codos* (elbows) whose exact length has been the subject of much debate. Most modern scholars use a figure somewhere between 560 and 574 millimeters. The tonnage formulas attempted to solve the problem of finding a cubic measurement for something other than a cube. The first part of the simplest formula calculated the square measure of a cross section of the ship. The square measure was then multiplied by the length on the first deck, giving a total measure for the hold in cubic *codos,* which was divided by 8 to yield *toneladas.* Adjustments in the simple formula allowed for the extra bracing, armaments, men, and provisions that distinguished ships on military duty from merchant vessels. When the same ship was gauged both ways, it measured about 14% larger as a warship than as a merchant ship. The Spanish government instituted a new set of formulas in 1613, rescinded it in 1618, and reinstituted it in 1633. Although the new set of formulas attempted to account more accurately for the capacity of the hull, it took quite a while to be widely used. Many official and private measurements of ships continued to use the formula established in 1590 well into the seventeenth century. Eventually, however, the new formulas prevailed.

Martínez-Hidalgo's configuration of the *Pinta* and the *Niña* were based on proportions for caravels in the sixteenth-century Portuguese *Livro nautico* by Fernando de Oliveira. That is certainly plausible, and the tonnages he estimates are plausible as well— about 61 *toneladas* for the *Pinta* and 53 for the *Niña.* Because he had in mind "light displacement tons," however, his measurements yield far larger tonnages when used in the formula for sixteenth-century Spanish ships. I argued in a 1986 conference paper that the ships he proposed are simply too large. Many other scholars agree, including the late John Patrick Sarsfield. Before his recent untimely death, Sarsfield commissioned construction of a replica of an early Iberian caravel in Brazil, where traditional shipbuilding methods still survive. The replica not only sails well but is widely thought to be the best approximation of early caravels yet devised.

Until more evidence is generated by nautical archeology, the best hope for arriving at plausible estimates of Columbus's ships and others of that epoch lies in the use of contemporary methods for measuring ship tonnages and in the study of contemporary ship configurations. A plausible configuration for the *Santa María* is the simple "as, dos, tres," the proportion common to merchant *naos* of the time, with the keel twice the beam, and the length three times the beam. The depth in the hold, from the lowest planked deck to the floor, was about half the beam. Caravels were somewhat slimmer and shallower in draft than *naos,* but we cannot be sure how much.

With estimated tonnages and configurations for Columbus's ships, I used a sixteenth-century formula for calculating ships' tonnages to derive a set of likely dimensions for each ship. The results are summarized in Table 1, along with comparative figures from Etayo and the 1992 replicas based on Martínez-Hidalgo's estimates.

Table 1

ESTIMATED CONFIGURATIONS OF COLUMBUS'S SHIPS / ESTIMATED TONNAGES OF COLUMBUS'S SHIPS

SHIP	SOURCE*	ESLORA (Length) (mts.)	(ft.)	(codos)	QUILLA (Keel) (mts.)	(ft.)	(codos)	MANGA (Beam) (mts.)	(ft.)	(codos)	PUNTAL (Depth) (mts.)	(ft.)	(codos)	DISPLACEMENT IN LIGHT CONDITIONS (TONS)	MAXIMUM DISPLACEMENT (TONS)	CALCULATED TONELADAS BY 16TH CENTURY FORMULA**
Santa María	Replica	26.60	86.45	47.15	16.10	52.33	28.54	7.96	25.87	14.11	3.24	10.53	5.74	104.65	223.88	238.86
	Phillips	17.77	57.75	31.50	11.85	38.49	21.00	5.92	19.25	10.50	2.96	9.62	5.25			108.53
	Etayo	14.13	45.92	25.05	10.15	33.00	18.00	5.75	18.70	10.20	4.31	14.01	7.64			122.01
Pinta	Replica	22.75	73.94	40.33	16.12	52.39	28.58	6.60	21.45	11.70	2.21	7.18	3.92	51.66	115.59	115.54
	Phillips	16.95	55.10	30.05	12.98	42.20	23.02	5.42	17.60	9.60	2.34	7.60	4.15			74.75
	Etayo	12.62	41.01	22.37	9.59	31.17	17.00	4.12	13.38	7.30	2.22	7.22	3.94			40.21
Niña	Replica	21.40	69.55	37.94	15.55	50.54	27.57	6.28	20.41	11.13	2.00	6.50	3.55	48.66	100.30	93.59
	Phillips	15.32	49.80	27.16	11.85	38.50	21.00	4.89	15.90	8.67	2.09	6.80	3.71			54.61
	Etayo	11.76	38.23	20.85	8.46	27.50	15.00	3.38	11.00	6.00	1.98	6.43	3.51			27.44

mts. = meters of 39 inches each

ft. = feet of 12 inches each

codos = the codo real of 22 inches each, used for shipbuilding

*Sources:

Replica = Official measurements of the replicas built by the Spanish government for 1992.

Phillips = Carla Rahn Phillips, "Sizes and Configurations of Spanish Ships in the Age of Discovery," in Columbus and His World, comp. Donald T. Gerace (Ft. Lauderdale, Fl, 1987).

Etayo = Carlos Etayo Elizondo, La expedicion de la "Nina II" (Barcelona, 1963).

**The official formula for measuring ships, calculated in codos, was: Puntal times Manga, divided by 2, times Eslora, which gave a figure in cubic codos. This was then divided by 8 to give a figure in Toneladas.

My method has the merit of estimating ships' dimensions that conform to tonnage formulas understood by contemporaries, to proportions of ships common at the time, and to the few mentions of Columbus's ships that have been found in documents of the time, including information about their crews. The late Alice Bache Gould painstakingly researched the lives of every man on Columbus's first voyage and was able to identify 87 of them, with 90 as a usable estimate for the total: 40 on the *Santa María*, 26 on the *Pinta*, and 24 on the *Niña*.

During the 1492 voyage Columbus often mentioned that his flagship (the *nao Santa María*) did not handle as well as either of the caravels, though all three ships carried three masts and a full rig for most of the outgoing voyage. It seems to have been fairly common in Columbus's time to experiment with sails and other equipment on board ships. The *Niña* was re-rigged with a fourth mast in 1498, though the sail plan it carried on those masts is not clear. Some four-masted caravels used lateen sails on all but the foremast. During the sixteenth century, full-rigged caravels used in Spain's transatlantic fleets could be as large as 150–200 *toneladas*. Smaller caravels persisted in the sixteenth century as well, having proved useful as coastal patrols, dispatch vessels, and light gunboats. Caravels thus showed great variety, not only in size, but also in rigging and equipment. The safest generalization is that the caravel was fairly long, narrow, and lightly built, relying on speed and agility rather than size and strength. Because of its adaptability, the caravel became one of the two most important ship types on the trans-Atlantic run to the Spanish Indies in the early sixteenth century.

The other important ship type on that run was the *nao,* in many ways the logical successor to the full-rigged carrack. Although "carrack" seems to have been a generic term for round merchant ships of the late fifteenth century, by the early sixteenth century the term often connoted an enormous ocean-going ship, sometimes as large as 1,000 *toneladas,* suitable for long trading voyages. Although large carracks were used by many European seafaring nations, they were particularly favored by the Portuguese for their sixteenth-century voyages to the East Indies. Because of their size and height above the water line, large carracks were virtual floating fortresses, easily able to defend themselves against poorly armed local enemies in the Indian Ocean. But large carracks were not ideal for conditions in much of Europe, nor for trade to the West Indies, which required numerous stops at small ports. The Spanish therefore developed full-rigged round ships that they called *naos* for their Indies trade. Spanish *naos* were somewhat larger than typical carracks of the late fifteenth century, but much smaller than the large Portuguese carracks of the sixteenth century. Nonetheless, the Spanish used the term *nao* to denote many different sizes of full-rigged round ships, even the large Portuguese carracks. This tendency to use the term *nao* as a generic designator has led to much confusion in studies of ship design during the Age of Discovery.

In general a *nao* was fairly large and wide, short in the keel and deep in the hold, as paintings of the era demonstrate. When the word *nao* first appeared in a Spanish royal chronicle in 1343, it seems to have denoted a warship, but later *naos* became best known as cargo carriers. After the initial Spanish voyages of discovery, the *nao* type of ship increased in importance on the Indies run, for several reasons. Crossing the Atlantic and the Caribbean to arrive at Spain's colonies required a ship of at least 50–60 *toneladas,* the size of Columbus's *Niña.* Smaller ships did not have enough space to carry provisions for the crew on that long a voyage. To make the crossing profitable required much larger ships. The vessels involved in regular long-distance trade needed enough space to carry not only crew, soldiers, and provisions, but also trade goods, passengers, and their belongings. The *nao* was large enough to carry cargo, strong and fast enough for naval warfare, and seaworthy enough for long voyages, although it was not as efficient as more specialized ships at any of those tasks.

As we have seen, hulks, caravels, and *naos* represented three distinctive types of ships that developed from the full-rigged vessels of the fifteenth century. By the late sixteenth century, every seafaring people in Europe had developed a range of characteristic sailing ships to serve their needs. Spain continued to use the caravel and the *nao* in its Indies trade, along with a variety of smaller ships, but the most characteristic vessel on the Indies run by the late sixteenth century was the galleon. Although it had features in common with each of the three general types of full-rigged ship defined above, it was essentially a hybrid, with a hull that combined features of the caravel and the *nao* and a name recalling the fighting prowess of the medieval galley—a long, narrow ship moved primarily by oars. Although the Spanish galleon of the sixteenth century was considerably larger than the caravel, it had a very similar profile. The forecastle was much lower than the aft castle, unlike most *naos* and carracks, giving the galleon as well as the caravel a low-slung crescent shape. It was full-rigged like the *carabela redonda,* but it featured a galley-style beak below the bowsprit, which the caravel usually lacked. Ships that could be either *carabelas redondas* or small galleons appeared in a map of the world made in Seville in 1529. By the late sixteenth century, the major differences between caravels and galleons were in the latter's greater size, heavier armament, and increased internal bracing for battle and rough seas. These characteristics brought the galleon close to the *nao,* although the galleon lacked the prominent forecastle that defined early *naos.*

The traditional *nao* of the medieval Mediterranean had served for both warfare and trade, but it needed strengthening to serve those same functions in the Atlantic. Castilian *naos* adopted a Flemish style of hull bracing in the early sixteenth century and a northern-style curved stern or round tuck, which the Spanish often referred to as a "monkey's behind" (*culo de mono*). A government decree in 1522 increased the quality and the quantity of armaments carried by *naos* on the Indies run, and other changes regulated mast height and sail volume, required bilge pumps, and established strict rules for the use of fire on board. Ships going to the Indies were also required to carry spare parts and tools for repairs, as well as sufficient provisions for increased crews on longer voyages. The forecastle for the *nao* also began to recede to facilitate handling the sails, bringing its shape closer to the galleon. Thus, conditions on voyages across the Atlantic led to changes that made the *nao* stronger and more seaworthy, able to serve both as a cargo carrier and as a warship.

The galleon took features from both the caravel and the *nao,* and, although it was more often associated with defense or warfare than with trade, it remained a multipurpose vessel. In numerous fleet lists from the late sixteenth century, the size and armaments of *naos* and galleons were very similar, and the same ship might be called a *nao* or a galleon interchangeably in the same document. The only clear distinction would seem to be that Spanish galleons were ships sailing for the crown or that had sailed for the crown as military vessels, whether or not they carried cargo as well. The Portuguese galleon was rarely used for cargo, assuming a more specialized military function. By the late sixteenth century the galleon had acquired its classic shape: a low, set-back forecastle, a high aft castle; a beak below the bowsprit; a high, flat stern and a square tuck like the caravel but unlike the round tuck of the *nao*; and full-rigging, complete with topsails on the fore and mainmasts. Interestingly, by the late sixteenth century the *nao* and even the carrack had adopted some of the same features, responding to the needs of long-distance ocean sailing. Given the lack of standard definitions of ship types and their continued use in a variety of tasks, the characteristics of individual historical ships cannot be assumed just because they were called by a particular name. For positive identification, we need documents that list a ship's measurements, and even those reveal little about the superstructure.

Fortunately, the methods of ship construction in use during the Age of Discovery are somewhat better known. Hull construction methods in southern Europe changed very little from late medieval times to the end of the era of the wooden sailing ship, relying on traditions, raw materials, and labor in regions devoted to shipbuilding. Spain had a Mediterranean tradition of shipbuilding, particularly in Barcelona, and Atlantic traditions on the Cantabrian coast and in the southwest. In all of Europe, craftsmen's skills continued to govern ship construction in the sixteenth century, but eventually the need was felt for a more scientific and standardized approach. Spurred by the demands of long-distance trade, Iberians wrote some of the first European treatises on ship construction. The Portuguese Fernando de Oliveira and the Spaniard Juan Escalante de Mendoza discussed the ideal proportions for ocean-going ships in manuscripts on navigation written in about 1565 and 1575, respectively. It was Diego García de Palacio, however, who published the first full-blown treatment of ship construction and design. His *Instrucción náuthica,* printed in Mexico City in 1587, gave detailed mathematical proportions for the hull and the rigging, as well as discussing ship construction, sailmaking, and other topics.

These early theorists helped to move ship design in a more scientific direction, but the actual construction process remained strongly traditional. The crucial first step was to select the wood. If a master builder or carpenter could arrange to go to the forests himself, so much the better. If the master carpenter did not supervise the cutting himself, he would select appropriate logs from the timber brought to the shipyards. The accepted wisdom was that trees should be cut during the winter when they had no leaves and little sap, and all the wood had to be dried and aged properly before use. In general, oak was preferred for most of the hull, pine (lighter than oak) for the superstructure, rot-resistant cedar or alder for the pumps, and other woods for other purposes. Roots were often used for treenails and dowels. Curved pieces of particular sizes and shapes were highly prized for bracing inside the hull. Planking could be cut from straight logs, with various widths for particular parts of the hull and superstructure, and the wood normally lost one-quarter in trimming it to size. There is some evidence that Spanish carpenters partly fashioned wood for ship construction in the forest, before it was hauled to the shore for assembly.

In some shipbuilding centers in Europe, such as medieval Barcelona and Venice, ship construction took place in vast stone buildings designed for the purpose. Such fixed installations were rarities, however. Many shipyards in the sixteenth century and thereafter were no more than selected sites along riverbanks or in protected harbors near the sea. In Spanish, a ship's carpenter was called *a carpintero de ribera* (riverbank carpenter), and the word for shipyard (*astillero*) denotes a place for building the braces (*astillas*) for a ship's frame. Quite large ocean-going ships were built in the open air, in Spain and elsewhere in Europe.

The actual construction of a large ship began by laying the keel, made of several pieces of joined heavy timber, forming the spine of the ship's body. In traditional shipbuilding, the keel was then braced by pieces of wood set into the ground, with additional bracing added as the ship took form. A curved stempost (*roda*) was attached to the front end of the keel, and a straight sternpost (*codaste*) was attached to the rear end, set at an angle leaning backward from the keel. The forward curve of the stempost extended farther from the front of the keel than the sternpost extended backward. The precise amount was calculated by dropping a plumb-line from a particular point on each post to the ground below, with the distance from the plumb-bob to the keel called the *lanzamiento*. The length of the keel was determined by the proportions established for the finished ship. As Juan Escalante observed in 1575, the moment the keel was laid in the *astillero,* the owner, the master builder, and each master carpenter should already know the mathematical proportions of the finished ship. Only in that way could each piece of wood have its proper place and the geometry of the ship be appropriate and pleasing to the eye.

During the sixteenth century, the use of explicit mathematical proportions for each part of the ship slowly gained ground from traditional methods that relied more on experience than on mathematics, yet even in the most traditional methods, geometry and standard proportions played a central role in ship construction. In Spanish shipbuilding, the key measure in the ship's configurations was the breadth of the hull at its widest point (*manga* or beam). From this measure, all the others followed in proportion, from the length of the keel (*quilla*), to the length of the ship at the level of the lower deck (*esloria*), to the depth of the hold (*puntal*), and the breadth of the floor (*plan*). Based on these five measures, the total tonnage of the ship could be calculated, according to a mathematical formulation.

Many other factors besides a ship's dimensions influenced how well it would sail, however. That is where the experience of both master carpenters and their subordinate shipwrights came into play. With minor variations, the ship rose from the keel in the time-honored fashion of skeleton construction in southern Europe. The largest and fullest set of ribs, called the master ribs (*cuaderna maestra*), seems to have been placed first, perpendicular to the keel and slightly forward of its midpoint. The master ribs were formed in a "U" shape from many separate pieces of wood, with a curve set by a combination of geometry and tradition. Historians and archeologists are still trying to understand how shipwrights calculated the curves of ribs at various points in the hull, and it is by no means certain that Portuguese and Spanish shipwrights used the same methods. Each part of a rib had a precise name in Spanish usage, from the bottom of the curve (*varenga*) to the top (*genol*). The maximum breadth of the master rib would be the maximum breadth of the finished ship. The next step was to form and attach a smaller set of ribs called the *aletas* to the sternpost. Shaped more like a "Y" than a "U," it was set anywhere from one-half to two-thirds the distance from the keel to the top of the sternpost, at the same angle to the keel as the sternpost itself. A piece of wood running from one rib of the *aletas* to the other through the sternpost was called the yoke (*yugo*), marking the division between the hull and the superstructure.

With the first two sets of ribs in place, a traditional Spanish shipbuilder could have formed the rest of the ship, shaping the curve of the hull by relying on his experienced eye. He would attach four thick but narrow strips of wood (ribbands or *vagaras*) to the ribs at the stern, the master ribs and the stem, curving them between each two points by eye or with the aid of measuring devices. The highest strip of wood traditionally was fullest at two points, about one-fourth from either end. Because each master rib was forward of the middle of the ship, it was closer to the point in front (the *mura*) than to the point in back (the *cuadra*). A set of ribs was placed at these two points, with the bottom of both ribs farther above the keel than the master ribs, extending downward in a shortened "Y" shape. This would reverse the curve of the hull from convex to concave in the sections forward and aft of the master ribs. The first four sets of ribs determined the shape of the hull. The rest of the ribs would be set at even intervals to fill in the skeletal framework and attached to the keel by a strong joined beam called the keelson (*sobrequilla*).

During the sixteenth century, workers in Spanish royal shipyards were provided with tools, but other workers seem to have had their own. Each carpenter needed a hatchet, a saw, three sizes of auger, a claw hammer, a sledgehammer, and two chisels. Each caulker needed a mallet; five sizes of caulking iron (*hierro*); a centering chisel (*gubia*); a rave-hook (*magujo*); a sledgehammer; a claw hammer; an oakum remover (*saca-estopa*); and three sizes of auger. The *cabillador,* who inserted the dowels that attached the planking, required augers, caulking-augers, gimlets (*taladros*), and sledgehammers. The tow or oakum for caulking, as well as dowels, grease, and all other materials required, were traditionally provided by the shipbuilder.

The duplication of several tools for different sorts of workers suggests the overlapping skills of shipwrights. Carpenters were responsible for preparing the wood to size and shape and for erecting the framework. Once the frame was ready to be planked, the carpenters moved on to the internal bracing and the decks, and the caulkers and *cabilladores* worked on attaching the hull planking. Special care needed to be taken to match the sizes of the planks with the nails and dowels used to attach them. Different sizes of plank were used for different parts of the ship, and, just as in modern woodworking, if a fastener were too thick it would split the plank. The dowels or treenails (*cabillas*) used in Spanish shipbuilding could be made either of wood or of iron. The wooden sort were always round, but the iron ones traditionally used in Basque shipbuilding could be either round or square. First a hole was drilled, sized to hold the dowel tightly without splitting the wood. Then the planks were steamed or soaked so they could be bent to fit, clamped in place, and fastened.

Caulking the seams between the planks followed, using methods that had been proven over the centuries. Tow (*estopa*) or hemp fiber (*cáñamo*) was forced into the open seams and other joints, knotholes, and cracks, as well as around nail and dowel holes. All had to be made as watertight as possible. In Vizcaya in the Spanish Basque country, knotholes and other flaws were placed facing the inside of the ship, putting the strongest face of the wood toward the sea. A foreman (*capataz*) supervised each step in the caulking process, but especially before the caulking was coated with tar. Once tar had been added to the seams, it was nearly impossible to see flaws in the caulking. As a final step, the entire hull was coated with a mixture of tar and some sort of grease, lard, or tallow to make it stick to the hull. Lacking animal fats, one could use heated pitch or pine tar, or a mixture called *alquitrán* made of pitch, grease, resin, and oil. *Alquitrán* may even have been superior to animal fat. In traditional Spanish practice, a ship was pushed into the water as soon as the lower part of the hull was planked and caulked from the keel up beyond the water line. The rest of the planking was attached with the ship afloat. Despite the care taken in every part of the work, leakage remained a major problem on most large ships; that is why pumps were standard equipment. During the sixteenth century, a bulkhead parallel to the keel divided the hold into two sections. A separate pump was needed for each side of the bulkhead.

The masts, spars, rigging, and sails came last, their proportions dictated by the general proportions of the ship. Shipbuilding treatises at the end of the sixteenth century were the first to give mathematical formulae for the relationships between hull, masts, yards, and sails, but their proportions were undoubtedly based on traditional practice. The mainmast, largest of the three masts in a full rig, was placed near the center of the ship, passing down through both decks and resting on the floor. It was braced by tapered wedges at the openings in the decks and held upright by standing rigging running from the top of the mast to the bowsprit and by tackle attached to the hull. The foremast rested on the stempost, lashed to the bowsprit and steadied by wedges at the opening in the decks. The bowsprit was set at about a 45 degree angle to the lower deck, and rested upon it. The mizzen mast, set toward the aft end of the ship, passed through the upper deck and rested on the lower deck, braced and stayed like the others.

Although iron and most of the wood for the hulls and superstructures were readily available in Spain, many other supplies were imported during the sixteenth century. This included some of the tar and pitch used for waterproofing, and the long timbers for the masts, all of which traditionally came from the Baltic. Tall trees were evidently still available in Spanish forests, but they were too far from the coasts to be supplied economically. Some of the sail canvas and hempen cables were supplied from within Spain, but they too were supplemented by foreign imports as the need for shipping strained local resources. Early in the sixteenth century, the cable of Calatayud in the province of Aragón was prized for its strength and durability, just as Vizcayan oak was preferred for the hull and Prussian pine for the masts.

The array of rigging, tackle, and hardware of all sorts displayed a dizzying variety, with each item designed for a specific task, aiding human muscles in the difficult work of handling a ship under sail.

As the sail plan became more complex, so did the rigging required to manipulate it. By the end of the sixteenth century, a typical ship on the Indies run would have had two sails each on the foremast and mainmast, and one sail each on the bowsprit and mizzen. Shortly after 1600 a topsail would often be added above the spritsail, and a third sail (topgallant) often appeared on the foremast, the mainmast, and sometimes even the bowsprit.

The overall configurations of each ship would determine the arrangements of the hold and the sizes and quantities of equipment on board. Most large ships in the sixteenth and early seventeenth centuries had two decks above the floor, with the hold divided into compartments for storage. The castles fore and aft provided sleeping quarters for officers and important passengers, and shelter for a limited number of crew and soldiers. It would have been rare to have sufficient shelter for all on board, however. Many of the ordinary seamen, apprentices, pages, and soldiers would have had to find places for themselves and their belongings on the open deck.

The adornment on ships sailing for Spain was much more subdued than we might assume. Because the ships were usually covered with tar and *alquitrán*, they would have appeared almost black, with a few touches of color (especially red) and gilding standing out dramatically against the dark hull. The flat face of the stern would have carried a painted image of the ship's namesake, usually a saint or other holy figure. On a royal galleon in the seventeenth century, a gilded lion rampant served as a figurehead beneath the beak, and gilded gallery railings adorned the stern. Royal ships would also have carried at least one painted linen flag bearing the royal coat of arms, but the overall image these ships projected was still austere. Some of the decoration also had a practical purpose. The red bunting strung along the wales and the lookout platforms during battle not only provided cover for the men fighting but also camouflaged the inevitable bloodstains during battle.

It was in ships like these, built on the coasts of Iberia, that the people and goods of Portugal, Spain and their empires sailed into the Atlantic and around the globe. They were part of the long tradition that had produced the full-rigged ship of the fourteenth and fifteenth centuries, and that would continue to produce seaworthy vessels for the Iberian empires. The evolution of ship design during the period from the fourteenth to the seventeenth centuries, as rapid as it was in relative terms, seems impossibly slow compared to the technological changes witnessed in the twentieth century. Nonetheless, by proceeding slowly and incrementally, shipbuilding pre-

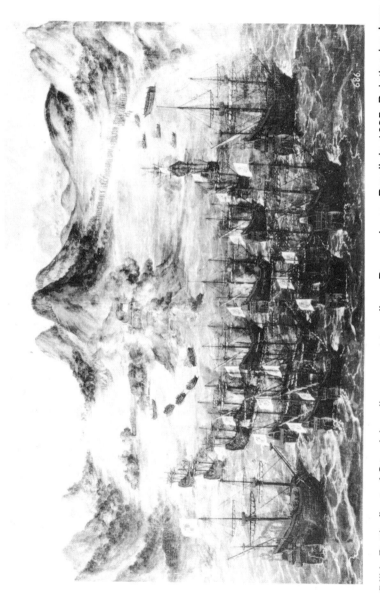

Figure XXIV. Battle fleet of Spanish galleons sent to relieve Pernambuco, Brazil, in 1635. Painting by Juan de la Corte. *Courtesy of the Museo Naval, Madrid.*

served the best of traditional designs and methods, changing only when change was warranted. Each nation developed versions of the sailing ship that best suited its needs. The Iberian powers and their empires were well served by a variety of large and small ships, but most characteristically for Portugal by the caravel, the carrack, and the galleon, and for Spain by the caravel, the *nao*, and the galleon during the Age of Discovery.

NOTES

1. T. C. Lethbridge, "Shipbuilding," in *A History of Technology,* ed. Charles Singer, et al., (Oxford: Oxford University Press, 1956) vol. II, p. 563.

2. Juan Escalante de Mendoza, *Itinerario de navegación de los mares y tierras occidentales* (Madrid, 1575), in *Disquisiciones náuticas,* ed. by Cesáreo Fernández Duro (Madrid: Sucesores de Rivadeneyra, 1876–81), 5:445.

Suggestions for Further Reading

Artiñano y de Galdácano, Gervasio. *La arquitecture naval española (en madera).* (Madrid, 1920).

Barker, Richard. "Shipshape for Discoveries and Return." *The Mariner's Mirror* 78 (November 1992): 433–47.

El buque en la armada española. (Madrid: Silex, 1981).

Cano, Tomé. *Arte para fabricar y aparejar naos.* (1611). Edited by Enrique Marco Dorta. (La Laguna, Canary Islands: Instituto de Estudios Canarios, 1964).

Casado Soto, Jose Luis. *Los barcos españoles del siglo XVI y la Gran Armada de 1588.* (Madrid: Editorial San Martín, 1988).

Edwards, Clinton R. "Design and Construction of Fifteenth-Century Iberian Ships: A Review," *The Mariner's Mirror* 78 (November 1992): 419–432.

Elbl, Martin, "The Portuguese Caravel and European Shipbuilding: Phases of Development and Diversity." *Revista da Universidade de Coimbra.* 33 (1985): 543—572.

Etayo Elizondo, Carlos. *Naos y carabelas de los descubrimientos y las naves de Colón.* (Pamplona, 1971).

García de Palacio, Diego. *Instrucción nautica para navegar (1587).* (Madrid: Cultura hispánica, 1944).

Goodale, Jerry. "Voyage of the Sarsfield *Niña.*" *Archeology* 45 (May–June 1992), pp. 42–43.

Gould, Alicia B. *Nueva lista documentada de los tripulantes de Colón en 1492.* (Madrid: Real Academia de la Historia, 1984).

Hasslöf, Olof. "Main Principles in the Technology of Ship-Building," in *Ships and Shipyards, Sailors and Fishermen.* Introduction to Maritime Ethnology. (Copenhagen: Copenhagen University Press, 1972).

Lane, Frederic Chapin. *Venetian Ships and Shipbuilders of the Renaissance.* (Baltimore: The Johns Hopkins University Press, 1934).

Lethbridge, T. C. "Shipbuilding." In *A History of Technology.* Edited by Charles Singer, et al. 7 vols. (Oxford: Oxford University Press, 1954–1978), 2: 563–588.

Lewis, Archibald and Timothy J. Runyan. *European Naval and Maritime History, 300–1500.* (Bloomington: Indiana University Press, 1985).

The Lore of Ships, rev. ed. (New York: Crescent, 1975), p. 18.

Lyon, Eugene. "15th Century Manuscript Yields First Look at Niña." *National Geographic* 170 (November 1986): 601–604.

Martínez-Hidalgo y Terán, José María. *Columbus's Ships.* Edited and translated by Howard I. Chapelle. (Barre, Mass.: Barre Publishing Co., 1966).

Morineau, Michel. *Jauges et méthodes de jauge anciennes et modernes.* (Paris: Armand Colin, 1966).

Phillips, Carla Rahn. *Six Galleons for the King of Spain. Imperial Defense in the Early Seventeenth Century.* (Baltimore, MD.: The Johns Hopkins University Press, 1986).

Phillips, Carla Rahn. "Size and Configurations of Spanish Ships in the Age of Discovery," *Proceedings of the First San Salvador Conference,* held Oct. 30–Nov. 3, 1986, comp. Donald T. Gerace (Ft. Lauderdale, Fla.: CCFL Bahamian Field Station, 1987.)

Rubin de Cervin, G. B. "The Age of Discovery." In *The Great Age of Sail,* ed. Joseph Jobé, trans. Michael Kelly. (Lausanne: Edita, 1967).

Rubio Serrano, José Luis. *Arquitectura de las naos y galeones de las flotas de Indias. I. (1492–1590). II. (1590–1690).* (Malaga: Ediciones Seyer, 1991).

Smith, Roger C. *Vanguard of Empire. Ships of Exploration in the Age of Columbus.* (Oxford and New York: Oxford University Press, 1993).

Unger, Richard W., ed. *Cogs, Caravels and Galleons: The Sailing Ship 1000-1650.* Conway's History of the Ship. (Annapolis: Naval Institute Press, 1994).

Unger, Richard W. *The Art of Medieval Technology: Images of Noah the Shipbuilder.* (New Brunswick, New Jersey: Rutgers University Press, 1991).

Unger, Richard. *The Ship in the Medieval Economy, 600–1600.* (Montreal: McGill-Queen's University Press, 1980).

Part IV
The World Encompassed

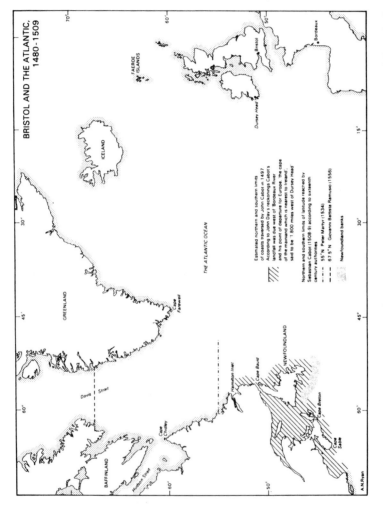

Figure XXV. Bristol and the Atlantic, 1480–1509. Originally drawn by A.N. Ryan for *Atlas of British Overseas Expansion* (London, 1991). *Reproduced by kind permission of the editor, Professor A.N. Porter, and the publisher, Routledge.*

14
BRISTOL, THE ATLANTIC AND NORTH AMERICA, 1480–1509
A. N. Ryan

Bristol in the fifteenth century was the outpost of English Atlantic endeavor. Bristol ships and foreign ships sailing to and from the port made it a focal point of oceanic trades which extended to Iceland in the north, to the Iberian peninsula in the south, to Madeira and possibly also to the Azores and Cape Verdes. The Iberian connections, especially those with Portugal, were a source of information about the Atlantic, and the islands thereof, some of it solidly based on Portuguese and Spanish, mainly Portuguese, observation and occupation, some resting upon the fragile foundations of legends, myths and alleged sightings in both the recent and remote past.

The expanding island world of the fifteenth-century Atlantic, including those islands awaiting discovery or rediscovery, was depicted upon contemporary marine charts. A feature of such charts as have survived is the small, circular Isle of Brasil situated to the west or southwest of Ireland at no great distance from the coast. It is indeed described by the English topographer, William Worcestre who died about 1481, as situated "in the western part of Ireland." By 1480 at the latest, however, there was already extant a new version of Brasil in a Catalan chart now in the Biblioteca Ambrosiana, Milan. Its creator's concept of the pre-Columbian north Atlantic is worthy of note. He displaced Iceland by moving it to the south of its real latitude and overlapped it with the latitude of Ireland. He preserved Brasil in its conventional position, though at a greater distance from the land. He also inserted a new Brasil: a much larger circular island far to the west of the small Brasil. The new Brasil was located to the north of the western edge of the Azores group and adjacent to a large rectangual island, named Illa Verde, which in shape strongly resembles conventional fifteenth-century deliniations of Antilia, the object of Portuguese searches and often called by them the Island of the Seven Cities, the alleged refuge of Christians who had fled the Iberian peninsula in the eighth century A.D. in the wake of the Moslem invasions. There are reasons to believe that the larger and more distant Brasil was the object of voyages of exploration from Bristol in the fifteenth century.

There was sufficient motivation for this activity. For much of the fifteenth century the Icelandic trade and the Islandic cod fishery were of interest to the English, not only at Bristol but also in the east coast ports. Some indication of Bristol's involvement in trade with Iceland may be gleaned from the royal licenses issued to trade there between 1439 and 1484, of which some 40% were for Bristol. Great numbers of vessels from all ports, however, sailed unlicensed. An- glo-Icelandic relations were not consistently amicable. There were allegations that young Icelanders were kidnapped by Englishmen and carried off to become servants or apprentices. As far as Bristol is concerned the only surviving evidence is that 48 or 49 Icelandic men and boys were household servants in the city in 1484. How and when they had got there we do not know, whether voluntarily or in- voluntarily. They were not necessarily doomed to remain in service throughout their lives. At least one of those listed in 1484, William Yslond, was by 1492 a naturalized Bristol merchant.

Whatever may have been the ups and downs of Anglo-Icelandic re- lations, Iceland was a reliable market for English cloth and a source of access to a relatively secure cod fishery during the greater part of the fifteenth century. This period of stability came to an end in the 1460s when the kings of Denmark, rulers of Iceland, began a shift of policy in favor of the Hanseatic League, a vigorous mercantile con- federation of north-German cites and ports which was dedicated to the monopolization of trade between the Eastland and Western Eu- rope via the Baltic and North Seas. Competition between the Eng- lish and the Hanseatic League gave rise to intermittent fighting. The situation further deteriorated following the appointment as governor of Iceland in 1478 of Diddrik Pining, a German, who waged systematic war against the English and denied them access to the ports they were wont to frequent. When King Henry VII of England visited Bristol in 1486, he was informed of the commercial depres- sion arising out of the enfeebled condition of trade with Iceland.

Already by the date of the king's visit, pioneers of Bristol and their associates from London were attempting to counter the depression by extending the established trade with the Iberian peninsula to the Atlantic islands and by discovering in the Atlantic fishing grounds free of Hanseatic competition. The seamen of Bristol, hardened by their experience in the Icelandic trade and fishery had no reason either to fear the Atlantic or to doubt their ability to find their way around it. It is true that as navigators they were unfamiliar with the new astronomical aids to navigation and the mathematical knowledge which underpinned them; but they were skilful pilots able to conduct a ship from place to place through the reasoned application of knowledge, acquired and inherited, of the seas through which they sailed and the ports at which they called.

One hundred years earlier Geoffrey Chaucer had written a portrait in verse of a man such as they: a ship's master from Dartmouth who joined the pilgrims gathered at Southwark for the journey to the shrine of St. Thomas at Canterbury. He is praised for his skill in calculating the tides and currents and the dangers likely to be encountered on the voyage and for his knowledge of the phases of the moon. He was said to know all the harbors from Gotland in the Baltic Sea to Cape Finisterre on the northwest corner of the Iberian peninsula, as well as all the creeks in Brittany and Spain. In his reckonings, "he had such dispatch that none from Hull to Carthage was his match."

In braving the northern Atlantic to get to Iceland and back fifteenth-century English seamen were above all dependent, like Chaucer's sea captain, upon the senses, particularly those of sight and hearing, and upon their ability to interpret as a guide to their whereabouts a wealth of knowledge and experience of the depth, when available, of the water, the color of the water, the prevailing wind, currents and tides and the lie of the land when in sight of it. Their principal instrument was the magnetic compass to control the course steered. The compass could be supplemented by observation with the naked eye in northern latitudes of the Pole Star as a guide to the heading of the ship: a method of navigation which pre-dated the compass and had been employed since times immemorial. A second, and indeed older, instrument was the lead line for sounding in shallower waters the depth of the sea and nature of its bottom: information which could yield an indication of the position of the ship and serve also as a warning of the proximity of dangerous shoaling. This skilled craft was not studied in academies or learned from books. It was passed down the generations by word of mouth and perfected, by those who survived, in the hard school of experience at sea. The skills it fostered were not outdated by the rise, later in England than in Iberia, of celestial navigation; they survived as essential ingredients of the art and practice of navigation.

To reach Iceland from the British Isles seamen had to make good a northwesterly track. To succeed in so doing they needed fair winds. Oceanic wind systems were learned by trial and error. Mastery over the new oceanic routes of the Age of Discovery was achieved through the discovery of the wind systems. The seamen of England were as much aware of this as were those of Portugal and Spain. They were the first to master the north Atlantic, if we leave aside the very different island-hopping techniques which had brought the Vikings to North America via Shetland, the Faeroes, Iceland and Greenland in the tenth century A.D. The prevailing Atlantic winds in the latitudes of the British Isles blew from the west and did not favor therefore ventures into the ocean. There was no northeast trade wind which was to waft Columbus in 33 days from the Canary Islands to his transatlantic landfall in 1492. However, during March, April, May and early June there were frequent northeasterly winds which enabled English seamen to enter the Icelandic trade and fishery and to progress to westward voyages into the Atlantic. Moreover, given the prevalence of westerlies, except during the short season which followed the vernal equinox, seamen could challenge the ocean in the confident hope of picking up a favorable wind for the return voyage.

Oceanic navigation was inconceivable without a reliable ship. The ships which sailed out of Bristol into the Atlantic were by modern standards ludicrously small. The only extant contemporary record of a voyage in 1480 in search of Brasil gives the size of the ship as 80 tons. Contemporary evidence concerning the voyage of the *Trinity* and the *George* in 1481 describes each one of them as "a ship or balinger." The term balinger eludes precise definition. It was applied to small and medium sized sailing ships of 30 to 120 tons which might be furnished with auxiliary oars. The famous *Matthew,* on board which John Cabot made a successful two-way crossing of the Atlantic in 1497, is reckoned to have been a three-masted ship of 60 tons manned by about 20 men. We must not, however, get the size of these ships out of proportion. As late as 1582 a government investigation into the availability for war service of suitable merchantmen revealed only two hundred and fifty ships of 80 tons or more and less than twenty of more than 200 tons in the entire English mercantile marine. Francis Drake's *Golden Hind,* formerly the *Pelican,* in which he circumnavigated the world during 1577–80 was of 150 tons. The exploits of English, French, Basque, Spanish and Portuguese fisherman in crossing the Atlantic to the Newfoundland Banks from the beginning of the sixteenth century in vessels which ranged from 20 to 80 tons are a testament to their basic seaworthiness.

However, in writing about early transoceanic navigation there is no room of complacency. Despite the improvements achieved in strengthening masts and hulls during the fifteenth century, these small wooden ships were fragile when pitted against the force of the winds and waves which overwhelmed so many of them. We need look no further than Bristol for an instance of disaster. In 1498 John Cabot sailed with the object of extending his discoveries of the previous year. Of the five ships under his command four seem to have perished. The only reported survivor was said to have "made land in Ireland in a great storm with the ship badly damaged."

A crucial technical advance still has to be considered. Extended voyages to the west in the latitudes of the British Isles were out of reach a century earlier owing to the limitations imposed by the masts and sails of English ships. Most small English ships, and most English ships were small, had a single main mast which supported a square sail. A ship so rigged could run only before a following wind, a limitation which could mean spells of immobilization. Additions to the masts and square sails could not solve the problem. A more significant development was the adoption by the Portuguese from the Arabs of the lateen sail—a triangular fore-and-aft sail—for use on the mizzenmast. This variation on the traditional square-sail rig of the lateen increased considerably, as the Portuguese demonstrated on their voyages in African waters, the sailing power and maneuverability of the vessels; for the lateen, unlike the square sail, released ships from total dependence upon following winds. By the later fifteenth century the lateen had spread to northern Europe and three masted vessels, such as is conjectured the *Matthew* of Bristol, hoisted the lateen at the stern of the ship.

The evidence available for the study of the Bristol voyages in the Atlantic in the late fifteenth and early sixteenth centuries is sparse and difficult to interpret. There are no contemporary logs or journals; no reports or letters written by participants; no surviving maps or charts drafted in their hands. The recovery of the evidence itself has been a slow business. Key English material relating to the voyage of 1481 from Bristol became available only in the early 1930s. The existence of a vital document relating to John Cabot's voyage of 1497 was unknown until the 1950s. Its unexpected discovery at Simancas by Dr. L. A. Vigneras first published by him in Spanish in the *Hispanic American Historical Review* (1956) and in English translation as "The Cape Breton Landfall 1494 or 1497" in the *Canadian Historical Review* (1957) offers grounds for hope that the account is not yet closed and that more precious evidence may yet come to light. In the meantime we must operate within the boundaries set by what we have. Legitimate speculation is valid, but we must not present ideas arising therefrom as though they were established fact.

Our first encounter with a voyage of Atlantic exploration from Bristol is a passage from the *Itinerario* of William Worcestre who claimed relationship with the Bristol merchant and shipowner John Jay. Recorded therein is a voyage by a ship of Jay, commanded by a sea captain named Lloyd, for "the Island of Brasyle on the west part of Ireland" from which the vessel and its crew returned safely after nine weeks at sea. Worcestre reports that they did not find the island, "but had been turned back by storms at sea." This rings true, even if for "storms" we read "adverse winds"; for by sailing into the Atlantic as late as July, Lloyd must have encountered the opposing westerlies.

Two authentic legal document of 1481 and 1483, the first discovered by W. E. C. Harrison in the Public Record Office in 1930, the second, in the same office by D. B. Quinn in 1931, testify to a voyage by the "ships or balingers" *Trinity* and *George* of Bristol in 1481 not for purposes of trade but "to serch and fynde a certain Isle called the Isle of Brasil." Neither document mentions the outcome of the voyage; nor has been there found in contemporary English records any reference to further voyages in search of Brasil during the 1480s.

For information about the activities of Bristol ships in the Atlantic in the interval between the voyage of 1481 and the voyage of John Cabot in 1497 we are dependent upon Pedro de Ayala, a Spanish diplomat in London. In a letter to his sovereigns, dated 1498, he reported that "for the last seven years the people of Bristol have equipped two, three [and] four caravels to go in search of the Island of Brasil and the Seven Cities according to the fancy of this Genoese." Although Ayala's information may not have been entirely reliable, it points to Bristolian voyages in the Atlantic in the years leading up to 1497 and implies that "this Genoese," John Cabot, was attracted to Bristol because he was aware of this activity and of Bristolian interest in the Isle of Brasil.

The precise identity of this isle remains uncertain. We have seen that it was a feature of many charts in the fourteenth and fifteenth centuries and that in the later fifteenth century a second, larger Brasil, situated much farther from Ireland to the west, had made its appearance. The concept of Brasil had nothing to do with Brazil of the Portuguese empire in Latin America. The name Brasil—the Isle of the Blessed—was derived from Irish visions, some of them mythological enough, of the Atlantic. We may be sure, however, that Thomas Croft, a Bristol customs official who was at the center of the case from which the legal documents of 1481 and 1483 emanate, and his associates were not spending money in a search for the Aran Islands off County Galway or the Blasket Islands off County Kerry, both of which groups can be seen from the mainland. Their Brasil was an island in the western Atlantic. Their search was inspired, not by contemporary Italian views, such as those of Columbus, of the Atlantic or Western Ocean as a gateway to Asia, but as a perceived necessity to ease economic pressures arising out of intensifying competition in the fishing grounds off Iceland through the discovery of new fishing grounds in the remoter west. The documents of 1481 and 1483 both stress the lading of salt on board the *Trinity* and *George* which can only mean that fishing was an object of the voyage. We have to allow for the probability that the English had obtained fragments of information from Icelandic and Azorean sources of the existence of fisheries.

A new phase in the history of exploration from Bristol opened with the arrival there of John Cabot which coincided, if we put our trust in Ayala, with intensive Atlantic activity. The evidence available about him indicates that he was Genoese by birth and Venetian by naturalization, that he was the same man as "Joan Caboto Montecalunya, the Venetian" who attempted to enter the service of Ferdinand of Aragan in 1492 as a harbor engineer at Valencia, having already been in Spain for two years, and that he peddled without success in the Iberian peninsula a project identical with that of Christopher Columbus. His failure to win acceptance was followed about 1494 by emigration to England. He arrived there equipped to graft on to the native English tradition of voyages in search of the isle of Brasil and the waters around it the Genoese vision of a westward passage to Asia.

The Letters Patent granted to Cabot and his young sons by Henry VII in March 1496 do not of course acknowledge this in as many words. They authorized him at his own proper costs and charges "to find, discover and investigate whatsoever islands, countries, regions or provinces of heathens and infidels, in whatsoever part of the world placed, which before this time were unknown to all Christians . . . We have given licence to set up our aforesaid banners and ensigns in any town, city, castle, island or mainland whatsoever, newly found by them." Of course it makes no sense to bring Cabot to England in a state of ignorance of the Bristol voyages. He may well have known more than we do about an Atlantic discovery underlying the

apparent intensification of effort in the 1490s noted by Ayala. Henry
VII, who had had earlier dealings with Bartholomew Columbus and
understood something of what was at stake, was also sufficiently
well informed to licence the new venture without risking any public
money in its support.

John Cabot made one successful return transatlantic voyage on
board the Bristol ship *Matthew* between late May and 6 August
1497, after having been forced to turn back in 1496. Were we dependent upon Cabot for an account of what he had set out to do and
what he had done, or at least, what he thought he had done, we
would be at a loss. As with the voyages of 1480 and 1481 we have
nothing which emanates directly from the participants. His claims,
however, must have impressed the king, for we find in the Household Books an item, dated 10/11 August, of a grant of £10:00 "to hym
that found the new Isle," followed by the grant of an annuity of
£20:00 on 13 December 1497.

Fortunately we are able to savor the Italian context from our
knowledge of communications between London, Venice and Milan.
A Venetian merchant Lorenzo Pasqualigo reported home on 23 August that "this Venetian of ours" claimed to have discovered "mainland 700 leagues away which is the country of the Grand Khan." In
the archives of the Duchy of Milan there is a note of news, dated 24
August, from London that a Venetian "has found two very large and
fertile new islands. He has also discovered the Seven Cities, 400
leagues from England on the western passage." Finally Raimondo
de Soncino, who had taken up residence as Milanese ambassador towards the end of August, reported on 18 December that "his Majesty
has gained a part of Asia, without a stroke of the sword."

One must question, however, any assumption that Cabot and his
English associates shared a common perception of the voyage; for
Soncino intimates some clash of aspirations between the Mediterranean navigator and the English pioneers. He reported that the
seas were swimming with fish which gave great satisfaction to the
English because they were thereby liberated from dependence upon
the Icelandic fishery. "But," he continued, "Messer Zoane has his
mind set upon even greater things, because he proposes to keep
along the coast from the place at which he landed, more and more
towards the east, until he reaches an island called Cipango situated
in the equinoctial region, where he believes all the spices of the
world have their origin, as well as the jewels." The hint that the English did not share the Mediterranean dream that the wealth of Asia
was within their grasp seems to be supported by events. Despite

Italian forecasts of a large scale expedition, generously backed by the king, to follow up the discovery, the expedition of 1498 was a relatively modest affair in which neither Henry VII nor English merchants invested extravagantly. Of this expedition all we know is that one ship out of five returned storm-beaten to Ireland and that John Cabot was never seen again.

Why this English skepticism, if that is what it was. Was it that the islanders were so ignorant of the geographical learning of Renaissance Italy that they could not comprehend, even remotely, Cabot's claim? Or can it be that they possessed, as a result of their own voyages, a grater experimental knowledge, than did the man from the Mediterranean world, of the Northwest Atlantic Ocean and its adjacent coasts: a knowledge which made it difficult for them to accept unreservedly an identification between those coasts and Asia? In an area full of doubts and confusions, the second explanation seems the more probable.

Further enlightenment may be found in the documentary discovery of L. A. Vigneras at Simancas, first published in 1956. This is known as the John Day Letter, John Day, also known as Hugh Say, was an English merchant with strong Castilian commercial and social connections. The letter addressed in late 1497 or early 1498 to the Lord Grand Admiral who was either the Grand Admiral of Castile or, perhaps more probably, the "Almirante Mayor," Christopher Columbus, can be seen from internal evidence to have been part of a series. It is important as the only account by a contemporary Englishman of the Cabot voyage which has so far come to light. From Day we learn that Cabot sailed from Bristol in May and being favored by an east-northeast wind made a transatlantic landfall, which we cannot identify, after 35 days at sea. According to Day's reckonings. Cabot spent about a month exploring the coast between "the southernmost part of the Island of the Seven Cities, said to be in the same latitude as the mouth of the Garonne River on the west coast of France" and "the cape nearest to Ireland," said to be in the same latitude as Dursey Head, Co. Kerry, Ireland and 1,800 miles distant from it. Making some allowance for error in Cabot's latitudinal calculations, we can set the outer limits of the coast surveyed as lying between Cape Sable to the south and Hamilton Inlet to the north. In the light of the evidence available this is a rational, though provisional, estimate.

Like the Italians resident in London Day reported plans for a large expedition, much larger than that which actually sailed, in 1498. Unlike them, he makes no mention of Cabot's claims to have reached Asia. He gives not the slightest hint of any inclinations on his own part to identify the "said land" with Asia. But he does state in a matter of fact way that the "cape of the said land was found and discovered in the past by the men from Bristol who found Brasil as your Lordship well knows. It was called the Island of Brasil, and it is assumed and believed to be the mainland that the men from Bristol found." This statement has given rise to legitimate speculation concerning the possibility of a pre-Cabotian, even a pre-Columbian, English discovery of North America.

Historians are haunted by the expression "in the past" [*en otros tiempos*]. Does it refer to the flurry of activity in the 1490s noted by Ayala, to some unrecorded voyage of the 1480s, to the voyage of 1481 or to a voyage of which no trace remains of an earlier date again? In the light of the evidence available none of these options regarding an earlier Bristolian discovery can be ruled out. The same evidence, however, like much historical evidence, created its own problems. Why, for example, if Day is correct in stating that the cape of the said land was found and discovered in the past by the men from Bristol was Cabot described in the grant of £10:00 as "hym that found the new Isle"? The term "new Isle," or variations upon it, is also used four times in the Household Books between 17 March and 11 April 1498 during preparations for the second Cabot expedition.

Samuel Eliot Morison, author of a famous biography of Christopher Columbus and historian of the European discovery of America, dismissed out of hand the idea of a pre-Cabotian transatlantic landfall, arguing that Henry VII would never have bestowed financial rewards upon Cabot for finding "the new Isle," if all he had done was to confirm an earlier Bristol discovery. But the evidence, taken in its totality, of the voyages of 1480 to 1497 is remarkably resistant to such hammer blows. The problems arising therefrom cannot be solved by denying in effect that they exist. Some attempt must be made to see whether Day's assertion of an earlier discovery can be reconciled with Henry VII's reaction to the 1497 discovery.

A provisional solution proposed by David B. Quinn, an internationally recognized authority on the history of the English and North America in pre-colonial and early colonial times, merits attention. Quinn's hypothesis is that the Bristolians found their Brasil between 1481 and 1491 and also found, as they had clearly hoped in 1481 they would find, a great fishery in the waters around it. He argues that they concentrated upon the exploitation of the fishery to the neglect of exploration and discovery, Brasil being primarily "a landmark for the fishing grounds" of the Grand Banks. It may well be that the annual departures in search of Brasil, mentioned by Ayala, were annual departures on fishing expeditions. Despite the avoidance of publicity, reports of an alleged discovery reached Spain where they were picked up by Cabot who saw in them an opportunity to promote his version of a voyage to Asia, hence his emigration to England. Cabot added a new dimension to English Atlantic endeavor. By surveying the coasts, by calculating through the use of celestial aids to navigation their latitude and by identifying, however erroneously, the land with Asia, Cabot achieved recognition as the discoverer. Although unprovable, this hypothesis makes sense of the limited facts at our disposal without doing violence to the evidence available.

In 1992 the attention of historians in Britain was directed by Dr. J. Witherington of the University of Lancaster to an article, "The Passing of King Arthur to the Island of Brasil in a Fifteenth-century Spanish Version of the Post-Vulgate *Roman de Graal*" in *Romania* (1971) by Harvey L. Sharrer. The "Spanish version" is that of an Arthurian text found in *Libro de las bienandanzas e fortunas,* a compendium of general and local historical lore, written between 1471 and 1476 by Lope Garcia de Salazar and preserved in a 1492 copy made by Cristobal de Mieres in the Academia de Historia in Madrid. A feature of the text is that Garcia de Salazar, who died in 1476, altered the traditional story of Arthur's passing to Avalon by substituting for Avalon the enchanted Isle of Brasil: enchanted, according to him, because the English reported that the island could be found only if sighted by the ship before it caught sight of the ship. Garcia de Salazar defended his belief in the existence of Brasil, as the last resting place of King Arthur, by reference to fourteenth- and fifteenth-century charts and reinforces his belief by reporting a visit there by a ship from Bristol.

He supplied circumstantial detail, recalling how the crew landed and took on board a load of firewood which on return to Bristol was recognized to be brasilwood and sold at a profit. However, attempts to rediscover the island in a quest of further profit were fruitless. The use by a fifteenth-century Basque antiquarian of a Bristol discovery of Brazil as a means of bolstering his version of Arthurian legend require investigation. This might involve extensive literary research into the circumstances in which the text was copied and into the possibility of interpolation. The use of the term "brazilwood" is awkward, since it seems to have been first used in 1500 when Yanez Pinzón was permitted by the crown to sell a quantity thereof after a voyage along the north coast of South America. The authenticity of the text and the validity of the circumstantial story seem to be in need of further testing. It is incredible that a ship from Bristol should have reached the area where brazilwood grows and returned safely at some date like the early 1470s. There is no need to be entirely negative. The story may reflect a garbled version of talk in the northern ports of Spain about the activity of Bristol vessels in the Atlantic. If this be so, we may have to push back by, perhaps, a decade from 1480 the beginning of the Bristolian enterprises in search of an Atlantic island or islands.

After 1498 any lingering idea that John Cabot had reached Asia was abandoned in England. By 1501–2 the English were talking of "the newe founde launde" and rewards were made by the king for services rendered there, as for example to "men of bristol that have bene in the new founde launde" (September 1502). A mariner "that brought haukes" was rewarded with ten shillings' [50 n.p.] and "an other that brought an Egle" with six shillings and eight pence' [33 n.p.].

A series of transatlantic voyages for purposes of trade, fishing and, possibly, further exploration of the area took place during 1501–5 under letters patent granted by Henry VII to syndicates of Bristol merchants with Azorean associates: an association which confirms that some Azoreans with an interest in the northwest Atlantic, perceived that they might win advantages for themselves through collaboration with Bristol. The Portuguese crown on the other hand viewed Bristol as a competitor in an area which it could hope, particularly following delineation of the so-called English coasts on the Juan de la Cosa world map of 1501, lay within its own demarcation under the terms of the treaty of Tordesillas with Spain of 1494. These aspirations prompted the tragic voyages of 1500–2 of the Corte-Real family of Terceira, two of whom Gaspar and Miguel, like John Cabot before them, were never seen again.

Of the English voyages made to North America under the charters of Henry VII little is known. It seems certain that English participation in the Newfoundland fishery was continuous; but for the commercial side of things the evidence is unrevealing, indicating only the import of novelty items such as those mentioned above and wild cats and popinjays. Dealings with the inhabitants of America are substantiated by a reference to the presence at the English court of two Amerindians, dressed in English clothes, in 1504. They had either been kidnapped or cajoled on board ship. In 1497 John Cabot had, according to John Day, no direct dealings with the inhabitants. He and a party landed, observed signs of human activity, obtained fresh water and retired without delay to the ship. Efforts to establish a profitable trade failed. The Company of Adventurers to the New Found Land collapsed, it would seem, in some acrimony. The last documented reference to it is dated 1506. Thus ended the first phase of English attempts to establish relations with the New World.

Sebastian Cabot, eldest son of John, was meanwhile performing shadowy service "in and about the fynding of the Newe founde landes" for which he was awarded a pension of £10:00 per annum in 1505. There is no documentation of what these services were. The only records of them and other services during the reign of Henry VII, on whose death in 1509 the pension expired, consist of legal documents appertaining to its payments during 1507–9 from which we can only conclude that Sebastian was out of the country for some of the time.

Sebastian can be seen as the representative of the Cabot interest in Bristol exploration and as an advocate of a renewal of his father's ambition to pass to Asia by way of the Atlantic. The idea that the 1497 landfall was the land of Grand Khan being no longer tenable, Sebastian's only hope of success was to sail beyond the new found land. This comes to light in the inadequately documented voyage of 1508–9 for knowledge of which we are dependent upon Sebastian himself. Sebastian's contribution to our knowledge does not take the form of contemporary written evidence.

He speaks to us largely through the sixteenth-century historians, Peter Martyr, author of *De Orbe Novo Decades* (1516) which was translated into English in 1555 by Richard Eden, and by Giovanni Battista Ramusio, author of *Navigationi et Vaiggi* (1556). If Sebastian Cabot's achievement in 1508–9 is unclear, it is because he, the chief witness, is unclear. In Martyr's version the area explored was the "Baccallaos because in the adjacent sea he found so great a quantity of a certain kind of great fish like tunnies." In Martyr's second version of 1534, it is specifically stated on the authority of Sebastian that he reached a latitude of 55°N., the sea bring full of large masses of ice. Ramusio, on the other hand, not only reported that Sebastian reached 67 1/2 degrees under our pole' but that "he firmly believed that by that way he could pass to Eastern Cathay." Given the discrepancies all we can be sure of is that Sebastian Cabot crowned his career in England, Spain and back in England by convincing many people in England and abroad that he had discovered the entry to a navigable passage around the new land to Asia. He thus created the concept of the Northwest Passage, in some respects the most enduring aspects of the Cabot family's legacy to the English.

Given the evidence available it is impossible to reach a definitive account of the Bristol voyages and the Bristol discoveries. Historians are faced again and again with evidence which points towards certain conclusions and then reveals itself as incapable of sustaining the burden of proof. It offers leads which they are invited to follow only to find that the leads peter out. A sound conclusion is that the enterprises launched from Bristol showed that late fifteenth-century English seamen could master the North Atlantic despite their rudimentary navigational skills, that they revealed North America to the world, whether before or after 1497 is currently unknowable, and that they opened an international industrial zone in the waters off Newfoundland where, as Soncino put it, the sea was swarming with fish.

SUGGESTIONS FOR FURTHER READING

Published Contemporary Sources

Quinn, D. B. (ed.). *New American World: A Documentary History of North America to 1612,* 5 vols. (New York, 1979), vol. I, chapters 9–12.

Williamson, J. A. (ed.). *The Cabot Voyages and Bristol Discovery under Henry VII with "The Cartography of the Voyages" by R. A. Skelton,* Hakluyt Society, 2nd series, vol. 120 (Cambridge, 1962).

Note that Richard Hakluyt, *The Principal Navigations, Voiages and Discoveries of the English Nation,* 3 vols. (London, 1598–1600), modern edition 12 vols. (Glasgow, 1903–5), contains contemporary accounts of sixteenth-century oceanic voyages by European seamen, most of them English.

Later Works

Andrews, K. R. *Trade, Plunder and Settlement: Maritime Enterprise and the Genesis of the British Empire, 1480–1630.* (Cambridge, 1984), chapter 1.

Cumming, W. P., D. B. Quinn, R. A. Skelton, *The Discovery of North America.* (London, 1971).

McGrath, P. "Bristol and America, 1480–1631," K. R. Andrews, N. P. Canny, P. E. H. Hair (eds.), *The Westward Enterprise* (Liverpool, 1978).

Morison, S. E. *The European Discovery of America: The Northern Voyages, A.D. 500–1600.* (New York and Oxford, 1971), chapters VI and VII.

Quinn, D. B. *England and the Discovery of America, 1481–1620.* (New York, 1974), chapters 1–5, including, with updated notes, "The Argument for the English Discovery of America between 1480 and 1494," from *The Geographical Journal,* vol. 127 (1961).

Quinn, D. B. *North America from Earliest Discovery to First Settlements: The Norse Voyages to 1612.* (New York, 1977), chapters 3–5.

Quinn, D. B. *Sebastian Cabot and Bristol Exploration,* Bristol branch of the Historical Association, 2nd revised edn. (Bristol, 1992).

Ruddock, A. A. "John Day of Bristol and the English Voyages across the Atlantic before 1497." *The Geographical Journal,* vol. 132 (1966).

Ruddock, A. A. "The Reputation of Sebastian Cabot," *Bulletin of the Institute of Historical Research,* vol. 47 (1974).

Sacks, D. H. *The Widening Gate: Bristol and the Atlantic Economy, 1450–1700.* (Berkeley and Oxford, 1991).

Sharrer, H. L. "The Passing of King Arthur to the Island of Brasil in a Fifteenth-Century Spanish Version of the Post-Vulgate *Roman de Graal,*" *Romania* (1971).

Vigneras, L. A. "New Light on the 1497 Cabot Voyage of America," *Hispanic-American Historical Review,* vol. 36 (1956).

Vigneras, L. A. "The Cape Breton Landfall: 1494 or 1497? Note on a Letter by John Day," *Canadian Historical Review,* vol. 38 (1957).

15

THE NEW WORLD AND ASIA, 1492–1606

A. N. Ryan

The Europeans who found America, coming as they did from a world without America, had no means of knowing what America was. After his return to Seville at the end of March 1493 from the first transatlantic voyage Christopher Columbus was addressed by the sovereigns of Castile and Aragon as "Admiral of the Ocean Sea, Viceroy and Governor of the Islands that he has discovered in the Indies." They thus accepted his claim to have succeeded in the "Enterprize of the Indies" without either defining what they understood by Indies or making any specific reference to Asia. The sovereigns and their advisers recognized the discovery as important and looked forward to its successful exploitation. They were also acutely aware of disagreements between geographical experts over the size of the globe and the distance between western Europe and east coast of Asia: the same disagreements which had played so significant a part during the negotiations which preceded the voyage of 1492.

Pietro Martire d'Anghiera, known to the English-speaking world as Peter Martyr, who was to become the first historian of the discoveries, adopted from the beginning a cautious approach. In a private letter of May 1493 he wrote that a few days ago "there returned from the Western Antipodes a certain Cristoforus Colonus, a Ligurian, who, because they thought what he said was fabulous, only got three ships from my sovereigns and those with difficulty." He continued by remarking that he had brought back proofs of special things, including gold. The term "Western Antipodes" was chosen by Martyr to distinguish between them and Asia, for later in the year he wrote that Columbus had sailed to the Western Antipodes, claimed to have sailed as far as the Indian coast and had discovered several islands. "These," he continued, "they think to be those whereof mention is made by cosmographers as lying beyond the

Western Ocean and adjacent to India. I do not wholly deny this, although the size of the globe suggests otherwise, for there are not wanting those who think the Indian coast to be but a short distance from the end of Spain."

Peter Marty's agnosticism had its adherents in both the Iberian peninsula and Italy, the countries where the news naturally attracted most attention in 1493. Dogmatism was also influential. There were those who identified the Indies, as Columbus seems to have done, with islands contiguous to some part of Asia: India, Cathay, China. Again there were those who rejected this identification out of hand on the ground that the size of the world was such that no ship could have sailed from the Canaries to Asia in 33 days. For such critics of Columbus the "Indies" were but an extension to the island world, real and fabled, of the fifteenth-century Atlantic Ocean. John II of Portugal, who, given the Portuguese interest in the unfolding of an ocean route to Asia around the southern extremity of Africa, had little choice in the matter, put his faith in the belief that the islands revealed by Columbus were, like the fabled Antillia, at best no more than a potential staging post on an immeasurably long haul to Asia. In the then state of knowledge, he could not envisage the emergence of a seemingly endless land mass barring the way to the Spaniards.

Whatever one thought of Columbus; whatever one thought of his "indies," their proximity to or distance from the "lands of the spices," the vital interests of the sovereigns of Spain and Portugal were at stake. Behind the festivities at Barcelona, where Columbus was honored and feted, the problem gnawed away at Ferdinand and Isabella as they made plans to assert their claims to priority of discovery over the Portuguese, as across the border it also gnawed away at João II. Isabella of Castile could hardly conceal her anxiety to get Columbus off to sea again at the head of a much more imposing expedition that that of 1492 and to obtain from him a chart which might serve to substantiate the Spanish claims.

During 1493 Spain and Portugal were active through their diplomats in Rome in quests for papal bulls which might register a demarcation satisfactory to their respective national interests. This badgering of Pope Alexander VI of the Spanish Borgia family (in whom the Portuguese understandably did not place unbounded confidence) was aimed by both powers at the acquisition of moral authority rather than legal right which the pope could not dispense. Both parties knew this and were already engaged in negotiations to assert their rights by priority of discovery against non-Iberian powers and to achieve a legal demarcation between their respective spheres of discovery. The negotiations led in 1494 to the treaty of Tordesillas, the principle clause of which was that the line of demarcation ran longitudinally across the world in the western hemisphere 370 leagues west of the Cape Verde Islands. The Spanish demarcation lay to the west of the agreed meridian; the Portuguese, who had by this time had rounded the Cape of Good Hope, but not yet crossed the Indian Ocean, to the east of it. The race to be first to Asia was on.

The treaty of Tordesillas reflected the ignorance and uncertainty which prevailed in 1494 concerning the Columbian discovery, particularly the geographical relationship between the islands recently unveiled and the Asia of Columbus's dreams and ambitions. It was for this reason that the negotiators, although dealing with partition of a sphere, confined themselves to the western hemisphere, declining to nominate a complementary meridian in the eastern hemisphere. Against this background both parties sought to make progress in the promotion of their actual and potential discoveries. For Spaniards, acting through Columbus himself and the Andalusian seamen sent out by the crown after 1499 to remedy the failure to translate into reality his claims to have found outlying islands of Asia, it was a baffling experience. As they pushed westwards and southwards from the first discoveries in the Caribbean, they encountered not open ocean, not even ocean littered with yet more islands, but an unbroken *tierra firme*. By the early sixteenth century the barrier to further advance extended from Honduras to the mouth of the Amazon and beyond. This was indeed a mysterious New World which rendered suspect the geographical assumptions upon which was based Martin Behaim's globe of 1492 with its promise of an easy passage to Asia, situated approximately in the longitudes of our America.

Some light was thrown on the problem by the Spanish adventurer, Vasco Núñez de Balboa, who, after forcing his way across the Isthmus of Panama became in September 1513 the first European to sight from America the Pacific Ocean, or as he called it the "Great South Sea." He automatically made the far reaching claim that all the lands and islands therein belonged to Spain.

The Portuguese meanwhile, holding by treaty the right to exploit the only known ocean route to the real Indies—that around the Cape of Good Hope—were making rapid strides. Vasco da Gama had crossed the Indian Ocean and reached Cochin in 1498. They proceeded to establish their power in the Indian Ocean through the creation, often with the aid of indigenous allies, of a network of naval bases. In the context, however, of the Tordesillas demarcation the most significant acquisition was that of Malacca by Afonso de Albuquerque in August 1511. Situated on the strait of the same name Malacca occupied a commercially strategic position on one of the world's great trading highways which linked the Indian Ocean with the South China Sea and the western fringe of the Pacific Ocean. It was also so situated as to enable shipping to exploit throughout the year the monsoon or seasonal wind system.

The seizure of Malacca was inspired by the Portuguese ambition to gain access to the Spice Islands proper, particularly those of the Moluccas which produced not only pepper but also cloves, nutmeg and mace. The Portuguese advance towards the Pacific Ocean, the dimensions of which could not at this time be calculated by Europeans, raised difficult questions, shelved by the negotiators in 1494, concerning the demarcation in the eastern hemisphere. To these questions there were no ready-made answers. Nobody knew the distance between the leading edge of Portuguese expansion and the New World, though the Portuguese were, officially at least, confident that, were a longitudinal meridian complementary to that in the Atlantic drawn across the Pacific, the Spice Islands would be found within their demarcation. Both sides considered themselves legally entitled to expand within their respective demarcations unless checked by a physical barrier, geographical reality, effective occupation by the other party or a combination of two or more of these factors.

The physical barrier confronting the Spaniards was a formidable obstacle to the satisfaction of the claim asserted by Balboa. Exploration of the coasts of Central and South America had so far revealed that the easterly bulge of what is now Brazil lay within the Portuguese demarcation in the western hemisphere, but had revealed no signs of either a strait through the landmass or the termination thereof. In 1514 the Spaniards resolved to make a further effort to enter Balboa's "Great South Sea." In November Juan Diaz de Solis, a former subject of Portugal and now *piloto mayor* of Spain, was commissioned to lead an expedition for the discovery of a route through South America or around its southern extremity leading to the south coast of the Isthmus of Panamá where he was to rendezvous with the governor Pedriás Dávila.

The experts at Seville had no firm knowledge of the longitudinal and latitudinal extent of South America nor the latitude of any strait, but they were by this time convinced that South America was distinct from Asia; and they also knew from the reports of Amerigo Vespucci on his voyage of 1501–2 in the Portuguese service that the east coast of South America crossed the line of demarcation in the latitude of 25°S so that any passage to the south of it belonged legally to Spain. The expedition sailed from Seville in October 1515. After rounding the bulge of Brazil it followed the southwesterly trend of the coast. After entering and examining the estuary of the Rio de la Plata, called by de Solis *el Mar Dulce*—"The Freshwater Sea"—the venture came to a grisly end. In February 1516 de Solis rashly went ashore with seven men, presumably to attempt communication with the inhabitants by whom they were seized, killed and eaten within sight of their helpless companions on board the ships. Two of the three ships got back to Seville in September 1516 to report the deaths of de Solis and his companions, the shipwreck of the third ship on the Brazilian coast and the discovery not of a strait but of a great river. The high cost of failure did not deter the Spaniards from launching a new search for the elusive passage within a few years.

The key figure in the resumption of the search was Ferdinand Magellan who was, like de Solis, a subject of Portugal. Magellan had hitherto pursued a career appropriate to a man of his social status in the Portuguese service. Born in northern Portugal about 1480 into a family of noble blood he entered the royal household as a page to King João II's queen Leonar and after 1495 held an appointment in the household of King Manuel I. In 1505 he sailed for the East under Francisco de Almeida, the first Portuguese viceroy to India, in search of honor, fame and fortune. During eight years of arduous service there under the commands of Almeida and Albuquerque he took part in operations at Goa and Malacca and was both wounded and shipwrecked. By the time of his return to Portugal in 1513, scarred, battle-hardened and, to some extent, disillusioned, he possessed a wealth of information about Asiatic trade and the Portuguese system.

He also acquired ideas about the distance between the Moluccas and the New World which were difficult to reconcile with official Portuguese geographical dogma and policy. In collaboration, it would seem, with his friend, Francisco Serrão, who held a position as adviser to the sultan of the clove producing island, Ternate, he developed doubts, as any able and intelligent man, though not any dedicated careerist, might well have done about the validity of Portuguese claims that the Moluccas lay within their demarcation.

These doubts gradually hardened into a false conviction that the Moluccas were situated in a longitude to the east of that estimated by the Portuguese and much nearer to the New World than had been thought. Magellan's errors were compounded by his adherence to the view that the world was smaller than it actually is, thus reducing further the distance between the Moluccas and the New World. Out of these convictions he conceived the enterprize which was to raise him from the obscurity of an increasingly frustrating career in the Portuguese service to the pinnacle of posthumous international fame in the Spanish service.

The road from Lisbon to Seville was paved with clashes of personality and disappointed expectations. Magellan is known to have incurred, for reasons not altogether clear, the disfavor of both the formidable Albuquerque and the equally formidable Manuel I. Relations with the monarch were hardly improved by allegations of corrupt conduct made against Magellan during a campaign in Morocco in which he had volunteered to fight in 1514. Although the charges were dropped, Magellan was faced in his mid-thirties with the dismal prospect of a humdrum career in the royal household: a prospect repugnant to a man consumed with ambition to achieve the fame and fortune which had so far eluded him.

Personality clashes must not be made to carry too great a burden of explanation. Magellan's ambition was to find a Southwest Passage through or around the New World with the aim of completing Columbus's enterprise of the Indies of 1492. He had no hope of achieving this ambition in the service of Portugal. The passage, if it existed, lay within the Spanish sector of the Tordesillas demarcation. The Portuguese had no reason to encourage, and many reasons to discourage, the revelation of a second passage to the Moluccas by the way of the New World. In October 1517 the king, apparently in a mood of indifference with regard to Magellan, allowed him to emigrate. He went to Seville and acquired citizenship in the hope as such of reviving his career.

He arrived at an opportune moment. Magellan's private ambition chimed in with the public ambitions of Spain. The collapse of the de Solis expedition had by no means rendered invalid the ideas of its sponsors. Influential people favored a resumption of the quest. They included Juan de Aranda, an official of the *Casa de Contratación* in Seville, Juan de Fonseca, bishop of Burgos, a member of the royal council and advocate of exploration to the southwest, and Cristóbal de Haro, a wealthy business magnate who had for many years been an agent in Lisbon of the German banking house of Fugger. He had left Portugal as a result of differences with Manuel I over policy.

Magellan was but one of a succession of foreigners employed by

Spain because of their knowledge and navigational skills: Columbus, Vespucci, Sebastian Cabot and de Solis. It looked for a time as if a leading position on the expedition would be allocated to Ruy Falerio, an associate of Magellan, who followed him over the border in December 1517. Faleiro, a cosmographer of some standing, had, like Magellan, no future in Portugal since his belief that the spiceries lay within the Spanish demarcation was tantamount to treason. In the event Faleiro was excluded from the expedition partly because of a reputation for instability, which was systematically exaggerated by Portuguese agents in Spain, and partly because of the reluctance of the Spaniards to confer upon two Portuguese a near monopoly of authority. The crown had also to take into account the possible resentment of Spanish candidates for high appointments at being passed over. Events on the voyage were to show how well founded were the royal concerns on this score.

The outcome was a significant reinforcement of Spanish influence in the leadership through the advancement of Juan de Cartagena of the Fonseca family. He became "chief factor of the fleet and captain of a ship, and treasurer and clerk of the fleet." As such he was responsible for business and financial affairs. He was also described as "persona conjuncta" with Magellan. As such his status was ambiguous. He can be seen as Magellan's deputy or second-in-command. In his own mind, however, and perhaps in the minds of influential Spaniards within the Fonseca circle, he was joint commander. At least he tried to behave so, though this could hardly be reconciled with the gist of Magellan's instructions from the king. The rise of Juan de Cartagena was a concession to xenophobic suspicions and resentments. It might well have wrecked the enterprise had the leadership been in hands other than those of the obdurately self-willed Magellan.

The expedition, financed mainly by the crown and victualed for two years, was made up of five ships; the *San Antonio* (120 tons), commanded by Juan de Cartagena; the *Trinidad* (110 tons) which was Magellan's flagship; the *Concepción* (90 tons), commanded by Gaspar de Quesada; the *Victoria* (85 tons), commanded by Luis de Mendoza; the *Santiago* (75 tons), commanded by Juan Serrano, an officer of Portuguese origins. The crews were multinational. Spaniards predominated among the 237 men embarked. Portuguese were well represented. The chief pilots were all of this nation. Their skills were indispensable. Difficulties of recruitment led to the enrollment of non-Iberian seamen: French, Italian, Flemings, Germans, men from the eastern Mediterranean, men of mixed blood and

one Englishman, Andrew of Bristol who, like so many of his ship-
mates, was destined to die in the Pacific Ocean.

One of the foreigners on board the *Trinidad* was listed as "Antonio Lombardo." Anthony of Lombardy was in fact Antonio Pigafetta,
a native of the Italian city of Vicenza, who arrived in Spain in the
entourage of the papal nuncio to the Spanish court. Hearing of the
proposed expedition, when on official duties at Barcelona, his imagination was so stirred that he hastened to Seville to volunteer for
service and succeeded in persuading Magellan to enlist him in June
1519 as a personal aide and supernumerary. Antonio Pigafetta is
singled out for special mention because of our indebtedness to him.
He was one of the handful of survivors who came ashore at Seville
in September 1522. The impulse which inspired him to embark also
inspired him to write a journal: the most complete and vivid account
of the voyage with perceptive comments about the non-European
peoples encountered thereon. It is a remarkable literary record of
what Samuel Eliot Morison in *The European Discovery of America:
The Southern Voyages, 1492–1616* has called the "most remarkable
voyage in recorded history."

The *Armada de Molucca,* as it was officially known, sailed from
Sanlúcar, the port of Seville, on 20 September 1519 and headed for
a transatlantic landfall to search for the elusive passage to Asia. After arriving off Rio de Janeiro on 13 December 1519, Magellan's first
assignment was to follow in the wake of de Solis and enter the estuary of the Rio de la Plata a thorough examination of which satisfied him that this was no passage or strait but the mouth of a river.
Pushing into the higher latitudes of the south Atlantic, Magellan entered the harbor of Port St. Julian in 49° 20′S on 31 March 1520. He
resolved to winter there.

In Port St. Julian, Magellan had to deal, as did Francis Drake on
his famous voyage of circumnavigation (1577–80), with a challenge
to his authority. In the case of Magellan, and the same was later to
be true of Drake, the challenge did not emanate from a turbulent
lower deck but from discontented and uneasy officers. The crisis of
leadership had developed in an atmosphere of anxiety and suspicion
which had been present since the departure from Sanlúcar and
probably even before that. Anxiety arose out of ignorance, in the
then state of knowledge, of what lay beyond the boundaries of the
known world into which they were being led. Suspicion was fueled
by the secrecy with which, for reasons which he saw as prudent,
Magellan shrouded his thoughts and his innermost beliefs. It was
exacerbated by distrust of his possible motives as a Portuguese. Am-

bition, displayed most ostentatiously by Juan de Cartagena, was directed against the subordination of Spanish officers to a foreign commander. Yet the mutiny was never purely and simply a clash between Spaniards and Portuguese. At its height, Gonzalo de Espinosa, the Spanish officer in charge of the shipboard soldiers, intervened decisively to support Magellan. At a later stage Estevão Gomes, the chief Portuguese pilot, seized command of the *San Antonio* and deserted after attempting unsuccessfully to persuade Magellan to return to Spain.

There were still many waverers on board when Magellan sailed from this desolate place in late August 1520 with four ships. The *Santiago* had been cast away and her crew rescued with difficulty during an earlier reconnaissance to the south. Left behind at Port St. Julian were the bodies of Quesada of the *Concepción,* tried and judicially executed, and Mendoza of *Victoria,* stabbed to death by Espinosa in a mutinous tussle. Juan de Cartagena and an unknown Spanish priest disappeared from history. They were marooned and abandoned to their respective fates, whatever they may have been. The farther south the expedition sailed off alien coasts in seas totally unknown to Europeans, the more dependent it became upon the will of Magellan. His secretive policy, hitherto a source of dissension, became an advantage to him; for he alone appeared to know where he was heading and how he was going to get there.

The breakthrough came at last on 21 October 1520 in latitude 52° 30′S where an inlet was found which turned out to be a strait. According to Pigafetta, Magellan's sense of conviction was critical at this juncture since everybody believed that this was yet another bay closed in all sides. Pigafetta's declaration of trust in Magellan should be treated with a measure of caution. He was neither a navigator nor a geographer and he believed that Magellan knew of the existence of the strait because he had consulted in the royal Portuguese archives a world map either made by Martin Behaim or based on his globe. Since the world of Martin Behaim was the non-American world of 1492, Pigafetta's belief belonged to a world of fantasy. Magellan had already sailed beyond the expected latitude of the strait, if it existed, and was running out of options. He could only hope after rounding Cape Virgins that the inlet would not turn out to be yet another bay or estuary.

The passage through the Strait of Magellan, as it was later to be called in honor of its discoverer, was difficult but by no means impassable. The distance between Cape Virgins on the Atlantic and Cape Pilar on the Pacific was 310 nautical miles. Magellan accom-

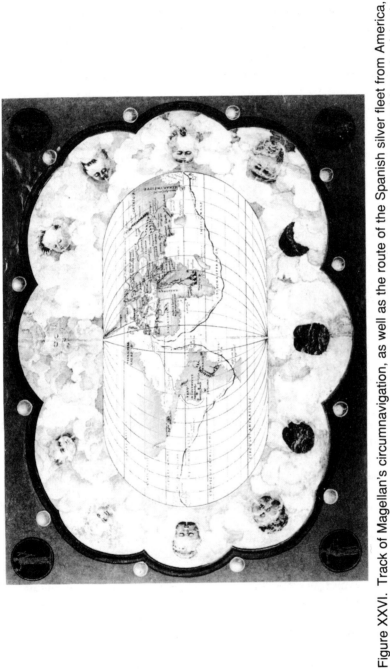

Figure XXVI. Track of Magellan's circumnavigation, as well as the route of the Spanish silver fleet from America, as shown on Battista Agnese's world map of 1543–45. The uncolored area stretching westward from the Atlantic coast of North America reflects Verrazzano's 1524–25 voyage, during which he saw water over the outer banks of North Carolina and thought that it was the Pacific Ocean. This map is part of atlas that the Emperor Charles V gave to his sixteen year old son, who in 1556 became King Philip II of Spain. *Courtesy of the John Carter Brown Library at Brown University.*

plished the passage in 38 days which included time spent in searching for the *San Antonio* after she had gone missing which for all Magellan ever knew was what had happened to her. The main obstacle was the prevailing westerly wind. This was particularly true of the second half of the strait between Cape Froward and Cape Pilar. It was narrow and flanked by mountainous coasts and offered few anchorages. The problems were increased by strong tidal currents. On this leg the wind often funneled up the rock-bound passage at great speed as most sixteenth-century navigators who attempted the strait were to discover. Of Magellan's successors to the end of the century only Francis Drake in 1578 was favored by the winds, making a passage of 16 days.

Among the recorded voyages of the sixteenth century, Drake's experience was unique. He was not the only navigator, however, to demonstrate the navigability of Magellan's discovery. The English privateer, Thomas Cavendish, passed Cape Virgins on January 1587 and completed the voyage to Cape Pilar in 49 days; in February 1593 Richard Hawkins, on a wartime sortie into the Pacific Ocean, entered the strait and completed the passage in 46 days. He was later to write a report, on the whole favorable, on its usefulness. Against these successes must be set grim episodes, the most disastrous of which was an expedition from Spain during 1525–27 led by Garcia Jofre de Loaysa and John Sebastián del Cano. It arrived off Cape Virgins on 24 January 1526 after a six month voyage. Baffled by continuous westerlies, often of gale force, Loaysa was unable to make an attempt to enter the strait until 5 April, arriving off Cape Pilar with the fleet in a state of material disintegration on 26 May, four and a half months after the arrival off Cape Virgins.

Another victim of the Strait of Magellan was the Englishman, John Chidley, who sailed from Plymouth in August 1589 on a mission to the Pacific. He battled for six weeks after entering the strait, passing beyond Cape Froward eight times and being just as often driven back. Before his death the attempt was abandoned. Few survivors of the original fleet of three ships and two pinnaces ever saw England again. Ill fortune also overtook Cavendish who, accompanied by the Arctic explorer John Davis, attempted to repeat his successful foray into the Pacific of 1587. After entering the strait in April 1592 they encountered persistent westerlies. In May Cavendish abandoned the effort. He was later to die at sea on the return voyage to England. Davis was more resolute. Twice in 1592 he managed to get beyond Cape Pilar; twice he was driven back into the strait by heavy westerly gales. After getting back to England with a skeleton crew Davis was to write that he "had seene and tested the frowardnesse of the place [the Strait of Magellan] with the great unlikelyhoode of any passage to be that way."

By the end of the sixteenth century the strait was the only known route between the Atlantic and the Pacific: the only known direct route from Europe to Asia except that around the Cape of Good Hope. However, despite Richard Hawkins's claim that it was navigable throughout the year, it was generally, and rightly, regarded as being of doubtful value as a commercial route since only in November, December and January was there likely to be any abatement of the westerly wind. Even Richard Hakluyt, the English maritime propagandist and historian, who, on learning Drake's passage through the strait, had hailed it as the "gate of entry into the treasure of both the East and West Indies" was later forced to concede that "the seeking of these Streights of Magellan is so dangerous, and the voyage so troublesome, that it seemth a matter almost impossible to be performed."

The Spaniards for their part encouraged the dissemination of such adverse opinions, not because they wanted to keep a monopoly over the strait as a trade route, but because they wanted to deter predatory foreign intruders, especially the English, from using it as a passage into the Pacific. The disappointing commercial returns from the hopes invested by the Spaniards were quite unforseen when Magellan, in his hour of triumph, named the headland to the south of Cape Pilar "Cape of Desire" and "entered into the pacific sea" on 28 November 1520.

During the crossing of the Pacific which followed, Magellan's misconceptions were cruelly exposed. By 1520 the idea that the New World and Asia were physically entangled, as Columbus had claimed, was largely abandoned, except perhaps with regard to America's most northern parts; but there was confusion, arising out of unsettled disputes over the size of the world, as to the distances involved. In 1520–21 Europeans discovered something of the true dimensions of the Pacific. This discovery was bought at a heavy cost in human life and suffering. It is best described by Pigafetta.

> We entered the Pacific Sea [so called because of the peace which reigned there] where we stayed three months and twenty days without taking on victuals or other refreshments, and we ate only old biscuit turned to powder all full of worms and stinking with the odour of the urine the Rats had made on it, after eating the good part. And we drank putrid yellow water. We also ate the hides of cattle which were very hard because of the sun, rain and wind. And we left them four or five days in the sea, then put

them for a little while over the coals. And so we ate them. Also rats which cost half a crown each one. And even so we could not find enough of them.

The dietetic deficiency made inevitable the spread of disease. Pigafetta noted the classic symptoms of scurvy, the swelling of the upper and lower gums, the loss of teeth and general enfeeblement, all of which led, if the symptoms were not reversed, to death. Scurvy was a scorbutic disease, caused by a lack of vitamin C in the diet. It could be remedied only by the intake of fresh food, particularly fresh fruit, green vegetables or citric juices. Magellan and his men had no access to such during the long haul from Cape Pilar to Guam. Nineteen men, including Andrew of Bristol, were reported dead by Pigafetta on board the three ships. The deaths were also noted of a Brazilian Indian and Patagonian from South America, victims of the well attested European practice of seizing indigenous people for punitive purposes and for exhibition on return home.

Although ravaged by intense physical suffering and threatened with extinction by starvation, the first European crossing of the Pacific was in a purely nautical sense a prosperous voyage. After working its way up the coast of what is now Chile the expedition entered warmer climes and picked up the southeast trade wind before which it steered diagonally on a west northwesterly heading across the Pacific. The weather was consistently fair; the wind reliable. Unfortunately the expedition's track took it clear of islands where food and drink might have been obtained. The equator was reached on 21 February and crossed on the same west northwesterly course. As the obvious way to the Moluccas was to steer due west along the equatorial latitude, Magellan's adherence to the diagonal course requires explanation. The most probable is that, given the enfeebled condition of the ships' crews Magellan prudently declined to venture into an area where the Portuguese were established in force until he had found refreshment and restored the stricken men to health.

The first transpacific landfall was made by Europeans on 6 March 1521 at Guam where supplies were obtained and where future standards of European behavior toward indigenous Pacific peoples were set by the savage punishments inflicted on them in revenge for acts of theft. Before departing on 9 March Magellan dubbed Guam the Island of Thieves. It is not possible to be dogmatic about the hopes and ambitions which drove Magellan forward during what turned out to be the last weeks of his life. Favored by the Northeast Trade Wind he steered more or less due west from Guam in a latitude well to the north of the Moluccas. He may well have intended to alter course and bear down upon them. Before he did so, however, he found the Philippine Islands or, as he called them in honor of the saint on whose day they were discovered [15 March], *Islas de San Lazaro.*

In the Philippines, Magellan conducted himself, in absence of a Portuguese presence, like a potential conqueror in the mold of Albuquerque, following the well-tried Portuguese practice in the East of gaining a footing in local politics through intervention, backed by displays of force and messianic zeal, in local conflicts. Having established a protective alliance with Humabon, the rajah of the island of Cebu, he sought to consolidate it by subduing recalcitrant vassals of Humabon in neighboring islets. On 26 April he attacked Lapulapu, the ruler of Mactan, in a badly botched combined operation. The invaders were repulsed and Magellan was killed. His body was never recovered and the final resting place of this unfulfilled and restless man is still unknown. A nineteenth-century monument to Magellan stands near the spot where he fell. Lapulapu is honored on Mactan by a statue dedicated to him as the first hero of Filipino resistance to foreign colonialism.

The defeat at Mactan and the death of Magellan undermined the credibility of the Spaniards as worthwhile collaborators in the eyes of Humabon and his court, destroyed the *raison d'être* of his opportunist policy of alliance with the foreign intruders and gave him grounds for ridding Cebu of them. This was achieved by the massacre at a banquet ashore on 1 May of 27 members of the expedition, including Duarte Barbosa and Juan Serrano who had been appointed to succeed Magellan as commanders. Much of the urgency inspired by Magellan seems to have vanished with his death. Nonetheless the decisions were made to make for the Moluccas and to destroy the *Concepción* on the ground that the 115 survivors were insufficient to work three ships. With the aid of local pilots, most of whom were kidnapped, the *Trinidad* and the *Victoria* made a leisurely voyage to the Moluccas arriving off the clove producing island of Tidore on 8 November 1521.

The Spaniards found themselves regarded by the local ruler as potential allies, or at lest counterweights, against the Portuguese whose commercial demands he found increasingly burdensome. In these circumstances they were able to negotiate the purchase of cloves; but they were quite unable to challenge the consolidated power of Portugal in the eastern seas. The only remaining hope for the remnants of the *Armada de Molucca* was to find a route home. It was agreed that the *Trinidad,* commanded by Espinosa who had done so much to save Magellan at Port St. Julian, should complete her repairs at Tidore before making a passage to the New World across the Pacific. Given the prevailing winds, of which of course the Spaniards were ignorant, this was an impossible task. Espinosa was obliged to surrender to the Portuguese. Most of his crew died in captivity. Only the commander and three others eventually returned to Spain. The *Victoria,* now commanded by the Basque seaman, Juan Sebastián del Cano, whose mutinous conduct at Port St. Julian had been pardoned by Magellan, achieved a permanent place in history's hall of fame by sailing across the Indian Ocean and round the Cape of Good Hope to complete the circumnavigation of the world. Eighteen men in a state of near starvation staggered ashore at Seville on 8 September 1522.

The first known circumnavigation in human history was an unforeseen outcome of an expedition designed to bring the Moluccas within the orbit of the New World. The grand design, based as it was upon false suppositions concerning the distances involved, was in a short term a failure. Following the disastrous Loaysa-del Cano voyage of 1525–27 the Spaniards had to recognize the unreliability of Magellan's route as a channel for commerce; in April 1529 by the treaty of Zaragoza, they conceded with some mental reservations, for nobody in the then state of knowledge could be absolutely certain, that the Moluccas lay within the Portuguese demarcation. In practice they were now free to focus their energies and ambitions upon the arduous business of taming the Pacific Ocean and turning it into a Spanish lake.

Until 1520–21 there was as far as Europeans were concerned no such thing as the Pacific Ocean, only a nameless, undefined and unmeasured void between the New World and the Spice islands. Although hitherto unknown to Europeans, the Pacific was populated by peoples who were distributed throughout its many island groups, most of which as time went on were found to be habited. The ancestors of these Micronesian and Polynesian peoples, not the Europeans, had been the first to make distant voyages within the Pacific. These ancient voyages in its central and southern regions had performed great feats of seamanship. The Polynesians are credited with having discovered and settled the Hawaiian islands by 400 A.D.

However, if by discovery we mean the recording in written and cartographic form of the places observed, of their relative positions and of the distances between them, then Pacific discovery was a European achievement. It was they, too, who solved the problem of how to cross the entire Pacific from east to west and west to east. Magellan's voyage from Spain to the Philippines was but the beginning of Pacific discovery which, like American discovery, was the work of centuries rather than of decades. The first great obstacle to exploration was the size of the ocean. It was described in 1523 by Maximillian Transylvanus in a brief account of the voyage, based on oral evidence supplied by survivors of the *Victoria,* as "a sea to vast that the human mind can scarcely grasp it." The vastness imposed unprecedented strains on the navigational techniques and logistical capacities of the age.

Contemporary navigators, even the most skilled and experienced, dealt in probabilities rather than in facts, owning to their inability with the available instruments to measure longitude, to their dependence upon eye and sense of movement (unlike the English, the Spaniards did not use, even in the later sixteenth century, the recently discovered log-line) to estimate the speed of the ship and hence the distance run from the last observed position and to reliance upon understanding of variation and sense of judgment with regard to the influence of drift and leeway to reach something like a sound assessment of the compass course made good.

Navigators were entitled to expect greater accuracy when it came to fixing the parallel of latitude on which the ship was situated for this could be ascertained by measuring at night the altitude of certain stars in both the northern and southern hemispheres and by day the altitude of the sun. Reliable instruments, the cross-staff, the astrolabe and the quadrant were available and there are many well attested examples in the sixteenth century among seamen of all nations of remarkably accurate readings. However, the observation of celestial bodies with early instruments was hardly an exact science. We are reminded by the remarkable Pedro Fernández de Quirós, who crossed and recrossed the Pacific twice between 1595 and 1606, of the frailties of astronavigation. "If four pilots," he wrote, "even though they be on land, observe the altitude of the sun or the stars with the same instruments, they will find a difference of more or of less, and seldom will their reckonings agree. And when they repeat their observations, they will find a new difference."

Navigational errors arising out of miscalculations of latitude and speed were compounded by the unsolved problem of how to measure longitude on transpacific voyages both eastwards and westwards. Knowledge of latitude provided the seaman with a position line; ignorance of longitude denied him knowledge of where he was on that position line. He could only make a reckoning, based on estimates of speeds and mean courses, of his distance run along the line of latitude and hence of his position. This lack of exactitude was for Quirós a source of anxiety. He declared that "only half the navigation [latitude] is known and by many the other half is ill understood."

Navigation, "an art," according to Quirós, "that does not admit of ignorance or carelessness," was flawed by ignorance. In the vast open spaces of the Pacific this gave rise to bizarre instances of places being "discovered" only to be lost or be misidentified. The overlapping careers of Alvaro de Mendaña and of Quirós himself illustrate the problem. In 1567 Mendaña was sent on a voyage from Callao in Peru to find rich islands, perhaps even a continent, allegedly situated, according to Inca legend, some 600 leagues to the west. After 80 days at sea he came upon an island group which he identified as King Solomon's Ophir and named the Solomon Islands. He never saw them again. In 1595 he headed to the west, this time with Quirós as pilot. So hazy were the concepts of distance, and hence of longitude, that confusion reigned. Mendaña identified the Marquesas Islands, just over half way from Peru to the Solomons, as the Solomons themselves, and recognized his error too late to retain confidence in his leadership. The Solomons were never found again by the Spaniards and remained hidden from European eyes until 1767. Pacific exploration before the second half of the eighteenth century, by which time scientific methods of fixing longitude had been discovered, has been admirably described by J. C. Beaglehole in *The Life of Captain James Cook* (1974) as a "history of faith, hope, accidental discovery, missed objectives, disillusionment, disaster."

Another obstacle to exploration of the Pacific were problems associated with the wind systems which had to be solved before decisive progress could be made either in linking the New World with Asia or in revealing the Pacific in its entirety. Westerly winds prevailed in both the northern and southern hemispheres of the Pacific beyond the latitudes of 30° in winter and 40° in summer. The trade wind areas were situated to the north and south of the equator. They blew from the northeast sector of the ocean in the northern hemisphere and from the southeast sector in the southern hemisphere. They were separated from each other by an area of calms in the region just north of the equator. Once this regular and reliable wind system was, along with its attendant currents, understood two-way transoceanic voyages, and hence transoceanic trade became feasible.

Hernan Cortés, conqueror of the Aztec empire and creator of New Spain (the modern Mexico), rather than Magellan whose route was destined to fall into disfavor, inspired the Spanish conquest of the

Pacific. New Spain provided both bases and shipbuilding yards in the New World from which to launch new enterprises. The first of these was led by his kinsman Alvaro de Saavedra, who sailed from Zihuatanejo on the Pacific coast of New Spain with two small caravels and a bergantina in October 1527 on a commercial mission to the Moluccas. Picking up the northeast trade wind Saavedra revealed the outward passage to the Moluccas which he reached via Guam and the Philippines after a voyage of five months in his flagship the *Florida,* the only ship to survive the crossing.

Saavedra managed to obtain some spices with the aid of survivors from Loaysa's expedition at Gilolo who were hanging on in the hope that the demarcation dispute with Portugal over the Moluccas would be settled in favor of Spain. Saavedra's task was to complete his mission by returning to New Spain with 70 quintals of spices. The plan was flawed by ignorance of the wind circulation around the Pacific. Saavedra knew that he could not return to the New World on a reciprocal track against the northeast trade; he did not know the latitudes of westerly winds. Two hit and miss searches resulted in Saavedra being driven back on both occasions to the Moluccas where he died and the *Florida,* leaky and structurally frail, was abandoned. This experience set the pattern of things until 1565. Few of the men who attempted the return voyage, and none of the ships, got back to New Spain. Sickness and shipwreck took a deadly toll.

During these years a shift in Spanish interests in the East gradually became apparent. Such lingering hopes as survived Zaragoza that the Portuguese presence in the Moluccas might be proved to be legally baseless gave way to a recognition that the Portuguese were too strongly entrenched there to be removed. This recognition was reinforced by awareness of how fragile were Spain's transpacific lines of communication. Guam and the Philippines came back into the picture as potential bases on the Asiatic perimeter of the ocean and as necessary supports for the establishment of Pacific hegemony.

The conquest of the Philippines was accompanied by the discovery of the westerly winds. Credit for the discovery belongs primarily to Andrés de Urdaneta, an Augustinian friar based in New Spain, who was personally instructed by Philip II of Spain in September 1559 to sail with a projected expedition to the Philippines which got to sea in November 1564. As a young layman, Urdaneta had sailed with del Cano on the 1525–27 expedition and was one of the survivors of the Pacific crossing who tried to retain a toehold in the

Moluccas. Seventeen years of age when he left Spain, he returned at the age of 28 with a reputation as a loyal servant, a competent navigator and something of an expert on the East. Posted to New Spain in 1539, he was ordained priest in 1552 and became noted for his missionary work. One can understand why his qualities and experience recommended him to Philip II for a place on the expedition.

After being present at the first stage of the conquest of the Philippines, the occupation of Magellan's Cebu in early 1565, Urdaneta boarded the *San Pablo* as pilot for the momentous voyage to New Spain which began on 1 June 1565. Although it seems improbable in an age when the problem of the return voyage was much discussed that Urdaneta reached his conclusion about the location of the belt of westerly winds independently of everybody else, he navigated the *San Pablo* with a remarkable sense of conviction. Heading out of Cebu in 10°N on the southwest monsoon wind (the Philippines lay within the monsoon wind system of the Indian Ocean) he made good a northeasterly track until he picked up in 39°50N the westerly winds which brought him to a Californian landfall in 34°N on 18 September and to a safe anchorage at Acapulco in New Spain in early October. He logged in all 11,600 miles. Urdaneta's discovery changed the world. 1567 witnessed the inaugural voyage of what came to be called the Manila galleon which annually made the round trip between Acapulco and the Philippines over the next 250 years. There was thus created a commercial system which embraced within its orbit China and Seville and brought to reality, in ways quite unforeseen by them, the visionary ambitions of Christopher Columbus and Ferdinand Magellan.

But if the Pacific north of the equator was gradually taking on a shape which is recognizable to us, the Pacific south of the equator continued to guard its secrets and remained an area, as it had been for the classical geographers of the ancient world, conceived of in imaginative, even metaphysical, terms. It was the supposed location of a tropical extension of the great southern landmass, *Terra Australis Incognita,* or to the more sanguine, *Terra Australis Nondum Cognita.* It appears as such on maps constructed in the sixteenth century, a good example being its depiction on the *Typus Orbis Terrarum,* world map of 1570 by the famous Flemish geographer, Abraham Ortelius. It continued to influence thought about the Pacific until the later eighteenth century.

In the sixteenth century the elucidation of the problem was frustrated by contemporary navigational problems and by the prevailing westerlies in the higher latitudes of the southern hemisphere, which impeded the passage of ships to the west in latitudes of the Pacific which were the supposed location of *Terra Australis* in its Pacific environment. The promising lines of enquiry initiated by Mendaña (1567) and Mendaña-Quirós (1595) petered out in the voyage from Peru led by Quirós in 1605–6 which clarified the relationship between New Guinea and the modern Australia but which ended in confusion and self-doubt as Quirós tormented by a growing uncertainty about his exact position, by the spread of sickness and by adverse winds abandoned the quest after making an effort to establish a New Jerusalem in the New Hebrides, the modern Vanuata.

Although Quirós bombarded the authorities until his death in 1615 with memorials in favor of locating and settling *Terra Australis,* Spanish interest in the establishment of colonies in far distant and largely unknown seas died with him, if it did not predecease him. The Spaniards had acquired in the face of enormous difficulties a patchy knowledge of this region. It was to remain until the age of James Cook in the second half of the eighteenth century an enigma. Mapmakers continued either to slave blank spaces or to depict mythical continents as substitutes for the factual void.

SUGGESTED FURTHER READING
Published Contemporary Sources

Cortés, Martín. *Arte of Navigation,* translated from the Spanish by Richard Eden (London, 1561). A facsimile reproduction for the John Carter Library with an introduction by D. W. Waters (New York, 1992).

Kelly, C., O. F. M. (ed.). *La Austrialia del Espíritu Santo: The Journal of Fray Martin de Munilla, O.F.M. and other documents relating to the Voyage of Pedro Fernández de Quirós to the South Sea (1605–1606) and the Franciscan Missionary Plan (1617–1627).* Hakluyt Society, 2nd. series, vols. 126–7 (Cambridge, 1966).

Nowell C. E. (ed.). *Magellan's Voyage around the World: Three Contemporary Accounts.* (Evanston, Ill., 1962).

The Voyage of Magellan. The Journal of Antonio Pigafetta. Facsimile of the earliest printed edition; translated into English by Paula S. Page. (Ann Arbor, 1969).

Pigafetta, Antonio. *Magellan's Voyage: A Narrative Account of the First Circumnavigation.* Translated into English and annotated with an introduction by R. A. Skelton. (New Haven, 1969).

Later Works

Beaglehole, J. C. *The Exploration of the Pacific.* (London, 1947).

Fernandez-Armesto, F. *Columbus.* (New York and Oxford, 1992).

Friis, H. R. (ed.). *The Pacific Basin: A History of its Geographical Exploration* (New York, 1967).

Jack-Hinton, C. *The Search for the Solomon Islands.* (London, 1969).

Morison, S. E. *The European Discovery of America: The Southern Voyages, 1492–1616.* (New York and Oxford, 1974).

Parry, J. H. *The Discovery of the Sea.* (New York, 1974).

Roditi, E. *Magellan of the Pacific.* (London, 1972).

Scammel, G. V. *The World Encompassed: The First European Maritime Empires, c. 800–1650.* (London, 1980), chapters 5–6.

Scammel, G. V. *The First Imperial Age: European Overseas Expansion, c. 1400–1715.* (London, 1989).

Spate, O. H. K. *The Spanish Lake.* (London, 1979).

Taylor, E. G. R. *The Haven-Finding Art: A History of Navigation from Odysseus to Captain Cook,* 2nd impression. (London, 1958).

Vigneras, L. A. *The Discovery of South America and the Andalusian Voyages.* (Chicago, 1976).

16

FRANCE AND THE ATLANTIC IN THE SIXTEENTH CENTURY

A. N. Ryan

The French response to the challenge of the Atlantic was led by seamen and entrepreneurs from ports on the northwestern and western coasts of the realm. Like the English, perhaps in imitation of them, they were lured by the transatlantic fisheries. Evidence of early activity is limited, but it is sufficient to support belief in French participation in the Newfoundland fishery as early as the first decade of the sixteenth century. Dates, however, are elusive.

There are guidelines, some more reliable than others. It was claimed in 1539 that the first crossings of the Atlantic were made by Bretons and Normans in 1504, that there was a transatlantic voyage by a ship of Honfleur in 1506 and that *Le Pensée* of Dieppe, fitted out by Jean Ango the Elder and commanded by Thomas Aubert, returned from *Terre-Neuve* [the New Land] with seven Amerindians on board in 1508. This report on the "seven savage men" brought to Normandy on board *La Pensée* is confirmed in an independent publication of 1512.

The first specific reference to a Breton ship in the waters off Newfoundland related to *La Jacquette* which sold a cargo of fish at Rouen in 1510. The reference occurs in a legal document of unimpeachable authenticity: a pardon granted by Louis XII of France to Guillaume Dobel, boatswain's mate of *La Jacquette,* who had been arrested following a fight on board the vessel which resulted in the death of Guillaume Garroche. *La Jacquette* was, however, hardly the first Breton ship to fish in Newfoundland waters. When Juan de Agramonte, a Catalan, was contracted in 1511 by the Spanish monarchy to sail from either Laredo or Santander "to discover the secret of the Newfoundland" he was under orders to employ Spanish seamen on board the two ships with the exception of two pilots to be recruited from Brittany. The Spaniards evidently believed that the Bretons were the most experienced Newfoundland pilots available.

Normans and Bretons were the pioneers of French involvement in the great Newfoundland cod fishery. They were followed by the French Basques of Bayonne and St. Jean de Luz and by seamen of La Rochelle and Bordeaux. In the 1520s the French were a force to be reckoned with in the Newfoundland fishery. They were aided by easy and relatively cheap access to the salt pans of Brittany and Biscay which enabled them to specialize in the "wet" or "green" fishery By this was meant the practice, favored in particular by the Normans, of cleaning and gutting the catch at sea and of salting it heavily in the hold in readiness for a quick return to Europe. It could be a hazardous enterprize, both a test, and a school, of seamanship. Ships employed in the "wet" fishery often sailed early in the year. After doing battle with the Atlantic westerlies, they were likely to encounter fog and icebergs on the Grand Banks. The commercial advantages were a modest outlay, a rapid turnover and, if the timing were right, the opportunity to make a second round trip in the year.

The French also participated in the "dry" fishery. This was an inshore operation which began in early June when the cod moved inshore toward Newfoundland. It was conducted from the boats and shallops of the fishing vessels. The catches were immediately put ashore. The fish, after being cleaned, gutted and lightly salted, were laid inside up on beds of small twigs and boughs on platforms known as flakes. Here through exposure to sun and wind they were gradually dried out, a technique which demanded much skill, attention and patience. The finished product was known as stockfish by the English, for whom the "dry" fishery was a compensation for their lack of easy access to cheap supplies of salt, and *morue* by the French. It was sealed in the holds of the fishing vessels for shipment to Europe, including the valuable Mediterranean market, at the end of the season. Most of the fleet was back in Europe by October at the latest. During the sixteenth century the French more than held their own in competition with the English, the Portuguese and the Spanish Basques. In 1580 Richard Hitchcock wrote in a commentary on the fishing industry in general of French involvement in the cod fishery that "there goeth out of Fraunce commonly five hundredth saile of shippes yearely in March to Newfoundlande, to fishe for Newland fishe, and comes home againe in August."

For the industry, colonization of Newfoundland was irrelevant. The eyes of both the controllers ashore and the seamen were fixed firmly on the business of profit making. Financial success did not call for permanent settlement with its potential troubles and expense. Participants in the "wet" fishery needed to call at Newfoundland before the home voyage to replenish stocks of water and wood; those in the "dry" fishery needed access to their flakes and rough quarters ashore in the summer months. There was no incentive for fishermen to brave the Newfoundland winter and much less again to surrender any part of their jealously guarded independence to a royal governor or a state company.

The French monarchy has been frequently criticized by historians for a failure to give to French maritime interests the sustained support it gave to her continental interests. Such truth as there may be in this criticism is by no means the whole truth. Monarchical France in the sixteenth century was not (indeed was it ever?) a homogeneous "national" state governed by an absolute ruler. Against the undoubted centralizing tendencies of the crown must be set the fierce particularism of the maritime provinces who followed independent policies in pursuit of independent interests without much regard to such ideas as might emanate from Paris. The tough pioneers who fished for cod off Newfoundland, hunted whales, walrus and seals further afield in the Strait of Belle Isle, the Gulf of St. Lawrence, on the Magdalen Islands and Sable Island and were the first to venture into the fur trade with coastal Amerindians, were Normans, Bretons, Rochellais and Basques before they were French. This maritime centrafugalism was accelerated in the second half of the century in Normandy and La Rochelle by the spread of Calvinism which heightened the sense of disaffection.

From the beginning these people had respect neither for the contents of papal bulls which conferred an aura of divine sanction upon the monopolistic claims of Spain and Portugal nor for the terms of the treaty of Tordesillas which purported to give them legal substance. Norman and Breton interlopers intruded into the waters of Portuguese Brazil at least as early as 1504, the first known vessel to arrive there, perhaps inadvertently, being *L'Espoir* of 120 tons which had sailed from Honfleur in June 1503. She was followed over the years by a succession of French ships. They were primarily in search of brazilwood, a source of red dyestuff much in demand by the textile industries of Dieppe and Rouen. A frieze depicting Brazilian Indians in the church of St. Jacques, Dieppe, originally in the Ango family's grand town house, bears witness to the sixteenth-century enterprises of the Normans.

During the first three decades of the sixteenth century Brazil was not effectively occupied by the Portuguese. French traders enjoyed easy access to coastal areas where brazilwood flourished and where the Indians were willing to trade in a barter economy. It may well be that by the mid-1520s there were more French than Portuguese ships involved in the trade. John III of Portugal, alarmed by the extent of French penetration, sent a naval force to take punitive action against them at Bahia and elsewhere: an event which prompted Jean Ango the Younger, fortified by a letter of marque from Francis I, to launch a privateering war against Portuguese shipping in the Atlantic. In 1531 a syndicate associated with Lyon and Marseille attempted to establish a permanent logwood settlement near Pernambuco. It was wiped out.

It is conceivable that had the French with full state backing made an all out effort to establish a colony in Brazil in the 1520s, when the Portuguese presence was ineffective, they may have created a New France in Latin America. This, however, may well be no more than retrospective wisdom. In the circumstances of the time the incentives were much less apparent. Prosperous trading was available without undertaking the burdens of occupation and full state backing of a financial and military kind was hardly feasible in an era which included the defeat at Pavia by the Habsburgs and the capture of Francis I.

Despite the setbacks of the 1520s and 1530s, French interlopers were able to maintain commercial relations with Brazilian Indians in areas where the Portuguese were thinly spread. The destruction of the Pernambuco station, however, had damaging effects upon French ambitions to achieve permanent settlements in Brazil. Not until 1555, by which time emigration from Portugal to Brazil was increasing steadily, did they try again. On 14 August of this year three ships, each of two hundred tons, manned in the main by Norman and Breton seamen, sailed from Dieppe for Brazil with a force of six hundred men. The expedition had the support of the king, Henry II, and enjoyed a measure of royal financial backing; it was inspired and led by Nicolas Durand de Villegagnon who had performed naval services for the crown and was Vice-Admiral of Brittany.

The site chosen for the settlement was the modern Governador island, of Guanabara Bay, Rio de Janeiro, which the expedition entered on 10 November 1555. Its economic basis was a flourishing trade in brazilwood and other woods. The success of the trade owed much to Villegagnon's skill and humanity in his relations with local Amerindians who traded in wood. Economic success was an essential condition of the colony's survival, but Villegagnon was looking for more than a secure transatlantic commercial outpost. He had a vision of a New France, *La France Antarctique,* in the tropical latitudes of the New World.

Villegagnon had sought and obtained the approval of the king, Henry II, for the enterprise; as a recent convert to Calvinism, he had also consulted Gaspard de Coligny, Admiral of France, a political leader of French Calvinism, and John Calvin himself. As tensions in France between Catholics and Calvinists sharpened, the three men saw in *La France Antarctique* a potential refuge from persecution at home of Calvinists. However, the expeditionary party of 1555 was made up of adherents of both confessions. Laudable though this may have been, it tended to reproduce in the Brazilian settlement the tensions already apparent in metropolitan France. Villegagnon's doctrinal and moral enthusiasms did nothing to calm things. The tendency was further reinforced by the arrival in March 1557 of new settlers accompanied by Calvinist preachers. During the confessional turmoil which followed, Villegagnon suddenly announced his reconversion to Catholicism and in 1559 he abandoned Governador and returned to France. His departure did not lead automatically to the end of the colony. Of much greater significance was the determination of the Portuguese, their confidence fortified by steady population growth, to rid Brazil of the intruders. They launched a successful military operation in 1560. Of those of the French who survived, many took refuge wilth the Amerindians with whom social bonds had been created since 1555 through commercial exchanges, intermarriage and cohabitation. The trade with France survived, but the history of *La France Antarctique* had run is course.

Like the English, the French failed in the sixteenth century to establish a permanent colony anywhere in the New World, though their contribution to the unveiling of North America was significant. This contribution was a product of their active interest in the discovery of a western oceanic route to Asia which dated from the early 1520s and coincided with the news of del Cano's circumnavigation of the world and Magellan's discovery of a passage between the Atlantic and Pacific Oceans. There existed at this time in Lyon a well-established Florentine colony of merchants, bankers and silk manufacturers which had associates in Paris and Rouen. It was interested in the discovery of a route, through or around the New World, to China with the aim of winning direct and independent access to sources of raw silk.

These aspirations come to light in a notarial document, dated Rouen, 23 March 1523, which reveals the existence of a close knit group and records that Jehan le Buatier, described as collector of the duty on silks at Lyon, his brother François and Antoine de Martigny, also of Lyon, had in hand sums of money which they intended to use in an expedition by sea to a place called the Indies in Cathay ["au lieu nommé les Indes en Kathaye"]. It is also recorded that they were associated in the venture by Jehan de Varrasenne, Thomassin Gadagne, Guillaume Naze, Robert Albisse, Anthoyne Gondy and Julien Bonacorey. All were said to be Florentine merchants which can mean either that they were natives of Florence or members of Florentine families established in Lyon.

Jehan de Varrasenne is one of several Gallicized variations of the name Giovanni da Verrazzano, a member of the Verrazzano family which had branches in Florence and Lyon. His place of birth—Florence or Lyon—is uncertain and knowledge of his earlier life (he was by this time in his late thirties) is sketchy. We can say little of it except that it is not unreasonable to assume that he had followed a career as merchant and seaman. There is tenuous evidence linking him with the voyage of *La Terre Neuve* in 1508 led by Thomas Aubert of Dieppe. If this could be substantiated, it might establish an early connection between him and the famous shipowners and *armateurs* of Dieppe and Rouen, the Ango family, and help to root him in Normandy. It was said of him in 1528 by a Portuguese official that he had spent time in Lisbon where he had known Magellan with whom he had crossed the border into Castile in 1517. According to Bernardo Carli, writing from Lyon in 1524 to his father in Florence, Verrazzano had spent several years—no dates are given—in the Levant.

Like other explorers of the "Age of Expansion," Verrazzano is, at least to us, a man of mystery. Whatever the truth about his past, he can be located with certainty in 1523 in Dieppe and Rouen where he enjoyed a sufficiently high reputation as to have obtained from Francis I, king of France, both a commission to lead a voyage of exploration and the provision of a royal warship *La Dauphine,* the master of which, Antoine de Conflams, was contracted by the king himself, not by the Lyon syndicate which otherwise financed the voyage.

We are dependent for our knowledge of Verrazzano's voyage of 1524 upon literary and cartographic evidence emanating from Verrazzano himself. The literary evidence is a letter addressed by Verrazzano from Dieppe on 8 July 1524 to Francis I.[1]

The expedition originally made up of four ships made a false start in the late summer of 1523. Sailing from Dieppe, it encountered westerly gales and "was forced by the fury of the winds to return in

distress to Brittany" with the loss of two ships. The voyage was resumed in early January 1524 by the two surviving ships, *La
Dauphine* and *La Normande* which was the property of Jean Ango.
Because of a mysterious "new plan," however, *La Normande* parted
company on unknown duties. *La Dauphine* set course for the New
World in search of a passage through or around it, somewhere to the
north of Florida, from off Madeira in latitude 32°N on 17 January
1524. After being driven off her intended track by a storm she made
a landfall a little to the south of Cape Fear in the second half of
March. A solitary ship operating in distant and unknown waters
was at risk of disappearing from history unless the navigation was
in the hands of able men.

Verrazzano and Conflans, who can hardly be left out of the assessment, were competent and methodical navigators. They proposed to adhere to their selected latitude in the belt of the northeast
trade winds with the object of making a landfall clear of Spanish
bases in the Caribbean, and on a parallel somewhere to the north of
which they expected to find a route leading to "Cathay and the extreme eastern coast of Asia." They kept a regular and, as far as we
can judge, reasonably accurate measurement of latitude by solar observations. They also wrestled, it would seem with less accuracy,
with the as yet unsolved problem of longitudinal reckonings. For
reckonings of where they were on their latitudinal position line they
were dependent upon estimates, methodically recorded, of the speed
of *La Dauphine*. Such estimates of distance run on longitudinal
crossings of the oceans in the sixteenth century were notoriously
subjective. Verrazzano and Conflans shared with Christopher
Columbus a predilection to exaggerate the speed and hence of the
distance made good and length of passage.

Verrazzano derived encouragement in his quest from observations of peoples and places during his reconnaissance of the North
American coastline from Florida to Cape Breton. While never confusing the New World with Asia, he was tempted to look for signs of
affinity and proximity between them. Amerindians encountered
close to the transatlantic landfall were said in respect to their cun-
ning and agility to resemble Orientals. The "most beautiful" people
of Narragansett Bay were described as having trinkets hanging
from their ears "as the orientals do." The forested lands adjacent to
the landfall—the "Forest of Laurels" and the "Field of Cedars on account of the beautiful cedar trees"—were praised for their appearance and fragrance. "We think," he wrote, "that they belong to the
orient by virtue of their surroundings and that they are not without

some kind of narcotic or aromatic liquor." This tendency, by no means peculiar to Verrazzano, of the professional explorers of the fifteenth and sixteenth centuries, to look for and to find evidence which chimed in with their expectations and aspirations, led almost inexorably to the "discovery" made on 25 March 1524 at a place named Annunciata.

It was from Annunciata, the modern Cape Lookout, that he got his first glimpse of "an isthmus one mile wide and about two hundred miles long, in which we could see the eastern sea from the ship, halfway between west and north. This is doubtless the one which goes around the tip of India, China and Cathay. We sailed along the isthmus, hoping all the time to find some strait or real promontory where the land might end to the north, and we could reach those blessed shores of Cathay." Verrazzano's "isthmus" was in reality the Carolina Outer Banks. His eastern sea, the false "Verrazzanian Sea," was from south to north Pamlico Sound, Roanoke Sound, Albemarle Sound and Currituck Sound. Viewed from the deck, or even the mast, of a 100-ton ship on the Atlantic side of the banks, the sounds could give the impression of an open sea divided from the Atlantic by a narrow isthmus. Verrazzano offered no explanation of why he did not investigate further the reality or otherwise of his first vivid impressions. Perhaps he was unwilling to risk his lone ship in shoaling water; perhaps he was satisfied that he had found what he had come to find in an area where he might expect to find it. Both considerations may have supplemented each other.

The illusion of the "Verrazzanian Sea," an extension of the Pacific Ocean over a great part of what is now the United States of America, found its way into sixteenth-century concepts of America largely through the efforts of the explorer's brother, Girolamo, and the Genoese cartographer, Visconte de Maggiolo. Maggiolo was first off the mark in 1527 with a world map which may have been personally influenced by Giovanni da Verrazzano himself.[2] Considered as attempts to record geographical reality, the maps of Girolamo da Verrazzano and of Maggiolo were seriously flawed, not only because of their depiction of the false sea but because of their conflicting and consistently erroneous calculations of latitude. They were nevertheless influential. Examples of their influence in the sixteenth century are the copper globe of 1530 by Robert de Bailley, of which one is in the Pierpont Morgan Library, the Battista Agnese oval world map of about 1544 in the John Carter Brown Library, Providence, Rhode Island (see p. 266) and Michael Lok's map of North America and the

North Atlantic which was printed by Richard Hakluyt in his *Divers Voyages touching the Discoverie of America* of 1582.

Verrazzanian cartography was never accepted universally in the sixteenth century and its influence tended to wane with the passing of the years. Battista Agnese dropped the "Verrazzanian Sea" from his work after 1552. Richard Hakluyt, likewise, excluded it from his edition of Peter Martyr's *De Orbe Novo,* published at Paris in 1587, only five years after printing it in his *Divers Voyages.* But the value of an ancient map as historical evidence does not depend upon its accuracy. The very misrepresentations of the Verrazzanian tradition testify to the difficulties encountered by Europeans in coming to terms with the reality of America during this early stage of its discovery. Their inherited mental picture of a world without America was an obstacle to its assimilation.

Although very much a man of his time in that he was less interested in the continent than in the ocean which lay somewhere beyond it, Verrazzano was the first European explorer to furnish a description of North America and the peoples whom he encountered there. He was also the first to find and describe briefly "a very agreeable place between two small but prominent hills" in a land called Angoulême. It was a practice of Verrazzano to bestow French names, often associated with the royal family, upon places worthy of mention in his narrative. The description is such that we can confidently identify the discovery as New York harbor, where his twentieth-century monument, the Verrazzano Bridge, appropriately stands today. Oddly enough he does not seem to have considered the possibility that the bay might have opened up a waterway to the Pacific; but he did note, before making an abrupt departure for security and navigational reasons, that "all the hills showed signs of minerals," a point always well worth making to their sponsors by sixteenth-century explorers.

After leaving New York Verrazzano cruised in sight of land along the coast of Long Island, sighted Block Island, called Aloysia after the king's mother, in unfavorable weather and entered Narragansett Bay, "Refugio" on the Verrazzanian maps, in search of rest and refreshment. *La Dauphine* was anchored, apparently on the advice of local people, in the harbor of Newport, Rhode Island. Of this land and its people, the Narrangansetts and Wamponoags, Verrazzano wrote with eloquence and admiration. According to Lawrence Wroth, it was the most detailed of his descriptions of the Amerindians of the Atlantic coast, the one in which he was most specific in describing their physical features and way of life. It was the first ethnological picture by a European of the indigenous people of what is now New England.

After a stay at Refugio of fifteen days, *La Dauphine* put to sea on 6 May 1524, rounded Cape Cod, where the shoals were perceived to be dangerous, doubly so in the absence of a consort. Verrazzano was unable to resume his practice of keeping the coast in sight until he had crossed Massachusetts Bay and fetched up on the coast of Maine, the inhabitants of which he considered objectionable. He was now reaching the end of his mission as he sailed up the coasts of Maine and Nova Scotia towards Cape Breton, whose northerly latitude he exaggerated, and Newfoundland. From this region he set course for Europe and reached Dieppe on 8 July.

Verrazzano's report to the king, with its emphasis upon the Atlantic seabord, gave little encouragement to the projects of the Lyon syndicate. It is questionable whether its members ever saw the annotated version which contained the reference to the isthmus, though they may have received verbal reports thereon. Whatever the truth, they do not figure among the financial sponsors of enterprises with which he was thereafter associated. The first of these, commissioned by Francis I, was a proposed voyage by four ships destined vaguely enough for certain unknown isles in the Indies. It was mainly financed by Alonce de Civille, a Spanish resident of Rouen, and his associates. Late in 1524, when preparations for sailing were well advanced, the ships were requisitioned by the king for war service.

The explorer's name was afterwards linked temporarily with the courts of England and Portugal and, more specifically, with a syndicate, a prominent member of which was Jean Ango, organized in 1526 by Philippe de Chabot, Admiral of France, which had a plan for a voyage to "spiceries in the Indies," presumably the Moluccas. The limited evidence permits us to conjecture that, after sailing from Honfleur, Verrazzano failed either to round the Cape of Good Hope or penetrate the Strait of Magellan and that he may, having reached the Cape, recrossed the Atlantic to Brazil in search of dyewood. Of his last voyage in 1528 we know even less than that of 1526–27. It seems to have been bound for Brazil. Verrazzano never returned. He may have been the victim, in sight of Girolamo stationed in a boat offshore, of cannibalistic Caribs somewhere in the West Indies.

Verrazzano's descent into tragedy after 1524 was paved with disappointed hopes. The record, insofar as it can be traced, indicates that neither Francis I, the Lyon syndicate, the entrepreneurs of Normandy nor the Admiral of France had any interest in a repeat of the search between Florida and Cape Breton for a route through or around the continent to Cathay. The promoters of the enterprises with which he was associated favored direct action against the Iberian powers by intrusion upon the routes over which they claimed monoplastic rights and by invasion of their establishments in the Orient and South America. His great scheme was relegated to the sidelines. The idea of a search in northern latitudes for a passage to Asia was not, however, abandoned by the French. It was resumed in 1534, inspired not by the fantasy of the "Verrazzanian Sea," but by the activities of fishermen in the Strait of Belle Isle, called by the French *"baye des Chasteaulx."* Here it seemed might be a passage leading to the penetration of the landmass. The royal commission to its commander was that he should "voyage and go to the New Lands and to pass the Strait of the Bay of Castles." Another contemporary document reports that he was "to discover certain islands and countries where there is said to be found a vast quantity of gold and other such things." Wrapped up in the conventional language of the day, Asia was the objective.

The leader of the voyage of 1534 was Jacques Cartier of St. Malo. Born in 1490, Cartier was an experienced mariner who had certainly sailed to the Newfoundland fisheries in the course of a busy career and very probably also to Brazil. Although not so shadowy a figure as, say, John Cabot or Verrazzano, we would like to know more about him. Of his confidence and competence, however, there is no room for doubt. As S. E. Morison points out in *The European Discovery of America: The Northern Voyages, A.D. 500–1600* (1971), Cartier made three voyages of discovery in difficult and dangerous, hitherto unknown, waters, entered and left some 50 hitherto unknown harbors without serious mishap and lost sailors only through disease contracted ashore.

He crossed the Atlantic in 1534 with aplomb. Sailing from St. Malo in latitude 48°39'N on 20 April he made a landfall off Cape Bonavista (latitude 48°42'N) in Newfoundland on 10 May. He must have been favored by a consistent easterly wind to have made so swift a passage. It might be argued that he had departed St. Malo too early and made too swift a passage, for on sighting the entrance to the Strait of Belle Isle on 27 May he not only encountered unfavorable weather but a "large number of icebergs." Further investigation was effectively postponed until early June.

The summer was spent in making a thorough survey of the Gulf of St. Lawrence which he charted in authoritative fashion. At the same time there are interesting indications that the launching of

Cartier's first voyage may well have owed something to information collected by French seamen who had preceded him there. Cartier and his men were not on their own in 1534, for they sighted a ship from La Rochelle fishing for cod. Cartier's first serious encounter with the Micmac Indians in early July in the *Baie des Chaleurs* is also instructive. Although there is no written evidence of any previous contacts, commercial or otherwise, the behavior of the Micmacs suggests that there might have been, for "there sprang out [of the canoes] and landed a large number of Indians, who set up a great clamour and made frequent signs to us to come on shore, holding up to us some furs on sticks." Once the French had decided that it was safe to go ashore, a barter trade followed.

Although Cartier considered it worthwhile to note in his report this trade with the Micmacs, he was mainly interested in the *Baie des Chaleurs* as a possible waterway giving access to a route to Asia. For this reason he explored it thoroughly, withdrawing only when he found that it was indeed a bay. His next encounter with Amerindians on the Gaspé peninsula was with Hurons who had come from the Quebec region for the summer season to fish. The exchanges between the two parties were commercially unproductive, but Cartier saw and heard enough, even if most of what he heard was unintelligible, to conclude that the Hurons might supply priceless information about the interior and its water passages, if communications between the two sides could be established. He therefore persuaded the chief, Donnaconna, by what means we are not told, to permit his son, Don Agaya, and another young Huron, Tagnoagny, to depart with him on the understanding they would be back next year. Cartier meant this. He hoped that they would acquire sufficient command of French as to be of service in the future.

On the arrival at St. Malo on 5 September, Cartier was able to make a positive report on the voyage of 1534. After leaving Gaspé, he had made good a northeasterly track towards Anticosti Island. Owing to thick fog he could not be sure whether Anticosti was an island or a peninsula. He explored its southeastern and northern coasts and found between Anticosti and the mainland, now part of the province of Quebec, a strait which he named the Strait of St. Peter. Its modern name is Jacques Cartier Passage. He was confident that this passage was the key to the penetration of North America by water.

This confidence was shared by Philippe de Chabot, by Cartier's backers in St. Malo and, since he made available three royal ships and some financial aid, the king himself. Chabot began preparations in early October 1534. The royal ships were *La Grande Hermine* (100–120 tons and 12 guns), *La Petite Hermine* (60 tons and 4 guns) and *L'Émerillon* (40 tons and 2 guns). They were manned by 112 officers and men, of whom some two-thirds belonged to St. Malo and of whom a dozen, including Macé Jalobert, commander of *La Petite Hermine,* were related to Cartier. In the sixteenth century, and later, regional and family solidarity offered some kind of insurance on long ocean voyages against the risk of disciplinary fragmentation, such as that which threatened Magellan in 1519–20 and Francis Drake in 1578 and that which destroyed Henry Hudson in 1611.

On 19 May 1535, Cartier on board *La Grande Hermine* led the fleet out of St. Malo on a fair wind "for the second voyage undertaken by the command and wish" of Francis I, "for the completion of the discovery of the western lands, lying under the same climate and parallels as the territories and kingdome of that prince, and by his orders already begun to be explored." Even in May and June boisterous westerly winds could blow up in the Atlantic as Cartier discovered, if he did not already know it, in 1535. The fleet was scattered. Newfoundland was not sighted by *La Grande Hermine* until 7 July and Blanc Sablon, the appointed rendezvous within the Strait of Belle Isle was reached on 15 July. The two remaining ships rejoined Cartier there on 6 July.

During the intense examination which followed of the islands and coasts of the Strait of Belle Isle and the Jacques Cartier Passage, the ships entered a good harbor in Quebec province on 10 August, the feast of St. Lawrence. It was accordingly named "Baie Sainct Laurins," the first use of a nomenclautre which became general usage later as the name of the gulf and of the great river, as he termed it, discovered by Cartier. On the subject of the river he listened to Don Agaya and Taignoagny, presumably by now able to make themselves understood in French, who told him that this was "the great river of Hochelaga and the route towards Canada, and that the river grew narrower as one approached Canada, and also that farther up the water became fresh, and that one could make one's way so far up the river that they had never heard of anyone reaching the head of it."

The young men added that one could only proceed along it in small boats. We cannot be sure just what Cartier made of this statement except that he searched for another strait before committing himself to the exploration of his "Great River." Sounding and charting as he moved up the St. Lawrence, Cartier's first major pause was at the mouth of the Charles River close by Stadacona, the base of Donnaconna and his people and site of the modern city of Quebec. Here the two larger ships were laid up and a fort constructed for purposes of defence. Cartier, on board *L'Émerillon,* sailed up the river to the Amerindian village of Hochelaga, about 1,000 miles from the open sea and somewhere on the site of what is now Montreal. Here on 3 October Cartier and his party climbed with local guides to the summit of "Mont Royal," from which they saw that the river extended far to the west from the point where they had left their longboats: a point they were unable to pass because of "the most violent rapid it is possible to see." The Lachine Rapids, as they were ironically named in the seventeenth century, put an end to Cartier's dream that the river was an open seaway to Asia.

On his return downriver to the anchorage called Sainte-Croix, near Stadacona, on 11 October, Cartier reinforced the defenses of the fort and, it being too late in the season to contemplate an Atlantic crossing, prepared to winter. Had he anticipated the severity of winter in the St. Lawrence valley and its threats to health, he may well have speeded up the reconnaissance of 1535. Being frozen up from mid-November until mid-April 1536 was a demoralizing experience. Lack of vitamin C in the available victuals put everybody's life at risk through the spread of scurvy. According to Cartier, 25 men died. And it is clear from his description of the symptoms that many survivors emerged from the ordeal with few or no teeth left in their heads. The expedition was saved from extinction by the fact that the Amerindians were also subject to the affliction during winter and that they had discovered a remedy in the leaves and bark of what they called the Annedda tree, most probably the Eastern White Cedar, which had anti-scorbutic properties. The history of modern Canada began when these properties were disclosed by the Amerindians to the stricken Europeans. Even so, Cartier was left with insufficient seamen to work the three ships. He was compelled to abandon the hull of *La Petite Hermine.*

Favored by good weather, the ships reached St. Malo on 16 July 1636. The report made it clear that the passage to Asia was blocked by the rapids above Hochelaga. The sense of urgency, so apparent in the autumn of 1534 that the search should be resumed as soon as possible, was missing. Cartier's report, however, aroused interest, as he intended that it should, in the Kingdom of Saguenay. Belief in its existence was based upon stories told by Don Agaya and Taignoagny, embroidered later by Donnaconna. All three were brought to France, along with a small party of young Amerindians, to promote Saguenay as a source of mineral wealth.

Saguenay was a kingdom of the mind, invented by the peoples of the St. Lawrence Valley to account for the supplies of Lake Superior copper which they received via the Ottawa and Saguenay rivers. It was transformed by the bullion-hungry French (as it would probably have been by other Europeans) into a land rich in precious stones and metals. From his third and last voyage to the St. Lawrence in 1541–42, Cartier returned to St. Malo with a quantity of stones and ore which he believed contained diamonds and gold. They proved to be of no value.

The exploitation of Saguenay, the precise location of which was a puzzle to the French, demanded the establishment of a permanent settlement. At this stage, however, a permanent settlement proved to be beyond their capacity. They had no experimental knowledge of the conduct of the fur trade of the interior. Participation therein was a condition of economic viability. Another problem was that of making the necessary adjustments to produce adequate quantities of appropriate crops to see them through the winter. It should be said that in this respect the French made a better showing than did the English who at Roanoke in the 1580s became pitifully dependent upon the Amerindians for supplies of food with damaging consequences for race relations. Given time, the French might have solved this problem. Time was denied them by the ferocity of the St. Lawrence winter. Neither Cartier in 1541–42 nor Jean François de La Rocque de Roberval, in charge of the support party, in 1542–43 was able to induce his followers (we cannot even be sure that either man tried very hard to so do) to endure a second winter in the frozen wilderness, especially given the proximity of increasingly suspicious Hurons.

The retreats of Cartier and de Roberval put an end to French colonizing ventures in the St. Lawrence until the first decade of the seventeenth century when Samuel de Champlain laid, with the backing of Henry IV, the permanent foundations of New France. During this long interval France never relinquished her claims nor abandoned her interests which were kept alive anonymously by fishermen and fur traders who did business with the inhabitants of both modern Canada and the United States of America.

Some of these traders may have penetrated the valley of the St. Lawrence before 1577 when the first official attempt since 1542–43 was made to revive a permanent French presence in North America through a commission granted by Henry III to a Breton nobleman,

Troilus de Merguëz, marquis de La Roche. He was authorized to acquire and exploit lands in the *Terres-Neuves* and in 1578 was appointed "*vice-roi des nouvelles terres.*" Nothing much came of this initiative until 1597 when De La Roche obtained permission to establish a colony, largely peopled by petty criminals and their guards, on Sable Island. It survived from 1598 to 1603 before being killed off through disciplinary disintegration. He was also nomimal leader of an expedition, directed in reality by Pierre Chauvin of Dieppe, for the establishment of a permanent foothold, the first on the mainland since 1543, at Tadoussac, a fur-trading center on the St. Lawrence near the mouth of the Saguenay river. This tiny settlement collapsed, as had its predecessors on the mainland, after the winter of 1600–1601.

More significant than these badly organized and ineffective attempts at settlement was the return of the French up the St. Lawrence. This may have happened earlier, but we are on sounder, if still somewhat uneven, ground for the 1580s and later. Basques, Bretons and Normans took advantage of the domestic boom in furs to trade regularly as collaborators and as rivals. Royal efforts to coordinate French commercial and colonial activities were frequently impeded by provincial particularism, notably that of the Bretons who favored free trade in opposition to protective royal monopolies, partly because they were able to identify some as Norman, partly because they objected to them in principle even when conferred upon individual Bretons. New France had a difficult birth.

A prominent role was played in the 1580s by the Noël family of St. Malo which included Jacques, a nephew of Cartier, and his two sons, Jean and Michel. In 1583, or maybe 1585, Jacques Noël sailed up the St. Lawrence to Hochelaga and looked down, like his uncle, on the river and the Lachine Rapids. Jean and Michel may well have done the same in 1587. French fur traders did not confine themselves to the St. Lawrence in this era. In 1583 Etienne Bellenger, a merchant of Rouen, made a profitable voyage to the Bay of Fundy and the coast of Maine.

The St. Lawrence, however, remained the chief French sphere of interest in North America. This was not because of the fur trade alone. An important element in the calculations of Champlain was the discovery of a western sea route to Asia. This would require access to a permanent settlement beyond the Lachine Rapids. Without such, expansion to the west was inconceivable. Whether the fur trade was seen as an argument for settlement is doubtful. Many of its participants, judging from the reaction to the attempted creation of royal monopolies, probably thought not. Henry IV on the other hand believed that, having emerged from the religious civil wars and the war with Spain of Philip II, France should match Spain by creating a New France in North America. He was also anxious to exert control over French subjects active there. It is doubtful whether in France there was a consensus in favor of an overseas empire. There were certainly no queues of "vexed and troubled" French men and women seeking passage to Canada. But there was sufficient informed opinion in support to warrant the effort.

It often seems as if historians, especially those working within the British tradition, regard as a central problem of sixteenth-century Atlantic history the need to explain the "failure" or the "unfilled promise" of the French effort. Conventional explanations on offer, French obsession with continental politics, the unsupportive attitude of the kings, civil and confessional strife in metropolitan France, appear on reflection as less than convincing. This is partly because these factors were hardly peculiar to France. It is mainly because the diagnosis of failure is itself defective.

In the North Atlantic French seamen were from the beginning to the fore in pioneering the greatest maritime industry of sixteenth-century Europe, the Newfoundland cod fishery, and in leading its extensions into the whaling grounds and seal and walrus colonies beyond. They were prominent in promoting the discovery, in the real sense of the term, of North America and, in pursuit of their own version of the mirage of the Northwest passage, revealed for the first time knowledge of the interior and its peoples up to 1,000 miles inland from the open sea. We are still in debt to the Norman cartographers and chart makers whose skills enhance our understanding of the process of North Atlantic and North American discovery.

In mid-Atlantic, French privateers (and pirates) launched the first battle of the Atlantic in history when raiders financed by the Ango family captured Spanish vessels bound from the Indies to Spain off the Azores in 1523 following the outbreak of war between France and the Habsburgs. This demonstration of strength was followed by the arrival in American and Azorean waters of wave upon wave of French raiders whose depredations compelled the Spaniards to organize a system of transatlantic convoy and the mobilization of the trade into annual fleets. In 1558 Henry II was considering a plan, probably proposed by Coligny, to send a combined force to the Caribbean to seize Panamá, storehouse of the silver shipped from Potosí.

Although not attempted because of the peace of Cateau Cambrésis (1559), the design anticipates in some respects the French Florida venture of 1562–5, sponsored by Coligny, with the acquiescence of Charles IX, and led by Jean Ribault and René Goulaine de Laudonnière. Its objects were twofold: the creation of a transatlantic refuge for Calvinists should the pressure for uniformity imperil their security in France (confessional strife could liberate energies for deployment in overseas ventures) and the establishment of a base or bases in Florida from which to launch attacks on the annual *flota*. Although the project ended in defeat, France was, as the Spaniards recognized, the only serious challenger to the Spanish colonial monopoly in America.

The same is true of the Portuguese monopoly in Brazil. Here the French breached the commercial barriers and traded for brazilwood throughout the sixteenth century. They also succeeded in the 1550s by establishing a settlement there—*La France Antarctique*—thus breaching temporarily at least the colonial monopoly. The survival intact of the transatlantic Iberian empires was a tribute to their durability, a fact of life discovered later by both the Dutch and the English. It is hardly proof that French maritime enterprise in the sixteenth century was in some ways flawed. Much less can we improve our understanding of it by assuming that we are dealing with a record of failure.

NOTES

1. Several versions of this letter are extant, the most complete being the Cèllere Codex, a twentieth-century discovery now in the Pierpont Morgan Library, New York, which contains annotations to the text added by Verrazzano. The most comprehensive scholarly edition in English thereof is *The Voyages of Giovanni da Verrazzano, 1524–1528* (1970) by Lawrence C. Wroth.

2. Maggiolo's map was destroyed at Milan during the war of 1939–45. Fortunately it had been reproduced in full size and color at the beginning of the twentieth century. Girolamo's map of 1529 is in the Vatican Library. A map of 1528 with additions up to 1540–42, which is attributed to him, is preserved in the National Maritime Museum, Greenwich.

SUGGESTIONS FOR FURTHER READING

Published Contemporary Sources

Biggar, H. P. (ed.). *The Precursors of Jacques Cartier*. (Ottawa, 1911).

Biggar, H. P. (ed.). *The Voyages of Jacques Cartier*. (Ottawa, 1924).

Biggar, H. P. (ed.). *A Collection of Documents relating to Jacques Cartier and the Sieur de Roberval.* (Ottawa, 1930).

Quinn, D. B. (ed.), *New American World: A Documentary History of North America to 1612,* 5 vols. (New York, 1979), vol. I, chapters 21, 22; vol. II, chapters 32–36, for French Florida, 1562–5.

Wroth, L. C. (ed.), *The Voyages of Giovanni da Verrazzano, 1524–1528.* (New Haven, 1970).

Later Works

Axtell, J. *After Columbus: Essays in the Ethnohistory of Colonial North America.* (New York and Oxford, 1988).

Boxer, C. R. *The Portuguese Seaborne Empire, 1415–1825.* (London, 1969).

Julien, C. A. *Les Voyages de découverte et les premiers establissements.* (Paris, 1948).

Lanctot, G. *A History of Canada,* vol. I. (Toronto, 1963).

Mollat, M. *Le Commerce Maritime Normand à la Fin du Moyen Âge.* (Paris, 1952).

Morison, S. E. *The European Discovery of America: The Northern Voyages, A.D. 500–1600.* (New York and Oxford, 1971), chapters IX, XI, XII, XIII.

Morison, S. E. *The European Discovery of America: The Southern Voyages, 1492–1616.* (New York and Oxford, 1974), chapter XXIV.

Quinn, D. B. *North America from Earliest Discovery to First Settlements: The Norse Voyages to 1612.* (New York, 1977), chapters 7, 8, 10.

Quinn, D. B. "The Attempted Colonization of Florida by the French, 1562–1565," *Explorers and Colonies: America, 1500–1625.* (London, 1990).

Quinn, D. B. "The Voyage of Etienne Bellenger to the Maritimes in 1583: A New Document," *ibid.*

Thrower, N. J. W. "New Light on the 1524 Voyage of Verrazzano," *Terrae Incognitae,* vol. 11 (1979).

Tomlinson, R. J. *The Struggle for Brazil: Portugal and "the French Interlopers."* (New York, 1970).

Trudel, M. *Histoire de la Nouvelle France: Les Vaines Tentatives, 1524–1603.* (Montreal, 1963).

Trudel, M. *The Beginnings of New France, 1524–1663.* (Toronto, 1973).

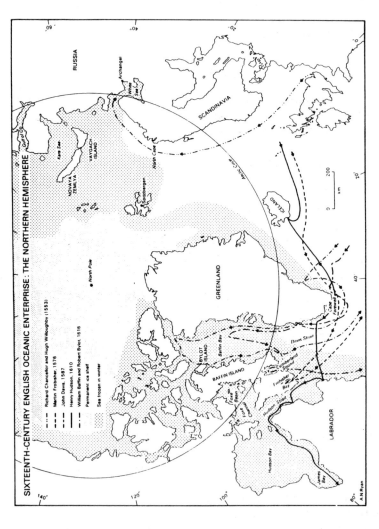

Figure XXVII. Sixteenth-Century English Oceanic Enterprise: The Norther Hemisphere. Originally drawn by A.N. Ryan for *Atlas of British Overseas Expansion* (London, 1991). *Reproduced by kind permission of the editor, Professor A.N. Porter, and the publisher, Routledge.*

17

"A NEW PASSAGE TO CATAIA": THE NORTHWEST PASSAGE IN EARLY MODERN ENGLISH HISTORY

A. N. Ryan

When I gave myself to the studie of Geographie, after I had perused and diligently scanned the descriptions of Europe, Asia and Afrike, and conferred them with the Mappes and Globes both Antique and Moderne I came in fine to the fourth parte of the worlde, commonly called America, which by all descriptions I founde to be an Islande environed round about with the Sea, having on the southside of it, the frete, or strayte of Magellan, on the West side Mare de sur, which Sea runenth towardes the North, separating it from the East parts of Asia, where the dominions of the Cataians are, On the East part our West Ocean, and on the Northside the sea that severeth it from Grondland, thorow which Northern seas, the passage lyeth, which I take now in hand to discover.

Thus reads the first paragraph of *A discourse of a discoverie for a new passage to Cataia,* first drafted in 1566 and "Imprinted at London by Henry Middleton, for Richarde Jhones, *Anno Damini, 1576.*" Its author was Sir Humphrey Gilbert, participant in Tudor wars in Ireland, advocate of English colonization and protagonist of a navigable northwest passage around America from the Atlantic into the Pacific. Gilbert belonged to a landed family in Devon which had significant maritime interests and associations. He was a nephew of Sir Arthur Champernoune, vice-admiral of Devon and a promoter of privateering. Gilbert's brother Adrian shared his pioneering spirit, as did his half-brother Walter Raleigh.

The writing and publication of the *Discourse* was inspired by a revival of interest in mid-sixteenth-century England in the discovery of a northern passage or passages to Asia, which had been largely dormant since Sebastian Cabot's voyage of 1508–9 and his entry into the service of Spain which lasted from 1512 to 1547. Lack of interest can be measured by the negative response to an offer by Sebastian Cabot during a visit to England in 1520–21 to lead an expedition to Cathay by the Northwest and by the indifference of both the crown and the city of London to Robert Thorne the Younger's "Declaration of the Indies" of 1527 which contained a proposal for a passage to Asia across the North Pole. Thorne was a link with the earlier Bristol enterprise, his father Robert the Elder having been a participant in the activities surrounding the new found land. The concept of a polar route was kept alive by Roger Barlowe, who had lived in Spain and sailed with Cabot to the River Plate in 1525–26, in a "Briefe Summe of Geographie" of 1541. It attracted no more political and financial support than Thorne's "Declaration of the Indies."

In the second half of the 1540s, however, things were different. The greater availability of capital, growing ambitions in both governmental and entrepreneurial circles to break into trades monopolized by the Spaniards and Portuguese, increasing awareness of the need to supplement the declining markets for English cloth in Europe by finding new outlets for the cloth industry elsewhere, all combined in an age of economic stress to encourage searches for new routes to distant places whereby England might compete effectively with the Iberian colonial powers. What little was known of the Arctic regions seemed to point to them as the location of convenient routes.

There was, however, despite the availability for consultation with the interested parties after 1547 of Sebastian Cabot no unanimous agreement in favor of the Northwest Passage. At a late hour in fact it was determined to attempt a passage around the North Cape of Norway and beyond Novaya Zemlya into the Kara Sea and so around Russia to Cathay: The Northeast Passage. The first attempt was made in 1553 under the command of Hugh Willoughby, who was frozen to death in the Arctic winter, with Richard Chancellor as navigator on board a second vessel. Chancellor entered the White Sea and found a settlement at St. Nicholas in the dominions of Tsar Ivan IV of Muscovy. The landfall led to successful negotiations for an Anglo-Russian commercial settlement and to the foundation in 1555 of the Muscovy Company whose charter conferred upon it monopolistic rights over navigation in the Arctic Seas. As we have no minutes of the consultations which preceded the voyage of 1553 we can only offer provisional explanations of the decision in favor of a search to the Northeast. It may well have been, as was suggested by Clement Adams, a professional associate of Cabot, an example of the influence of business factors. Experience at the beginning of the century had shown a distinct lack of trading opportunities in North America, whereas it might at least be hoped that markets for English cloth existed in the territories flanking a Northeast Passage. This consideration was justified, somewhat unexpectedly, by the English discovery of Russia and the opening of trade via the White Sea.

The company continued to promote exploration to the east of the White Sea. In 1556 its young servants, Stephen and William Borough, attempted a reconnaissance as far as the mouth of the River Ob, but failed to get beyond Vaygach Island near Novaya Zemlya. Arthur Pett and George Jackman struggled into the Kara Sea in 1580 only to find themselves, like the Boroughs, blocked by a barrier of ice. Later again in 1608 Henry Hudson was forced to turn back without entering the Kara Sea. The formidability of the ice-fields encouraged advocates of the Northwest Passage to challenge the Muscovy Company's monopolistic claims over all navigation in the northern seas with the aim of launching a sustained search for a Northwest Passage. The legal wrangles gave birth to Gilbert's promotional literature which was originally written in 1566 to support his arguments in debate with Anthony Jenkinson of the Muscovy Company before the Privy Council: a debate from which the company emerged with its monopoly intact.

The discourse is an erudite work, lavishly garnished with acknowledgments to respected authorities ranging from Plato and Pliny to "al the best modern Geographers," including Gemma Frisius, to Giovanni da Verrazzano, who had surveyed the coast of North America in 1524 for Francis I of France and was said by Gilbert as having heard at Nova Francia that "there was a great sea at Saguinay, whereof the ende was not knowen, which they presupposed to be the passage to Cataia" and to Sebastian Cabot himself.

Gilbert's valiant attempt to prove by authority, by reason, by experience of "sundry men's travails," by circumstance and by dubious history concerning Indians "driven upon the coastes of Germania" in the age of Frederick Barbarossa was flawed by defective geographical concepts. This was hardly his own fault. In the 1560s, and indeed for a long time to come, the latitudinal and longitudinal extents of North America were unknown with the result that estimates of distance were no more than guesses. The Arctic Ocean and its contents were also unknown with the result that cartographers were faced with a choice between cutting off North America with the northern boundary of their maps or of depicting an unbroken northern coastline bordering an open sea, the supposed Northwest Passage, in the manner favoured by the famous sixteenth-century geographical masters, Gemma Frisius and Abraham Ortelius. Gilbert's map, which accompanied the discourse, was clearly influenced by them both.

Gilbert's geographical ideas were by no means eccentric in sixteenth-century England. The concept of a commodious Northwest Passage in the approximate latitudes of the British Isles was welcomed as an attractive alternative to the long hauls to Asia around Africa or through the Strait of Magellan. Although growing awareness of geographical reality compelled promoters and participants to accept that the passage would have to be sought in higher latitudes than those envisaged by Gilbert, the English launched expeditions, funded by private investors, over a period of nearly 60 years in search of the elusive passage. The aim of the voyages between 1576 and 1632 was to translate theory into practice by conclusively demonstrating the existence of a commercially feasible route.

The commercial driving force was Michael Lok, member of a London business family which had been prominent for many years in ventures to expand English overseas trade beyond its traditional boundaries. He had much to do with overcoming the resistance of the Muscovy Company to any relaxation of its monopolistic rights and with raising sufficient capital to finance a voyage. Lok also entered into an alliance with 37-year old Martin Frobisher. Frobisher, a tough and unscrupulous Yorkshire-born seaman, was known to Lok through having served in his youth on the Guinea coast of Africa under Captain John Lok, Michael's brother. In his subsequent career at sea Frobisher had acquired an unsavoury reputation as a pirate; but he was known to be both resolute and durable and to be anxious for employment as a leader of a hazardous expedition to the Northwest.

The expedition sailed from Ratcliffe within the River Thames on 7 June 1576. Modestly funded, it consisted of three vessels, the *Gabriel* (30 tons), with Frobisher on board, the *Michael* (30 tons) and a pinnace, manned by four men; which was lost off Shetland in rough weather. According to the journal, in effect the log, of Christopher Hall, master of the *Gabriel,* the two surviving ships set course across the Atlantic from off Shetland and were generally favored by wind and weather until off Greenland. Hall, who gave his name to Hall Peninsula on Baffin Island, was an able and methodical navigator.

Expecting, as did Martin Frobisher, Humphrey Gilbert and, more authoritatively again, John Dee, the famous cosmographer and mathematician, to find the passage between 60°N and 63°N Hall kept a careful record of his reckonings of latitude. He is an early example, as far as England is concerned, of a scientific navigator, obtaining the latitude of the ship by observations with the cross staff of the altitudes of the sun by day and the Pole Star by night. The star was less of an aid than the sun because of its faintness during the short nights of summer in the high northern latitudes. Hall also recorded his estimates of the distance run and noted changes in the variations of the magnetic compass.

When the east coast of Greenland, "rising like pinnacles of steeples, all covered with snow" was sighted on 11 July, the ships were by Hall's calculations on track. They found themselves confronted, however, by an ice-bound coast with fog closing in. At this stage the master and crew of the *Micheal* dropped out and returned home to report on 1 September that the *Gabriel* was cast away. Frobisher, justifying his reputation for durability, pushed on through dangerously high seas and made a landfall off Resolution Island on 20 July. His next discovery was an inlet, now known as Frobisher Bay, on the southeast coast of Baffin Island, by Hall's accurate reckoning in 62°02′N.

If the latitudinal reckonings were admirable throughout the crossing, the geographical misconceptions were woeful. The flawed geography of Frobisher and Hall led them to misidentify Greenland as the mythical island of Frisland. This misconception occurred because they accepted as authentic, a chart published in Venice by Nicolo Zeno in 1558 (to be fair, men more learned than they also accepted it), which he claimed had been compiled by his ancestors, Nicolo and Antonio Zeno, in 1380. Much of it, including Frisland and other islands, was pure invention. Zeno also included a peninsular Greenland extending from Europe and located to the northwest of its actual position. By trusting so misleading an aid to Arctic exploration, Frobisher virtually lost whatever chance he may have had of solving the problem of the relationship between the real Greenland and North America.

Geographical fantasy continued to influence events. George Best, who wrote from personal experience the fullest account of the Frobisher voyages, described Frobisher Bay as "a great gutte, bay or passage deviding as it were two major lands or continents assunder." After entering the bay, which he explored to a distance of about 150 miles, Frobisher was even more positive. He claimed to have

upon either hand "a great mayne or continent" and judged the land
on his right hand, as he sailed up the bay, to be Asia and "there to
devided from the firme of America which lyeth upon the left hand
over against the same." Without penetrating the bay to its upper
limits because of ice, Frobisher had found what he had expected to
find and what he had been commissioned to find: a spacious passage
to the north of America leading westward to Cathay, the land on the
right being the mythical Horn of Asia. "This place he named," wrote
Best, "after his name Frobishers Streytes, lyke as Magellanus at the
Southwest ende of the worlde, havying discovered the passage to the
South Sea . . . called the same straites Magellans steightes."

Fortified by his defective geography, Frobisher claimed on return
to England to have discovered the entrance to the passage. He reinforced his claim by exhibiting an unfortunate Inuit man who was
said to resemble the Samoyeds whom men of the Muscovy company
had seen during the Northeast Passage searches. He did not live
long. Christopher Hall seems to have been of a similar opinion, describing the Inuit as being "like to Tartars, with long blacke haire,
broad faces, and flatte noses, and tawnie in colour, wearing Seale
skinnes, and so do the women, not differing in the fashion, but the
women are marked in the face with blewe streekes downe the
cheekes and round the eies."

On the basis of these speculations Lok succeeded in obtaining a
renewal and enlargement of his licence and set about launching a
Cathay Company which attracted subscriptions from Queen Elizabeth I, who made available for service the *Aid,* a three masted royal
warship of 200 tons, and from courtiers, including the lord treasurer, William Cecil, Lord Burghley. Before the second expedition
was ready for sea, word began to spread, apparently with the support of Lok, that rock brought back home from the mouth of the supposed strait contained gold. The prospect of a gold find in an area remote from the transatlantic bases of Spanish power unleashed
cravings which had little to do with the discovery of a Northwest
Passage. Frobisher and his men dedicated themselves in 1577 and
again in 1578 largely to the loading of rock from the area called by
the queen Meta Incognita.

The expedition of 1578 was the largest to have left the shores of
England for a transatlantic destination: a fleet 15 ships, drawn from
a wide range of English ports, led by the *Aid* with the *Gabriel* and
Michael in attendance. Most of the vessels were to serve as trans-
ports of cargoes of "ore." Although tests on that brought back in
1576–77 were inconclusive, the so-called experts being unable to

agree on its worth, the enterprise was well backed financially by members of the court. Amidst talk of the establishment of a permanent mining settlement at Meta Incognita, Frobisher led his ships out of Harwich on 31 May, sighted Greenland, still convinced that it was the mythical Frisland, on 20 June and came off Resolution Island on 2 July in bitterly cold and stormy weather.

At this stage Frobisher might have associated his name with a great discovery. In the dismal weather conditions which restricted opportunities for the fixing of latitude by observation of the sun or Pole Star a navigational error caused Frobisher to miss Frobisher Bay and enter what became known as the "Mistaken Straits" which, from all contemporary descriptions, cannot have been other than Hudson Strait. He sailed up it for some 180 miles before turning back and was convinced that he had found the true passage. But the passage no longer enjoyed priority. The main business of the wretched summer was the mining of "ore" which began at Kodlunarn Island and other places on 1 August.

Ten of his ships having been laden, Frobisher returned to England to find on arrival that the Cathay Company was in tatters and that Michael Lok was under siege. Exhaustive tests of the "ore" at Bristol and Deptford had conclusively demonstrated the absence of any trace of gold or silver in which so much hope and money had been invested. Lok, though far from ruined, lost heavily; other contributors, including the queen, came out poorer than when they went in. On the positive side, the English had shown that they could mobilize sufficient capital to sustain a hazardous overseas venture and that they could organize shipping on a fairly large scale. But, even laying aside the financial fiasco arising out of credulity and incompetence, Frobisher hardly advanced confidence in the reality of the Northwest Passage. When he sailed away from Meta Incognita in 1578, he sailed away from it for the last time.

The most pathetic victims of the enterprise, however, were five Englishmen and four Inuit. Anglo-Inuit relations were governed on both sides by curiosity, by no means consistently hostile, and wariness. They were not helped by the language barrier, nor by the assumption that primitive non-European people must be morally inferior to Europeans. In this strained atmosphere breakdowns in relations were a recurrent danger. The five Englishmen were victims in the first instance at least of disobedience to sensible orders. They were instructed to row ashore an Inuit who had been entertained on board the *Gabriel* with the proviso that they should land him at a distance from where the mass of the Inuit was assembled.

They carried out the first part of their orders, but ignored the second and fell into the hands of local people. Despite negotiations in 1576 and again in 1577 they were never seen again. Inuit folk memory has it that they eventually built a boat and sailed away.

Mention has already been made of the death at London in 1576 of the Inuit brought back by Frobisher as evidence of success in the search for a Northwest Passage. He was not the last of his people to die in England. In 1577, the English having failed to negotiate the release of their fellow countrymen, attempted to do so by force. In the skirmishes which ensured some Inuit were killed, Frobisher was wounded in the buttock by an arrow and an Inuit man, in his kayak, a woman, mistakenly believed to be his wife, and her child were seized. They were brought to England in the hope, according to Best, of being of service in spreading knowledge of their language. At Bristol the man gave demonstrations in his kayak. Unfortunately during the crossing of the Atlantic he had broken a rib which had punctured a lung and caused his death. The woman died a few days later. The child was taken to London, but did not live for long. Their memorial is an entry in the parish registers of the church of St. Stephen in Bristol: "Collichang a heathen man buried the 8th. of November; Egnock a heathen woman buried the 12th. of November."

After the financial fiasco of 1578–79 the only people willing the venture capital in voyages to the northwest were those who still believed that a Northwest Passage awaited discovery. Adrian Gilbert, younger brother of Humphrey, shared his brother's faith, as did the intellectually influential John Dee, and Walter Raleigh. In 1583 Adrian Gilbert obtained a royal patent to seek a passage by way of the Arctic seas to China and the Moluccas on behalf of himself and "certain Honourable personages and worthy Gentlemen of the Court and Countrey, with divers worshipful Marchants of London and the West Countrey." The chief financier of the projected discovery was William Sanderson, a merchant of London. At a political level the enterprise enjoyed the backing of Sir Francis Walsingham, the anti-Spanish principal secretary of Queen Elizabeth I.

For "Captaine and chiefe Pilot of this exployt" Gilbert turned to a fellow Devonian, John Davis of Sandridge, near Dartmouth, who, though of humbler social origins than the Gilberts, had acquired a high professional reputation as a seaman and navigator. Davis led the barks *Sunneshine* (50 tons) and *Moonshine* (35 tons) out of Dartmouth on 7 June 1585 and 20 July "fell upon the shore which in ancient time was called Greenland, five hundred leagues distant from the Durseys [Dursey Head, Co. Kerry, Ireland] Westnorthwest

Northerly." Rounding Cape Farewell, Cape Desolation as he called it, Davis began the exploration of the ice-free waters of the west coast of Greenland as far as the modern Godthåb or Nuuk (which he called Gilbert Sound), thereafter crossing the strait, which now bears his name, to a point on Baffin Island just within the Arctic circle. He discovered, but did not at this stage fully explore, Cumberland Sound, situated to the north of Frobisher Bay. Cumberland Sound was for Davis "our hoped straight." But with the end of August fast approaching and "not knowing the length of the straight and the dangers thereof, we tooke it our best course to returne with notice of our good successe for this small time to search." This was not an unfair claim. He had established more clearly the geographical relationship between Greenland and North America, thus clearly up a major misconception of Frobisher, and provided grounds for a renewal of hope in the existence of a passage.

In Davis's own mind there was little or no doubt. Despite his talents as chartmaker, explorer and navigator, he had seen in 1585, like Frobisher in 1576 and like other sixteenth-century navigators, what he expected to see. He impressed potential contributors. A number of Exeter merchants threw in their lot with Sanderson. Yet Davis produced no new evidence in 1586 to support his ideas regarding the discovery of a passage through Cumberland Sound. He inexplicably failed to explore it thoroughly despite crossing Davis Strait from West Greenland as in 1585. The truth may well be that he was experiencing a change of mind about the location of an open passage. Conversations, conducted in sign language with the Greenland Inuit, pointed in his opinion to the existence of an open sea to the north. This interpretation of events receives support from Davis's conduct in 1587.

The expedition of 1587 received less financial support than that of 1586, not surprisingly in view of the lack of positive findings. Provision had to be made for fishing as a means of helping to cover the cost. As "Chiefe Captaine and Pilot generall, for the discoverie of a passage to the Isles of Molucca, or the coast of China," Davis sailed from Dartmouth on 19 May and arrived off Godthåb on 14 June. After a ritual exchange of goods with the Inuit, with whom his relations were robust and, given the difficulties for both parties, remarkably amicable, David drove north. "Now having coasted the land," wrote John Janes "which we called London coast, from the 21 of this present [June] till the 30, the Sea open all to the Westwards and Northwards, the land on starboard side East from us, the winde shifted to the North, whereupon we left that that shore, naming the same Hope Sanderson, and shaped our course West, and ranne 40 leagues and better without the sight of any land." The site of Hope Sanderson is in latitude 72°46'N. How far he would have got had the wind not changed and whether he would have returned home are unanswerable questions.

By turning west, Davis was heading again for Baffin Island. On this leg of the voyage he was impeded by the Middle Pack, the ice barrier in Baffin Bay, and was forced to alter course to the south. He noted, however, that there was no ice towards the north, "but a great sea, free, large very salt and blew and of an unassailable depth." He thereafter explored Cumberland Sound, rediscovered Frobisher Bay, which he named Lumley's Inlet, and sighted, but did not examine Frobisher's "Mistaken Straits." He returned home convinced, as he reported to Sanderson in a letter from Sandridge of 16 September, that having found the sea open and forty leagues between land and land, "the passage is most probable, the execution easie, as at my coming you shall fully know." But Davis had seen Davis Strait and Baffin Bay for the last time. Declining financial support, the war with Spain and the death of Walsingham, its principal political prop, terminated the enterprise. The search was not renewed until the early seventeenth century.

Davis's account of the voyages of 1585–87 was published in 1595 as *The Worlde's Hydrographical Description* which was a declaration of belief, based upon reason and observation, in the existence of the passage and a statement of the advantages which England would obtain from its being discovered. After service against Spain in 1588–89, Davis was eager to resume the search. In 1591 he teamed up with Thomas Cavendish, a landed adventurer from Suffolk, who had circumnavigated the world during 1586–88 and taken the rich Spanish galleon *Santa Ana* off Cape San Lucas, California, in November 1587. Cavendish's aims in 1591 were to plunder Spanish ships in the Pacific and establish direct trade with China or Japan via the Strait of Magellan. He needed the services of Davis as a navigator and chartmaker to pilot the ships through the hazardous strait.

Davis, who contributed a ship jointly owned by himself and Adrian Gilbert, had another object. The arrangement with Cavendish was that Davis should part company off California "to search that Northwest discovery upon the backe parts of America." In other words he intended to look for the supposed Strait of Anian, the exit from the Northwest Passage into the Pacific Ocean. Francis Drake, when working his way up the Pacific coast of North America in 1579, during what turned out to be a voyage of circumnavigation, had entertained the same idea. He was thwarted by the fact that the Strait of Anian could not be found in a sufficiently low latitude to encourage hopes of a swift and secure passage around America for the *Golden Hind* and her cargo of booty. The Cavendish-Davis expedition failed to enter the Pacific. It struggled through the strait of Magellan, but was driven back by foul weather and adverse winds. Davis made a second attempt which suffered the same fate. He returned home in 1593 (Cavendish died at sea) convinced of "the great unlikelyhoode of any passage to be that way" [the Strait of Magellan].

Davis is remembered chiefly for the voyages of 1585–87, the harsh voyage of 1591–93 and later voyages in both Dutch and English service to the Indian Ocean by way of the Cape of Good Hope. He should also be remembered as author of *The Seamans Secrets* (1593), the first published treatise on the practice of navigation to be written by a professional English seaman. It was not the first book of its kind to be written by an Englishman; that honor belongs to *A Regiment For the Sea* published in 1574 by William Bourne of Gravesend. Davis, however, was the first seaman to write for his fellow seamen. The publication of these books is an indicator of English progress in the theory and practice of oceanic navigation in the second half of the sixteenth century. As late as 1561 the only available navigational text book was Richard Eden's recent translation into English of *Breve compendio de la sphera y de la arte de navigar* from the Spanish of Martin Cortés.

Davis's contribution was practical as well as theoretical. He stressed in *The Seamans Secrets* the importance of celestial observations as an aid to navigation, listing among the instruments "necessary for the execution of this excellent skill" the cross staff, the quadrant and the astrolabe. Of these three instruments he recommended the cross staff as being more likely to produce accurate results when observations were made from the deck of a moving ship. By means of such observations the navigator could identify the latitude of the ship, as Hall had done when bringing the *Gabriel* across the Atlantic to Baffin Island in 1576. In the northern hemisphere this was done either by measuring the altitude of the sun by day or of *Stella Polaris* (the Pole Star) by night. Davis's experience in the higher latitudes of the North Atlantic encouraged him to improve the accuracy of the cross staff. In these latitudes the long summer daylight meant that opportunities of measuring the altitude of *Stella Polaris* might not occur. This put a premium upon accurate observations of the sun. For this reason Davis devised a variant of the cross staff called the back staff (later known as the Davis or English quadrant) which enabled the observer with his back to the sun to focus upon the horizon and to bring it into line with the shadow cast by the sun. It had the advantage that the observer was spared the glare of the sun and relieved of the almost insurmountable difficulty of sighting simultaneously the sun and the horizon. The back staff remained a standard nautical instrument until its replacement after 1731 by John Hadley's reflecting quadrant.

In the 1580 edition of *A Regiment for the Sea*, William Bourne offered advice which, if heeded, might have put English expectations regarding the Northwest Passage on a more realistic basis. Although he suspected that the *"Frobishers Streights"* led nowhere, he did not reject the possibility that "there may be passage there about" These views may well have reflected those of his stepson, John Beare, master, under George Best, of the *Anne Francis* on the second and third Frobisher voyages. Bourne, however, did not regard the discovery of a passage, assuming that such existed near Meta Incognita, as the solution to the problem. Rather like fifteenth-century Portuguese and Spanish critics of Christopher Columbus's "Enterprize of the Indies," he believed that the distance involved in any voyage to Cathay or the Moluccas by a Northwest Passage was much greater than that envisaged by the promoters. He warned that the distance between the entry to the passage and the exit therefrom into the Pacific could not be less than 1,000 leagues.

Despite this sobering estimate and the failures of Frobisher and Davis to find a way through, there was a revival of interest, led by the English East India Company, in the Northwest Passage in the first decade of the seventeenth century. The company had been granted a charter in December 1600 to compete with the Dutch and Portuguese in the Eastern Seas, including the Spice Islands. Its first voyage was directed around the Cape of Good Hope, which was to become in the long term its standard route; but the company's directors recognized that the Northwest Passage, if navigable, offered a quicker and safer route than the haul around Africa. They were also anxious less English interlopers might to the company's disadvantage discover the passage and they were worried by signs of Danish and Dutch interest in the area which, if it came to anything, might bring foreign powers into the passage.

In 1602 Captain George Waymouth was ordered to search for the passage. He examined the coasts of Labrador and Baffin Island between 55° and 63°N. and entered what was soon to be called Hudson

Strait in dismal weather. His journal for July and August contains frequent references to fog, snow, ice and fierce winds. The crews of the two ships, *Discovery* (70 tons) and *Godspeed* (60 tons) lost their appetite for exploration and compelled Waymouth to return to England. This incident, by no means the only one of its kind in the series of northwest voyages, illustrates the extent to which leaders were dependent upon the goodwill of their followers. Physically isolated and unsupported by either the power of the state or the disciplinary traditions of a professional naval service, they had little or no room for maneuver if faced by a hostile majority verdict against continued combat with the perils of the sea.

The next move was made in 1606 by the East India and Muscovy Companies acting in collaboration as the Society of English Merchants for the Discovery of New Trades. It appointed as leader John Knight who had sailed in 1605 on an expedition to Davis Strait and Greenland largely, it would seem, in search of traces of the defunct Norse Greenland settlement in the service of Christian IV, king of Denmark. On 19 June, Knight in the *Hopewell* (40 tons) "descryed the Land of America which riseth like eight Ilands . . . I observed the latitude and found my selfe to be in 56. degrees and 48. minutes." Within a few days the *Hopewell* was grounded by ice and storms on the coast of Labrador and was eventually refloated and sufficiently repaired for the voyage home. She returned without Knight and three of the crew, who had gone ashore, armed, on 26 June, were observed to crest a hill and were never seen again. It is presumed that they were killed by Inuit, by now "salvagions [savages]" and "man-eaters," who also carried out attacks upon the rest of the crew. In the light of Waymouth's experience the survivors were, at the behest of the promoters, examined before the High Court of Admiralty, but nothing emerged to substantiate such suspicions of their conduct as may have been entertained.

The wave of interest in the passage in countries on both sides of the North Sea culminated in the discovery of Hudson Bay. Henry Hudson was a professional navigator and explorer whose services were much in demand. In 1607–8 he was employed by the Muscovy Company to discover Robert Thorne's transpolar passage to Cathay and the Northeast Passage. His searches were blocked, like those of his predecessors, by ice and, it would seem, in 1608 by reluctance of the mariners to proceed into the icefields. On these voyages he added significantly to knowledge of Spitzbergen and the fish-laden seas around it. 1609 found him in the service of the Dutch East India Company when he sailed on the *Halve Moen* from Amsterdam to find a Northeast Passage beyond Novaya Zemlya, an enterprise which was bedeviled by the obstructive attitude of his Anglo-Dutch crew. Perhaps Hudson's own strength of commitment was limited. He had come to believe in the existence of a passage through temperate latitudes to the north of Virginia. Instead of putting back to Amsterdam he crossed the Atlantic, entered the Hudson River, discovered New York harbor and explored up river to modern Albany before deciding that this was not the passage. He still hoped to reach an agreement with the Dutch East India Company in 1610 for a resumption of the search.

Like many explorers of the Age of Discovery Hudson was less concerned with national interests than with the promotion of his own career and the satisfaction of his own exploratory ambitions. However, national considerations came into play. Hudson was forbidden to go to the Dutch Republic and found himself appointed by a syndicate, which included magnates of the East India and Muscovy Companies, to lead an expedition to the Northwest Passage. He sailed in April 1610 on board the *Discovery* (55 tons) with a crew, which numbered among it Abacuk Pricket as representative of the promoters, of 22 men and 2 boys. Crossing the Atlantic by way of the Orkneys, Shetland, the Faeros, Iceland and Greenland he passed through Frobisher's "Mistaken Streights [Hudson Strait]" and entered the great bay now named after him on 3 August. After working his way southward down its east side Hudson became embayed at the head of what would later be called James Bay on 1 November and was frozen in.

In June 1611, with the *Discovery* clear of the ice, shortage of food, sickness and clashes of personality broke the fragile bonds of discipline. Hudson, his son and seven other men were put adrift in a pinnace. Their exact fate is unknown. Those still on board the *Discovery* included three key figures: Robert Juet who had sailed as mate to Hudson until, having incurred the distrust of Hudson, he was demoted, Robert Bylot, Juet's successor as mate, who took over as master following the mutiny, and Abacuk Pricket. The *Discovery* got back with only nine survivors on board. Four of the crew were killed by Inuit after having gone ashore in search of food and Juet died at sea.

The impression given by the survivors, of whom Pricket was the most astute, is of the mutiny as an act of desperate men faced with a choice between the death of all through starvation and the survival of some at the expense of those in so weak a condition that their chances of living were remote. The impression was also given of the need to distinguish between Henry Greene, William Wilson, two of the four men killed by the Inuit, and Robert Juet, all described as prime movers of the mutiny and those, the survivors, who acquiesced "to save some from Starving." The survivors were examined at Trinity House in 1611 and proceedings against them were initiated by the High Court of Admiralty in 1614. The available evidence, all of it supplied by themselves, pointed unerringly neither to their innocence nor to their guilt. They were officially cleared in 1618.

The dilatory nature of the proceedings seems to have reflected from the beginning a feeling that they may have been pushed beyond the limits of endurance. It also reflected an awareness that Bylot and Pricket could be of service to the "Governor and Company of the Merchants of London, Discoverers of the Northwest Passage," the foundation of which early in 1612 was inspired by faith in the existence of the passage beyond the strait through which Hudson had passed. The company launched two major ventures, as well as minor ones, into the bay. The first under Captain Thomas Button, who had done service in the navy, sailed in April 1612, having Bylot and Pricket on board. His instructions were to search for Hudson, which was perfunctorily performed, and to find the passage. He was ordered as well to winter at a suitable place in the southern part of the bay, should it be found advantageous to do so "for we assure our selfe by God's grace you will not returne, without either the good Newes of a passage, or sufficient assurance of an impossibility." Having examined much of the west coast of the bay and having lost many men from sickness, probably scurvy, during the winter, Button returned home in September 1613, without "good Newes" and also without "assurance of an impossibility."

The door through the bay was effectively closed on the company in 1615 by William Baffin and Bylot. Baffin, an experienced navigator with experience in the seas around Greenland and Spitzbergen, was remarkable for his meticulous observation and recording of the facts as he saw them. After a thorough examination of the bay he informed the company of his opinion that, if a passage did exist, it was more likely to be found "upp fretum Davis." The company took him at his word and sent him and Bylot up Davis Strait in March 1616 on board the *Discovery,* now on her sixth voyage to the northwest. The expedition sailed beyond Davis's Hope Sanderson to a height of 78°N, the highest latitude reached until 1853. On its way south down what is now called Baffin Bay, Baffin sighted when in 74°20′ N what appeared to be an ice-bound bay on his west side. He named it Lancaster Sound after Sir James Lancaster of the East India Company, a prominent supporter of the Northwest Passage project. In reality Lancaster Sound was the gateway to the intricate chain of channels through which Roald Amundsen was to sail in his conquest of the Northwest Passage during 1903–6. Baffin had no means of knowing this. "There is no passage," he wrote, "nor hope of passage in the north of Davis Straights." With these words he brought in effect an end to the brief history of the Northwest Passage Company.

The final curtain came down on this phase of English Arctic explorations in 1631–32 when two expeditions went to Hudson Bay. The first, commanded by Thomas James of Bristol and backed by the Bristol Society of Merchants Adventurers in the hope of enjoying "such priviledges and immunities (if the passage bee discovered) as are graunted to any others," sailed on 3 May 1631. The second commanded by 45-year-old Luke Foxe, a master mariner of Hull, sailed from London on 5 May. Foxe, though he made no claims to scholarship, was a friend of Henry Briggs, a famous Oxford mathematician and author of a treatise on the Northwest Passage, from whom he had received instruction in mathematics and navigation. He sailed with the support of London merchants and, through the influence of Briggs, with a measure of royal patronage.

Both explorers added to geographical knowledge, but neither found evidence calculated to rekindle the declining faith in Hudson Bay as the way to Cathay. They left their names on the maps and charts: Foxe Basin, Foxe Channel and James Bay, where Hudson had wintered in 1610–11. After returning to England, Foxe in 1631, James in 1632, they set about recording their experiences and their opinions. James was first into print with his literary gem, *The Strange and Dangerous Voyage of Captain Thomas James* (1633). Foxe followed with *North-West Foxe* (1635), geographically and historically speaking a more solid work. The two books share an honored place with those of George Best and John Davis in the literature of man and the sea in an epoch of daring endeavor.

Although the English may have a serious claim through the Bristol circle to have invented the idea of passage or passages to Asia across the Arctic Sea, they were not alone in attempting to circumnavigate or bisect the North American landmass. The Corte Real and Barcelos families of Portugal had an interest in the possibility of a passage which dated back to the beginnings of the sixteenth century. There is evidence of activity in the region by both families from their bases in the Azores during the 1560s and 1570s. Estévan Gomes, a Portuguese in the service of Spain, made a detailed reconnaissance of the New England coast in 1524–25 but found nothing to encourage further Spanish investigations. The French were also active. Giovanni da Verrazzano in 1524 and Jacques Cartier in the 1530s and 1540s led expeditions to North America, the initial aim of which was to find a route from the Atlantic to the Pacific. In the early seventeenth century Samuel de Champlain listed among the motives for the achievement of a permanent French settlement in Canada the hope "of attaining more easily to the completion of this enterprise since the voyage would begin in this land beyond the ocean, along which the search for the desired passage is to be made." Danish and Dutch interest in the Arctic, both to the west and east, is well attested in the late sixteenth and early seventeenth centuries. The most serious effort by the Danes to locate the Northwest Passage was the voyage of Jens Munk who sailed from Copenhagen with two ships and 64 men in May 1619. He entered Hudson Bay and wintered at the mouth of Churchill River where all but three of the crews died. Munk and two companions returned to Copenhagen in the smaller of the two ships in September 1620. The voyage might be written off as entirely unproductive were it not that Munk's illustrative material made significant additions to the cartography of Hudson Bay.

The illusions that a short and easy passage awaited discovery to the north of the American landmass was certainly not peculiarly English; but from the 1570s onwards they identified themselves with it with an ardor hardly evident elsewhere. For that minority of sixteenth-century Englishmen who believed that oceanic endeavor was the key to fortune, the North American landmass was on the whole an unattractive prospect compared with that of a sea route to Asia and the riches expected to accrue therefrom. American colonization, though it had its advocates, was slow to gain recognition as a national priority, a fact well illustrated by the tardy logistical support to the ill-fated Roanoke colony in the 1580s and survival by only the narrowest margin of the Jamestown colony in the early seventeenth century. It was when sufficient numbers of English men and women found reasons, social, religious and economic, from the 1620s onwards to emigrate to the New World in search of a new life that North America became something more than an obstacle to a passage to Asia.

As an obstacle it proved to be insuperable in the period up to 1632, in the eighteenth century when the search was revived and again in the nineteenth century when an intensive, almost obsessive, search culminated in the deaths of Sir John Franklin and all his men during 1845–48. In late Tudor and early Stuart times, English seamen sailed on an impossible mission. Ships manned by crews of 20 to 30 men, many of them reluctant to pass between icebergs to a point of no return, and victualled for 6, 12, or 18 months, had no chance of circumnavigating North America during the short season when the seas were open. The chief beneficiaries of the English defeat in the icefields were the Inuit, the threat to whose social structure and culture from the intruders was lifted for several centuries.

Even in defeat, however, the English balance sheet contained some healthy features. They cross and recrossed the North Atlantic with steadily increasing confidence, and fortified by their advancing aptitude for oceanic navigation, made transatlantic landfalls with increasing accuracy. They pushed beyond the latitudes reached by other Europeans, familiarizing themselves with the seas beyond the Arctic circle and adding significantly to knowledge of the North American seaboard. The penetration of Hudson Bay, though it revealed no passage, led to the foundation of 1670 of the Hudson Bay Company which outlived all the other English chartered companies of the sixteenth and seventeenth centuries and survived into the twentieth century. Yet, when all is said and done, the English effort to emulate the Spaniards and Portuguese by discovering their own passage to the East was blocked in a series of dead ends. John Old-mixon in *The British Empire in America,* published in the reign of Queen Anne, made the apt comment, "thus we see all the Adventurers made to the North West were in Hopes of passing to China, but that is a Discovery as latent as the Philosophers Stone, the perpetual Motion or the Longitude."

SUGGESTIONS FOR FURTHER READING

Published Contemporary Sources

Christy, Miller (ed.). *The Voyages of Captain Luke Foxe of Hull and Captain Thomas James of Bristol, in search of a north-west passage, in 1631–32.* (London: Hakluyt Society, 1st. series, vols. 88–89, 1894).

Davis, John. *The Seamans Secrets,* 5th. edition (1633). A facsimile reproduction for the John Carter Brown Library with an introduction by A. N. Ryan. (New York, 1992).

Gilbert, Sir Humphrey. "A Discourse of a Discovery for a New Passage to Catia," D. B. Quinn (ed.), *The Voyages and Colonising Enterprises of Sir Humphrey Gilbert,* vol. I. (London: Hakluyt Society, 2nd. series, vols. 83–4, 1940).

Markham, A. H. (ed.). *The Voyages and Works of John Davis the Navigator.* (London, Hakluyt Society, 1st series, vol. 59, 1880).

Quinn, D. B. (ed.). *New American World: A Documentary History of North America to 1612,* 5 vols. (New York 1979), vol. IV.

Stefansson, V. (ed.). *The Three Voyages of Martin Frobisher,* 2 vols. (London, 1938).

Taylor, E. G. R. (ed.). *A Regiment for the Sea and other writings on Navigation by William Bourne of Gravesend, a gunner (c. 1535–1582* (London: Hakluyt Society, 2nd series, 1963).

Later Works

Abbe, E. C. and F. J. Gillis. "Henry Hudson and the Early Exploration and Mapping of Hudson Bay, 1610 to 1631," J. Parker (ed.), *Merchants and Scholars: Essays in the History of Exploration and Trade.* (Minneapolis, Minn., 1965).

Andrews, K. R. *Trade Plunder and Settlement: Maritime Enterprise and the Genesis of the British Empire, 1480–1630.* (Cambridge, 1984).

Asher, G. M. *Henry Hudson the Navigator.* (London, 1860).

Dodge, E. S. *Northwest by Sea.* (New York, 1961).

McIntyre, R. "William Sanderson: Elizabethan Financier of Discovery," *William and Mary Quarterly,* vol. 13 (1956).

Markham, C. R. *Life of John Davis.* (London, 1891).

Morison, S. E. *The European Discovery of America: The Northern Voyages A.D. 500–1600.* (New York and Oxford, 1971), chapters xv, xvi and xviii.

Quinn, D. B. *North America from Earliest Discovery to First Settlements: The Norse Voyages to 1612.* (New York, 1977), chapters 3, 4, and 5.

Taylor, E. G. R. "The Voyages of Martin Frobisher," *The Geographical Journal,* vol. 91 (1938).

Taylor, E. G. R. *Tudor Geography, 1485–1583.* (London, 1930).

Wallis, Helen 'The First English Globe: A Recent Discovery', *Geographical Journal,* vol. 117 (1951).

Wallis, Helen. "Further Light on the Molyneux Globes," *ibid.,* vol. 121 (1955).

Waters, D. W. *The Art of Navigation in England in Elizabethan and Early Stuart Times.* (London, 1958).

INDEX